History of the
HARTFORD CONVENTION

Da Capo Press Reprints in

AMERICAN CONSTITUTIONAL AND LEGAL HISTORY

GENERAL EDITOR: LEONARD W. LEVY
Brandeis University

History of the
HARTFORD CONVENTION

*With A Review of the Policy of the
United States Government Which Led to the
War of 1812*

By Theodore Dwight

DA CAPO PRESS • NEW YORK • 1970

A Da Capo Press Reprint Edition

This Da Capo Press edition of
History of the Hartford Convention
is an unabridged republication of the first edition
published in New York and Boston in 1833.

Library of Congress Catalog Card Number 77-99474

SBN 306-71855-3

Published by Da Capo Press
A Division of Plenum Publishing Corporation
227 West 17th Street, New York, N.Y. 10011
All Rights Reserved

Manufactured in the United States of America

HISTORY

OF THE

HARTFORD CONVENTION:

WITH A

REVIEW OF THE POLICY

OF THE

UNITED STATES GOVERNMENT,

WHICH LED TO THE

WAR OF 1812.

BY THEODORE DWIGHT,

SECRETARY OF THE CONVENTION.

Published by N. & J. WHITE,

NEW-YORK;

And RUSSELL, ODIORNE, & Co.

BOSTON.

D. Fanshaw, Printer.

....

1833.

HISTORY

OF THE

HARTFORD CONVENTION.

No political subject that has ever occupied the attention, or excited the feelings of the great body of the people of these United States, has ever been the theme of more gross misrepresentation, or more constant reproach, than the assembly of delegates from several of the New-England states, which met at Hartford, in the state of Connecticut, in December, 1814, commonly called the "Hartford Convention." It has been reviled by multitudes of persons who were totally unacquainted with its objects, and its proceedings, and by not a few who probably were ignorant even of the geographical position of the place where the convention was held. And it was sufficient for those who were somewhat better informed, but equally regardless of truth and justice, that it afforded an opportunity to kindle the resentments of party against men whose talents they feared, whose respectability they could not but acknowledge, whose integrity they dare not impeach, and the purity of whose principles they had not the courage even to question. A great proportion of those who, at the present time, think themselves well employed in railing at the Hartford Convention, were school-boys at the time of its session, and, of course, incapable of forming opinions entitled to the least respect in regard to the objects which it had in view, or of the manner in which its duties were performed. In the meantime, men of more age, and greater opportunities for acquiring knowledge, have stood calmly by, and have coolly heard the general falsehoods and slanders that have been uttered against the convention, giving them at least their countenance, if not their direct and positive support.

In these, and in various other ways, the Hartford Convention, from the time of its coming together to the present hour, has been the general topic of reproach and calumny, as well as of the most unfounded and unprincipled misrepresentation and falsehood.

In the meantime, very little has been done, or even attempted, by any person, to stem the general torrent of reproach by which that assembly have been assailed. Conscious of their own integrity, and the purity of their motives and objects, the members, with a single exception, have remained silent and tranquil, amidst the long series of efforts to provoke them to engage in a vindication of their characters and conduct. One able and influential member of the convention, a number of years since, published a clear and satisfactory account of its objects and its proceedings. But it was deemed sufficient for those who did not believe the accusations which had been so lavishly preferred against that body, and who, of course, had no intention of engaging seriously in a discussion of the general subject, to reply, that the author of the vindication was one of the accused, and on trial upon the charge of sedition, at least, if not meditated treason, against the United States, and therefore not entitled to credit.

This mode of replying to an unanswerable vindication of the convention, as might have been expected, satisfied the feelings of interested and devoted partizans ; of course, that publication had no tendency to check the utterance or the circulation of party virulence, or vulgar detraction. Revilings of the convention have been continued in common conversation, in newspapers, in Fourth of July orations, in festive toasts, and bacchanalian revelries and songs. And finally, when driven from every other topic on which to support false principles by unfounded argumentation, grave senators and representatives of the United States, have introduced the threadbare subject of the Hartford Convention into debate, in the legislative halls of the nation, when engaged in discussing the weighty concerns of this extensive republic, and united with those of inferior standing and character, in villifying the Hartford Convention.

Occurrences of this kind, with others of a more serious and portentous description, seemed to indicate, in a clear and convincing manner, that the time had arrived when the public at large should be better informed on the subject of this convention. The objects for the accomplishment of which it had originally been convened, and the able and most satisfactory exhibition of their labors contained in their report, which was published by them to the world at the moment of their adjournment, have long been lost sight of, and forgotten. With this is connected the extraordinary circumstance, that besides the members themselves, no individual, except a single executive officer of the body, had any means of knowing what passed during their session. That officer was the only disinterested witness of what was transacted by the convention. He was present throughout every sitting, witnessed every debate, heard every speech, was acquainted with every motion and every proposition, and carefully noted the result of every vote on every question. He, therefore, of necessity was, ever has been, and still is, the only person, except the members, who had the opportunity to know, from personal observation, every thing that occurred. His testimony, therefore, must be admitted and received, unless he can be discredited, his testimony invalidated, or its force entirely destroyed.

Previously to entering upon the immediate history of

the convention, it will be necessary to review the policy
and measures of the national government, which eventually led to the war between this country and Great Britain ; as it was that war which induced the New-England
states to call the convention.

After the formation of the Constitution of the United
States by the Convention of 1787, and before its adoption
by the several states, the country became divided into two
political parties—THE FRIENDS and THE ENEMIES of that
constitution. The former, being in favour of the establishment of a federal government, according to the plan de-
lineated in the constitution, naturally took the name of
Federalists. Those who were opposed to the constitution,
and the form of government which it contained, as naturally took the name of Anti-federalists. Under these titles,
when the constitution had been adopted, and was about to
commence its operations, these parties took the field, and
arrayed themselves, both in congress and in the country,
under their several banners. The Federalists, that is, the
friends of the new constitution and government, were for
the first eight years the majority, and of course were able
to pursue the policy, and adopt the measures, which in
their judgment were best calculated to promote the great
interests of the Union. At their head, by the unanimous
vote of the nation, was placed the illustrious WASHING-
TON, who had led their armies to victory in the war of
independence, and who was now designated by the whole
body of the people as their civil leader and guide, and the
protector of their rights and liberties. No person who is
not old enough to remember the feelings of 1789, can
realize the deep emotions of that most interesting period,
the hopes that were enkindled by the reappearance of this
great man upon the stage of active usefulness, and of the
confidence that was reposed in his talents, his wisdom, the
purity of his character, and the disinterestedness of his
patriotism. Congress assembled, and the government was

organized. Among the members of the legislative houses, were to be found those who had attended the convention of 1787, and assisted in forming the constitution under which they were convened to deliberate on the highest interests of the Union. Among them were the names of Strong, King, Ellsworth, Johnson, Sherman, Madison, Langdon, Few, Paterson, Read, Baldwin, and Gilman— all members of the convention. These men could not fail of being thoroughly acquainted with the constitution, in all its parts and provisions, the views which were entertained of its character and principles by the convention, and which had been fully explained and discussed before the state conventions by which it had been approved and ratified. They were also associated, in the Senate and House of Representatives, with others from different parts of the Union, and of the highest reputation for public spirit and talents, many of whom had, either in the council or in the field, assisted in vindicating the rights and achieving the independence of their country. Among the latter were R. Morris, Carroll, R. H. Lee, Izard, Schuyler, Benson, Boudinot, Fitzsimmons, Sedgwick, Sturges, Trumbull, Ames, and Wadsworth. On men of this description, devolved the task of commencing operations under the new and untried system of government, which had been established by the great body of the people over this infant republic. No collection of statesmen or patriots were ever placed in a more sublime or responsible situation. On their wisdom, integrity, patriotism, and virtue, under the blessing of Heaven, depended not only the freedom, the prosperity, and the happiness of the unnumbered millions who might hereafter inhabit this emancipated portion of the western continent, but the result of the great experiment which was about to be made, whether there was virtue enough in men to support a system of free, elective, representative government.

The attempt was made, and it was successful. During

the two successive periods of General Washington's administration, the cardinal principles of the government were ascertained and established, and a general system of national policy was marked out and pursued, which has regulated and controlled the important concerns of the national government to the present day. At the first session of the first congress, a judicial system was formed with such skill and wisdom, that forty year's experience approves and sanctions, in the fullest manner, the soundness of its principles and the practical wisdom and utility of its general character and provisions. A financial system, devised by the extraordinary mind, and matured by the intuitive discernment of Hamilton, was adopted, the great principles of which have been in operation through all the vicissitudes of party which the country has experienced, and are still in force. The funding system was also adopted by the first congress, which as strongly displayed the wisdom, as it did the justice of the government. The national Bank, an institution indispensably necessary to the government as well as to the country at large, was another important measure of this administration. The organization of the militia, and the formation of a navy, were objects of its constant attention and solicitude. In short, it may be said, without danger of its being seriously controverted by men of intelligence and character, that the great principles of policy which have led the nation onward to reputation, respectability, prosperity, and power, were proposed and adopted under the administration of Washington, and were the fruits of the combined wisdom, profound forecast, and disinterested patriotism of himself and his associates in the councils of the nation. He was the great leader, and they were members, of that class of politicians who were called Federalists—a body of men who have been the objects of vulgar reproach and popular calumny from the time the government was formed, down to the present period.

The acknowledged head of the Anti-federal party was Thomas Jefferson. At the time when the convention which formed the constitution were in session, and until its adoption by nine of the states, Mr. Jefferson was absent from the country in France, where he had resided as the ambassador of the United States for a number of years. As his character and conduct will be found to be intimately connected with the subject of this work, it will be necessary to devote some time to an examination of his political career, from the time of his return from Europe, until the expiration of his administration of the national government.

This gentleman came into public life at an early age; and after having been once initiated in political pursuits, he devoted to them a large portion of the residue of his days. His mind was of a visionary and speculative cast ;— he was somewhat enthusiastic in his notions of government, ambitious in his disposition, and fanciful in his opinions of the nature and principles of government. By a long course of watchful discipline, he had obtained a strict command over his temper, which enabled him to wear a smooth and plausible exterior to persons of all descriptions with whom he was called to mingle or associate. Having been chairman of the committee of the congress of 1776, by whom the Declaration of Independence was drawn up, that faet gave him a degree of celebrity, which the mere style of composition in that celebrated document would not, under other circumstances, have secured to its author. At the same time, he had the reputation of being a scholar as well as a statesman; and more deference was paid to him, in both respects, than the true state of the case called for, or in strictness would warrant. His knowledge of men, however, was profound; he understood the art of gaining and retaining popular favour beyond any other politician either of ancient or modern times. Whilst he was apparently familiar with those who were about him, he was capable of deep dissimulation; and though he had at his command

a multitude of devoted agents, he was generally his own
adviser and counsellor. If, by any untoward circumstance,
he found himself in the power of any individual to such an
extent as to endanger his standing in the community, he
took care to secure that individual to his interests, by an
obligation so strong as to be relieved of all serious apprehensions of a future exposure. In addition to all his other
characteristics, during his long residence in France, he had
become thoroughly imbued with the principles of the infidel
philosophy which prevailed in that kingdom, and extensively over the continent of Europe, previously to and
during the French revolution. This fact, in connection
with the belief that his views of government were of a
wild and visionary character, destroyed the confidence of
a large portion of his most intelligent countrymen in him
as a politician, as well as a moralist and a Christian.

Mr. Jefferson was in Paris when the constitution was
published. He early declared himself not pleased with
the system of government which it contained. On the
13th of November, 1787, in a letter to John Adams, he
said—"How do you like our new constitution? I confess
there are things in it which stagger all my dispositions to
subscribe to what such an assembly has proposed. The
house of federal representatives will not be adequate to
the management of affairs either foreign or federal. Their
president seems a bad edition of a Polish king. He may
be elected from four years to four years, for life. Reason
and experience prove to us, that a chief magistrate, so
continuable, is an office for life. When one or two generations shall have proved that this is an office for life, it
becomes, on every succession, worthy of intrigue, of
bribery, of force, and even of foreign interference. It
will be of great consequence to France and England, to
have America governed by a *Galloman* or an Angloman.
Once in office, and possessing the military force of the
Union, without the aid or check of a council, he would not

be easily dethroned, even if the people could be induced to withdraw their votes from him. I wish that, at the end of the four years, they had made him forever ineligible a second time. Indeed, I think all the good of this new constitution might have been couched in three or four new articles to be added to the good, old, and venerable fabric, which should have been preserved even as a religious relique."

In a letter of the same date to Colonel Smith, he says—" I do not know whether it is to yourself or Mr. Adams I am to give my thanks for the copy of the new constitution. I beg leave, through you, to place them where due. It will yet be three weeks before I shall receive them from America. There are very good articles in it, and very bad. I do not know which preponderate. What we have lately read in the history of Holland, in the chapter on the Stadtholder, would have sufficed to set me against a chief eligible for a long duration, if I had ever been disposed toward one : and what we have always read of the election of Polish kings, should have forever excluded the idea of one continuable for life. Wonderful is the effect of impudent and persevering lying. The British ministry have so long hired their gazetteers to repeat, and model into every form, lies about our being in anarchy, that the world has at length believed them, the English nation has believed them, the ministers themselves have come to believe them, and what is more wonderful, we have believed them ourselves. Yet where does this anarchy exist, except in the single instance of Massachusetts ? And can history produce an instance of rebellion so honorably conducted ? I say nothing of its motives. They were founded in ignorance, not wickedness. *God forbid we should ever be twenty years without such a rebellion.* The people cannot be all, and always well informed. The part which is wrong will be discontented in proportion to the facts they misconceive. *If they remain in quiet under*

*such misconceptions, it is a lethargy, the forerunner of death
to public liberty.* We have had thirteen states independent
for eleven years. There has been one rebellion. That
comes to one rebellion in a century and a half for each
state. What country before ever existed a century and
a half without a rebellion? *And what country can preserve its liberties, if its rulers are not warned from time to
time that this people preserve the spirit of resistance?* Let
them take arms. The remedy is to set them right as to
facts, pardon, and pacify them. *What signify a few lives
lost in a century or two? The tree of liberty must be refreshed
from time to time with the blood of patriots and tyrants. It
is its natural manure.* "

In a letter to William Carmichael, dated December
11th, 1787, he says—"Our new constitution is powerfully
attacked in the American newspapers. The objections
are, that its effect would be to form the thirteen states into
one ; that proposing to melt all down into a general government, they have fenced the people by no declaration of
rights ; they have not renounced the power of keeping a
standing army ; they have not secured the liberty of the
press ; they have reserved the power of abolishing trials
by jury in civil cases ; they have proposed that the laws of
the federal legislatures shall be paramount to the laws and
constitutions of the states; they have abandoned rotation
in office ; and particularly their president may be re-
elected from four years to four years, for life, so as to render him a king for life, like a king of Poland; and they
have not given him either the check or aid of a council.
To these they add calculations of expense, &c. &c. to
frighten the people. You will perceive that those objections
are serious, and some of them not without foundation."

The subject is alluded to subsequently in a variety of
letters to different correspondents, in the course of which
he confines his objections principally to the omission of a

bill or declaration of rights, and the re-eligibility of the president.

Enough has been quoted to show that Mr. Jefferson was not friendly to the constitution ; and some of his sentiments were of a nature to shake the confidence of its friends in the soundness of his general political principles. Of this description were his remarks on the Massachusetts insurrection. So far from considering rebellion against government an evil, he viewed it as a benefit—as a necessary ingredient in the republican character, and highly useful in its tendency to warn rulers, from time to time, that the people possessed the spirit of resistance. And particularly would the public feelings be shocked at the cold-blooded indifference with which he inquires, " What signify a few lives lost in a century or two ?" and the additional remark, that " *The tree of liberty must be refreshed* from time to time *with the blood of patriots and tyrants. It is its natural manure.*" This language would better become a Turkish Sultan, or the chief of a Tartar horde, than a distinguished republican, who had been born and educated in a Christian country, and enjoyed all the advantages to be derived from civilization, literature, and science.

In September, 1789, Mr. Jefferson left Paris, on his return to the United States. On the 15th of December, of that year, he wrote the following letter to General Washington :

" *Chesterfield, December* 15, 1789.

" To the President.

" Sir,—I have received at this place the honor of your letters of October the 13th, and November the 30th, and am truly flattered by your nomination of me to the very dignified office of Secretary of State, for which permit me here to return you my humble thanks. Could any circumstance seduce me to overlook the disproportion between its duties and my talents, it would be the encouragement of

your choice. But when I contemplate the extent of that
office, embracing as it does the principal mass of domestic
administration, together with the foreign, I cannot be insensible of my inequality to it; and I should enter on it
with gloomy forebodings from the criticisms and censures
of a public, just, indeed, in their intentions, but sometimes
misinformed and misled, and always too respectable to be
neglected. I cannot but foresee the possibility that this
may end disagreeably for me, who having no motive to
public service but the public satisfaction, would certainly
retire the moment that satisfaction should appear to lan-
guish. On the other hand, I feel a degree of familiarity
with the duties of my present office, as far at least as I
am capable of understanding its duties. The ground I
have already passed over, enables me to see my way into
that which is before me. The change of government too,
taking place in the country where it is exercised, seems to
open a possibility of procuring from the new rulers some
new advantages in commerce, which may be agreeable to
our countrymen. So that, as far as my fears, my hopes,
or my inclinations might enter into this question, I confess
they would not lead me to prefer a change.

" But it is not for an individual to choose his post. You
are to marshal us as may best be for the public good; and
it is only in the case of its being indifferent to you, that I
would avail myself of the option you have so kindly offered
in your letter. If you think it better to transfer me to
another post, my inclination must be no obstacle; nor shall
it be, if there is any desire to suppress the office I now
hold, or to reduce its grade. In either of these cases, be
so good as to signify to me by another line your ultimate
wish, and I shall conform to it cordially. If it should be
to remain at New-York, my chief comfort will be to work
under your eye, my only shelter the authority of your
name, and the wisdom of measures to be dictated by you
and implicitly executed by me. Whatever you may be

pleased to decide, I do not see that the matters which have called me hither will permit me to shorten the stay I originally asked; that is to say, to set out on my journey northward till the month of March. As early as possible in that month, I shall have the honor of paying my respects to you in New-York. In the mean time, I have that of tendering to you the homage of those sentiments of respectful attachment with which I am, Sir,

" Your most obedient, and most humble servant,

" TH. JEFFERSON."

This letter will show with what feelings of esteem and respect for General Washington Mr. Jefferson professedly accepted the appointment of Secretary of State. It may hereafter appear with what degree of sincerity these professions were made ; and it is important to the object of this work, that it should be borne in mind by the reader, because one end which the writer has in view in preparing it is, to enable the community to form a more just estimate of his principles and character.

By adverting to that part of Mr. Jefferson's writings, published since his death, which bears the singular and awkward title of " *Ana*," it appears by his own declarations, that immediately upon entering upon the duties of his office, he became an opposer of some of the principal measures of the government. He says—

" I returned from that mission (to France) in the first year of the new government, having landed in Virginia in December, 1789, and proceeded to New-York in March, 1790, to enter on the office of Secretary of State. Here, certainly, I found a state of things which, of all I had ever contemplated, I the least expected. I had left France in the first year of her revolution, in the fervor of natural rights, and zeal for reformation. My conscientious devotion to those rights could not be heightened, but it had been aroused and excited by daily exercise. The presi-

dent received me cordially, and my colleagues, and the circle of principal citizens, apparently with welcome. The
courtesies of dinner parties given me, as a stranger newly
arrived among them, placed me at once in their familiar
society. But I cannot describe the wonder and mortification with which the table conversations filled me. Politics were the chief topic, and *a preference of a kingly over a
republican government, was evidently the favorite sentiment.*
An apostate I could not be, *nor yet a hypocrite;* and I
found myself, for the most part, the only advocate on the
republican side of the question, unless among the guests
there chanced to be some members of that party from the
legislative houses. Hamilton's financial system had then
passed. It had two objects : 1. As a puzzle, to exclude
popular understanding and inquiry ; 2. As a *machine for
the corruption of the legislature;* for he avowed the opinion,
that man could be governed by one of two motives only,
force, or interest ; force, he observed, in this country, was
out of the question ; and the interests, therefore, of the
members, must be laid hold of to keep the legislature in
unison with the executive. And with grief and shame it
must be acknowledged that his machine was not without
effect ; that even in this, the birth of our government, some
members were found sordid enough to bend their duty to
their interests, and to look after personal, rather than
public good."

Another measure of great importance, which Mr. Jefferson strongly disapproved, was the assumption of the state
debts. Nothing could be more just or more reasonable
than this act of the general government. The exertions of
different states had necessarily been unequal, and in the
same proportion their expenses had been increased. But
those expenses had all been incurred in the common cause ;
and that cause having been successful, nothing could be
more just than that the debts thus incurred should be borne
by the nation. Mr. Jefferson, however, stigmatizes the

measure as corrupt. "The more debt," he says, "Hamilton could rake up, the more plunder for his mercenaries." And he closes a long series of opprobrious remarks upon the subject, and upon the manner in which, according to his opinion, it was carried, by saying—"This added to the number of votaries to the Treasury, and made its chief the master of every vote in the legislature, which might give to the government the direction suited to his political views."

The bank was another measure which did not meet with Mr. Jefferson's support.

After remarking on these various subjects, he says, "Nor was this an opposition to General Washington. He was true to the republican charge confided to him, and has solemnly and repeatedly protested to me, in our conversations, that he would lose the last drop of his blood in support of it; and he did this the oftener, and with the more earnestness, because he knew my suspicions of Hamilton's designs against it, and wished to quiet them. For he was not aware of the drift, or of the effect of Hamilton's schemes. Unversed in financial projects, and calculations, and budgets, his approbation of them was bottomed on his confidence in the man.

"But Hamilton was not only a monarchist, but for a monarchy bottomed on corruption." And he then gives an account of a conversation which he says took place at a meeting of the Vice-president and the heads of departments, in the course of which the British constitution was alluded to; and in regard to which he says—"Mr. Adams observed, 'Purge that constitution of its corruption, and give to its popular branch equality of representation, and it would be the most perfect constitution ever devised by the wit of man.' Hamilton paused, and observed, 'Purge it of its corruption, and give to its popular branch equality of representation, and it would become an *impracticable* government; as it stands at present, with all its

supposed defects, it is the most perfect government which
ever existed."

The Funding System was one of the great measures
that distinguished General Washington's administration.
It was devised by Hamilton, and has ever been considered
as reflecting the highest credit upon his talents and patriotism. No man labored with more zeal or ability to
procure the adoption of the constitution than this great
statesman. The Federalist, of which he was one of the
principal writers, and contributed the largest share, has
long been considered as a standard work on the constitution, and is now resorted to as an authority of the highest
respectability and character, respecting the true principles
and construction of that instrument. The system of revenue adopted under General Washington, was also the work
of this distinguished financier ; and so nearly perfect was
it found to be in practice, amidst all the changes and
violence of party, and under the administration of those
individuals who were originally opposed to its adoption,
that they severally found it necessary, when placed at the
head of the government, to pursue the system which he had
devised. Even Mr. Jefferson himself, during the eight years
that he held the office of chief magistrate, never ventured to
adopt a new system of finance, but adhered, in all its essential particulars, to that devised by Hamilton. And yet,
from the moment he came into the executive department
of the government, and was associated with Hamilton
and others in establishing the principles of the constitution,
it appears, by his own evidence, that he was endeavoring
to destroy the reputation and influence of that great statesman, by secret slanders, and insidious suggestions against
his political integrity and orthodoxy. The article from
which the foregoing citations are taken, was not written at
the moment—it was not the record of events as they occurred from day to day : it bears date in 1818—nearly thirty
years after most of those events took place, and fourteen

years after General Hamilton had been consigned to the tomb. A more extraordinary instance of vindictive, personal, or political hostility, probably cannot be mentioned.

This work, however, has not been undertaken with the view of vindicating the character of General Hamilton from the aspersions of Mr. Jefferson. That duty devolves on others ; and it is a gratification to know that the task is in a fair way to be performed by those, who, it is presumed, will see that it is done faithfully. Mr. Jefferson's " Writings" have been referred to for the purpose of showing his original dislike of the constitution, his opposition to the most important measures of the government at its first organization, and his inveterate hostility to the most able, upright and disinterested expounders of the constitution. Among these was Alexander Hamilton. The mode of attack upon this distinguished individual, and equally distinguished public benefactor, was no less insidious than it was unjust and calumnious. It was to represent him not only as unfriendly to the constitution, in the formation and adoption of which he was one of the intelligent, active, and influential agents, but as a monarchist—an enemy to republicanism itself. In the quotations which have already been made from his " Ana," he says General Hamilton " was not only a monarchist, but for a monarchy bottomed on corruption." And he professes to repeat declarations of a similar kind, made openly by General Hamilton at a dinner party, when Mr. Jefferson himself was present. Assertions of this kind, unsupported by any other evidence than his own declarations, are not worthy of credit. General Hamilton was too well acquainted with Mr. Jefferson's feeling toward him, and of his disposition to undermine and destroy him, thus voluntarily and unnecessarily to place himself in his power. In some instances, in the course of his " Ana," other names are introduced as corroborating witnesses in support of some of the charges against General Hamilton. It is difficult to disprove posthumous testimony by positive evidence, especially when the parties, as well as the witnesses, are in their graves ; but several of the individuals, named by Mr. Jefferson as the persons from whom he derived a knowledge of the conversations and declarations of General Hamilton, will add no strength to the evidence; they are not worthy of belief in a case of this kind.

That General Hamilton was an enemy to the very nature of the government, in the formation of which he had assisted so zealously and so faithfully, in procuring the adoption of which he had laboured with as much talent, and with as much effect, as any other man in the United States, and in developing and establishing the great principles of which, his exertions were inferior to those of no other individual, will not at this late period be credited.

That Mr. Jefferson wished, by secret measures, and a train of artful and insidious means, to destroy his great rival, no person acquainted with his history, conduct, and character, can doubt. It comported with his policy to lay the charge of monarchical feelings and sentiments against him, because his object was to avail himself of the prejudices of the people against Great Britain, which the war of independence had excited, and which time had not allayed, to raise himself to popularity and power. When the French revolution had advanced far enough to enlist the feelings of a portion of our countrymen in their favour, on the ground that the nation was endeavouring to throw off a despotism, and establish a republican government, another portion of them considered the principles they avowed, and the course they pursued, as dangerous to the very existence of civilized society. Mr. Jefferson declares in his "*Ana*," as above quoted, that he " had left France in the first year of her revolution, in the fervor of natural rights and zeal for reformation." His devotion to those rights, he says, " could not be heightened, but it had been aroused and excited by daily exercise." Accordingly he became, at a very early period, the leader of the party in this country, who, in the utmost warmth of feeling, espoused the cause of revolutionary France. To render himself the more conspicuous, he found it expedient to stigmatize those who entertained different sentiments from himself, as the enemies of republicanism, and of course, as the friends of monarchy. The meaning of this charge was, that they were the friends of Great Britain and the British government. Hence proceeded the charges of a monarchical propensity in Mr. Adams and General Hamilton, specimens of which have been already adduced. But it was soon found necessary to go greater lengths than this. To pave the way for a gradual attempt to undermine the popularity of General Washington, and to shake the public confidence in his patriotism and integrity, a similar effort was made to involve him in a similar accusation. The plan adopted to accomplish this object, was to represent him as having a bias toward Great Britain, and against France. If Mr. Jefferson, who had espoused the side of revolutionary France, could succeed in making the country believe that General Washington had taken sides with Great Britain against France, in the great controversy that was then convulsing Europe, it would follow almost as a necessary consequence, that he would be considered as the enemy of freedom, and the friend of monarchical government. In his correspondence, published since his death, there is the following letter :

" To P. Mazzei.

" *Monticello, April* 24, 1796.

" My dear Friend—The aspect of our politics has wonderfully changed since you left us. In place of that noble love of liberty and republican government which carried us triumphantly through the war, an Anglican monarchical and aristocratical party has sprung up, whose

avowed object is to draw over us the substance, as they
have already done the forms, of the British government.
The main body of our citizens, however, remain true to
their republican principles : the whole landed interest is
republican, and so is a great mass of talents. *Against us
are the* EXECUTIVE, the judiciary, two out of three branches
of the legislature, all the officers of the government, all
who want to be officers, all timid men who prefer the
calm of despotism to the boisterous sea of liberty, British
merchants, and Americans trading on British capitals,
speculators and holders in the banks and public funds, a
contrivance invented for the purposes of corruption, and
for assimilating us in all things to the rotten as well as
the sound parts of the British model. It would give you
a fever were I to name to you the apostates who have
gone over to these heresies, men who were Samsons in
the field and Solomons in the council, but who have had
their heads shorn by the harlot England. In short, we
are likely to preserve the liberty we have obtained only
by unremitting labors and perils. But we shall preserve
it ; and our mass of weight and wealth on the good side
is so great, as to leave no danger that force will ever be
attempted against us. We have only to awake, and snap
the Lilliputian cords with which they have been entangling
us during the first sleep which succeeded our labors."

When this letter first appeared in the United States, it
was in the following form :

" Our political situation is prodigiously changed since
you left us. Instead of that noble love of liberty, and that
republican government which carried us through the dangers of the war, an anglo-monarchic-aristocratic party
has arisen. Their avowed object is, to impose on us the
substance, as they have already given us the *form,* of the
British government. Nevertheless, the principal body of
our citizens remain faithful to republican principles, as
also the men of talents. We have against us (republicans)

the executive power, the judiciary, (two of the three branches of our government,) all the officers of government, all who are seeking for offices, all timid men, who prefer the calm of despotism to the tempestuous sea of liberty, the British merchants, and the Americans who trade on British capitals, the speculators, persons interested in the bank, and public funds. [Establishments invented with views of corruption, and to assimilate us to the British model in its worst parts.] I should give you a fever, if I should name the apostates who have embraced these heresies, men who were Solomons in council, and Samsons in combat, but whose hair has been cut off by the whore England.

" They would wrest from us that liberty which we have obtained by so much labor and peril; but we shall preserve it. Our mass of weight and riches are so powerful, that we have nothing to fear from any attempt against us by force. It is sufficient that we guard ourselves, and that we break the Lilliputian ties by which they have bound us, in the first slumbers which have succeeded our labors. It suffices that we arrest the progress of that system of ingratitude and injustice toward France, from which they would alienate us, to bring us under British influence."

It may easily be imagined, that the appearance of this extraordinary article in the United States, was calculated to disturb the feelings of Mr. Jefferson. Such an attack as it contained on the character of General Washington, as well as upon his coadjutors, could not pass unnoticed; and it obviously placed the writer of it in a perplexing and inextricable dilemma. Accordingly, in a letter addressed to Mr. Madison, dated August 3d, 1797, he thus unbosomed himself :

" The variety of other topics the day I was with you, kept out of sight the letter to Mazzei imputed to me in the papers, the general substance of which is mine, though the diction has been considerably altered and varied in the course of its translations from French into Italian, from Italian into French, and from French into English. I first met with it at Bladensburg, and for a moment conceived I must take the field of the public papers. I could not disavow it wholly, because the greatest part was mine in substance, though not in form. I could not avow it as it stood, because the form was not mine, and, in one place, the substance was very materially falsified. This, then, would render explanations necessary; nay, it would render proofs of the whole necessary, and draw me at length into a publication of all (even the secret) transactions of the administration, while I was of it; and embroil me personally with every member of the executive and the judiciary, and with others still. I soon decided in my own mind to be entirely silent. I consulted with several friends at Philadelphia, who, every one of them, were clearly against my avowing or disavowing, and some of them conjured me most earnestly to let nothing provoke me to it. I corrected, in conversation with them, a substantial misrepresentation in the copy published. The original has a sentiment like this, (for I have it not before me,) " They are endeavoring to submit us to the substance, as they already have to the *forms* of the British government; meaning by *forms*, the birthdays, levees, processions to parliament, inauguration pomposities, &c. But the copy published says, ' as they have already submitted us to the *form* of the British,' &c.; making me express hostility to the form of our government, that is to say, to the constitution itself; for this is really the difference of the word *form*, used in singular or plural, in that phrase, in the English language. Now it would be impossible for me to explain this publicly, without bringing on a personal difference between General Washington and myself, which nothing before the publication of this letter has ever done. It would embroil me also with all those with whom his character is still popular, that is to say, with nine-tenths

of the United States; and what good would be obtained
by avowing the letter with the necessary explanations?
Very little, indeed, in my opinion, to counterbalance a
good deal of harm. From my silence in this instance, it
cannot be inferred that I am afraid to own the general sentiments of the letter. If I am subject to either imputation, it is to avowing such sentiments too frankly both in
private and public, often when there is no necessity for it,
merely because *I disdain every thing like duplicity.* Still,
however, I am open to conviction. Think for me on the
occasion, and advise me what to do, and confer with Colonel Monroe on the subject."

This letter, take which version of it we may, discloses
the secret of Mr. Jefferson's policy. It was to represent
the federal party as monarchists, and aristocrats, enemies
to republicanism, and therefore devoted to the interests
of Great Britain, and hostile to those of France. No man
ever understood more perfectly the effect of names upon
the minds of partizans, than this great champion of modern
republicanism; and hence he informs his friend Mazzei,
that *the Federalists were a body of Anglo-Monarchic-Aris-
tocrats, and himself and his friends were Republicans.*

Nobody will be surprised to find, that the publication of
his letter in the newspapers of the United States, gave
Mr. Jefferson uneasiness. The man who had the hardi-
hood to accuse General Washington with being an aristo-
crat and a monarchist, and particularly, with being devoted
to British influence and interests, must have possessed a
degree of mental courage not often found in the human
constitution. And it is perfectly apparent that this was
the circumstance which so greatly embarrassed him, when
determining the important question whether it would be
most for his own advantage to come before the public, and
endeavour to explain away the obvious meaning of his
letter, or to observe a strict, and more prudent silence,
and leave the world to form their own conclusions. He

finally resolved on the latter, making his explanations only
to his confidential friends, and leaving them in such a form,
that they might pass, with his other posthumous works,
to future generations.

A little attention to the subject will show, that he
adopted the most prudent course. Mr. Jefferson's attempt
to give a different meaning to his own language, is entirely
unsatisfactory. In the letter, as first published in the
newspapers, it is said—" Our *political situation* is prodigiously changed since you left us." In the version of it
in his posthumous works, it is—" The *aspect* of *our politics*
has wonderfully changed since you left us." Not having
the original, either in Italian or French, it is not practicable at this time to say which is most correct. But there
is a material difference between the expressions " Our
political condition," and " the aspect of our politics." The
first has an immediate and obvious reference to the situation of the country at large, as connected with the general
government, and the character of that government ; the
other relates merely to the measures of the government.
The first, if in any degree to be deplored, must be considered as permanent; the last, as referring to mere
legislative acts, which in their nature were transitory.
The next sentence shows, conclusively, that it was the
character of the government, and not merely its measures,
that were alluded to. " Instead of that noble love of
liberty, and that *republican government*, which carried us
through the dangers of the war, an Anglo-Monarchic-
Aristocratic party has arisen." The " republican government which carried us through the dangers of the war,"
was the " old confederation," as it is usually called. The
change that had taken place was in the system of government—in the substitution of something else in the place of
the confederation. By turning back to Mr. Jefferson's
letter to Mr. Adams, dated November 13th, 1787, we shall
find him using the following language—" How do you like

our new constitution? I confess there are things in it
which stagger all my dispositions to subscribe to what such
an assembly has proposed." He then enumerates several
objections, and says—" I think all the good of this new
constitution might have been couched in three or four new
articles *to be added to the good, old, and venerable fabric,*
which should have been preserved even as a religious
relique." It is obvious, therefore, that his affections were
placed on the "good, old" confederation; and when he
complains of the prodigious alteration that had taken place
in our political condition since Mr. Mazzei had left us, he
must have had reference to the new constitution.

This is further manifest from the language which immediately follows. He declares in the letter as first published,
that the " avowed object of the party to which he has alluded,
is, *to impose on us* the *substance,* as they have already given
us the *form* of the British government." In the letter as
published in his works, he blends the two sentences together, and after mentioning the Anglo party, varies the passage above quoted, by saying—"whose avowed object is
to draw over us the *substance,* as they have already done the
forms, of the British government." The British government consists of three estates—a hereditary monarchy, a
hereditary House of Peers, and an elective House of Commons—or in other words, of King, Lords, and Commons.
Our government consists of a President, Senate, and House
of Representatives—all elective, though for different periods. One objection urged, on various occasions, against
the adoption of the constitution, was its resemblance, in
the particulars just mentioned, to the British government.
Among others, Mr. Jefferson was pointedly opposed to the
re-eligibility of the executive. He compared it to the case
of the king of Poland, and thought there ought to have
been a provision prohibiting the re-election of any individual to that office. The people of the states, however,
concluded that their liberties would not be exposed to any

imminent hazard, under a system where all the officers, executive and legislative, were elective, and they took the constitution as it was. And great as Mr. Jefferson's fears of danger to freedom were from this quarter, he eventually overcame them so far as to suffer himself to be placed in the office of chief magistrate twice, without any apparent misgivings of mind or conscience. Now it is scarcely possible for any unbiassed mind to believe, that he had not immediate reference to this part of our constitution, when he remarked, that the "Anglo-Monarchic-Aristocratic" party were endeavouring to impose upon the nation "*the substance*, as *they had already* given it *the form*, of the British government." These three cardinal branches of the British government, viz. "Kings, Lords, and Commons," are all the form there is to that government. All the residue of what is called by themselves their constitution, consists of unwritten and prescriptive usages, sometimes called laws of parliament, which never were reduced to form, and certainly never were adopted in *the form* of a constitution.

Mr. Jefferson, in his letter to Mr. Madison, attempts to give a totally different meaning to this part of his letter. He says, "The original has *a sentiment* like this, (for I have it not before me,) They are endeavouring to *submit us* to the substance, as they already have to the *forms*, of the British government ; meaning by *forms*, the birth-days, levees, processions to parliament, inauguration pompositics, &c. For this is really the meaning of the word *form*, used in the singular or plural, in that phrase, in the English language." We do not believe that any person, well acquainted with the English language, ever made use of such an awkward and senseless expression as that above cited—They are endeavouring to *submit us to the substance*. As Mr. Jefferson always was considered a scholar, the internal evidence derived from this singular phraseology is sufficient to warrant the conclusion that it was adopted here for the occasion.

But the application of the expression form, or even forms, of the British government, to the practise of observing birth-days, holding levees, of moving in procession to parliament, or the pomposities of inaugurations, is downright absurdity. These ceremonious customs are no part of the government, either in Great Britain, or in the United States. They may be childish, they may be pompous, they may be servile and adulatory, but they are not proceedings, either in form or substance, of the government. Nor has the word form or forms any such legitimate meaning. This explanation was doubtless contrived for future use, and not to be made public; and it is not at all surprising that Mr. Jefferson found there were serious difficulties in the way of a public exposure of his meaning, if this was all the explanation he had to give. The course he adopted, which was to observe a strict silence, was far more discreet. A more weak and unsatisfactory attempt to evade a plain and obvious difficulty has rarely been made.

The next sentence in the letter as first published is, " Nevertheless, the principal body of our citizens remain faithful to republican principles, as also the men of talents." In the letter in Mr. Jefferson's works, it stands thus— " The main body of our citizens, however, remain true to their republican principles; the whole landed interest is republican, and so is a great mass of talents." Now it may be safely said, that no mistake in translation can possibly account for the diversity that appears in these two sentences. Without noticing the difference between the first and last members of the two sentences, the expression—" the whole landed interest is republican "—is entirely wanting in the letter as first published. This must have been wilfully suppressed in the first letter, if it was in the original—a circumstance that is not to be credited, because no possible motive can be assigned for such an act. The inference then must be, that it was introduced into the copy left for posthumous publication, to help the general appearance of mistranslation, and to countenance and give plausibility to other alterations of more importance.

The letter as first published, then proceeds—"We have against us (republicans) *the Executive Power*, the Judiciary, (*two of the three branches of our government,*) all the officers of government, all who are seeking for offices, all timid men, who prefer the calm of despotism to the tempestuous sea of liberty, the British merchants, and the Americans who trade on British capitals, the speculators, persons interested in the Bank and Public Funds, [establishments invented with views of corruption, and to assimilate us to the British model in its corrupt parts.] In the letter in Mr. Jefferson's works, it stands thus—"Against us are the executive, the judiciary, *two out of three branches of the legislature;* all the officers of government, all who want to be officers, all timid men who prefer the calm of despotism to the boisterous sea of liberty, British merchants, and Americans trading on British capitals, speculators and holders in the banks and public funds, a contrivance invented for the purposes of corruption, and for assimilating us in all things to the rotten as well as the sound parts of the British model.

It is impossible to avoid the conclusion, that the article published in the form of a letter to Mazzei, in Mr. Jefferson's works, from which the last extract is taken, is not a correct transcript of the original, but was prepared to answer a specific purpose. No person will be persuaded that Mr. Jefferson ever called the executive and the judiciary " *two out of three branches of the legislature.*" The language of the letter first published is correct—" *two of the three branches of our government.*" Again he says, " speculators and holders in *the banks.*" There was but one national bank, and reference must be made to national banks alone. The first letter has it correctly—the Bank.

The fact that banks are mentioned in the last, is decisive proof that the first is the most accurate translation.

There is an expression here which is so strikingly characteristic of the author, that it ought not to pass unnoticed. Mr. Jefferson says, " We have against *us republicans*—all timid men who prefer the calm of despotism to the tempestuous sea of liberty." In the second letter it is "the boisterous sea of liberty." It will be borne in mind, the "timid men" here spoken of, were not inhabitants of France, or England, but of these United States, then under the mild, and peaceable, and prosperous influence of the government which they had so recently adopted, and the beneficial effects of which they were then realizing in a most gratifying degree. That a man of his temperament should call such a state of things, under such a government, the calm of despotism, is not a little extraordinary. But it will be recollected, that in a letter quoted in the former part of this work, when speaking of the insurrection in Massachusetts, he said, "God forbid we should ever be twenty years without such a rebellion." " And what country can preserve its liberties, if its rulers are not warned from time to time, that this people preserve the spirit of resistance ? Let them take arms."—" What signify a few lives lost in a century or two ? *The tree of liberty must be refreshed from time to time with the blood of patriots and tyrants. It is its natural manure.*" After reading these sentiments and expressions, no person can be surprised to find that Mr. Jefferson should prefer the tumults, the distresses, and the bloodshed of insurrections, to the peace, the tranquillity, and the social happiness, which are enjoyed under a mild, beneficent, well-regulated, and well-administered government. No man of sound mind, and virtuous principles, will envy him his choice.

But the most extraordinary expression in this letter is the declaration, that the republicans, that is, Mr. Jefferson and his political partizans, were opposed by *the executive* and *the judiciary.* When this allegation was made, and it is contained in both versions of the letter, the chief executive magistrate of the United States was GEORGE WASHINGTON. George Washington led the armies of the United States through the revolutionary war ; and during the whole of that arduous and distressing conflict, discovered military skill and talents of the highest order. Under all circumstances, and in all situations, he manifested the most pure and devoted patriotism ; and after having seen his country victorious, and its independence acknowledged, even by the adversary with whom he had so long and so successfully contended, in a manner that excited the surprise and the admiration not only of his own country, but of the civilized world, he surrendered the power with which he had been clothed, and which he had so long exercised, into the hands of those from whom he received it, and retired to private life amidst the applauses, and loaded with the gratitude and benedictions of his fellow citizens. When it was found that the government which had carried the nation through the war, was insufficient for the exigencies of peace, he again lent his whole talents andi nfluence to the formation and adoption of a new system, better calculated for the wants, and better suited to the promotion of the great interests of the union. As soon as that system was adopted by the nation, he was called by the spontaneous, and unanimous voice of his countrymen, to the office of chief magistrate ; which call was renewed, with the same unanimity, on a second occasion ; at the end of which, after having addressed his fellow citizens in a train of the warmest affection, the purest patriotism, and the most elevated political morality and eloquence, he declined being again a candidate for office, and crowned with the highest honours which a free people could confer on their most respected and revered citizen, bade a final adieu to all further active engagement in the public affairs of the government and country. The life of this great man passed without a stain. The annals of nations contain no account of a more unimpeachable character, either in military or civil life. And what adds much to the splendour of his reputation, he was as highly distinguished as a statesman, as he had previously been as a soldier. In both he was illustrious in the most exalted sense of the word ; while in private life, he was, in an exemplary degree, amiable and virtuous, beloved by his most intimate friends, and respected and venerated by an enlarged and highly respectable circle of neighbours and acquaintance.

Such was the man who was stigmatized in this letter to a foreigner, residing in a distant quarter of the globe, as a member of an " Anglo-monarchic-aristocratic party" in this country, whose " *avowed* object was to impose on us the substance, as they had already given us the form, of the British government." General Washington's republicanism is here expressly denied, notwithstanding he had risked more, suffered more, and made greater exertions, to support and establish the republican character, principles, and government of his country, than any other individual in it.

After having thus attempted to fix upon General Washington the reproach of being a monarchist, and of enmity to the Constitution of the United States, Mr. Jefferson proceeds to say of the monarchical party, of which he obviously considered General Washington as the head, " They would wrest from us that liberty which *we* have obtained by so much labor and peril ; but we shall preserve it. Our mass of weight and riches are so powerful, that we have nothing to fear from any attempt against us by force." In the letter, *as published* in his works, this passage stands thus : " In short, we are likely to preserve the liberty we have obtained only by unremitting labors and perils. But we shall preserve it; and our mass of weight and wealth on the good side is so great as to leave no danger that force will ever be attempted against us." In the first place, it may be again remarked, that no man, even of ordinary understanding and capacity, will ever believe that the difference of phraseology between these two versions of this part of the letter, was caused by a mere mistake in the translation. The first implies a full expectation that force might be used to destroy our liberties. It says, " They would *wrest* from us that liberty," &c. The second, that we are likely to preserve the liberty we have obtained," &c. without a suggestion of any attempt *to wrest* it from us.

The letter, however, states the manner in which our liberties are to be preserved. It says—" It is sufficient that we guard ourselves, and that we break the Lilliputian ties by which they have bound us, in the first slumbers which have succeeded our labours." In the letter in the published works, this sentence is thus expressed—" We have only to awake and snap the Lilliputian cords with which they have been entangling us during the first step which succeeded our labors." This can be considered in no other light, than that of referring to the Constitution of the United States. It has already appeared, by the language used in a variety of instances in his letters that have been quoted, that Mr. Jefferson had strong objections to the constitution, and that in his judgment, " all that was good in it might have been included in three or four articles," added to the old confederation. As it was, the government was too strong for his taste. The first slumbers which succeeded the labours of the country in achieving its independence, must mean the period between the peace of 1783, and the adoption of the constitution. This constitution was " *the Lilliputian tie*" by which the nation had been bound, while in a fit of drowsiness; but which must be broken, to insure its safety from bondage. This passage will assist the community in forming a just estimate of Mr. Jefferson's regard for the constitution, and of the government which it provided, and over which he was destined at a future day to preside. This constitution General Washington assisted in forming; he recommended it strongly to the adoption of the country; and he devoted his great talents and influence for eight years to the developement of its principles, and the establishment of its operations; and was laboriously engaged in these patriotic labours at the moment when Mr. Jefferson was thus secretly calumniating his character, and impeaching his integrity; and at the same time declaring, that our liberties could only be preserved by the destruction of the constitution.

But Mr. Jefferson had still another machine to make use of in accomplishing our deliverance from the dangers with which our liberties were surrounded, and by which our freedom was threatened. " It suffices," says the letter first published, " that we arrest the progress of that system of ingratitude, and injustice *towards France*, from which they would alienate us, *to bring us under British influence*," &c.

Here is to be found the great governing principle of Mr. Jefferson's political conduct.—*It was* FRIENDSHIP FOR FRANCE and ENMITY TO GREAT BRITAIN. Those who did not adopt his sentiments, and pursue his system of policy, were monarchists and aristocrats; and those who agreed with him, and placed themselves under his direction and influence, were republicans.

It should be mentioned as one of the singular circumstances which attend this letter, that the sentence last quoted from it is entirely omitted in that published in the posthumous works. It would seem very strange that the person who translated Mr. Mazzei's letter, should not only have added this sentence, and then finished with an &c. as if there had been something still further, if, as Mr. Jefferson would have it understood by leaving a copy of it to be published after his death, no such sentence was in the original.

That this attack upon the reputation of General Washington, was the result of a political calculation, and intended to answer the selfish and ambitious purposes of Mr. Jefferson, cannot for a moment be doubted. It has been seen, that General Washington, at the first organization of the government, appointed him Secretary of State. Mr. Jefferson's letters, on various occasions, are full of expressions of respect and regard for General Washington. He left that office at the close of the year 1793, and retired to his residence at Monticello, in Virginia. There he wrote, in 1818, the first article in that collection of "Ana," as it now stands in his book. This, it will be observed, was more than twenty years after the date of his letter to Mazzei. In that, when speaking of General Hamilton's influence, arising from the Bank, and other measures, and alluding to his monarchical principles, he says—" Here then was the real ground of the opposition which was made to the course of his administration. Its object was to preserve the legislature pure and independent of the executive, to restrain the administration to republican forms and principles, and not permit the constitution to be construed into a monarchy, and to be warped in practice, into all the principles and pollutions of their favorite English model. Nor was this an opposition to General Washington. He was true to the republican charge confided to him ; and has solemnly and repeatedly protested to me, in our conversation, that he would lose the last drop of his blood in support of it."

In the month of February, 1791, the House of Representatives of the United States passed a resolution calling on the Secretary of State [Mr. Jefferson] " to report to congress the nature and extent of the privileges and restrictions of the commercial intercourse of the United States with foreign nations, and the measures which he should think proper to be adopted for the improvement of the commerce and navigation of the same." This report was not delivered until December, 1793; and on the last day of that month Mr. Jefferson resigned his office. On the 4th of January following, the house resolved itself into a committee of the whole on the report above alluded to, " when Mr. Madison laid on the table a series of resolutions for the consideration of the members."

" These memorable resolutions," says Judge Marshall, in his Life of Washington, " almost completely embraced the idea of the report. They imposed an additional duty on the manufactures, and on the tonnage of vessels, of nations having no commercial treaty with the United States; while they reduced the duties already imposed by law on the tonnage of vessels belonging to nations having such commercial treaty; and they reciprocated the restrictions which were imposed on American navigation."

Mr. Pitkin, in his " Political and Civil History of the United States," when alluding to this subject, says, " This report of Mr. Jefferson formed the basis of the celebrated commercial resolutions, as they were called, submitted to the house by Mr. Madison early in January, 1794. The substance of the first of these resolutions was, that the interest of the United States would be promoted by further restrictions and higher duties, in certain cases, on the *manufactures* and *navigation* of foreign nations. The additional duties were to be laid on certain articles manufactured by those European nations *which had no commercial treaties with the United States.*" " The last of the resolutions declared, that provision ought to be made for ascertaining the losses sustained by American citizens, from the operation of particular regulations of any country contravening the law of nations; and that these losses be reimbursed, in the first instance, out of the additional duties on the manufactures and vessels of the nations establishing such regulations."

A long debate ensued on these resolutions, in the course of which, Mr. Fitzsimmons, a member from Pennsylvania, moved that in their operations they should extend to all nations. This motion was met by one from Mr. Nicholas, of Virginia, the object of which was to exempt all nations from their operation except Great Britain.

" In discussing these resolutions," says Mr. Pitkin, " a wide range was taken ; their *political* as well as *commercial* effects upon foreign nations, were brought into view. In the course of the debate it was soon apparent, that their political bearing was considered as the most important, particularly on that nation to which its operation was finally limited, by the motion of Mr. Nicholas."

Judge Marshall gives a more extended sketch of the debate. The advocates of the resolutions said, they " conceived it impracticable to do justice to the interests of the United States without some allusion to politics ;" and after a long discussion of the character and effects of the resolutions, " It was denied that any real advantage was derived from the extensive credit given by the merchants of Great Britain. On the contrary the use made of British capital was pronounced a great political evil. It increased the unfavourable balance of trade, discouraged domestic manufactures, and promoted luxury. But its greatest mischief was, that it favored a system of British influence, which was dangerous to their political security."

" It was said to be proper in deciding the question under debate, to take into view political, as well as commercial considerations. Ill will and jealousy had at all times been the predominant features of the conduct of England to the United States. That government had grossly violated the treaty of peace, had declined a commercial treaty, had instigated the Indians to raise the tomahawk and scalping knife against American citizens, had let loose the Algerines upon their unprotected commerce, and had insulted their flag, and pillaged their trade in every quarter of the world. These facts being notorious, it was astonishing to hear gentlemen ask how had Britain injured their commerce?

" The conduct of France, on the contrary, had been warm and friendly. That nation had respected American rights, and had offered to enter into commercial arrangements on the liberal basis of perfect reciprocity.

" In contrasting the ability of the two nations to support a commercial conflict, it was said Great Britain, tottering under the weight of a king, a court, a nobility, a priesthood, armies, navies, debts, and all the complicated machinery of oppression which serves to increase the number of unproductive, and lessen the number of productive hands; at this moment engaged in a foreign war; taxation already carried to the ultimatum of financial device; the ability of the people already displayed in the payment of taxes constituting a political phenomenon; all prove the debility of the system and the decrepitude of old age. On the other hand, the United States, in the flower of youth; increasing in hands; increasing in wealth; and although an imitative policy has unfortunately prevailed in the erection of a funded debt, in the establishment of an army, in the establishment of a navy, and all the paper machinery for increasing the number of unproductive, and lessening the number of productive hands; yet the operation of natural causes has, as yet, in some degree, countervailed their influence, and still furnishes a great superiority in comparison with Great Britain."

" The present time was declared to be peculiarly favourable to the views of the United States. It was only while their enemy was embarrassed with a dangerous foreign war, that they could hope for the establishment of just and equal principles."

The real object of this report by the Secretary of State, and of the resolutions introduced by Mr. Madison, was stated in the course of the debate upon the latter. " The discussion of this subject, it was said, " has assumed an appearance which must be surprising to a stranger, and painful in the extreme to ourselves. The supreme legislature of the United States is seriously deliberating, not upon the welfare of our own citizens, but upon the relative circumstances of two European nations; and this deliberation has not for its object the relative benefits of their markets to us, but which form of government is best and most like our own, which people feel the greatest affection for us, and what measures we can adopt which will best humble one, and exalt the other.

" The primary motive of these resolutions, as acknowledged by their defenders, is not the increase of our agriculture, manufactures, or navigation, but to humble Great Britain, and build up France."

And such was unquestionably their real character and object. But the intended operation of them, and of the language and sentiments uttered respecting them in debate, was so clear and explicit, that they could not be mistaken, and therefore they could not fail of producing their designed effect upon the feelings of the British government and people. Nor could they be viewed in any other light, than as expressing great hostility to the interests of that nation, and strong partiality to those of France. And hence may be discerned the first traces of that system of policy towards Great Britain, which originated with Mr. Jefferson, and was steadily pursued by him through the remainder of his political life, and by his immediate successor in the administration of the national government, until it terminated in the war of 1812.

To establish the truth of the position just advanced, it will be necessary to give a historical account of the measures of the government, relating to the general subject, under the administrations of Mr. Jefferson and Mr. Madison. The facts which will be adduced, will be derived from the public records and state papers, or from other sources equally authentic and creditable.

In April, 1794, Mr. Jay, then Chief Justice of the United States, was appointed minister extraordinary to the court of Great Britain. This mission was strongly disliked by the party of which Mr. Jefferson was the acknowledged leader. But notwithstanding their disapprobation it was pursued; and in November following, a treaty was concluded, in which the great causes of uneasiness and animosity between the two nations were adjusted, and a foundation laid for their future peace, harmony, and friendship. As soon as the news reached this country that such a treaty had been concluded and signed, and long before its contents were known, there was a great degree of excitement among what Mr. Jefferson called the republican party. Notwithstanding all the clamour, the treaty was submitted to the Senate, who advised its ratification, with the exception of one article. One member of that body, however, in violation of the injunction of secrecy under which they acted, and before the treaty was signed by the President, published it in a newspaper. Immediately upon its appearance, the country was thrown into a ferment, and every possible effort was made to induce the President to reject it. Meetings were held, violent resolutions were passed, and inflammatory addresses were made, and circulated, with the hope, if not the expectation, of overawing that dignified and inflexible magistrate and patriot, and of inducing him to withhold his final approbation from the treaty. The attempts all failed;—the treaty was ratified; and the nation derived from it numerous and substantial benefits.

But it met the most decided disapprobation of Mr. Jefferson. In a letter to Mann Page, dated August 30th, 1795, he says—" I do not believe with the Rochefoucaults and Montaignes, that fourteen out of fifteen men are rogues. I believe a great abatement from that proportion may be made in favour of general honesty. But I have always found that *rogues would be uppermost,* and I do not know that the proportion is too strong for the higher orders, and for those who, rising above the swinish multitude, always contrive to nestle themselves into the places of power and profit. These rogues set out with stealing the people's good opinion, and then steal from them the right of withdrawing it, by contriving laws and associations against the power of the people themselves. Our part of the country is in a considerable fermentation on what they suspect to be a recent roguery of this kind. They say that while all hands were below deck, mending sails, splicing ropes, and every one at his own business, and the captain in his cabin attending to his log-book and chart, *a rogue of a pilot* has run them into an enemy's port. But metaphor apart, there is much dissatisfaction *with Mr. Jay and his treaty.*" In a letter to William B. Giles, dated December 31, 1795, he says—" I am well pleased with the manner in which your house have testified their sense of the treaty : while their refusal to pass the original clause of the reported answer proved their condemnation, the contrivance to let it disappear silently respected appearances in favour of the president, who errs as other men do, but errs with integrity." In a letter to Edward Rutledge, dated November 30th, 1795, he says—" I join with you in thinking the treaty an execrable thing. But both negotiators must have understood, that as there were articles in it which could not be carried into execution without the aid of the legislatures on both sides, therefore it must be referred to them, and that these legislatures, being free agents, would not give it their support if they disapproved of it. I trust the popular branch of our legislature will disapprove of it, and thus rid us of *an infamous act*, which is really nothing more than a treaty of alliance between England and the Anglomen of this country, against the legislature and people of the United States."

This animosity against the treaty cannot be accounted for, on the ground that it was not a beneficial measure to the nation. After the excitement which its publication and ratification produced had subsided, its advantages were realized and acknowledged ; and it may be said with safety, that no subsequent arrangement between the two nations has ever been as beneficial to the United States as this. But it removed many sources of difficulty—the western posts, which the British had retained in violation of the treaty of 1783, were surrendered ; and the commerce of the country was greatly benefited. And it was calculated to remove a variety of causes of uneasiness, of complaint, of interference, and of recrimination, between the nations, and therefore was thoroughly reprobated by Mr. Jefferson. And it appears, by the last quotation from his letters, that rather than have it established, and go into operation, he would have rejoiced if the House of Representatives had encroached upon the constitutional prerogative of the President and Senate, and withheld the necessary legislative aid to carry its provisions into effect. The constitution authorizes the President, by and with the advice and consent of the Senate, to make treaties ; and treaties, when constitutionally made, are declared to be the supreme law of the land. Of course, when thus made, if they require legislative acts to carry them into effect, the legislature are bound by their constitutional duty, to pass such laws ; otherwise the supreme law of the land may be rendered inoperative, and be defeated, by one branch of the government. This bold experiment, Mr. Jefferson would have been gratified to see made, rather than have peace and friendship established between this country and Great Britain.

Nor is the coarse attack upon Mr. Jay's character, by Mr. Jefferson, in his letter above quoted, the least reprehensible circumstance in his conduct in relation to this treaty. Mr. Jay was one of the most pure and virtuous patriots that this country ever produced. His talents were of a very high order, his public services were of the most

meritorious and disinterested description, and his public
and private reputation without reproach. Yet, with an air
of levity, approaching jocularity, he is represented by Mr.
Jefferson as one of those fortunate *"rogues,"* who contrive
to keep themselves uppermost in the world,—one who had
been guilty of an "infamous act" in making the treaty.
Happy would it have been for his calumniator, if his character had been equally pure, and his services equally disinterested and patriotic.

When Mr. Jefferson came into office as chief magistrate
of the Union, in 1801, Rufus King was minister from the
United States to Great Britain.   In June, 1802, that gentleman was instructed to adjust the boundary line between
the two nations; and in May, 1803, in pursuance of his
instructions, he concluded a convention with that government.   A dispute on this subject had existed between the
two countries, from the ratification of the treaty of peace
in 1783, to the date of the above mentioned convention.
In forming this convention, it is known that Mr. King's
views were fully acceded to by the British commissioner,
Lord Hawkesbury, the latter having left the draft of the
convention to Mr. King, and fully approved of that which
he prepared.   In a message of the President of the United
States to Congress, dated October 17, 1803, is the following passage—" A further knowledge of the ground, in the
north-eastern and north-western angles of the United
States, has evinced that the boundaries established by the
treaty of Paris, between the British territories and ours
in those parts, were too imperfectly described to be susceptible of execution.   It has therefore been thought
worthy of attention for preserving and cherishing the harmony and useful intercourse subsisting between the two
nations, to remove by timely arrangements, what unfavourable incidents might otherwise render a ground of
future misunderstanding.   A convention has therefore
been entered into, which provides for a practicable demar-

cation of those limits, to the satisfaction of both parties. The following is a copy of a letter from Mr. King, which accompanied the convention, when it was transmitted to the United States government——

"*London, May* 13, 1803.

" SIR,—I have the honour to transmit herewith the convention which I yesterday signed in triplicate with Lord Hawkesbury relative to our boundaries. The convention does not vary in any thing material from the tenour of my instructions. The line through the bay of Passamaquoddy secures our interest in that quarter. The provision for running, instead of describing, the line between the northwest corner of Nova Scotia and the source of Connecticut river, has been inserted as well on account of the progress of the British settlements towards the source of the Connecticut, as of the difficulty in agreeing upon any new description of the manner of running this line without more exact information than is at present possessed of the geography of the country.

" The source of the Mississippi nearest to the Lake of the Woods, according to Mackenzie's report, will be found about twenty-nine miles to the westward of any part of that lake, which is represented to be nearly circular. Hence a direct line between the northwesternmost part of the lake, and the nearest source of the Mississippi, which is preferred by this government, has appeared to me equally advantageous with the lines we had proposed.

"RUFUS KING."

On the 24th of October, one week after the delivery of the message to Congress, from which the passage above quoted is taken, Mr. Jefferson submitted this convention to the Senate, accompanied by the following message :—

" I lay before you the convention signed on the 12th day of May last, between the United States and Great

Britain, for settling their boundaries in the north-eastern and north-western parts of the United States, which was mentioned in my general message of the 17th instant; together with such papers relating thereto as may enable you to determine whether you will advise and consent to its ratification."

A letter from Mr. Madison, Secretary of State, to Mr. Monroe, minister at Great Britain, dated February 14th, 1801, contains the following passage:—

"You will herewith receive the ratification, by the President and Senate, of the convention with the British government, signed on the 12th of May, 1803, with an exception of the 5th article. Should the British government accede to this change in the instrument, you will proceed to an exchange of ratifications, and transmit the one received without delay, in order that the proper steps may be taken for carrying the convention into effect."

"The objection to the fifth article appears to have arisen from the posteriority of the signature and ratification of this convention to those of the last convention with France, ceding Louisiana to the United States, and from a presumption that the line to be run in pursuance of the fifth article, might thence be found or alledged to abridge the northern extent of that acquisition."

Then follow a series of reasons intended to show why the British government ought not to make objections to the alterations proposed by ours.

"First. It would be unreasonable that any advantage against the United States should be constructively authorized by the posteriority of the dates in question, the instructions given to enter into the convention, and the understanding of the parties at the time of signing it, having no reference whatever to any territorial rights of the United States acquired by the previous convention with France, but referring merely to the territorial rights as understood at the date of the instructions for and signature of the British convention. The copy of a letter from Mr. King, hereto annexed, is precise and conclusive on this subject.

" Secondly. If the fifth article be expunged, the north boundary of Louisiana will, as is reasonable, remain the same in the hands of the United States as it was in the hands of France, and may be adjusted and established according to the principles and authorities which would in that case have been applicable.

" Fourthly. Laying aside, however, all the objections to the fifth article, the proper extension of a dividing line in that quarter will be equally open for friendly negociation after, as without, agreeing to the other parts of the convention, and considering the remoteness of the time at which such a line will become actually necessary, the postponement of it is of little consequence. The truth is that the British government seemed at one time to favour this delay, and the instructions given by the United States readily acquiesced in it."

It will be recollected, that in the message to Congress, on the 17th of October, 1803, from which we have just quoted a passage, Mr. Jefferson speaks of this convention as one that would give satisfaction to all parties. It seems, however, not to have been ratified, although it was submitted to the Senate for their approbation only one week after the date of the abovementioned message to Congress. All that can be ascertained respecting the causes of its rejection, are to be found in the above cited letter from the Secretary of State to Mr. Monroe, where the principal ground appears to be that it might in some way affect our concerns *with France.* By its rejection, however, the dispute about the boundary line was left unadjusted, and has remained so to this day.

Mr. Jay's treaty expired in 1804. As the country had experienced its beneficial effects for ten years, it was reasonable to expect that it would have been renewed at the

earliest opportunity. On the 7th of August, 1804, Mr.
Monroe, then ambassador from the United States to Great
Britain, wrote a letter on that subject to Mr. Madison,
then Secretary of State, from which the following are extracts.

" I received a note from Lord Harrowby on the 3d instant, requesting me to call on him at his office the next
day, which I did. His lordship asked me, in what light
was our treaty viewed by our government ? I replied that
it had been ratified with the exception of the fifth article,
as I had informed him on a former occasion. He observed
that he meant the treaty of 1794, which by one of its
stipulations was to expire two years after the signature of
preliminary articles for concluding the then existing war
between Great Britain and France. He wished to know
whether we considered the treaty as actually expired. I
said that I did presume there could be but one opinion on
that point in respect to the commercial part of the treaty,
which was, that it had expired : that the first ten articles
were made permanent ; that other articles had been executed, but then, being limited to a definite period which
had passed, must be considered as having expired with it."

After a further detail of the conversation, the letter
proceeds—

" He asked, how far it would be agreeable to our government to stipulate, that *the treaty of* 1794 *should remain
in force until two years should expire after the conclusion of
the present war ?* I told his lordship that I had no power
to agree to such a proposal ; that the President, animated
by a sincere desire to cherish and perpetuate the friendly
relations subsisting between the two countries, had been
disposed to *postpone the regulation of their general commercial system till the period should arrive, when each party,
enjoying the blessings of peace, might find itself at liberty to
pay the subject the attention it merited ;* that he wished those
regulations to be founded in the permanent interests, justly

and liberally viewed, of both countries ; that he sought for the present only to remove certain topics which produced irritation in the intercourse, such as the impressment of seamen, and in our commerce with other powers, parties to the present war, according to a project which I had the honor to present to his predecessor some months since, with which I presumed his lordship was acquainted. He seemed desirous to decline any conversation on this latter subject, though it was clearly to be inferred, from what he said, to be his opinion, that the policy which our government seemed disposed to pursue in respect to the general system, could not otherwise than be agreeable to his. He then added, that *his government might probably, for the present, adopt the treaty of* 1794, *as the rule in its own concerns, or in respect to duties on importations from our country,* and, as I understood him, all other subjects to which it extended ; in which case, he said, if the treaty had expired, the ministry would take the responsibility on itself, as there would be no law to sanction the measure : that in so doing, he presumed that the measure would be well received by our government, and a similar practice, in what concerned Great Britain, reciprocated. I observed, that on that particular topic I had no authority to say any thing specially, the proposal being altogether new and unexpected ; that I should communicate it to you ; and that I doubted not that it would be considered by the President with the attention it merited. Not wishing, however, to authorize an inference, that that treaty should ever form a basis of a future one between the two countries, I repeated some remarks which I had made to Lord Hawkesbury in the interview which we had just before he left the department of foreign affairs, by observing that *in forming a new treaty we must begin de novo;* that America was a young and thriving country ; that at the time that treaty was formed, she had little experience of her relations with foreign powers ; that ten years had since elapsed, a great portion

of the term within which she had held the rank of a separate and independent nation, and exercised the powers
belonging to it ; that our interests were better understood
on both sides at this time than they then were ; that the
treaty was known to contain things that neither liked ;
that I spoke with confidence on that point on our part ;
that in making a new treaty we might ingraft from that
into it what suited us, omit what we disliked, and add
what the experience of our respective interests might suggest to be proper ; and being equally anxious to preclude
the inference of any sanction to the maritime pretensions
under that treaty, in respect to neutral commerce, I deemed it proper to advert again to the project, which I had
presented some time since, for the regulation of those
points, to notice its contents, and express an earnest wish
that his lordship would find leisure, and be disposed to act
on it. He excused himself again from entering into this
subject, from the weight and urgency of other business,
the difficulty of the subject, and other general remarks of
the kind."

By this correspondence it appears, that it was a part
of Mr. Jefferson's policy, whenever Mr. Jay's treaty
should expire, not to renew it. There were undoubtedly
personal reasons for the adoption of this course. Mr. Jefferson, as has been seen, considered that treaty as an execrable measure, and regarded its ratification as opposed
to the interests of revolutionary France, to which he was,
in heart and soul, devoted. The advantages of the treaty
had been so fully realized, that it was natural to expect
that our government would have yielded at once to the
offer of the British ministry to renew it. Their willingness to form a new treaty, upon the principles of Mr.
Jay's, was repeatedly expressed, first by Lord Hawkesbury, in April, 1804, and afterwards by Lord Harrowby,
in August of the same year. Lord Hawkesbury, in a conversation with Mr. Monroe, " went so far as to express a

wish that the principles of the treaty of 1794 might be
adopted in the convention, which it was then proposed to
make; and Lord Harrowby informed him, " that his government might probably, for the present, adopt the treaty
of 1794, as the rule in its own concerns, or in respect to
importations from our country, and as he understood him,
all other subjects to which it extended." He even went
further, and said, if the treaty had expired (about which
Lord Harrowby appeared to doubt) the ministry would
take the responsibility on itself, as there would be no law
to sanction the measure." But Mr. Monroe, acting under
his instructions, was not willing to authorize even an inference, that the treaty of 1794 should ever form the basis
of a future one, repeated to him the remarks he had previously made to Lord Hawkesbury, and observed, that in
forming a new one, we must begin *de novo*—that we were
then but little experienced in our relations with foreign
countries; that our interests were better understood on
both sides than when the treaty was made—and that in
making a new one, we might introduce into it what suited
us, omit what we disliked, and add what experience might
suggest to be proper.

The idea that the agents on the part of the United
States, in this attempt at negotiation, understood the
interests of their country more thoroughly than those connected with the negotiation of 1794, is but little short of
ludicrous. The treaty negotiated by Mr. Jay, in its operation and effects, proved to be a most beneficial one to
the country; and it is a little remarkable, that no subsequent arrangement with Great Britain has been equally
advantageous. Under Mr. Jefferson's directions, an effort
was constantly made to procure some provision against
impressment—an object, certainly of great importance to
our country. But, when it was found impracticable to
induce the British government to enter into stipulations on
that subject, it might well be doubted whether it was good

policy, by insisting upon an impracticable measure, to
sacrifice all the other advantages which must necessarily
arise from a just and reasonable commercial treaty with
that nation. To this day such a stipulation has not been
obtained ; but the disadvantages experienced by the trade
of the United States, for the want of a treaty like that
negotiated by Mr. Jay, have been numerous, and greatly
detrimental. Those advantages were lost by not renewing
that treaty; and the treaty was not renewed, it is believed
the facts will warrant the declaration, because it comported with Mr. Jefferson's policy, at all times, to keep
alive a controversy with Great Britain.

In April, 1806, William Pinkney, of Maryland, was
appointed joint commissioner with Mr. Monroe, for the
purpose of settling all matters of difference between the
United States and Great Britain, "relative to wrongs
committed between the parties on the high seas, or other
waters, and for establishing the principles of navigation
and commerce between them."   Their negotiations were
held under the ministry of Mr. Fox, who was considered
as a great friend to the United States.   Owing to his
sickness, the business on the part of the British government was placed in the hands of his nephew, Lord Holland, and Lord Auckland.   On the 11th of September,
1806,.the American commissioners wrote to the secretary
of state, giving him an account of their first interview with
the noblemen abovementioned, in which, when noticing the
matter of impressment, they say—"On the impressment
subject it was soon apparent they (Lords Holland and
Auckland) felt the strongest repugnance to a formal renunciation or abandonment of their claim to take from our
vessels on the high seas such seamen as should appear to
be their own subjects."   And such was the answer, from
first to last, to every attempt to come to a formal arrangement on this perplexing subject. Every ministry of Great
Britain, however differently disposed on many other sub-

jects, on this thought and acted alike. With all the evidence that they possessed of the impracticability of negotiating successfully on this topic, Mr. Jefferson made it the turning point of all his efforts. In pursuance of this determination, on the 3d of February, 1807, Mr. Madison, secretary of state, wrote to Messrs. Monroe and Pinkney, and after having alluded to the matter of impressments, said—

"In the mean time, the President has, with all those friendly and conciliatory dispositions which produced your mission, and pervade your instructions, weighed the arrangement held out in your last letter, which contemplates a formal adjustment of the other topics under discussion, and an informal understanding only on that of impressment. The result of his deliberations which I am now to state to you, is, that it does not comport with his views of the national sentiment, or the legislative policy, that any treaty should be entered into with the British government which, whilst on every other point it is limited to, or short of strict right, would include no article providing for a case which both in principle and practice, is so feelingly connected with the honour and sovereignty of the nation, as well as with its fair interests; and indeed with the peace of both nations.

"The President thinks it more eligible, under all circumstances, that if no satisfactory or formal stipulation on the subject of impressment be attainable, the negotiation should be made to terminate without any formal compact whatever."

On the 3d of January, 1807, Messrs. Monroe and Pinkney wrote to the Secretary of State, saying—"We have the honour to transmit to you a treaty, which we concluded with the British commissioners on the 31st of December. Although we had entertained great confidence from the commencement of the negotiation, that such would be its result, it was not till the 27th, that we were able to make any satisfactory arrangement of several of the most important points that were involved in it. *A large proportion of the provisions of this treaty,—no less than eleven of its articles—was taken from that of* 1794." After giving an account of the various articles, those gentlemen say—

" We are sorry to add that this treaty contains no provision against the impressment of our seamen. Our despatch of the 11th of November, communicated to you the result of our labours on that subject, and our opinion that, although this government did not feel itself at liberty to relinquish, formally by treaty, its claim to search our merchant vessels for British seamen, its practice would, nevertheless, be essentially, if not completely abandoned. That opinion has been since confirmed by frequent conferences on the subject with the British commissioners, who have repeatedly assured us, that, in their judgment, we were made as secure against the exercise of their pretension by the policy which their government had adopted in regard to that very delicate and important question, as we could have been made by treaty."

This treaty was received at Washington the beginning of March, 1807, but was never even submitted to the Senate for their advice and consent to its ratification. On the 20th of May following, Mr. Madison wrote to Messrs. Monroe and Pinkney on the subject. The following is an extract from his letter :—

" The President has seen in your exertions to accomplish the great objects of your instructions, ample proofs of that zeal and patriotism in which he confided ; and feels deep regret that your success has not corresponded with the reasonableness of your propositions, and the ability with which they were supported. He laments more especially that the British government has not yielded to the just and cogent considerations which forbid the practice of its cruisers in visiting and impressing the crews of our vessels, covered by an independent flag, and guarded by the laws of the high seas, which ought to be sacred with all nations.

" The President continues to regard this subject in the light in which it has been pressed on the justice and friendship of Great Britain. He cannot reconcile it with his duty to our sea-faring citizens, or with the sensibility or sovereignty of the nation to recognise even constructively, a principle that would expose on the high seas their liberty, their lives, every thing, in a word, that is dearest to the human heart, to the capricious or interested sentences which may be pronounced against their allegiance by officers of a foreign government, whom neither the laws of nations, nor even the laws of that government, will allow to decide on the ownership or character of the minutest article of property found in a like situation."

" It is considered, moreover, by the President, the more reasonable, that the necessary concession in this case should be made by Great Britain, rather than by the United States, on the double consideration, first, that a concession on our part would violate both a moral and political duty of the government to our citizens, which would not be the case on the other side ; secondly, that a greater number of American citizens, than of British subjects, are in fact impressed from our vessels ; and that, consequently more of wrong is done to the United States than of right to Great Britain, taking even her own claim for the criterion.

" On these grounds, the President is constrained to decline any arrangement, formal or informal, which does not comprise a provision against impressments from American vessels on the high seas, and which would, notwithstanding, be a bar to legislative measures, such as Congress have thought, or may think proper to adopt for controlling that species of aggression."

" That you may the more fully understand his impressions and purposes, I will explain the alterations which are

to be regarded as essential, and proceed then to such observations on the several articles as will show the other
alterations which are to be attempted, and the degree of
importance respectively attached to them.

" *Without a provision against impressments, substantially
such as is contemplated in your original instructions, no treaty
is to be concluded.*"

After a long series of instructions, and remarks, relative
to the manner of conducting the negociation, and of the
concessions that may, if necessary, be made, it is said—

" Should the concession, (relating to the employment of
seamen belonging to the respective countries,) contrary to
all expectation, not succeed, even as to the essential objects, the course prescribed by prudence will be to signify
your purpose of transmitting ther esult to your government,
avoiding carefully any language or appearance of hostile
anticipations ; and receiving and transmitting, at the same
time, any overtures which may be made on the other side,
with a view to bring about an accommodation. As long
as negociation can be honourably protracted, it is a resource to be preferred under existing circumstances, to the
peremptory alternative of improper concessions, or inevitable collisions."

Thus, it is apparent, that this treaty was rejected pri-
marily on the ground, that no arrangement was made in
it to prevent the impressment of seamen. Of the importance of such an arrangement, had it been practicable,
there can be no difference of opinion among the inhabitants
of the United States. But when it was perfectly ascertained, that no stipulations on that subject could be obtained, that every successive cabinet in England had agreed
on this point, and the question only remained for our administration to determine, whether all the relations of the
two nations, and impressments with them, should be left
in a loose, undefined, and irritating condition, or all except
that should be satisfactorily adjusted, leaving that for fu-

ture consideration, no reasonable doubt can be entertained that the latter course should have been pursued. It will be recollected that the standing reason urged by Great Britain, against yielding the principle that our flag should protect the crew was, that she was struggling against the power of revolutionary France for her existence, and depended on her navy for her safety ; and that under such circumstances she could not admit the force of mere abstract principles—self-preservation being with her the highest object of consideration. There certainly was much force in this objection on her part, to treating on that specific point, at that critical period. That Mr. Jefferson should feel differently from the British statesmen, was perfectly natural. It has been shown that his governing principle in politics was, animosity against Great Britain, and attachment to France. It was well known, that from the strong national resemblance between Britons and Americans, and particularly from the identity of language, great difficulty would exist in distinguishing between American citizens and British subjects ; and this was one argument strongly urged against negotiation on this subject. But a clue to Mr. Jefferson's feelings towards that nation, may be discovered in his works published since his death, beyond the passages already quoted. The following is a letter to William B. Giles :—

" Monticello, April 27, 1795.
" DEAR SIR,—Your favour of the 16th came to hand by the last post. I sincerely congratulate you on the great prosperity of our two first allies, the French and the Dutch. If I could but see them now at peace with the rest of their continent, *I should have but little doubt of dining with Pichegru in London next autumn ; for I believe I should be tempted to leave my clover for awhile, to go and hail the dawn of liberty and republicanism in that island.*"

This is the language of Mr. Jefferson, when writing to an intimate and confidential friend. What must have been the principles and the heart of the man, who, from mere political feelings and resentments, could talk with such an air of levity, on such a subject? Wishing to dine with Pichegru in London, necessarily implied a wish that he might, as well as a belief that he would, be able to invade, overrun, and conquer Great Britain. That is, because the people of that nation preferred the government under which they lived, and which had been the means of elevating their country to a far greater height of freedom, prosperity, power, and renown, than any other European nation ever enjoyed, to Mr. Jefferson's notions of republicanism, he would have subjected them to all the miseries and horrors of an invading and victorious army, and to the tremendous consequences which must necessarily follow such a state of things, in such a country. Fortunately for Europe, and the interests of the civilized world, he was disappointed of the pleasure to be derived from such a festive entertainment. The French were not able to conquer Great Britain, and of course Pichegru had no opportunity of inviting his republican friends in other parts of the world to dine with him in London, and to heighten the hilarity of the entertainment, by witnessing the pillage and butcheries which must have attended a conquest over such a city.

Mr. Monroe, after the conclusion of the treaty, returned to the United States. As might have been expected, he considered himself as having been harshly dealt with in relation to it. On the 10th of March, 1808, Mr. Jefferson wrote to him on that subject. Among other things he says—

" You complain of the manner in which the treaty was received. But what was that manner? I cannot suppose you to have given a moment's credit to the stuff which was crowded in all sorts of forms into the public papers, or to the thousand speeches they put into my mouth, not a word of which I had ever uttered. I was not insensible at the time of the views to mischief, with which these lies were fabricated. But my confidence was firm, that neither yourself nor the British government, equally outraged by them, would believe me capable of making the editors of newspapers the confidants of my speeches or opinions. The fact was this. The treaty was communicated to us by Mr. Erskine on the day Congress was to rise. Two of the senators inquired of me in the evening, whether it was my purpose to detain them on account of the treaty. My answer was, ' that it was not ; that the treaty containing no provision against the impressment of our seamen, and being accompanied by a kind of protestation of the British ministers, which would leave that government free to consider it as a treaty or no treaty, according to their own convenience, I should not give them the trouble of deliberating on it.' This was substantially, and almost verbally what I said whenever spoken to about it, and I never failed when the occasion would admit of it, to justify yourself and Mr. Pinkney, by expressing my conviction, that *it was all that could be obtained from the British government ;* that you had told their commissioners that your government could not be pledged to ratify, because *it was contrary to their instructions;* of course, that it should be considered but as a *project;* and in this light I stated it publicly in my message to congress on the opening of the session."

Some time after his return, Mr. Monroe addressed a letter to Mr. Madison, giving a detailed account of the difficulties which the commissioners met with in the negotiations, the light in which he viewed various provisions in the treaty, and the sentiments which he entertained of its general character. That letter was dated at Richmond, Virginia, February 23, 1808. The following are extracts from it—

" The impressment of seamen from our merchant vessels is a topic which claims a primary attention, from the
order which it holds in your letter, but more especially
from some important considerations that are connected
with it. The idea entertained by the public is, that the
rights of the United States were abandoned by the American commissioners in the late negotiation, and that their
seamen were left by tacit acquiescence, if not by formal
renunciation, to depend, for their safety, on the mercy of
the British cruisers. I have, on the contrary, always believed, and still do believe, that the ground on which that
interest was placed by the paper of the British commissioners of November 8, 1806, and the explanations which
accompanied it, was both honourable and advantageous to
the United States ; that it contained a concession in their
favour, on the part of Great Britain, on the great principle
in contestation, never before made by a formal and obligatory act of the government, which was highly favourable
to their interest ; and that it also imposed on her the obligation to conform her practice under it, till a more complete arrangement should be concluded, to the just claims
of the United States." " The British paper states that
the king was not prepared to disclaim or derogate from a
right on which the security of the British navy might
essentially depend, especially in a conjuncture when he
was engaged in wars which enforced the necessity of the
most vigilant attention to the preservation and supply
of his naval force ; that he had directed his commissioners
to give to the commissioners of the United States the most
positive assurances that instructions had been given, and
should be repeated and enforced, to observe the greatest caution in the impressing of British seamen, to preserve the citizens of the United States from molestation
or injury, and that immediate and prompt redress should
be afforded on any representation of injury sustained by
them. It then proposes to postpone the article relative to

impressment on account of the difficulties which were experienced in arranging any article on that subject, and to proceed to conclude a treaty on the other points that were embraced by the negotiation. As a motive to such postponement, and the condition of it, it assures us that the British commissioners were instructed still to entertain the discussion of any plan which could be devised to secure the interests of both states without injury to the rights of either.

" By this paper, it is evident that the rights of the United States were expressly to be reserved, and not abandoned, as has been most erroneously supposed; that the negotiation on the subject of impressment was to be postponed for a limited time, and for a special object only, and to be revived as soon as that object was accomplished; and, in the interim, that the practice of impressment was to correspond essentially with the views and interests of the United States. It is, indeed, evident, from a correct view of the contents of that paper, that Great Britain refused to *disclaim* or *derogate* only from what she called her right, as it also is, that as her refusal was made applicable to a crisis of extraordinary peril, it authorized the reasonable expectation, if not the just claim, that even in that the accommodation desired would be hereafter yielded.

" In our letter to you of November 11, which accompanied the paper under consideration, and in that of January 3, which was forwarded with the treaty, these sentiments were fully confirmed. In that of November 11, we communicated one important fact, which left no doubt of the sense in which it was intended by the British commissioners that that paper should be construed by us. In calling your attention to the passage which treats of impressment, in reference to the practice which should be observed in future, we remarked that the terms " high seas" were not mentioned in it, and added that we knew that the omission had been intentional. It was impossible that those terms could have been omitted intentionally *with our knowledge*, for any purpose other than to admit a construction that it was intended that impressments should be confined to the land. I do not mean to imply that it was understood between the British commissioners and us, that Great Britain should abandon the practice of impressment on the high seas altogether. I mean, however, distinctly to state, that it was understood that the practice heretofore pursued by her should be abandoned, and that no impressment should be made on the high seas under the obligation of that paper, except in cases of an extraordinary nature, to which no general prohibition against it could be construed fairly to extend. The cases to which I allude were described in our letter of November 11. They suppose, a British ship of war and a merchant vessel of the United States, lying in the Tagus or some other port, the desertion of some of the sailors from the ship of war to the merchant vessel, and the sailing of the latter with such deserters on board, they being British subjects. It was admitted that no general prohibition against impressment could be construed to sanction such cases of injustice and fraud; and to such cases it was understood that the practice should in future be confined.

"It is a just claim on our part, that the explanations which were given of that paper by the British commissioners when they presented it to us, and afterwards while the negotiation was depending, which we communicated to you in due order of time, should be taken into view, in a fair estimate of our conduct in that transaction. As the arrangement which they proposed was of an informal nature, resting on an understanding between the parties in a certain degree confidential, it could not otherwise than happen that such explanations would be given us in the course of the business, of the views of their government in regard to it. And if an arrangement by informal understanding is admissible in any case between nations, it was our duty to receive those explanations, to give them the weight to which they were justly entitled, and to communicate them to you, with our impression of the extent of the obligation which they imposed. It is in that mode only that what is called an informal understanding between nations can be entered into. It presumes a want of precision in the written documents connected with it, which is supplied by mutual explanations and confidence. Reduce the transaction to form, and it becomes a treaty. That an informal understanding was an admissible mode of arranging this interest with Great Britain, is made sufficiently evident by your letter of February 3, 1807, in reply to ours of November 11, of the preceding year.

" Without relying, however, on the explanations that were given by the British commissioners of the import of that paper, or of the course which their government intended to pursue under it, it is fair to remark on the paper itself, that as by it the rights of the parties were reserved, and the negotiation might be continued on this particular topic, after a treaty should be formed on the others, Great Britain was bound not to trespass on those rights while that negotiation was depending ; and in case she did trespass on them, in any the slightest degree, the United States would be justified in breaking off the negotiation, and appealing to force in vindication of their rights. The mere circumstance of entertaining an amicable negotiation by one party for the adjustment of a controversy, where no right had been acknowledged in it by the other, gives to the latter a just claim to such a forbearance on the part of the former. But the entertainment of a negotiation for the express purpose of securing interests sanctioned by acknowledged rights, makes such claim irresistible. We were, therefore, decidedly of opinion, that the paper of the British commissioners placed the interest of impressment on ground which it was both safe and honourable for the United States to admit: that in short it gave their government the command of the subject for every necessary and useful purpose. Attached to the treaty, it was the basis or condition on which the treaty rested. Strong in its character in their favour on the great question of right, and admitting a favourable construction on others, it placed them on more elevated ground in those respects than they had held before; and by keeping the negotiation open to obtain a more complete adjustment, the administration was armed with the most effectual means of securing it. By this arrangement the government possessed a power to coerce without being compelled to assume the character belonging to coercion, and it was able to give effect to that power without violating the relations of amity between the countries. The right to break off the negotiation and appeal to force, could never be lost sight of in any discussion on the subject; while there was no obligation to make that appeal till necessity compelled it. If Great Britain conformed her practice to the rule prescribed by the paper of November 8, and the explanations which accompanied it, our government might rest on that ground with advantage; but if she departed from that rule, and a favourable opportunity offered for the accomplishment of a more complete and satisfactory arrangement, by a decisive effort, it would be at liberty to seize such opportunity for the advantage of the country."

Large quotations have been made from this important document, not merely for the purpose of showing the grounds on which the United States commissioners acted in forming and concluding the treaty, but with the view of establishing the proposition, that Mr. Jefferson had no sincere disposition fully and finally to adjust the sources of uneasiness and irritation between this country and Great Britain. It will be recollected, that the great reason for rejecting this treaty, without even submitting it to the Senate, who were in session when it was received, was, that it contained no article providing against impressment.

The other important subjects of negotiation were adjusted in it; and had the treaty been ratified, there is no reason to doubt that the war of 1812 might have been avoided. And there is too much reason to believe, that it was from an apprehension that the Senate might have advised to its ratification, that their opinion on the subject was not requested. It was, however, rejected, for the reason principally that there was no positive provision against impressment, under a full knowledge that no such provision could be obtained; but, at the same time with an informal understanding, as appears by Mr. Monroe's letter, that the practice should be avoided. The right they would not disclaim; but they would essentially abstain from its exercise.

Had the interests of the country alone been consulted, if there had not been something else in view, it is difficult to imagine any good reason for refusing to adjust all the subjects of dispute between this country and Great Britain, *except one.* If every thing had been concluded except impressment, the United States would have been placed in no worse situation as it regarded that. On the contrary, their condition would have been more favourable, both in relation to the practice, and to future negotiation. Besides, even that matter, by the informal understanding between the British government and Messrs. Monroe and Pinckney, was much more eligibly disposed of, than it could have been if left in the situation in which it had previously stood. That it would have been no worse for the United States, is most decisively proved by the fact, that from that day to this, no arrangement, formal nor informal, against impressment, has been made with Great Britain; nor, on other points of difference, have there ever been more advantageous terms obtained for the United States than were then offered and rejected.

In June, 1807, the attack of the British frigate Leopard, upon the United States frigate Chesapeake, occurred.

The first information which Mr. Monroe, our minister at London, received of this transaction, was through a note from Mr. Canning, dated July 25th, 1807. On the 29th of July Mr. Monroe addressed a note to Mr. Canning, calling his attention to this aggression on the sovereignty of the United States; and after having stated the case, he remarked—"I might state other examples of great indignity and outrage, many of which are of recent date, to which the United States have been exposed off their coast, and even within several of their harbours, from the British squadron; but it is improper to mingle them with the present more serious cause of complaint;" and he concluded his letter by saying—"I have called your attention to this subject, in full confidence that his majesty's government will see, in the act complained of, a flagrant abuse of its own authority, and that it will not hesitate to enable me to communicate to my government, without delay, a frank disavowal of the principle on which it was made, and its assurance that the officer who is responsible for it—shall suffer the punishment which so unexampled an aggression on the sovereignty of a neutral nation justly deserves."

This letter was answered by Mr. Canning on the 3d of August. After noticing the general subject of Mr. Monroe's note he remarks—"If, therefore, the statement in your note should prove to be correct, and to contain all the circumstances of the case, upon which complaint is intended to be made, and if it shall appear that the act of his majesty's officers rested on no other grounds than the simple and unqualified assertion of the pretension above referred to, his majesty has no difficulty in disowning that act, and will have no difficulty in manifesting his displeasure at the conduct of his officers.

" With respect to the other causes of complaint [whatever they may be] which are hinted at in your note, I perfectly agree with you, in the sentiment which you express, as to the propriety of not involving them in a question which is of itself of sufficient importance to claim a separate and most serious consideration."

On the 2d of July, Mr. Jefferson, President of the United States, issued a proclamation requiring all armed vessels belonging to the King of Great Britain, then in the ports or harbours of the United States, immediately to depart therefrom, and interdicting their entrance into those ports and harbours. Mr. Canning having received from the British minister an unofficial copy of this document, immediately, upon the 8th of August, wrote to Mr. Monroe, for the purpose of ascertaining whether it was genuine, or not, and received for answer, on the 9th, that Mr. Monroe had not heard from his government on the subject ; but expected, in a few days to be instructed to make a communication to the British government in regard to it. On the 7th of September, Mr. Monroe made a long communication to Mr. Canning respecting the attack on the Chesapeake. On the 23d of September Mr. Canning replied, and in the commencement of his note made the following remarks—" Before I proceed to observe upon that part of it which relates more immediately to the question now at issue between our two governments, I am commanded, in the first instance, to express the surprise which is felt at the total omission of a subject upon which I had already been commanded to apply to you for information, the proclamation purported to have been issued by the President of the United States. Of this paper, when last I addressed you upon it, you professed not to have any knowledge beyond what the ordinary channels of public information afforded, nor any authority to declare it to be authentic. I feel it an indispensable duty to renew my inquiry on this subject. The answer which I may receive from you is by no means unimportant to the settlement of the discussion which has arisen from the encounter between the Leopard and the Chesapeake.

" The whole of the question arising out of that transaction, is in fact no other than a question as to the amount of reparation due by his majesty for the unauthorized act of his officer : and you will, therefore, readily perceive that, in so far as the government of the United States have thought proper to take that reparation into their own hands, and to resort to measures of retaliation previously to any direct application to the British government, or to the British minister in America for redress, in so far the British government is entitled to take such measures into account, and to consider them in the estimate of reparation which is acknowledged to have been originally due.

" The total exclusion of all ships of war belonging to one of the two belligerent parties, while the ships of war of the other were protected by the harbours of the neutral power, would furnish no light ground of complaint against that neutral, if considered in any other point of view than as a measure of retaliation for a previous injury : and so considered, it cannot but be necessary to take it into account in the adjustment of the original dispute.

" I am, therefore, distinctly to repeat the inquiry, whether you are now enabled to declare, sir, that the proclamation is to be considered as the authentic act of your government ? and, if so, I am further to inquire whether you are authorized to notify the intention of your government to withdraw that proclamation, on the knowledge of his majesty's disavowal of the act which occasioned its publication ?"

After a long series of remarks and reasoning on the subject of impressment, and the difficulties attending a modification of the practice, Mr. Canning says—" Whether any arrangement can be devised, by which this practice may admit of modification, without prejudice to the essential rights and interests of Great Britain, is a question, which, as I have already said, the British government may, at a proper season, be ready to entertain ; but, whether the consent of Great Britain to the entering into such a discussion, shall be extorted as the price of an amicable adjustment, as the condition of being admitted to make honourable reparation for an injury, is a question of quite a different sort, and one which can be answered no otherwise than by an unqualified refusal.

" I earnestly recommend to you, therefore, to consider, whether the instructions which you have received from your government may not leave you at liberty to come to an adjustment of the case of the Leopard and the Chesapeake, independently of the other question, with which it appears to have been unnecessarily connected.

" If your instructions leave you no discretion, I cannot press you to act in contradiction to them. In that case there can be no advantage in pursuing a discussion which you are not authorized to conclude ; and I shall have only to regret, that the disposition of his majesty to terminate that difference amicably and satisfactorily, is for the present rendered unavailing.

" In that case, his majesty, in pursuance of the disposition of which he has given such signal proofs, will lose no time in sending a minister to America, furnished with the necessary instructions and powers for bringing this unfortunate dispute to a conclusion, consistent with the harmony subsisting between Great Britain and the United States. But, in order to avoid the inconvenience which has arisen, from the mixt nature of your instructions, that minister will not be empowered to entertain, as connected with this subject, any proposition respecting the search of merchant vessels."

On the 29th of September Mr. Monroe wrote a long answer to Mr. Canning's letter, in which, among other things, he says—" You inform me, that his majesty has determined, in case my instructions do not permit me to separate the late aggression from the general practice of impressment, to transfer the business to the United States, by committing it to a minister who shall be sent there with full powers to conclude it. To that measure I am far

from being disposed to raise any obstacle, and shall immediately apprise my government of the decision to adopt it."

In a short time after the date of the letter from which
the quotation immediately preceding was taken, the following note was addressed to Mr. Canning by Mr. Monroe.

            " *Portland Place, October* 9, 1807.

" To MR. CANNING,

" Mr. Monroe presents his compliments to Mr. Canning,
and requests that he will be so good as to inform him,
whether it is intended, that the minister, whom his majesty
proposes to send to the government of the United States,
shall be employed in a special mission without having any
connection immediate or eventual with the ordinary legation. Mr. Monroe has inferred from Mr. Canning's note,
that the mission will be of the special nature above described, but he will be much obliged to Mr. Canning to
inform him whether he has taken a correct view of the
measure. Mr. Monroe would also be happy to know of
Mr. Canning at what time it is expected the minister will
sail for the United States. Mr. Canning will be sensible
that Mr. Monroe's motive in requesting this information
is, that he may be enabled to communicate it without delay
to his government, the propriety of which, he is persuaded,
Mr. Canning will readily admit."

            " *Foreign Office, October* 10, 1807.

" From MR. CANNING,

" Mr. Canning presents his compliments to Mr. Monroe,
and in acknowledging the honour of his note of yesterday,
has great pleasure in assuring him that he is at all times
ready to answer any inquiries to which Mr. Monroe at-
taches any importance, and which it is in Mr. Canning's
power to answer with precision, without public inconvenience. But it is not in Mr. Canning's power to state with
confidence what may be the eventual determination of his

majesty in respect to the permanent mission in America. The mission of the minister whom his majesty is now about to send will certainly be limited *in the first instance* to the discussion of the question of the Chesapeake."

After Mr. Rose's arrival at Washington, he addressed a letter to Mr. Madison, then Secretary of State, dated January 26, 1808, from which the following passages are copied :

" Having had the honour to state to you, that I am expressly precluded by my instructions from entering upon any negotiation for the adjustment of the differences arising from the encounter of his majesty's ship Leopard and the frigate of the United States, the Chesapeake, as long as the proclamation of the President of the United States, of the 2d of July, 1807, shall be in force, I beg leave to offer you such farther explanation of the nature of that condition, as appears to me calculated to place the motives, under which it has been enjoined to me thus to bring it forward, in their true light."

After a series of remarks, he says—" I may add, that if his majesty has not commanded me to enter into the discussion of the other causes of complaint, stated to arise from the conduct of his naval commanders in these seas, prior to the encounter of the Leopard and Chesapeake, it was because it has been deemed improper to mingle them, whatever may be their merits, with the present matter, so much more interesting and important in its nature ; an opinion originally and distinctly expressed by Mr. Monroe, and assented to by Mr. Secretary Canning. But if, upon this more recent and more weighty matter of discussion, upon which the proclamation mainly and materially rests, his majesty's amicable intentions are unequivocally evinced, it is sufficiently clear, that no hostile disposition can be supposed to exist on his part, nor can any views be attributed to his government, such as, requiring to be counteracted by mea-

sures of precaution, could be deduced from transactions
which preceded that encounter."

To this Mr. Madison replied in a long letter, dated
March 5, in which he goes into a review of all the causes
of complaint on the part of the United States, against the
British Government, arising from the conduct of the naval
officers of that kingdom ; coming down in regular course
to the attack upon the Chesapeake by the Leopard; and
saying—that "it is sufficient to remark, that the conclusive evidence which this event added to that which had
preceded, of the uncontrolled excesses of the British naval
commanders, in insulting our sovereignty, and abusing our
hospitality, determined the President to extend to all
British armed ships the precaution heretofore applied to a
few by name, of interdicting to them the use and privileges
of our harbours and waters."———

"The President, having interposed this precautionary
interdict, lost no time in instructing the minister plenipotentiary of the United States to represent to the British
government the signal aggression which had been committed on their sovereignty and their flag, and to require
the satisfaction due for it ; indulging the expectation, that
his Britannic majesty would at once perceive it to be the
truest magnanimity, as well as the strictest justice, to
offer that prompt and full expiation of an acknowledged
wrong, which would re-establish and improve, both in fact
and in feeling, the state of things which it had violated."
The Secretary of State finally comes to the point between
him and Mr. Rose, the revocation of the proclamation—
"The proclamation [he says] is considered as a hostile
measure, and a discontinuance of it, as due to the discontinuance of the aggression which led to it.

It has been sufficiently shown that the proclamation, as
appears on the face of it, was produced by a train of
occurrences terminating in the attack on the American
frigate, and not by this last alone. To a demand, there-

fore, that the proclamation be revoked, it would be perfectly fair to oppose a demand, that redress be first given for the numerous irregularities which preceded the aggression on the American frigate, as well as for this particular aggression, and that effectual controul be interposed against repetitions of them. And as no such redress has been given for the past, notwithstanding the lapse of time which has taken place, nor any such security for the future, notwithstanding the undiminished reasonableness of it, it follows that a continuance of the proclamation would be consistent with an entire discontinuance of one only of the occurrences from which it proceeded. But it is not necessary to avail the argument of this view of the case, although of itself entirely conclusive. Had the proclamation been founded on the single aggression committed on the Chesapeake, and were it admitted, that the discontinuance of that aggression merely gave a claim to the discontinuance of the proclamation, the claim would be defeated by the incontestible fact, that that aggression has not been discontinued. It has never ceased to exist; and is in existence at this moment. Need I remind you, Sir, that the seizure and asportation of the seamen belonging to the crew of the Chesapeake entered into the very essence of that aggression, that, with an exception of the victim to a trial, forbidden by the most solemn considerations, and greatly aggravating the guilt of its author, the seamen in question are still retained, and consequently that the aggression, if in no other respect, is by that act alone continued and in force. " If the views which have been taken of the subject have the justness which they claim, they will have shown that on no ground whatever can an annulment of the proclamation of July 2d be reasonably required, as a preliminary to the negotiation with which you are charged. On the contrary, it clearly results, from a recurrence to the causes and objects of the proclamation, that, as was at first intimated, the strongest sanctions of Great Britain herself would support the demand, that, previous to a discussion of the proclamation, due satisfaction should be made to the United States; that this satisfaction ought to extend to all the wrongs which preceded and produced that act; and that even limiting the merits of the question to the single relation of the proclamation to the wrong committed in the attack on the American frigate, and deciding the question on the principle that a discontinuance of the latter required of right a discontinuance of the former, nothing appears that does not leave such a preliminary destitute of every foundation which could be assumed for it.

" With a right to draw this conclusion, the President might have instructed me to close this communication with the reply stated in the beginning of it; and perhaps in taking this course, he would only have consulted a sensibility, to which most governments would, in such a case, have yielded. But adhering to the moderation by which he has been invariably guided, and anxious to rescue the two nations from the circumstances under which an abortive issue to your mission necessarily places them, he has authorized me, in the event of your disclosing the terms of reparation which you believe will be satisfactory, and on its appearing that they are so, to consider this evidence of the justice of his Britannic majesty as a pledge for an effectual interposition with respect to all the abuses against a recurrence of which the proclamation was meant to provide, and to proceed to concert with you a revocation of that act, bearing the same date with the act of reparation, to which the United States are entitled.

" *I am not unaware, sir, that according to the view which you appear to have taken of your instructions, such a course of proceeding has not been contemplated by them.* It is possible, nevertheless, that a re-examination, in a spirit, in which I am well pursuaded it will be made, may discover them to be not inflexible to a proposition in so high a degree liberal and conciliatory. In every event, the President will have manifested his willingness to meet your government on a ground of accommodation, which spares to its feelings, however misapplied he may deem them, every concession, not essentially due to those which must be equally respected, and consequently will have demonstrated that the very ineligible posture given to so important a subject in the relations of the two countries, by the unsuccessful termination of your mission, can be referred to no other source than the rigorous restrictions under which it was to be executed."

On the 17th of March, Mr. Rose replied to the foregoing communication, informing Mr. Madison that he was "under the necessity of declining to enter into the terms of negotiation, which, by direction of the President of the United States," Mr. Madison had offered; and saying, "I do not feel myself competent, in the present instance, to depart from the instructions, which I stated in my letter of the 26th of January last, and which preclude me from acceding to the condition thus proposed." He then proceeds further and says—

"I should add, that I am absolutely prohibited from entering upon matters unconnected with the specifick object I am authorized to discuss, much less can I thus give any pledge concerning them. The condition suggested, moreover, leads to the direct inference, that the proclamation of the President of the United States of the 2d of July, 1807, is maintained either as an equivalent for reparation for the time being, or as a compulsion to make it.

"It is with the more profound regret that I feel myself under the necessity of declaring, that I am unable to act upon the terms thus proposed, as it becomes my duty to inform you, in conformity to my instructions, that on the rejection of the demand stated in my former letter, on the part of his majesty, my mission is terminated."

Thus another opportunity to adjust at least one, and perhaps several important subjects of dispute and complaint between the United States and Great Britain, was lost, in consequence of Mr. Jefferson's refusing to yield a mere point of etiquette, respecting the recal of the proclamation which he had issued, to say the least, precipitately, and which he was forewarned by the British government, would prevent an adjustment of the affair of the frigate Chesapeake, if continued in force. It is not to be believed, if he had been sincerely desirous of establishing a solid and permanent friendship (political friendship is here meant) between the two nations, that he would have failed of accomplishing that object on such slender a pretext as that which put an end to Mr. Rose's mission.

That he did not entertain such a wish is evident, not only from the manner in which the negotiation with Mr. Rose was conducted, and the grounds on which it was concluded; but from the circumstance, that a direct attempt was made by the Secretary of State, in his correspondence with him, to induce Mr. Rose to depart from his instructions, and enter upon the discussion of subjects which he was expressly ordered by his government not to meddle with. Mr. Madison, in his letter of the 5th of March, from which several extracts have been made, after using every effort in his power to induce Mr. Rose to violate his instructions, says in a passage already recited— " I am not unaware, sir, that according to the view which you appear to have taken of your instructions, such a course of proceeding has not been contemplated by them. It is possible, nevertheless, that a re-examination, in a spirit, in which I am well persuaded it will be made, may discover them to be not inflexible to a proposition in so high a degree liberal and conciliatory." This cannot be considered as any thing more or less than a direct proposition to the British minister to violate his instructions ; and this must have been with a perfect knowledge on the part of Mr. Madison, that any treaty or arrangement made under such circumstances would be rejected by the British government, because made in violation of his instructions.

The conduct of Mr. Canning, when corresponding with Mr. Monroe, was marked by a different disposition. After a long discussion of the difficulties between the countries, Mr. Canning said—"I earnestly recommend to you therefore, to consider, whether the instructions which you have received from your government may not leave you at liberty to come to an adjustment of the case of the Leopard and the Chesapeake, independently of the other question with which it appears to have been unnecessarily connected. If your instructions leave you no discretion, I cannot press you to act in contradiction to them."

On the 13th of November, 1811, more than four years after the affair between the British frigate Leopard and the American frigate Chesapeake, the following message and correspondence relating to that subject were transmitted to congress by the President of the United States.

" I communicate to congress copies of a correspondence between the envoy extraordinary and minister plenipotentiary of Great Britain and the Secretary of State, relating to the aggression committed by a British ship of war on the United States frigate Chesapeake, by which it will be seen that that subject of difference between the two countries is terminated by an offer of reparation which has been acceded to."

" *Washington, October* 30, 1811.

" MR. FOSTER to MR. MONROE.

SIR,—I had already the honour to mention to you, that I came to this country furnished with instructions from his royal highness the prince regent, in the name and on the behalf of his majesty, for the purpose of proceeding to a final adjustment of the differences which have arisen between Great Britain and the United States of America, in the affair of the Chesapeake frigate, and I had also that of acquainting you with the necessity, under which I found myself, of suspending the execution of those instructions in consequence of my not having perceived that any steps whatever were taken by the American government to clear up the circumstances of an event which threatened so materially to interrupt the harmony subsisting between our two countries, as that which occurred in the month of last May, between the United States' ship President and his majesty's ship Little Belt, when every evidence before his majesty's government seemed to show that a most evident and wanton outrage had been committed on a British sloop of war by an American commodore.

" A court of inquiry, however, as you informed me in your letter of the 11th instant, has since been held by order of the President of the United States, on the conduct of Commodore Rodgers, and this preliminary to further discussion on the subject being all that I asked in the first instance, as due to the friendship subsisting between the two states, I have now the honour to acquaint you that I am ready to proceed in the truest spirit of conciliation to lay before you the terms of reparation which his royal highness has commanded me to propose to the United States' government, and only wait to know when it will suit your convenience to enter upon the discussion."

Mr. Monroe replied to this letter on the following day.

" *Department of State, October* 31, 1811.

" MR. MONROE to MR. FOSTER.

" SIR,—I have just had the honour to receive your letter of the 30th of this month.

" I am glad to find that the communication which I had the honour to make to you on the 11th instant relative to the court of inquiry, which was the subject of it, is viewed by you in the favourable light which you have stated.

" Although I regret that the proposition which you now make in consequence of that communication has been delayed to the present moment, I am ready to receive the terms of it whenever you may think proper to communicate them. Permit me to add, that the pleasure of finding them satisfactory will be duly augmented, if they should be introductory to a removal of all the differences depending between our two countries, the hope of which is so little encouraged by your past correspondence. A prospect of such a result will be embraced, on my part, with a spirit of conciliation equal to that which has been expressed by you."

" *Washington, November* 1, 1811.

" MR. FOSTER to MR. MONROE.

" SIR,—In pursuance of the orders which I have received from his royal highness the prince regent, in the name and on the behalf of his majesty, for the purpose of proceeding to a final adjustment of the differences which have arisen between Great Britain and the United States, in the affair of the Chesapeake frigate, I have the honour to acquaint you—

" First, that I am instructed to repeat to the American government the prompt disavowal made by his majesty (and recited in Mr. Erskine's note of April 17th, 1809, to Mr. Smith,) on being apprized of the unauthorized act of the officer in command of his naval forces on the coast of America, whose recall from a highly important and honourable command immediately ensued as a mark of his majesty's disapprobation.

" Secondly, that I am authorized to offer, in addition to that disavowal, on the part of his royal highness, the immediate restoration, as far as circumstances will admit, of the men who, in consequence of Admiral Berkeley's orders, were forcibly taken out of the Chesapeake, to the vessel from which they were taken: or, if that ship should be no longer in commission, to such seaport of the United States as the American government may name for the purpose.

" Thirdly, that I am also authorized to offer to the American government a suitable pecuniary provision for the sufferers in consequence of the attack on the Chesapeake, including the families of those seamen who unfortunately fell in the action, and of the wounded survivors.

" These honourable propositions, I can assure you, sir, are made with the sincere desire that they may prove satisfactory to the government of the United States, and I trust they will meet with that amicable reception which their conciliatory nature entitles them to. I need scarcely add how cordially I join with you in the wish, that they might prove introductory to a removal of all the differences depending between our two countries."

" *November* 12*th*, 1811.

" MR. MONROE to MR. FOSTER.

" SIR,—I have had the honour to receive your letter of 1st November, and to lay it before the President. It is much to be regretted that the reparation due for such an aggression as that committed on the United States frigate Chesapeake should have been so long delayed; nor could the translation of the offending officer from one command to another, be regarded as constituting a part of a reparation otherwise satisfactory; considering however the existing circumstances of the case, and the early and amicable attention paid to it by his royal highness the prince regent, the president accedes to the proposition contained in your letter, and in so doing your government will, I am persuaded, see a proof of the conciliatory disposition by which the President has been actuated."

It is a little remarkable, that this final adjustment of a question about which so much had been said and done, should have been accompanied by such uncourteous and undignified language as that at the close of the foregoing letters. It seems as if it was studiously designed to irritate the British government, even when nothing could be gained by it.

On the 16th of May, 1806, Mr. Fox, then prime minister of Great Britain, addressed the following note to Mr. Monroe, the United States envoy at London :—

" Downing-street, May 16, 1806.

" The undersigned, his majesty's principal secretary of state for foreign affairs, has received his majesty's commands to acquaint Mr. Monroe, that the king, taking into consideration the new and extraordinary means resorted to by the enemy for the purpose of distressing the commerce of his subjects, has thought fit to direct, that the necessary measures should be taken for the blockade of the coast, rivers, and ports, from the river Elbe to the port of Brest, both inclusive, and the said coast, rivers, and ports, are and must be considered as blockaded ; but that his majesty is pleased to declare, that such blockade shall not extend to prevent neutral ships and vessels, laden with goods not being the property of his majesty's enemies, and not being contraband of war, from approaching the said coast, and entering into and sailing from the said rivers and ports, (save and except the coast, rivers and ports, from Ostend to the river Seine, already in a state of strict and rigorous blockade, and which are to be considered as so continued,) provided the said ships and vessels so approaching and entering (except as aforesaid) shall not have been laden at any port belonging to or in the possession of any of his majesty's enemies, and that the said ships and vessels, so sailing from the said rivers and ports (except as aforesaid) shall not be destined to any port belonging to or in the possession of any of his majesty's enemies, nor have previously broken the blockade.

" Mr. Monroe is therefore requested to apprise the American consuls and merchants residing in England, that the coast, rivers, and ports above mentioned, must be considered as being in a state of blockade, and that from this time all the measures, authorized by the law of na-

tions and the respective treaties between his majesty and
the different neutral powers, will be adopted and executed
with respect to vessels attempting to violate the said
blockade after this notice."

On the 17th of May, Mr. Monroe wrote to the Secretary of State, and communicated this note from Mr. Fox;
and in the course of his letter made the following remarks :—

" Early this morning I received from Mr. Fox a note, a
copy of which is enclosed, which you will perceive embraces explicitly a principal subject depending between
our governments, though in rather a singular mode. A
similar communication is, I presume, made to the other
ministers, though of that I have no information. The
note is couched in terms of restraint, and professes to extend the blockade further than was heretofore done; nevertheless it takes it from many ports already blockaded, indeed from all east of Ostend and west of the Seine, except
in articles contraband of war and enemies' property, which
are seizable without a blockade. And in like form of exception, considering every enemy as one power, it admits
the trade of neutrals, within the same limit, to be free, in
the productions of enemies colonies, in every but the direct
route between the colony and the parent country. I have,
however, been too short a time in the possession of this
paper to trace it in all its consequences in regard to this
question. It cannot be doubted that the note was drawn
by the government in reference to the question, and if intended by the cabinet as a foundation on which Mr. Fox
is authorized to form a treaty, and obtained by him for
the purpose, *it must be viewed in a very favourable light.*
It seems clearly *to put an end to further seizures, on the
principle which has been heretofore in contestation.*"

On the 20th of May Mr. Monroe wrote again to the
Secretary of State. The following is an extract from his
letter. " From what I could collect, I have been strength-

ened in the opinion which I communicated to you in my last, that Mr. Fox's note of the 16th was drawn with a view to a principal question with the United States, I mean that of the trade with enemies' colonies. It embraces, it is true, other objects, particularly the commerce with Prussia, and the north generally, whose ports it opens to neutral powers, under whose flag British manufactures will find a market there. *In this particular, especially, the measure promises to be highly satisfactory to the commercial interest, and it may have been the primary object of the government.*"

On the 21st of November, 1806, Bonaparte issued his decree, commonly called the Berlin decree, from the fact that it bears date from the Prussian capital.

" *Imperial Decree of the 21st of November,* 1806.

" ART. 1. The British islands are declared in a state of blockade.

2. All commerce and correspondence with the British islands are prohibited. In consequence, letters or packets, addressed either to England, to an Englishman, or in the English language, shall not pass through the post office, and shall be seized.

3. Every subject of England, of whatever rank and condition soever, who shall be found in the countries occupied by our troops, or by those of our allies, shall be made a prisoner of war.

4. All magazines, merchandise, or property whatsoever, belonging to a subject of England, shall be declared lawful prize.

5. The trade in English merchandise is forbidden; all merchandise belonging to England, or coming from its manufactories and colonies, is declared lawful prize.

6. One half of the proceeds of the confiscation of the merchandise and property, declared good prize by the preceding articles, shall be applied to indemnify the mer-

chants for the losses which they have suffered by the capture of merchant vessels by English cruisers.

7. No vessel coming directly from England, or from the English colonies, or having been there since the publication of the present decree, shall be received into any port.

8. Every vessel contravening the above clause, by means of a false declaration, shall be seized, and the vessel and cargo confiscated as if they were English property.

9. Our tribunal of prizes at Paris is charged with the definitive adjudication of all the controversies which may arise within our empire, or in the countries occupied by the French army relative to the execution of the present decree. Our tribunal of prizes at Milan shall be charged with the definitive adjudication of the said controversies, which may arise within the extent of our kingdom of Italy.

10. The present decree shall be communicated by our minister of exterior relations, to the kings of Spain, of Naples, of Holland, and of Etruria, and to our allies, whose subjects, like ours, are the victims of the injustice and the barbarism of the English maritime laws. Our ministers of exterior relations, of war, of marine, of finances, of police, and our post masters general, are charged each, in what concerns him, with the execution of the present decree."

On the 11th of November, 1807, a new order in council was issued by the British government, in which it is declared, "that all the ports and places of France and her allies, or of any other country at war with his majesty, and other ports and places in Europe, from which, although not at war with his majesty, the British flag is excluded, and all ports or places in the colonies belonging to his majesty's enemies, shall from henceforth be subject to the same restrictions, in point of trade and navigation, with the exceptions hereinafter mentioned, as if the same were actually blockaded by his majesty's naval forces in the most strict and rigorous manner : and it is hereby further ordered and declared, that all trade in articles, which are of the produce or manufacture of the said countries or colonies, together with all goods and merchandise on board, and all articles of the produce or manufacture of the said countries or colonies, shall be captured and condemned as prize to the captors."

The order contained various other provisions, not necessary to the object of this work, all professedly founded upon the idea of retaliation for the French decree alluded to, and to the extravagant assumptions of power, and gross violation of principle, and the rights of neutrals.

To meet this measure of the British government, the Emperor of France, on the 11th of December, 1807, issued a new decree from his imperial palace at Milan, which from that circumstance has been called the Milan Decree. After a preamble, it declares—

" Art. 1. Every ship, to whatever nation it may belong, that shall have submitted to be searched by an English ship, or on a voyage to England, or shall have paid any tax whatsoever to the English government, is thereby and for that alone, declared to be *denationalized*, to have forfeited the protection of its king, and to have become English property.

2. Whether the ships thus *denationalized* by the arbitrary measures of the English government, enter into our ports, or those of our allies, or whether they fall into the hands of our ships of war, or of our privateers, they are declared to be good and lawful prizes.

3. The British islands are declared to be in a state of blockade, both by land and sea. Every ship of whatever nation, or whatsoever the nature of its cargo may be, that sails from the ports of England, or those of the English colonies, and of the countries occupied by English troops, and proceeding to England, or to the English colonies, or

to countries occupied by English troops, is good and lawful prize, as contrary to the present decree, and may be captured by our ships of war, or our privateers, and adjudged to the captor.

4. These measures, which are resorted to only in just retaliation of the barbarous system adopted by England, which assimilates its legislation to that of Algiers, shall cease to have any effect with respect to all nations who shall have the firmness to compel the English government to respect their flag. They shall continue to be rigorously in force, as long as that government does not return to the principle of the law of nations, which regulates the relations of civilized states in a state of war. The provisions of the present decree shall be abrogated and null, in fact, as soon as the English abide again by the principles of the law of nations, which are also the principles of justice and of honour."

These British orders in council, and French decrees, were all in force at the time the negotiation with Mr. Erskine commenced, and were just subjects of uneasiness, complaint and remonstrance, on the part of the United States. Property to a large amount, belonging to American citizens, and not liable to condemnation or capture under the well established principles of the laws of nations, was taken and confiscated by both parties; and it almost seemed as if the warfare which was raging between the two most refined and civilized nations in Europe, would degenerate into downright piracy and barbarism.

On the 18th of December, 1807, Mr. Jefferson communicated to both houses of Congress the following message—

" The communications now made, showing the great and increasing dangers with which our vessels, our seamen, and merchandise, are threatened on the high seas and elsewhere, from the belligerent powers of Europe, and it being of the greatest importance to keep in safety these essential resources, I deem it my duty to recommend the subject to the consideration of Congress, who will doubt-less perceive all the advantages which may be expected from an inhibition of the departure of our vessels from the ports of the United States.

" Their wisdom will also see the necessity of making every preparation for whatever events may grow out of the present crisis."

The only documents published in the state papers as having accompanied this message, were,

1. An " Extract of a letter from the (French) Grand Judge, Minister of Justice, to the Imperial Attorney General for the Council of Prizes ;"—of which the following is a translation—

" *Paris, Sept.* 18, 1807.

" SIR,—I have submitted to his majesty the emperor and king the doubts raised by his excellency the minister of marine and colonies, on the extent of certain dispositions of the imperial decree of the 21st of November, 1806, which has declared the British isles in a state of blockade. The following are his majesty's intentions on the points in question :

1st. May vessels of war, by virtue of the imperial decree of the 21st November last, seize on board neutral vessels either English property, or even all merchandise proceeding from the English manufactories or territory ?

Answer. His majesty has intimated, that as he did not think proper to express any exception in his decree, there is no ground for making any in its execution, in relation to any whomsoever (a l'égard de qui que ce peut être.)

2dly. His majesty has postponed a decision on the question whether armed French vessels ought to capture neutral vessels bound to or from England, even when they have no English merchandise on board.

REGNIER."

And 2. A document cut from an English newspaper, the London Gazette of October 17, purporting to be a proclamation by the king of Great Britain, " for recalling and prohibiting British seamen from serving foreign princes and states," and dated October 16, 1807. This document concluded in the following manner—

" And we do hereby notify, that all such our subjects as aforesaid, who have voluntarily entered, or shall enter, or voluntarily continue to serve on board of any ships of war belonging to any foreign state at enmity with us, are and will be guilty of high treason : and we do by this our royal proclamation declare, that they shall be punished with the utmost severity of the law."

In a speech of Mr. Pickering, a member of the Senate of the United States from Massachusetts, on a resolution to repeal all the embargo laws, on the 30th of November, 1808, in allusion to the act of Congress of December, 1807, laying the embargo, the following remarks are to be found—

" Of the French papers supposed to be brought by the Revenge, none were communicated to Congress, save a *letter dated September 24th, 1807, from General Armstrong to M. Champagny, and his answer of the 7th of October,* relative to the Berlin decree, and a letter from Regnier, minister of justice, to Champagny, giving the emperor's interpretation of that decree. These three papers, with a newspaper copy of a proclamation of the king of Great Britain, issued in the same October, were all the papers communicated by the President to Congress, as the grounds on which he recommended the embargo. These papers, he said, " showed the great and increasing dangers with which our vessels, our seamen and merchandise were threatened on the high seas and elsewhere, from the belligerent powers of Europe."

These remarks of Mr. Pickering were made in debate in the Senate, within less than a year from the date of the message recommending an embargo, and of course, as they were not denied or questioned, they must be taken to be correct. It is certainly a singular circumstance, if they were correct, that none of the documents alluded to are published with the message recommending the embargo, except Regnier's letter, and the British proclamation recalling their seamen. In the same volume of " state papers," published by Wait & Sons, four hundred pages farther advanced in the volume, are to be found Regnier's letter of the 18th of September, 1807, General Armstrong's letter of September 24th to the minister of foreign relations, and Champagny's answer of October 7th. Why they were not published with the message with which they were communicated to Congress, and more especially how they came to be placed where they are, are matters that we cannot explain. General Armstrong's letter is as follows—

" Paris, Sept. 24, 1807.

" SIR,—I have this moment learned that a new and extended construction, highly injurious to the commerce of the United States, was about to be given to the imperial decree of the 21st of November last. It is therefore incumbent upon me to ask from your excellency an explanation of his majesty's views in relation to this subject, and particularly whether it be his majesty's intention, in any degree, to infract the obligations of the treaty now subsisting between the United States and the French empire?

" JOHN ARMSTRONG.

" His Excellency the Minister of
    Foreign Relations."

The following is M. Champagny's answer—

" Fontainbleau, Oct. 7, 1807.

" SIR,—You did me the honour, on the 24th of September, to request me to send you some explanations as to the execution of the decree of blockade of the British islands, as to vessels of the United States.

" The provisions of all the regulations and treaties relative to a state of blockade have appeared applicable to the existing circumstance, and it results from the explanations which have been addressed to me by the imperial procureur general of the council of prizes, that his majesty has considered every neutral vessel, going from English ports, with cargoes of English merchandise, or of English origin, as lawfully seizable by French armed vessels.

" The decree of blockade has been now issued eleven months. The principal powers of Europe, far from protesting against its provisions, have adopted them. They have perceived that its execution must be complete, to render it more effectual, and it has seemed easy to reconcile the measure with the observance of treaties, especially at a time when the infractions, by England, of the rights of all maritime powers, render their interests common, and tend to unite them in support of the same cause.

" Champagny."

" His Excellency General Armstrong,
   Minister Plen. of the U. States."

It is perfectly apparent, from the examination of these several documents, that no *new facts* appeared respecting the policy or measures of Great Britain, which justified or called for an embargo. The proclamation, allowing it to have been a genuine state paper, showed no new or additional marks of animosity against the United States, or their commerce. It appears to have been a mere measure of precaution for the security of their seamen. The aggravated spirit of hostility towards this country, and its commercial interests, was to be found only in the French documents. But as the French had at that time very little external commerce, and but few vessels of any description afloat, and Great Britain had the command of the ocean ; under such circumstances, it was doubtless thought necessary, if for nothing else, to appease the feelings of his imperial majesty of France, to adopt a measure which should involve Great Britain as well as France, in its operations. And hence the British proclamation was introduced, as furnishing evidence of " the great and *increasing* dangers with which our vessels, our seamen, and merchandise were threatened on the high seas and elsewhere from the belligerent powers of Europe."

The remark in the President's message, as far as it related to this document, was not true. There is nothing in the British proclamation which showed the slightest increase of danger to our vessels, seamen, or merchandise.

That our commerce had suffered great injustice from the British orders of council, there can be no doubt ; and there never was, it is presumed, any disposition among the opposers of the embargo, to excuse or vindicate that injustice. But great as it was, it in a variety of respects fell far short of the atrocious conduct of France towards us. After the naval power of France had been destroyed by the British, and the nation was in effect driven from the ocean, it became an object of the highest importance to Bonaparte to prevent all commercial intercourse between Great Britain and the continent. To accomplish this, he undertook to establish his famous Continental System—which was nothing less than an attempt, by the most arbitrary and oppressive measures, to shut out all British trade, merchandise, produce, and manufactures, from the nations on the continent. His decrees, issued at Berlin, Milan, and Rambouillet, were parts of the machinery by which he intended to carry his project into effect. It is perfectly clear from the nature of the case, that in prosecuting this project, it must have been his intention from the beginning to disregard every principle of law, justice, and humanity, that might stand in his way. As a large part of the neutral trade of the world was carried on through American vessels, it was necessary for his purposes either to drive us from our neutrality, or render the trade so hazardous as to induce us to withdraw from it. And there is much evidence in the proceedings of our government, to show, that as far as his measures could be carried into effect against Great Britain, without too great a sacrifice on our part, Mr. Jefferson and his partisans were willing he should succeed. Many proofs of his animosity against Great Britain, and of his partiality for France, will be found in this history. And whoever will take the pains to examine the public state papers of the Congress of the United States, or the Memoirs and Correspondence of Mr. Jefferson, published since his death, will find abundant evidence of that animosity towards the one, and that partiality towards the other. In addition to the evidence derived from these sources, of his abject subserviency to France, further proof may be adduced, from a pamphlet published about the same period, of these transactions, entitled, " FURTHER SUPPRESSED DOCUMENTS ;" from which is copied the following article :—

" *Extract of a letter from Mr. Armstrong to Mr. Madison.*

" *February* 22, 1808.

" Mr. Patterson offering so good a conveyance that I cannot but employ it. Nothing has occurred here since the date of my public dispatches (the 17th) to give to our business an aspect more favourable than it then had ; but on the other hand, I have come to the knowledge of two facts which I think sufficiently show the decided character of the Emperor's policy with regard to us. These are first, that in a Council of Administration held a few days past, when it was proposed to modify the Decrees of November, 1806, and December, 1807, (though the proposition was supported by the whole weight of the Council,) he became highly indignant, and declared that these *decrees* should *suffer no change*—and that *the Americans should be com-*

pelled to take the positive character of either allies or enemies :
2d, that on the 27th of January last, twelve days after
Mr. Champagny's written assurances that *these Decrees
should work no change in the property sequestered* until our
discussions with England were brought to a close, and *seven
days before he reported to me verbally these very assurances,*
the Emperor had by a special decision *confiscated two of
our ships and their cargoes,* (the Julius Henry and the Ju-
niata,) for want merely of a document not required by any
law or usage of the commerce in which they had been engaged. This act was taken, as I am informed on a general
report of sequestered cases, amounting to one hundred and
sixty, and which, at present prices, will yield upwards of
one hundred millions of francs, a sum whose magnitude
alone renders hopeless all attempts at saving it—Danes,
Portuguese, and Americans, will be the principal sufferers.
*If I am right in supposing that the emperor has definitively
taken his ground, I cannot be wrong in concluding that you
will immediately take yours.*"

Here is decisive evidence of Bonaparte's object in issuing and enforcing his decrees. It was *to compel the United
States to become either his allies, or his enemies ;* and hence,
when urged to modify those decrees by his Council of
Administration, he became indignant, and declared they
should suffer no change.

In this same publication of " Suppressed Documents,"
is the following letter—

" *London, January 26th,* 1808.

" From MR. PINKNEY to MR. MADISON.

" SIR,—I had the honour to receive this morning your
letter of the 23d of last month, inclosing a copy of a message from the President to Congress, and of their act in
pursuance of it, laying an embargo on our vessels and
exports. It appeared to be my duty to lose no time in

giving such explanations to the British government, of this wise and salutary measure, as your letter suggests. And accordingly I went to Downing-street immediately, and had a short conference with Mr. Canning, who received my explanations with *great apparent satisfaction*, and took occasion *to express the most friendly disposition towards our country*. I availed myself of this opportunity, to mention a subject of some importance, connected with the late orders in council.

"I had been told, that American vessels coming into British ports under warning, could not obtain any document to enable them to return to the United States, in the event of its being found imprudent, either to deposit their cargoes, or to resume their original voyages, although they are not prohibited from returning, yet as the warning is endorsed on their papers, the return may be hazardous, without some British documents to prove compliance with it and give security to the voyage. Mr. C. took a note of what I said, and assured me that whatever was necessary *to give the facility in question, would be done without delay ;* and he added, that *it was their sincere wish to show, in every thing connected with the orders in council, which only necessity had compelled them to adopt, their anxiety to accommodate them, as far as was consistent with their object, to the feelings and interest of the American government and people.*"

It is difficult to imagine why these documents were kept hidden from the public eye, unless it was the fear that the country at large, from the difference of style and sentiment between the two, would form opinions unfavourable to the policy which our government were pursuing in relation to the two countries. The tone of the French emperor, as conveyed in the letter of General Armstrong, was imperious, and insolent. He would force the United States to take the positive character of either allies, or enemies— he became highly indignant, and would suffer no change in his decrees—showing conclusively, that his object was to make them answer his own purposes, regardless of their effects upon the United States.

By Mr. Pinkney's letter to Mr. Madison, it appears, that when the former communicated to Mr. Canning, the British minister, the information that Congress had established the embargo, the latter "received his explanations with great apparent satisfaction, and took occasion to express the most friendly disposition towards our country."

It is not necessary to show in what manner these " suppressed documents" were obtained for publication. It is enough for the public to know that they were obtained, and that they are genuine. Of the latter fact they may rest assured ; the author having been furnished with the most satisfactory evidence of the fact—so much so, that it will not be questioned by those by whose order they were kept back from the public.

In a report of the committee on foreign relations in the House of Representatives, bearing date November 22d, 1808, is the following passage—

" It was on the 18th of September, 1807, that a new construction of the decree took place ; an instruction having on that day been transmitted to the council of prizes by the minister of justice, by which that court was informed, that French armed vessels were authorized, under that decree, to seize without exception, in neutral vessels, either English property, or merchandise of English growth or manufacture. An immediate explanation having been asked from the French minister of foreign relations, he confirmed, in his answer of the 7th of October, 1807, the determination of his government to adopt that construction. Its first application took place on the 10th of the same month, in the case of the Horizon, of which the minister of the United States was not informed until the month of November ; and on the twelfth of that month he presented a spirited remonstrance against that infraction of the neutral rights of the United States. He had, in the mean while, transmitted to America the instruction to the council of prizes of the 18th of September. This was received on the   of December ; and a copy of the decision in the case of the Horizon having at the same time reached government, the President, aware of the consequences which would follow that new state of things, communicated immediately to Congress the alteration of the French decree, and recommended the embargo, which was accordingly laid on the 22d of December, 1807 ; *at which time it was well understood, in this country, the British orders of council of November preceding had issued, although they were not officially communicated to our government.*"

In the " Suppressed Documents," to which reference has been made, there is a letter from General Armstrong, in which some remarks are made which may probably explain the reason why those papers were not suffered to see the light. The following is an extract from it—

" *30th August*, 1808.

" We have somewhat overrated our means of coercion of the two great belligerents to a course of justice. The embargo is a measure calculated above any other, to keep us whole, and keep us in peace, but *beyond this you must not count upon it. Here it is not felt, and in England* (in the midst of the more interesting events of the day) *it is forgotten.*"

However lightly it was esteemed as a measure of coercion in France, and however speedily it passed out of mind in England, it is very certain that its full force was felt at home, and it bore too hardly upon the public prosperity, as well as upon private enterprise, to be either slighted or disregarded. Upon finding a strong spirit of opposition to its principles, as well as to its provisions, in January, 1809, Congress passed an act to enforce and make it more effectual, which excited a great deal of feeling, and no inconsiderable degree of alarm through a large part of the

country ; and probably this measure had considerable
efficacy in accomplishing the repeal of the embargo law,
and of introducing the non-intercourse act in its place.
But in this, as in almost all other cases of importance
under Mr. Jefferson's administration, it is necessary to examine closely into the subject, in order to ascertain whether the reasons given to the public for the recommendation of his measures are the genuine ones, and whether
there is not something kept out of sight, which, if discovered, might give a different aspect to the matter in hand.
It has been seen by the letter from General Armstrong to
Mr. Madison, copied from the suppressed documents, dated
February 22d, 1808, that Bonaparte had declared that the
United States should be compelled to take the positive
character of either allies or enemies. In Mr. Jefferson's
Works, published since his death, is a letter to Robert L.
Livingston, dated Washington, October 15th, 1808, from
which the following is a quotation :—

" Your letter of September the 22d waited here for my
return, and it is not till now that I have been able to acknowledge it. The explanation of his principles, given
you by the French Emperor, in conversation, is correct, as
far as it goes. He does not wish us to go to war with
England, knowing we have no ships to carry on that war.
To submit to pay to England the tribute on our commerce
which she demands by her orders of council, would be to
aid her in the war against him, and would give him just
ground to declare war with us. He concludes, therefore, as
every rational man must, that *the embargo, the only remaining alternative, was a wise measure.* These are acknowledged principles, and should circumstances arise
which may offer advantage to our country in making them
public, we shall avail ourselves of them. But as it is not
usual nor agreeable to governments to bring their conversations before the public, I think it would be well to consider this on your part as confidential, leaving to the govern-

ment to retain or make it public, as the general good may require.   Had the Emperor gone further, and said that he condemned our vessels going voluntarily into his ports in breach of his municipal laws, we might have admitted it rigorously legal, though not friendly.   But his condemnation of vessels taken on the high seas by his privateers, and carried involuntarily into his ports, is justifiable by no law, *is piracy*, and this is the wrong we complain of against him."

Who, after reading this language from Mr. Jefferson, can hesitate as to the real object which he intended to accomplish by establishing an embargo?   No other course would have answered the purpose he had in view, which obviously was, not the avoidance of dangers to our seamen, vessels, and merchandise, but to injure Great Britain, and benefit Bonaparte.   It would not benefit him if we were to go to war with Great Britain, because such a war must be to a great extent a war upon the ocean, and we had no ships to meet her there.   If we submitted to the terms which Great Britain demanded, it would be nothing less than paying tribute to her, which would aid her in carrying on her war with France, and therefore would be injurious to his majesty the Emperor, and would give him just cause of complaint against us.   " He (that is Bonaparte) concludes, *as every rational man must*, that *the embargo*, the only remaining alternative, *was a wise measure*." In what respect wise?   Not for the protection of our seamen, vessels, and merchandise, for neither of them are alluded to in these remarks, but wise for the purposes for which it was intended—*to benefit France, and injure Great Britain.*

It is to be regretted that the letter from Mr. Livingston, to which the foregoing is an answer, was not published.   It might have disclosed other facts and circumstances besides those mentioned and referred to in the answer.   But the latter contains clear and unquestionable evidence, that in the adoption of this measure it was the object of Mr. Jefferson to throw the weight of this country, as far as he then dared to venture, into the scale of France, and against that of Great Britain. It appears in Bonaparte's opinion, as well as his own, that the best, and indeed the only thing we could then do to aid the French, in their warfare against Great Britain, was to establish an embargo. Accordingly Mr. Jefferson recommended such a measure. But in bringing it before Congress he not only concealed his real motives in doing it, but he gave to Congress false reasons for introducing it to their consideration. Such conduct, when detected, and exposed, would destroy all confidence in any man, in the relations of private life. It is far more dangerous, and more to be condemned in the ruler of a great nation, whose influence must of necessity be great, and whose example cannot fail to produce a powerful effect upon the community at large. But the opportunity to prosecute his favourite political system towards the two great hostile nations of Europe was too flattering to be lost, and he improved it in the manner that has·been related. He did all he could, in a secret manner, to forward the views and promote the interests of France, and to injure and depress those of Great Britain.

Mr. Jefferson's caution to Mr. Livingston on the propriety on his part of observing secrecy with respect to the remarks of Bonaparte, on the subject of the policy of our government towards Great Britain and France, was strikingly characteristic. The *principles* advanced by the emperor are acknowledged to be sound; and should circumstances arise, which may offer advantages to our country in making them public, we shall avail ourselves of them. But as it is not usual, *nor agreeable* to governments to bring their conversations before the public, I think it will be well to consider this on your part *as confidential,* leaving to the government to retain or make it public, as the public good may require." That he should not be desirons of having this decisive evidence of Bonaparte's opinion in favour of the embargo, in preference to any other course which the case presented, and the irresistible presumption which the conversation furnishes that our administration were shaping their measures in such a manner as to promote the interests of France, published to the country, and the world, is not strange. It would ill comport with the professions which our government were constantly making of impartiality between the two belligerent powers, and certainly furnish Great Britain with unanswerable reasons for treating us as a secret and insidious enemy.

And as a decisive proof of the entire and absolute subserviency of Mr. Jefferson's feelings as well as conduct to Bonaparte's policy and interests, he says—"Had the emperor gone further, and said that he condemned our vessels going voluntarily into his ports in breach of his *municipal laws*, we might have admitted it rigorously legal, though not friendly." This, it is presumed, was the principle on which Bonaparte acted, when under his Rambouillet decree, he sequestered and confiscated, for the benefit of his privy purse, the immense amount of American property which was in his ports at the time that decree was promulgated, and for which he never made any remuneration, considering it undoubtedly as "*rigorously legal.*"

But what must be thought of the nature and strength of Mr. Jefferson's devoted attachment to France, when in his private intercourse and communications with his confidential friends, he makes use of such language as that in the closing part of this letter—"But his condemnation of our vessels taken on the high seas by his privateers, and carried involuntarily into his ports, is justifiable by no law, *is piracy.*" In all the complaints against Great Britain, nothing has been alledged of a more aggravated character than this. And yet, the general spirit and tenor of the correspondence with France, on the subject of her decrees, and the depredations upon our commerce under them, was, during the administration of Mr. Jefferson and Mr. Madison, tame, abject, and supplicatory, obviously dictated by strong apprehensions of giving offence, and expressed under the influence of servility and fear.

Mr. Madison came into office in March, 1809. Mr. Jefferson had bequeathed to him a series of difficulties and embarrassments with Great Britain, from which it was a perplexing task to extricate the country, and which, if suffered to remain in the predicament they were in at the time he left the presidency, could scarcely fail to involve it in deeper calamities. It has been shown in what manner the negotiation with Mr. Rose was defeated by an attempt to induce him to transcend his instructions, and take up controversies to which they did not extend. Upon Mr. Madison's accession to the government, the British minister in this country was the honourable David M. Erskine, son of Lord Chancellor Erskine, a member of the Whig cabinet under Mr. Fox's administration. This gentleman was inexperienced in diplomatic services, and was not distinguished by any uncommon talents, natural or acquired; but that he was extremely desirous of adjusting the difficulties between the two countries, cannot be doubted. On the 17th of April, 1809, about six weeks after Mr. Madison's inauguration as President of the United States, he addressed a letter to Mr. Smith, Secretary of State of the United States, of which the following is a copy—

" *Washington, April* 17*th*, 1809.

" SIR,—I have the honour to inform you that I have received his majesty's commands, to represent to the government of the United States, that his majesty is animated by the most sincere desire for an adjustment of the differences which have unhappily so long prevailed between the two countries, the recapitulation of which might have

a tendency to impede, if not prevent an amicable understanding.

" It having been represented to his majesty's government, that the Congress of the United States, in their proceedings at the opening of the last session, had evinced an
intention of passing certain laws, which would place the
relations of Great Britain with the United States upon an
equal footing, in all respects, with the other belligerent
powers ; I have accordingly received his majesty's commands, in the event of such laws taking place, to offer on
the part of his majesty, an honourable reparation for the
aggression committed by a British naval officer in the
attack on the United States frigate Chesapeake.

" Considering the act passed by the Congress of the
United States on the 1st of March, (usually termed the
non-intercourse act) as having produced a state of equality in the relations of the two belligerent powers with
respect to the United States, I have to submit, conformably to instructions, for the consideration of the American
government, such terms of satisfaction and reparation, as
his majesty is induced to believe will be accepted in the
same spirit of conciliation with which they are proposed.

" In addition to the prompt disavowal made by his majesty, on being apprized of the unauthorized act committed
by his naval officer, whose recall, as a mark of the king's
displeasure, from an highly important and honourable
command immediately ensued ; his majesty is willing to
restore the men forcibly taken out of the Chesapeake, and
if acceptable to the American government, to make a
suitable provision for the unfortunate sufferers on that
occasion."

This letter was answered by the Secretary of State on
the same day, and the propositions were accepted by the
government. On the following day, viz. the 18th of April,
Mr Erskine addressed a second letter to Mr. Smith, in

which, after alluding to what had previously occurred, added the following—

" On these grounds and expectations, I am instructed to communicate to the American government, his majesty's determination of sending to the United States an envoy extraordinary, invested with full powers to conclude a treaty on all the points of the relations between the two countries.

" In the mean time, with a view to contribute to the attainment of so desirable an object, his majesty would be willing to withdraw his orders in council of January and November 1807, so far as respects the United States, in the persuasion that the President would issue a proclamation for the renewal of the intercourse with Great Britain, and that whatever difference of opinion should arise in the interpretation of the terms of such an agreement, will be removed in the proposed negotiation."

On the same day Mr. Smith wrote the following letter to Mr. Erskine—

" Department of State, April 18*th,* 1809.

" SIR,—The note which I had the honour of receiving from you this day, I lost no time in laying before the President, who being sincerely desirous of a satisfactory adjustment of the differences unhappily existing between Great Britain and the United States, has authorized me to assure you, that he will meet with a disposition correspondent with that of his Britannick majesty, the determination of his majesty to send to the United States a special envoy, invested with full powers to conclude a treaty on all the points of the relations between the two countries.

" I am further authorized to assure you, that in case his Britannick majesty should, in the mean time, withdraw his orders in council of January and November, 1807, so far as respects the United States, the President will not fail to issue a proclamation by virtue of the authority, and for the purposes specified in the eleventh section of the statute, commonly called the non-intercourse act."

To this, on the succeeding day, the following answer was returned by Mr. Erskine—

"*Washington, April 19th,* 1809.

" SIR,—In consequence of the acceptance, by the President, as stated in your letter dated the 18th inst. of the proposals made by me on the part of his majesty, in my letter of the same day, for the renewal of the intercourse between the respective countries, I am authorized to declare that his majesty's orders in council of January and November, 1807, will have been withdrawn, as respects the United States on the 10th day of June next."

On the same day Mr. Smith replied in the following letter—

" *Department of State, April* 19, 1809.

"SIR,—Having laid before the President your note of this day, containing an assurance, that his Britannick majesty will, on the tenth day of June next, have withdrawn his orders in council of January and November, 1807, so far as respects the United States, I have the honour of informing you that the President will accordingly, and in pursuance of the eleventh section of the statute, commonly called the non-intercourse act, issue a proclamation, so that the trade of the United States with Great Britain may on the same day be renewed, in the manner provided in the said section."

In pursuance of this arrangement with the British Envoy, the following document was issued on the same day—

" *By the President of the United States of America.*

"A PROCLAMATION.

" Whereas it is provided by the 11th section of the act

of Congress, entitled 'An act to interdict the commercial intercourse between the United States and Great Britain and France, and their dependencies, and for other purposes; that in case either France or Great Britain shall so revoke or modify her edicts, as that they shall cease to violate the neutral commerce of the United States;' the President is authorized to declare the same by proclamation, after which the trade suspended by the said act, and by an act laying an embargo on all ships and vessels in the ports and harbours of the United States, and the several acts supplementary thereto, may be renewed with the nation so doing. And whereas the Honourable David Montague Erskine, his Britannick majesty's envoy extraordinary and minister plenipotentiary, has by the order and in the name of his sovereign declared to this government, that the British orders in council of January and November, 1807, will have been withdrawn, as respects the United States, on the 10th day of June next.

"Now therefore, I, James Madison, President of the United States, do hereby proclaim, that the orders in council aforesaid, will have been withdrawn on the said tenth day of June next; after which day the trade of the United States with Great Britain, as suspended by the act of Congress abovementioned, and an act laying an embargo on all ships and vessels in the ports and harbours of the United States, and the several acts supplementary thereto, may be renewed.

"Given under my hand and the seal of the United States, at Washington, the 19th day of April, A. D. 1809, and of the independence of the United States the thirty-third.

"JAMES MADISON.

"By the President. R. Smith, Secretary of State."

The news of this arrangement was received throughout the Union with the highest degree of gratification; and the general exultation furnished decisive evidence of the strong desire of all descriptions of persons and a great proportion of the politicians, to be at peace with Great Britain. In order to adapt the laws to the new state of things, Congress were convened in May following, and in addressing his message to both Houses, the President informed them that it afforded him much satisfaction to be able to communicate the commencement of a favourable change in our foreign relations; the critical state of which had induced a session of Congress at that early period. After recapitulating what had occurred in regard to the arrangement with Mr. Erskine, the message says,

" The revision of our commercial laws, proper *to adapt them to the arrangement which has taken place with Great Britain,* will doubtless engage the early attention of Congress."

In pursuance of this recommendation the laws necessary for the occasion were passed, and the country was gratified with the prospect of an unshackled and undisturbed prosecution of their commercial pursuits. In a short time, however, intelligence was received, that the British government had disclaimed the arrangement, on the broad ground that their agent had violated his instructions, and that the negociation was carried on, and the arrangement concluded, without authority; and in consequence thereof the minister was recalled. Upon receiving this information, a second proclamation was issued, bearing date the 3rd of August, 1809, by the President of the United States, declaring that the orders in council had not been withdrawn, agreeably to the arrangement with Mr. Erskine, and therefore the acts of Congress which had been suspended, were to be considered as in force.

It has just been remarked, that the arrangement, the history of which has been given, was rejected by the British government, on the ground that Mr. Erskine transcended, or violated his instructions. It is understood to be the fact, not only with reference to Great Britain, but other countries, for governments to withhold their sanctions from treaties and conventions concluded in this manner. The principle is recognized by our government. And it is perfectly evident that such must be the case, or there would be no security in the negotiations between governments. Like all other acts under delegated authority, it is binding on the principal when performed within the scope of the commission granted to the agent.

An inquiry necessarily arises here, whether our government were acquainted with the extent of Mr. Erskine's instructions, before, or at the time of the negotiation. The dates of the correspondence between the Secretary of State and Mr. Erskine show, that the business was hurried in a very extraordinary manner. The letters on both sides were all written, the arrangement concluded, and the proclamation founded upon that arrangement, was issued in the course of three days. On the 31st of July, 1809, Mr. Erskine communicated to Mr. Smith, Secretary of State, the information that the British government had not confirmed the arrangement; at the same time, expressing the conviction which he entertained at the time of making it, that he had conformed to his majesty's wishes, and to the spirit at least of his instructions. On the 9th of August the Secretary of State addressed a letter to Mr. Erskine, requesting an explanation of some communications contained in a letter from him to his government, respecting conversations with Mr. Madison, Mr. Gallatin, and Mr. Smith, on the affairs of the United States and Great Britain; and after noticing several distinct subjects of inquiry relating to these conversations, he says—" I, however, would remark, that had you deemed it proper to have communicated *in extenso* this letter, [from Mr. Canning to Mr. Erskine,] it would have been impossible for the President to have perceived in its conditions, or in its spirit, that conciliatory disposition which had been professed, and which, it was hoped, had really existed." Mr. Erskine replied to this letter of Mr. Smith, on the 14th of August, and in the course of his answer, after having noticed the several subjects of inquiry, he said—" Under these circumstances, therefore, finding that I could not obtain the recognitions specified in Mr. Canning's despatch, of the 23d of January, (which formed but *one part* of his instructions to me,) in the formal manner required, I considered that it would be in vain to lay before the government of the United States the despatch in question, which I was at *liberty* to have done *in extenso* had I thought proper : but as I had such strong grounds for believing that the object of his majesty's government could be attained, though in a different manner, and the spirit, at least, of my several letters of instructions be fully complied with, I felt a thorough conviction upon my mind, that I should be acting in conformity with his majesty's wishes, and accordingly concluded the late provisional agreement on his majesty's behalf with the government of the United States."

These remarks, on the one side and the other, are doubtless intended to convey the idea, that at the time of the negotiation, and until after the conclusion of the arrangement, our government were not made acquainted with the nature and extent of Mr. Erskine's instructions, but that they depended on his understanding of both.   Among the documents connected with this subject, is a letter, dated May 27, 1809, from Mr. Canning to Mr. Pinkney, the United States minister at London, in which is the following passage—

" Having had the honour to read to you *in extenso*, the instructions with which Mr. Erskine was furnished, it is not necessary for me to enter into any explanation of those points in which Mr. Erskine has acted not only not in conformity, but in direct contradiction to them."

From this passage it is apparent, that our government were, or might have been made acquainted with the nature and extent of Mr. Erskine's instructions. It was so clearly their duty to have ascertained this most important point, before entering on the negotiation, that it is not easy to imagine they could have passed it by, unless there were specific reasons for their remaining in ignorance concerning them. It has been seen, that in the negotiation with Mr. Rose, notwithstanding his instructions were strictly confined to a single object, and this fact was distinctly made known to Mr. Monroe before Mr. Rose left England, and as distinctly communicated to our government after his arrival, and before the negotiation was opened, still, with a full knowledge of this fact, immediately upon entering upon a discussion of the subject of Mr. Rose's mission, the first attempt of the Secretary of State was to draw him into a consideration of other subjects of controversy, which were not only not included in his commission, but which he was expressly prohibited from discussing. And this was attempted with a perfect knowledge on the part of our government, that if a treaty, or an arrangement had been entered into by Mr. Rose, in violation of his instructions, his government would disclaim it, even if it should not otherwise be objectionable. No explanation can be given for this course of conduct on the part of our government, except the plain, and as it is believed undeniable fact, that they did not wish to adjust the difficulties between the two nations. In consequence of the determination by our government not to negotiate, unless Mr. Rose would violate his instructions, and extend the negotiation to topics not included in his commission, it was discontinued, and reparation in the matter of the Leopard and the Chesapeake left undecided.

In the case of Mr. Erskine, the negotiation was one of great importance. Mr. Madison had just entered upon the office of President of the United States. Mr. Jefferson had left the government surrounded with difficulties and embarrassments. The foreign commerce of the country, under the system of embargo and non-intercourse, was destroyed, and all the various branches of domestic industry—agricultural, mercantile, and mechanical, were in a state of deep depression, or stagnation; and the community were becoming very uneasy under privations which were not only unnecessary, but extremely injurious and oppressive. Under such circumstances, it was a stroke of good policy in him, at his entrance upon the duties of chief magistrate, to excite popular feeling in favour of his administration; and nothing would be more likely to produce such an effect, than the adoption of measures which would relieve the nation from the multiplied evils of the restrictive policy. And it required no extraordinary degree of foresight to discern, that if such an arrangement as was contemplated with Mr. Erskine should be accomplished, that it would be cordially welcomed throughout the country, and render the new chief magistrate universally popular. At the same time, if the arrangement should be rejected by the British government, whatever the cause for refusing to ratify it might be, it could hardly fail to rouse a spirit of resentment in the United States, of a proportionate extent with the gratification which the adjustment had excited.

The chances of a favourable result towards the popularity of the administration were altogether in their favour. If Mr. Erskine's instructions should, upon being disclosed, warrant the arrangement, the measure would be hailed as highly beneficial to the country. If not, and the treaty should be rejected by Great Britain, the indignation of our country would be raised to a high pitch against that government, and would open an easy way to such further measures as our government might think proper to adopt. If the extent of the instructions was known to our government, before entering upon the negotiation, the subsequent proceedings were a fraud upon the nation. If it was not known, it was a most culpable omission on the part of the administration to engage in the negotiation in a state of ignorance respecting this indispensable fact, because the consequences could not, in the event of a want of authority, be otherwise than injurious to the nation.

An attempt was made to induce Mr. Erskine to say that he had not disclosed his instructions. His answer is equivocal, and leaves the point undecided. Whether he did or did not, does not seem to be a matter of much importance. They were shown to Mr. Pinkney in London, *in extenso;* and it is hardly to be supposed that he could have failed to communicate their contents to the government at Washington. If known to them, the course pursued by them was in the highest degree unworthy, and deceptive, because they must have known that any arrangement made in violation of instructions would be rejected for that reason only, if there had been no other. Nor can any good excuse be given for that ignorance, if it actually existed. The government ought to have known the extent of the minister's powers before they entered upon the negotiation.

The rejection of the arrangement by the British, though declared to be upon the ground of a departure from, or a violation of instructions, produced its natural effects in the country. Upon receiving intelligence of the fact, the President issued his proclamation, declaring the non-intercourse laws again in force : the feelings of the community were greatly excited, and a strong spirit of resentment was enkindled towards Great Britain.

Mr. Erskine having been recalled, Mr. Francis James Jackson was sent to the United States as his successor. The date of the first correspondence with him is prefixed to a letter from the Secretary of State, of the 9th of October, 1809. In this letter, the Secretary adverts to certain conversations which had taken place between him and Mr. Jackson, and states what he understood to be the purport of them; and adds, that " To avoid the misconceptions incident to oral proceedings, I have also the honour

to intimate that it is thought expedient that our further discussions on the present occasion be in the written form."
Mr. Jackson protested against this determination, as unprecedented in the annals of diplomacy, but consented to
go on with the business of his mission, rather than to have
it suspended until he could send home for further directions. In the course of his letter he remarks—"It was
not known when I left England, whether Mr. Erskine had,
according to the liberty allowed him, communicated to
you *in extenso* his original instructions. It now appears
that he did not. But in reverting to his official correspondence, and particularly to a despatch addressed on the
20th of April to his majesty's Secretary of State for
foreign affairs, I find that he there states, that he had
submitted to your consideration the three conditions spe
cified in those instructions, as the groundwork of an arrangement which, according to information received from
this country, it was thought in England might be made
with a prospect of great mutual advantage. Mr. Erskine
then reports *verbatim et seriatim* your observations upon
each of the three conditions, and the reasons which induced
you to think that others might be substituted in lieu of
them. It may have been concluded between you that these
latter were an equivalent for the original conditions; but
the very act of substitution evidently shows that those original conditions were in fact very explicitly communicated
to you, and by you of course laid before the President for
his consideration. I need hardly add, that the difference
between these conditions and those contained in the arrangement of the 18th and 19th of April, is sufficiently
obvious to require no elucidation; nor need I draw the
conclusion, which I consider as admitted by all absence of
complaint on the part of the American government, viz.
that under such circumstances his majesty had an undoubted and incontrovertible right to disavow the act of his
minister. I must here allude to a supposition which you

have more than once mentioned to me, and by which, if it had any the slightest foundation, this right might, perhaps, have been in some degree affected. You have informed me that you understood that Mr. Erskine had two sets of instructions, by which to regulate his conduct; and that upon one of them, which had not been communicated either to you or to the publick, was to be rested the justification of the terms finally agreed upon between you and him. It is my duty, Sir, solemnly to declare to you, and through you to the President, that the despatch from Mr. Canning to Mr. Erskine, which you have made the basis of an official correspondence with the latter minister, and which was read by the former to the American minister in London, is the only despatch by which the conditions were prescribed to Mr. Erskine for the conclusion of an arrangement with this country on the matter to which it relates."

A very long letter from Mr. Smith, Secretary of State, in answer to Mr. Jackson, bears date October 19. It is a laboured attempt to obtain a diplomatic victory over the British ambassador, on the subjects of dispute between the two governments. But the latter appears to have been thoroughly versed in his business; and no advantage was gained over him by Mr. Secretary Smith, in the argument. Owing perhaps to the disappointment which was experienced from this quarter, or to the long continuance of the discussion, more warmth of feeling began to be manifest. The controversy, at length, seemed to turn upon the nature and extent of the instructions given by the British government—whether Mr. Erskine acted under a limited, or what was called a full power. It was contended by Mr. Smith that Mr. Erskine supposed he had authority to make the arrangement, and that the British government were in honour bound to ratify it. Mr. Jackson, in a letter to Mr. Smith, of the 23d of October, says—" I have, therefore, no hesitation in informing you, that his majesty was pleased to disavow the agreement

concluded between you and Mr. Erskine, because it was
concluded in violation of that gentleman's instructions, and
altogether without authority to subscribe to the terms of
it. These instructions, I now understand by your letter,
as well as from the obvious deduction which I took the
liberty of making in mine of the 11th inst. were at the
time, in substance, made known to you; no stronger illustration, therefore, can be given of the deviation from them
which occurred, than by a reference to the terms of your
agreement."

On the 1st of November the Secretary of State replied
to Mr. Jackson. The following is an extract from his letter
" For the first time it is now disclosed that the subjects
arranged with this government by your predecessor, are
held to be not within the authority of a minister plenipotentiary, and that not having had a ' full power distinct from
that authority, his transactions on those subjects might of
right be disavowed by his government.' This disclosure,
so contrary to every antecedent supposition and just inference, gives a new aspect to this business. If the
authority of your predecessor did not embrace the subjects
in question, so as to bind his government, it necessarily
follows, that the only credentials yet presented by you,
being the same with those presented by him, give you no
authority to bind it ; and that the exhibition of a ' full
power' for that purpose, such as you doubtless are furnished with, is become an indispensable preliminary to
further negotiation ; or to speak more strictly, was required in the first instance by the view of the matter now
disclosed by you. Negotiation without this preliminary
would not only be a departure from the principle of equality which is the essential basis of it, but would moreover
be a disregard of the precautions and of the self-respect
enjoined on the attention of the United States by the circumstances which have hitherto taken place.

" I need scarcely add, that in the full power alluded to,

as a preliminary to negotiation, is not intended to be included either the whole extent or any part of your instructions for the exercise of it. These of course, as you have justly remarked, remain subject to your own discretion.

" I abstain from making any particular animadversions on several irrelevant and improper allusions in your letter, not at all comporting with the professed disposition to adjust in an amicable manner the differences unhappily subsisting between the two countries. But it would be improper to conclude the few observations to which I purposely limit myself, without adverting to your repetition of a language implying a knowledge on the part of this government that the instructions of your predecessor did not authorize the arrangement formed by him. After the explicit and peremptory asseveration that this government had no such knowledge, and that with such a knowledge no such arrangement would have been entered into, the view which you have again presented of the subject, makes it my duty to apprize you, that such insinuations are inadmissible in the intercourse of a foreign minister with a government that understands what it owes to itself."

Mr. Jackson replied to this letter on the 4th of November; and in the course of his remarks, says—" In his despatch of the 23d of January, Mr. Secretary Canning distinctly says to Mr. Erskine, 'upon receiving through you, on the part of the American government, a distinct and official recognition of the three abovementioned conditions, his majesty will lose no time in sending to America a minister fully empowered to consign them to a formal and regular treaty.'

" This minister would, of course, have been provided with a full power; but Mr. Erskine was to be guided by his instructions, and had the agreement concluded here been conformable to them, it would without doubt have been ratified by his majesty. I must beg your very particular attention to the circumstance that his majesty's ratification has been withheld, not because the agreement was concluded without a full power, but because it was altogether irreconcileable to the instructions on which it was professedly founded. The question of the full power was introduced by yourself to give weight, by a quotation from a highly respected author, to your complaint of the disavowal; in answer to which I observed that the quotation did not apply, as Mr. Erskine had no full power. Never did I imagine, or any where attempt to rest, the right of disavowal upon that circumstance : indubitably his agreement would nevertheless have been ratified, had not the instructions, which in this case took the place of a full power, been violated."————

"I am concerned to be obliged a second time to appeal to those principles of publick law, under the sanction and protection of which I was sent to this country. Where there is not freedom of communication in the form substituted for the more usual one of verbal discussion, there can be little useful intercourse between ministers ; and one, at least, of the epithets, which you have thought proper to apply to my last letter, is such as necessarily abridges that freedom. That any thing therein contained may be irrelevant to the subject, it is of course competent in you to endeavour to show ; and as far as you succeed in so doing, in so far will my argument lose of its validity ; but as to the propriety of my allusions, you must allow me to acknowledge only the decision of my own sovereign, whose commands I obey, and to whom alone I can consider myself responsible."————

" You will find that in my correspondence with you, I have carefully avoided drawing conclusions that did not necessarily follow from the premises advanced by me, and last of all should I think of uttering an insinuation, where I was unable to substantiate a fact. To facts, such as I have become acquainted with them, I have scrupulously adhered, and in so doing I must continue, whenever the good faith of his majesty's government is called in question, to vindicate its honour and dignity in the manner that appears to me best calculated for that purpose."

To this letter the Secretary of State made the following answer—

"*Department of State, November* 8, 1809.

"SIR,—In my letter of the 19th ultimo, I stated to you that the declaration in your letter of the 11th, that the despatch from Mr. Canning to Mr. Erskine, of the 23d of January, was the only despatch by which the conditions were prescribed to Mr. Erskine for the conclusion of an arrangement on the matter to which it related, was then for the first time made to this government. And it was added that if that despatch had been communicated at the time of the arrangement, or if it had been known that the propositions contained in it, were the only ones on which he was authorized to make an arrangement, the arrangement would not have been made.

"In my letter of the 1st instant, adverting to the repetition in your letter of the 23d ultimo, of a language implying a knowledge in this government that the instructions of your predecessor did not authorize the arrangement formed by him, an intimation was distinctly given to you that, after the explicit and peremptory asseveration that this government had not any such knowledge, and that with such a knowledge, such an arrangement would not have been made, no such insinuation could be admitted by this government.

"Finding that in your reply of the 4th instant, you have used a language which cannot be understood but as reiterating and even aggravating the same gross insinuation, it only remains in order to preclude opportunities which are thus abused, to inform you, that no further communications will be received from you, and that the necessity of this determination will, without delay, be made known to your government. In the mean time, a ready attention will be given to any communications, affecting the interests of the two nations, through any other channel that may be substituted. I have the honour to be, &c.

"R. SMITH."

Great pains were taken to excite the public feelings on this occasion. Mr. Jackson was accused of having insulted the government, and popular resentment was roused to so high a pitch, that it was considered hardly safe for him to travel through the country. On the 11th of November the following note was communicated to the Secretary of State—

" Mr. Oakley, his majesty's secretary of legation, is desired by Mr. Jackson to state to the Secretary of State, that, as Mr. Jackson has been already once most grossly insulted by the inhabitants of the town of Hampton, in the unprovoked language of abuse held by them to several officers bearing the king's uniform, when those officers were themselves violently assaulted, and put in imminent danger ; he conceives it to be indispensible to the safety of himself, of the gentlemen attached to his mission, and of his family, during the remainder of their stay in the United States, to be provided with special passports or safe-guards from the American government. This is the more necessary, since some of the newspapers of the United States are daily using language whose only tendency can be to excite the people to commit violence upon Mr. Jackson's person."

Congress met in November ; and on the 29th of that month the President's message was sent to both houses. After giving a history of the failure of the arrangement with Mr. Erskine, and mentioning his recall, the appointment of a new minister, and referring to the state of things in the attempt to open a negotiation with him, the message says—The correspondence "will show also, that forgetting the respect due to all governments, he did not refrain from imputations on this, which required that no further communications should be received from him."

If there are any persons who have been well acquainted with the course of the administration under Mr. Madison, who believe that the arrangement with Mr. Erskine was made with sincerity and good faith on the part of our government, and with an expectation that it would be ratified, and carried into effect by the British government, they will of course give him credit for this professed attempt to adjust the difficulties between the two nations. But persons of a different description, who view the whole proceeding as a political manœuvre, intended to gain popularity to a new chief magistrate in the first place, and in the result of its being rejected by the British government, to excite the resentment of the country against that government, will come to a different conclusion,—one very far from being favourable to the frankness and political candour of the head of our government.

At all events, it left the subject of controversy between the two nations, which gave rise to the negotiation, open and undecided. Its consequences will be more fully ascertained hereafter.

In the maritime war of retaliation which Great Britain and France were carrying on against each other by decrees and orders in council, it was of course an object of each to charge its origin upon the other. In a letter from Count Champagny to General Armstrong, dated August 22d, 1809, he says—" Let England revoke her declarations of blockade against France; France will revoke her decree of blockade against England. Let England revoke her orders in council of the 11th of November, 1807, the decree of Milan will fall of itself. American commerce will then have regained all its liberty, and it will be sure of finding favour and protection in the ports of France. But it is for the United States to bring on these happy results. Can a nation that wishes to remain free and sovereign, even balance between some temporary interests, and the great interests of its independence, and the maintenance of its honour, of its sovereignty, and of its dignity ?"

Having failed in the negotiation with Mr. Erskine, of obtaining a revocation of the British orders in council of January and November, 1807, the President's proclamation replaced the intercourse between the countries upon the same footing upon which it stood previously to the opening of that negotiation. It was then thought expedient by the American government to make an experiment with France, for the purpose of inducing the government of that nation to repeal the Berlin and Milan decrees. On the 1st of December, 1809, the Secretary of State addressed a letter to General Armstrong, of which the following is an extract :—

" Inclosed you have five copies of the President's message and of its accompanying documents. They will afford you a view of the existing state of things here, and particularly of the ground taken in the correspondence of the British minister. You will perceive that the deliberations of congress at their present session cannot but be embarrassed by the painful consideration, that the two principal belligerents have been, for some time, alike regardless of our neutral rights, and that they manifest no disposition to relinquish, in any degree, their unreasonable pretensions.

" You will also herewith receive a copy of a letter to Mr. Pinkney, which will show the light in which M. Champagny's letter is viewed by the President, and at the same time the course of proceeding prescribed to our minister in London. You will of course understand it to be wished that you should ascertain the meaning of the French government, *as to the condition on which it has been proposed to revoke the Berlin decree.* On the principle which seems to be assumed by M. Champagny, nothing more ought to be required than a recall by Great Britain of her proclamation or illegal blockades, which are of a date prior to that of the Berlin decree, or a formal decla-

ration that they are not now in force. Should this be done
and be followed by an annulment of all the decrees and
orders in chronological order, and Great Britain should
afterwards put in force old, or proclaim new blockades,
contrary to the law of nations, it would produce questions
between her and the United States, which the French government is bound to leave to the United States, at least
until it shall find it necessary to bring forward complaints
of an acquiescence on our part, not consistent with the
neutrality professed by us."

On the 25th of January, 1810, General Armstrong
wrote the following letter to Mr. Pinkney :—

" A letter from Mr. Secretary Smith of the 1st of December last, made it my duty to inquire of his excellency
the duke of Cadore, what were the conditions on which his
majesty the emperor would annul his decree, commonly
called the Berlin decree, and whether if *Great Britain revoked her blockades of a date anterior to that decree*, his
majesty would consent to revoke the said decree.   To
these questions I have this day received the following answer, which I hasten to convey to you by a special mes-
senger.

ANSWER.

" *The only condition* required for the revocation, by his
majesty the emperor, of the decree of Berlin, will be a
previous revocation by the British government of her
blockades of France, or part of France, [*such as that from
the Elbe to Brest, &c.*] of a date anterior to that of the
aforesaid decree."

On the 28th of January, 1810, General Armstrong
wrote the following letter to the Secretary of State.

" In conformity to the suggestions contained in your
letter of the first of December, 1809, I demanded whether,
if Great Britain revoked her blockades of a date anterior
to the decree, commonly called the Berlin decree, his ma-

jesty the emperor would consent to revoke the said decree."
To which the minister answered, that " *the only condition
required for the revocation, by his majesty*, of the decree of
Berlin, will be a previous revocation by the British government of her blockade of France, or part of France,
[such as that from the Elbe to Brest, &c.] of a date anterior to that of the aforesaid decree ; and that if the British
government would then recall the orders in council which
had occasioned the decree of Milan, that decree should
also be annulled."

On the 11th of November, 1809, Mr. Smith, Secretary
of State, wrote a letter to Mr. Pinkney, from which the
following is an extract :—

"From the enclosed copy of a letter from M. Champagny to General Armstrong, it appears that the French
government has taken a ground in relation to the British
violation of our neutral rights, not the same with that heretofore taken, and which it is proper you should be acquainted with. You will observe that the terms stating
the condition on which the Berlin decree will be revoked,
are not free from obscurity. They admit the construction, however, that if Great Britain will annul her illegal
blockades as distinct from her orders in council, such as the
blockade from the Elbe to Brest, &c. prior to the Berlin
decree, and perhaps of subsequent date, but still distinct
from her orders in council, that France will put an end to
her Berlin decree, or at least the illegal part of it. Whilst
therefore it becomes important to take proper steps, as
will be done, through General Armstrong, to ascertain the
real and precise meaning of M. Champagny's letter, it is
important also that your interposition should be used to
ascertain the actual state of the British blockades, distinct
from the orders in council, whether merely on paper or
otherwise illegal, and whether prior or subsequent to the
Berlin decree, and to feel the pulse of the British government on the propriety of putting them out of the way, in

order to give force to our call on France to prepare the way for a repeal of the orders in council, by her repeal of that decree.

" In the execution of this task, I rely on the judgment and delicacy by which I am persuaded you will be guided, and on your keeping in mind the desire of this government to *entangle itself as little as possible in the question of priority* in the violation of our neutral rights, and to commit itself as little as possible to either belligerent as to the course to be taken with the other.

" If it should be found that no illegal blockades are now in force, and so declared by Great Britain, or that the British government is ready to revoke and withdraw all such as may not be consistent with the definition of blockade in the Russian treaty of June, 1801, it will be desirable that you lose no time in giving the information to General Armstrong, and whatever may be the result of your inquiries, that you hasten a communication of it to me."

It is very apparent from the tenor of these letters, that the course which the government was pursuing, was not a little embarrassing to them. The British blockade of May, 1806, was prior in date to the French decree of Berlin. And it was an object of great importance, in the view of the French government, to have it understood, that the Berlin decree was issued in order to retaliate upon the British government for the blockading order abovementioned. But that order had not been considered by the government of the United States as a violation of their neutral rights, at least so far as to make it the subject of any formal or serious complaint. It will be recollected, that in the correspondence between Mr. Monroe and Mr. Fox in regard to it, at the time when the measure was adopted, the former, as well as the latter of those statesmen viewed it as rather advantageous to neutrals than otherwise. But after the failure of the arrangement with Mr. Erskine, it was a matter of deep concern with our government to endeavour to adjust their difficulties at least with France ; or by attempting to play off one of the belligerents against the other, to bring one, if not both of them to terms. For this purpose, General Armstrong was directed to apply to the French government, to ascertain on what terms his imperial majesty would consent to revoke the Berlin decree. His instructions, however, made it necessary for him to do something more than ask the simple general question, on what terms his majesty the emperor would annul that decree ; he was directed to inquire " whether, *if Great Britain revoked her blockades of a date anterior to that decree,* his majesty would consent to revoke the said decree ?" The only blockading order of a date prior to the Berlin decree, that appears to have formed the subject of complaint on the part of France, was that of May, 1806. Of course, as might have been, and doubtless was expected, the answer to the inquiry was, as has been already cited—" The only condition required for the revocation, by his majesty the emperor, of the decree of Berlin, will be the previous revocation by the British government of her blockades of France, or part of France, [such as that from the Elbe to Brest, &c.] of a date anterior to the aforesaid decree." It is very easy to see that the correspondence with the British government, under these circumstances, would be attended with no inconsiderable difficulty.

In a letter from the Secretary of State to Mr. Pinkney, dated July 2d, 1810, he says—

" As the British government had constantly alleged that the Berlin decree was the original aggression on our neutral commerce, that her orders in council were but a retaliation on that decree, and had, moreover, on that ground, asserted an obligation on the United States to take effectual measures against the decree, as a preliminary to a repeal of the orders, nothing could be more reasonable than to expect, that the condition, in the shape last presented, would be readily accepted. The President is, therefore, equally disappointed and dissatisfied at the abortiveness of your correspondence with Lord Wellesley on this important subject. He entirely approves the determination you took to resume it, with a view to the special and immediate obligation lying on the British government to cancel the illegal blockades; and you are instructed, in case the answer to your letter of the 30th of April should not be satisfactory, to represent to the British government, in terms temperate but explicit, that the United States consider themselves authorized by strict and unquestionable right, as well as supported by the principles heretofore applied by Great Britain to the case, in claiming and expecting a revocation of the illegal blockades of France, of a date prior to that of the Berlin decree, as preparatory to a further demand of the revocation of that decree.

" It ought not to be presumed that the British government, in reply to such a representation, will contend that a blockade, like that of May, 1806, from the Elbe to Brest, a coast of not less than one thousand miles, proclaimed four years since, without having been at any time attempted to be duly executed by the application of a naval force, is a blockade conformable to the law of nations and consistent with neutral rights."

On the 19th of October, 1810, the Secretary of State wrote again to Mr. Pinkney, on the same subject. The following is an extract from his letter—

" Your despatch of the 24th of August, enclosing a newspaper statement of a letter from the Duke of Cadore to General Armstrong, notifying a revocation of the Berlin and Milan decrees, has been received. It ought not to be doubted that this step of the French government will be followed by a repeal, on the part of the British government, of its orders in council. And if a termination of the crisis between Great Britain and the United States be really intended, the repeal ought to include the system of paper blockades, which differ in name only from the retaliatory system comprised in the orders in council. From the complexion of the British prints, not to mention other considerations, the paper blockades may however not be abandoned. There is hence a prospect that the United States may be brought to issue with Great Britain on the legality of such blockades. In such case, as. it cannot be expected that the United States, founded as they are in law and in right, can acquiesce in the validity of the British practice, it lies with the British government to remove the difficulty."

Our government having demanded of Great Britain, the revocation of her blockading orders prior to the Berlin decree, and particularly that of May, 1806, as a condition of renewing commercial intercourse with that nation, but without success ; it became an object with Mr. Madison to adjust, if possible, his difficulties with France. The style and temper in which the correspondence in relation to France were essentially different from that which regarded Great Britain. With the latter it was peremptory, and dogmatical. With the former it was in the language of great moderation, not to say of humility and submission. It has been seen by one of the foregoing extracts, that having insisted, in the first place, upon the revocation of the blockading order of May, 1806, our government had advanced a step further, and claimed that the repeal ought to include the whole system of paper blockades.

On the 26th of July, 1811, Mr. Monroe, Secretary of State, addressed a letter to Joel Barlow, who had been appointed minister to France, from which the following extracts are made—After referring to the events which had occurred respecting the revocation of the French decrees, and the issuing of the President's proclamation, suspending the non-intercourse law as it regarded France, it is said—

"This declaration of the emperor of France was considered a sufficient ground for the President to act on. It was explicit, as to its object, and equally so as to its import. The decrees of Berlin and Milan, which had violated our neutral rights, were said to be repealed, to take effect at a subsequent day, at no distant period, the interval apparently intended to allow full time for the communication of the measure to this government. The declaration had, too, all the formality which such an act could admit of, being through the official organ on both sides, from the French minister of foreign affairs to the minister plenipotentiary of the United States, at Paris.

"In consequence of this note from the French minister of foreign affairs, of the 5th of August, 1810, the President proceeded on the 2d of November following, to issue the proclamation enjoined by the act of May 1, of the same year, to declare that all the restrictions imposed by it should cease and be discontinued, in relation to France and her dependencies ; and. in confirmation of the proclamation of the President, the Congress did, on the 2d of March, 1811, pass an act, whereby the non-importation system provided for by the 3d, &c. sections of the act entitled &c. was declared to be in force against Great Britain, her colonies and dependencies, &c." As Great Britain did not revoke or modify her edicts, in the manner proposed, the fifth provision had no effect.

"I will now inquire whether France has performed her part of this arrangement.

"It is understood that the blockade of the British isles is revoked. The revocation having been officially declared, and no vessels trading to them having been condemned or taken on the high seas, it is fair to conclude that the measure is relinquished. It appears too, that no American vessel has been condemned in France for having been visited at sea by an English ship, or for having been searched or carried into England, or subjected to impositions there. On the sea, therefore, France is understood to have changed her system.

"Although such is the light in which the conduct of France is viewed in regard to the neutral commerce of the United States since the 1st of November last, it will nevertheless be proper for you to investigate fully the whole subject, and see that nothing has been or shall be omitted on her part, in future, which the United States have a right to claim.

" Your early and particular attention will be drawn to the great subject of the commercial relation which is to subsist between the United States. The President expects that the commerce of the United States will be placed, in the ports of France, on such a footing as to afford to it a fair market, and to the industry and enterprise of their people a reasonable encouragement. An arrangement to this effect was looked for immediately after the revocation of the decrees ; but it appears from the documents in this department, that that was not the case: on the contrary, that our commerce *has been subjected to the greatest discouragement,* or rather to *the most oppressive restraints;* that the vessels which carried coffee, sugar, &c. &c. though sailing directly from the United States to a French port, were held in a state of sequestration, on the principle that the trade was prohibited, and that the importation of those articles was not only unlawful, but criminal ; that even the vessels which carried the unquestionable productions of the United States were exposed to great and expensive delays, to tedious investigations in unusual forms, and to exorbitant duties.   In short, that *the ordinary usages of commerce between friendly nations were abandoned.*

" When it was announced that the decrees of Berlin and Milan were revoked, the revocation to take effect on the 1st of November last, it was natural for our merchants to rush into the ports of France to take advantage of a market to which they thought they were invited.   All these restraints, therefore, have been unjust in regard to the parties who suffered by them ; nor can they be reconciled to the respect which was due to this government. If France had wished to exclude the American commerce from her ports, she ought to have declared it to this government in explicit terms, in which case due notice would have been given of it to the American merchants, who would either have avoided her ports, or gone there at their own hazard. But to suffer them to enter her ports, under such circumstances, and to detain them there, under any pretext whatever, cannot be justified. It is not known to what extent the injuries resulting from those delays have been carried. It is evident, however, that for every injury thus sustained, the parties are entitled to reparation.

" If the ports of France and her allies are not opened to the commerce of the United States on a liberal scale and on fair conditions, of what avail to them, it may be asked, will be the revocation of the British orders in council? In contending for the revocation of those orders, so far as it was an object of interest, the United States had in view a trade with the continent. It was a fair and legitimate object and worth contending for while France encouraged it ; but if she shuts her ports on our commerce, or burdens it with heavy duties, that motive is at an end."

" You will see the injustice, and endeavour to prevent the necessity of bringing, in return for American cargoes sold in France, an equal amount in the produce or manufactures of that country. No such obligation is imposed on French merchants trading to the United States. They enjoy the liberty of selling their cargoes for cash, and taking back what they please from this country in return, and the right ought to be reciprocal.

" It is indispensible that the trade be free ; and that all American citizens engaged in it be placed on the same footing ; and with this view, that the system of carrying it on by licenses granted by French agents, be immediately annulled. You must make it distinctly understood by the French government, that the United States cannot submit to that system, as it tends to sacrifice one part of the community to another, and to give a corrupt influence to the agents of a foreign power in our towns, which is in every view incompatible with the principles of our government. It was presumed that this system had been abandoned some time since, as a letter from the duke of Cadore, of —— to Mr .Russel, gave assurance of it. Should it, however, be still maintained, you will not fail to bring the subject without delay before the French government, and to urge its immediate abandonment. The President having long since expressed his strong disapprobation of it, and requested that the consuls would discontinue it, it is probable, if they still disregard his injunction, that he may find it necessary to revoke their exequaturs. I mention this that you may be able to explain the motive to such a measure, should it take place, which, without such explanation, might probably be viewed in a mistaken light by the French government."

" You will be able to ascertain the various other claims which the United States have on France for injuries done to their citizens, under decrees of a subsequent date to those of Berlin and Milan, and you will likewise use your best exertions to obtain an indemnity for them. It is presumed that the French government will be disposed to do justice for all these injuries. In looking to the future, the past ought to be fairly and honourably adjusted. If that is not done, much dissatisfaction will remain here, which cannot fail to produce a very unfavourable effect on the relations which are to subsist in future between the two countries.

" The first of these latter decrees bears date at Bayonne, on the 17th of March, 1808, by which many American vessels and their cargoes were seized and carried into France, and others which had entered her ports in the fair course of trade, were seized and sequestered, or confiscated by her government. It was pretended in vindication of this measure, that as, under our embargo law, no American vessel could navigate the ocean, all those who were found on it were trading on British account, and lawful prize. The fact, however, was otherwise."————

" The Rambouillet decree was a still more unjustifiable aggression on the rights of the United States, and invasion of the property of their citizens. It bears date on the 23d of March, 1810, and made a sweep of all American property within the reach of the French power. It was also retrospective, extending back to the 20th of May, 1809. By this decree every American vessel and cargo, even those which had been delivered up to the owners by compromise with the captors, was seized and sold. The law of March 1st, 1809, commonly called the non-intercourse law, was the pretext for this measure, which was intended as an act of reprisal. It requires no reasoning to show the injustice of this pretension. Our law regulated the trade of the United States with other powers, particularly with France and Great Britain, and was such a law as every nation had a right to adopt. It was duly promulgated and reasonable notice given of it to other powers. It was also impartial as it related to the belligerents. The condemnation of such vessels of France or England as came into the ports of the United States in breach of this law, was strictly proper, and could afford no cause of complaint to either power. The seizure of so vast a property as was laid hold of under that pretext by the French government, places the transaction in a very clear light. If an indemnity had been sought for an imputed injury, the measure of the injury should have been ascertained, and the indemnity proportioned to it. But in this case no injury had been sustained on principle. A trifling loss only had been incurred, and for that loss all the American property which could be found was seized, involving in indiscriminate ruin innocent merchants who had entered the ports of France in a fair course of trade. It is proper that you should make it distinctly known to the French government that the claim to a just reparation for these spoliations cannot be relinquished, and that a delay in making it will produce very high dissatisfaction with this government, and people of these states.

" It has been intimated that the French government would be willing to make this reparation, provided the United States would make one in return for the vessels and property condemned under and in breach of our non-intercourse law. Although the proposition was objectionable in many views, yet this government consented to it, to save so great a mass of the property of our citizens. An instruction for this purpose was given to your predecessor, which you are authorized to carry into effect.

" The influence of France has been exerted to the injury of the United States in all the countries to which her power has extended. In Spain, Holland, and Naples, it has been most sensibly felt. In each of those countries the vessels and cargoes of American merchants were seized and confiscated under various decrees founded in different pretexts, none of which had even the semblance of right to support them. As the United States never injured France, that plea must fail ; and that they had injured either of those powers was never pretended. You will be furnished with the documents which relate to these aggressions, and you will claim of the French government an indemnity for them.

" The United States have also just cause of complaint against France for many injuries that were committed by persons acting under her authority. Of these the most distinguished, and least justifiable, are the examples which occurred of burning the vessels of our citizens at sea. Their atrocity forbids the imputation of them to the government. To it, however, the United States must look for reparation, which you will accordingly claim.''

The letter from which these passages are taken, was

written in July, 1811—about nine months after the pretended revocation of the Berlin and Milan decrees. It contains a black catalogue of charges against the French government, the most outrageous of which, both as it regards the principle on which it was founded, and the amount of property piratically seized and confiscated, was that of the proceedings under the Rambouillet decree. That decree had been issued, and those confiscations had been adjudged more than seven months prior to the pretended revocation of the Berlin and Milan decrees; no remuneration had been made, or even promised, before that revocation, and yet President Madison, upon receiving information that his majesty the emperor of France had issued his decree respecting the revocation of the Berlin and Milan decrees, immediately suspended the non-intercourse law with regard to France, and thus opened the way, by encouraging the renewal of the trade with that country, for further depredations, and a renewed series of piracies upon our commerce. But because Bonaparte demanded the repeal of the British blockading order of May, 1806, as the only condition on which he would consent to revoke those decrees, our government condescended to demand that measure of the British, as the only terms on which the trade with that country could be renewed. And it was by insisting on this pre-requisite, that the war of 1812 was eventually produced.

In addition to the passages quoted from the foregoing letter, the following is a letter addressed by the Secretary of State to Mr. Barlow, then minister at Paris, dated July 14, 1812—

" The President has seen with great surprise and concern that the government of France had made no accommodation to the United States on any of the important and just grounds of complaint to which you had called its attention, according to your instructions, given at the time of your departure, and repeated in several communications since. It appears that the same oppressive restraints

on our commerce were still in force; that the system of
license was persevered in; that indemnity had not been
made for spoliations, nor any pledge given to inspire confidence that any would be made.   More recent wrongs,
on the contrary, and of a very outrageous character, have
been added to those with which you were acquainted when
you left the United States.   By documents forwarded to
you in my letter of the 21st of March, you were informed
of the waste of our commerce, made by a squadron from
Nantz, in January last, which burnt many of our vessels
trading to the Peninsula.   For these you were also instructed to demand redress.

"It is hoped that the government of France, regarding
with a prudent foresight the probable course of events,
will have some sensibility to its interest, if it has none to
the claims of justice, on the part of this country."

The task of reconciling the expressions in this letter,
with the declarations so often made and repeated by our
government to that of Great Britain, when calling upon
the latter to revoke their orders of council, on the grounds
of an engagement to proceed *pari passu* with France in
repealing her decrees which violated our neutral rights,
must be left to those who are not easily staggered with
inconsistencies, or disturbed with contradictions.   It is a
task which any man not immediately interested in the
result, and who wishes to preserve a reputation for veracity, will not undertake, or covet.

On the 27th of July, 1811, Mr. Monroe communicated
in a letter to Jonathan Russell, his appointment as charge
d'affaires of the United States at London.   Mr. Russell
reached London in November of that year.   On the 14th
of February, 1812, he wrote to Mr. Monroe, that at that
time there had been exhibited no evidence of a disposition
on the part of the British government to repeal the orders
in council.   On the 9th of the same month, he also wrote
as follows—"I have the honour to transmit to you enclosed,
a copy of a letter, dated 29th ult. from Mr. Barlow, and a

copy of the note in which I yesterday communicated that letter to the Marquis Wellesley.

" Although *the proof of the revocation of the French decrees, contained in the letter of Mr. Barlow, is, when taken by itself, of no very conclusive character,* yet it ought, when connected with that previously exhibited to this government, to be admitted as satisfactorily establishing that revocation; and in this view I have thought it to be my duty to present it here."

On the 4th of March, 1812, Mr. Russell wrote a letter to Mr. Monroe, from which the following is copied—

" Since my letters of the 19th and 22d ultimo, which I trust will have extinguished all expectation of any change here, the motion of Lord Landsdown on the 28th of February, and that of Mr. Brougham yesterday, have been severally debated in the respective houses of parliament. I attended the discussions on both, and if any thing was wanting to prove the inflexible determination of the present ministry to persevere in the orders in council without modification or relaxation, the declarations of the leading members of administration on these occasions must place it beyond the possibility of a doubt. In both houses these leaders expressed a disposition to forbear to canvass, in the present state of our relations, the conduct of the United States towards England, as it could not be done without reproaching her in a manner to increase the actual irritation, and to do away what Lord Bathurst stated to be the *feeble* hopes of preventing war.

" In the house of commons, Mr. Rose virtually confessed that the orders in council were maintained to promote the trade of England at the expense of neutrals, and as a measure of commercial rivalry with the United States. When Mr. Canning inveighed against this new (he must have meant newly acknowledged) ground of defending these orders, and contended that they could be justified only on the principle of retaliation, on which they were avowedly

instituted, and that they were intended to produce the
effects of an actual blockade, and liable to all the incidents of such blockade—that is, that they were meant
only to distress the enemy—and that Great Britain had
no right to defeat this operation by an intercourse with
that enemy which she denied to neutrals; Mr. Percival
replied, " that the orders were still supported on the
principle of retaliation, but that this very principle involved
the license trade ; for as France by her decrees had said
that no nation should trade with her which traded with
England, England retorted, that no country should trade
with France but through England. He asserted that
neither the partial nor even the total repeal of the Berlin
and Milan decrees, as they related to America, or to any
other nation, or *all* other nations, would form any claim
on the British government, while the *continental system*, so
called, continued in operation. He denied that this system
or any part of the Berlin and Milan decrees were merely
municipal. They had not been adopted in time of peace
with a view to internal regulation, but in a time of war,
with a hostile purpose towards England. Every clause
and particle of them were to be considered of a nature
entirely belligerent, and as such, requiring resistance and
authorising retaliation on the part of Great Britain. It
was idle and absurd to suppose that Great Britain was
bound, in acting on the principle of retaliation in these
times, to return exactly and in form *like for like*, and to
choose the object and fashion the mode of executing it precisely by the measures of the enemy. In adopting these measures, France had broken through all the restraints imposed
by the laws of nations, and trodden under foot the great
conventional code received by the civilized world as prescribing rules for its conduct in war as well as in peace.
In this state of things England was not bound any longer
to shackle herself with this code, and by so doing become
the unresisting victim of the violence of her enemy, but she

was herself released from the laws of nations, and left at liberty to resort to any means within her power to injure and distress that enemy, and to bring it back to an observance of the *jus gentium* which it had so egregiously and wantonly violated. Nor was England to be restricted any more in the *extent* than in the *form* of retaliation; but she had a right, both as to the quantity and manner, to inflict upon the enemy all the evil in her power, until this enemy should retrace its steps, and renounce, not only verbally but practically, its decrees, its continental system, and every other of its belligerent measures incompatible with the old acknowledged laws of nations. Whatever neutrals might suffer from the retaliatory measures of England, was purely incidental, and as no injustice was intended to them, they had a right to complain of none ; and he rejoiced to observe that no charge of such injustice had that night been brought forward in the house. As England was contending for the defence of her maritime rights, and for the preservation of her national existence, which essentially depended on the maintenance of those rights, she could not be expected, in the prosecution of this great and primary interest, to arrest or vary her course, to listen to the pretensions of neutral nations, or to remove the evils, however they might be regretted, which the imperious policy of the times indirectly and unintentionally extended to them.

" As the newspapers of this morning give but a very imperfect report of this speech of Mr. Percival, I have thought it to be my duty to present you with a more particular account of the doctrines which were maintained in it, and which so vitally affect the rights and interests of the United States.

" I no longer entertain a hope that we can honourably avoid war."

On the 30th of May, 1812, Mr. Foster addressed a long letter to Mr. Monroe, in which he reviewed the whole ground of controversy between the United States and Great Britain. This document is too long to be copied in full. It commences in the following manner—

" Notwithstanding the discouraging nature of the conversation which I had the honour to have with you a few days since at your office, and the circumstance of your continued silence in regard to two letters from me, furnishing additional proof of the existence of the French decrees, nevertheless there does now appear such clear and convincing evidence in the report of the duke of Bassano, dated the 10th of March, of the present year, of those decrees having not only never been rescinded, but of their being recently extended and aggravated in the republication of them contained in that instrument, that I cannot but imagine it will seem most important to the President that it should be communicated to Congress, without delay, in the present interesting crisis of their deliberations ; and therefore hasten to fulfil the instructions of my government, in laying before the government of the United States the enclosed Moniteur of the 16th of last March, in which is contained that report, as it was made to the ruler of France, and communicated to the conservative senate.

" This report confirms, if any thing were wanting to confirm, in the most unequivocal manner, the repeated assertions of Great Britain, that the Berlin and Milan decrees have never been revoked, however some partial and insidious relaxations of them may have been made in a few instances, as an encouragement to America to adopt a system beneficial to France, and injurious to Great Britain, while the conditions on which alone it has been declared that those decrees will ever be revoked, are here explained and amplified in a manner to leave us no hope of Bonaparte having any disposition to renounce the system of injustice which he has pursued, so as to make it possible for Great Britain to give up the defensive measures she has been obliged to resort to.

"I need not remind you, sir, how often it has in vain been urged by Great Britain, that a copy of the instrument should be produced, by which the decrees of Bonaparte were said to be repealed, and how much it has been desired that America should explicitly state that she did not adopt the conditions on which the repeal was offered.

"It is now manifest that there was never more than a conditional offer of repeal made by France, which we had a right to complain that America should have asked us to recognise as absolute, and which, if accepted in its extent by America, would only have formed fresh matter of complaint, and a new ground for declining her demands."

Mr. Foster then attempts to show, by a series of argumentation, that the Berlin and Milan decrees had not in fact been revoked; and he then proceeds as follows:—

"I will not now trouble you, sir, with many observations relative to the blockade of May, 1806, as the legality of that blockade, assuming the blockading force to have been sufficient to enforce it, has latterly not been questioned by you.

"I will merely remark that it was impossible Great Britain should receive, otherwise than with the utmost jealousy, the unexpected demand made by America for the repeal of the blockade as well as of the orders in council, when it appeared to be made subsequent to, if not in consequence of, one of the conditions in Bonaparte's pretended repeal of his decrees, which condition was our renouncing what he calls ' our new principles of blockade;' that the demand on the part of America was additional and new, is sufficiently proved by a reference to the overture of Mr. Pinkney, as well as from the terms on which Mr. Erskine had arranged the dispute with America relative to the orders in council. In that arrangement nothing was brought forward with regard to this blockade. America would have been contented at that time without any reference to it. It certainly is not more a grievance, or an injustice, now, than it was then. Why then is the renunciation of that blockade insisted upon now, if it was not necessary to insist upon it then? It is difficult to find any answer but by reference to subsequent communications between France and America, and a disposition in America to countenance France in requiring the disavowal of this blockade, and the principles upon which it rested, as the condition *sine qua non* of the repeal of the Berlin and Milan decrees. It seems to have become an object with America, only because it was prescribed as a condition by France.

"On this blockade, and the principles and rights upon which it was founded, Bonaparte appears to rest the justification of all his measures for abolishing neutrality, and for the invasion of every state which is not ready, with him, to wage a war of extermination against the commerce of Great Britain.

"America, therefore, no doubt saw the necessity of demanding its renunciation, but she will now see that it is in reality vain either for America or Great Britain to expect an actual repeal of the French decrees, until Great Britain renounces, first, the basis, viz. the blockade of 1806, on which Bonaparte has been pleased to found them; next, the right of retaliation as subsequently acted upon in the orders in council; further, until she is ready to receive the treaty of Utrecht, interpreted and applied by the duke of Bassano's report as the universal law of nations; and finally, till she abjures all the principles of maritime law which support her established rights, now more than ever essential to her existence as a nation."

"I am commanded, sir, to express on the part of his royal highness the prince regent, that while his royal highness entertains the most sincere desire to conciliate America, he yet can never concede that the blockade of May, 1806, could justly be made the foundation, as it avowedly has been, for the decrees of Bonaparte; and further, that the British government must ever consider the principles on which that blockade rested, (accompanied as it was by an adequate blockading force,) to have been strictly consonant to the established law of nations, and a legitimate instance of the practice which it recognises.

"Secondly, that Great Britain must continue to reject the other spurious doctrines promulgated by France in the duke of Bassano's report, as binding upon all nations. She cannot admit, as a true declaration of public law, that free ships make free goods, nor the converse of that proposition, that enemy's ships destroy the character of neutral property in the cargo : she cannot consent, by the adoption of such a principle, to deliver absolutely the commerce of France from the pressure of the naval power of Great Britain, and by the abuse of the neutral flag, to allow her enemy to obtain, without the expense of sustaining a navy for the trade and property of French subjects, a degree of freedom and security, which even the commerce of her own subjects cannot find under the protection of the British navy.———

"She cannot admit, as a principle of public law, that arms and military stores are alone contraband of war, and that ship timber and naval stores are excluded from that description. Neither can she admit without retaliation, that the mere fact of commercial intercourse with British ports and subjects should be made a crime in all nations, and that the armies and decrees of France should be directed to enforce a principle so new and unheard of in war.

"Great Britain feels, that to relinquish her just measures of self-defence and retaliation, would be to surrender the best means of her own preservation and rights, and with them the rights of other nations, so long as France maintains and acts upon such principles."

Such was the state of things between the United States and Great Britain, at the beginning of June, 1812, that it was apparent the former were resolved on a war with the latter. On the 1st of June, the President of the United States transmitted a message to Congress, in which he reviewed the difficulties which had occurred, and those which then existed, and described in strong language the aggressions with which we had been visited by that nation. Towards the conclusion he makes the following remarks—

" Such is the spectacle of injuries and indignities which have been heaped on our country; and such the crisis which its unexampled forbearance and conciliatory efforts have not been able to avert. It might, at least, have been expected, that an enlightened nation, if less urged by moral obligations, or invited by friendly dispositions on the part of the United States, would have found, in its true interest alone, a sufficient motive to respect their rights and their tranquility on the high seas; that an enlarged policy could have favoured that free and general circulation of commerce, in which the British nation is at all times interested, and which, in times of war, is the best alleviation of its calamities to herself, as well as to other belligerents; and more especially that the British cabinet would not, for the sake of a precarious and surreptitious intercourse with hostile markets, have persevered in a course of measures which necessarily put at hazard the invaluable market of a great and growing country, disposed to cultivate the mutual advantages of an active commerce.

" Other councils have prevailed. Our moderation and conciliation have had no other effect than to encourage perseverance, and to enlarge pretensions. We behold our seafaring citizens still the daily victims of lawless violence committed on the great common highway of nations, even within sight of the country which owes them protection. We behold our vessels, freighted with the products of our soil and industry, or returning with the honest proceeds of them, wrested from their lawful destinations, confiscated by prize courts, no longer the organs of public law, but the instruments of arbitrary edicts; and their unfortunate crews dispersed and lost, or forced or inveigled, in British ports, into British fleets; whilst arguments are employed, in support of these aggressions, which have no foundation but in a principle equally supporting a claim to regulate our external commerce in all cases whatsoever.

"We behold, in fine, on the side of Great Britain, a state of war against the United States; and on the side of the United States, a state of peace towards Great Britain.

" Whether the United States shall continue passive under these progressive usurpations, and these accumulating wrongs; or, opposing force to force in defence of their national rights, shall commit a just cause into the hands of the Almighty Disposer of events; avoiding all connections which might entangle it in the contests or views of other powers, and preserving a constant readiness to concur in an honourable re-establishment of peace and friendship, is a solemn question, which the constitution wisely confides to the legislative department of the government. In recommending it to their early deliberations, I am happy in the assurance, that the decision will be worthy the enlightened and patriotic councils of a virtuous, a free, and a powerful nation."

On the 3d of June, the Committee on Foreign Relations of the House of Representatives made a long report on the foregoing message. After recapitulating various charges of aggression upon our neutral rights by the British nation, the committee in their manifesto say—

" In May, 1806, the whole coast of the continent, from the Elbe to Brest, inclusive, was declared to be in a state of blockade. By this act, the well established principles of the law of nations, principles which have served for ages as guides, and fixed the boundary between the rights of belligerents and neutrals, were violated. By the law of nations, as recognised by Great Britain herself, no blockade is lawful unless it be sustained by the application of

an adequate force ; and that an adequate force was applied
to this blockade, in its full extent, ought not to be pretended.   Whether Great Britain was able to maintain legally,
so extensive a blockade, considering the war in which she
is engaged, requiring such extensive naval operations, is
a question which it is not necessary at this time to examine. It is sufficient to be known that such force was not
applied, and this is evident from the terms of the blockade
itself, by which, comparatively, an inconsiderable portion
of the coast only was declared to be in a state of strict
and rigorous blockade.   The objection to the measure is
not diminished by that circumstance.   If the force was not
applied, the blockade was unlawful, from whatever cause
the failure might proceed.   The belligerent who institutes
the blockade cannot absolve itself from the obligation to
apply the force, under any pretext whatever.   For a belligerent to relax a blockade which it could not maintain,
with a view to absolve itself from the obligation to maintain it, would be a refinement in injustice, not less insulting to the understanding than repugnant to the law of nations.   To claim merit for the mitigation of an evil which
the party either had not the power, or found it inconvenient to inflict, would be a new mode of encroaching on
neutral rights.   Your committee think it just to remark,
that *this act of the British government does not appear to
have been adopted in the sense in which it has been since construed.*   On consideration of all the circumstances attending the measure, and particularly the character of the distinguished statesman who announced it, *we are persuaded
that it was conceived in a spirit of conciliation, and intended
to lead to an accommodation of all differences between the
United States and Great Britain.*   His death disappointed
that hope, and the act has since become subservient to
other purposes.   It has been made by his successors a pretext for that vast system of usurpation which has so long
oppressed and harassed our commerce.

" The next act of the British government which claims
our attention, is the order of council of January 7, 1807, by
which neutral powers are prohibited trading from one port
to another of France, or her allies, or any other country
with which Great Britain might not freely trade.   By this
order, the pretension of England, heretofore disclaimed
by every other power, to prohibit neutrals disposing of
parts of their cargoes at different ports of the same enemy,
is revived, and with vast accumulation of injury.   Every
enemy, however great the number, or distant from each
other, is considered one, and the like trade even with
powers at peace with England, who, from motives of
policy, had excluded or restrained her commerce, was also
prohibited.   In this act, the British government evidently
disclaimed all regard for neutral rights.   Aware that the
measures authorized by it could find no pretext in any
belligerent right, none was urged.   To prohibit the sale
of our produce, consisting of innocent articles, at any port
of a belligerent, not blockaded ; to consider every belligerent as one, and subject neutrals to the same restraints
with all, as if there was but one, were bold encroachments.
But to restrain, or in any manner interfere with our commerce with neutral nations, with whom Great Britain was
at peace, and against whom she had no justifiable cause of
war, for the sole reason that they restrained or excluded
from their ports her commerce, was utterly incompatible
with the pacific relations subsisting between the two
countries.

" We proceed to bring into view the British order in
council of November 11, 1807, which superseded every
other order, and consummated that system of hostility on
the commerce of the United States which has been since
so steadily pursued.   By this order, all France, and her
allies, and every other country at war with Great Britain,
or with which she was not at war, from which the British
flag was excluded, and all the colonies of her enemies, were

subjected to the same restrictions as if they were actually blockaded in the most strict and rigorous manner ; and all trade in articles, the produce and manufacture of the said countries and colonies, and the vessels engaged in it, were subjected to capture and condemnation as lawful prize. To this order certain exceptions were made, which we forbear to notice, because they were not adopted from a regard to neutral rights, but were dictated by policy to promote the commerce of England, and so far as they related to neutral powers, were said to emanate from the clemency of the British government.

" It would be superfluous in your committee to state, that by this order the British government declared direct and positive war against the United States. The dominion of the ocean was completely usurped by it, all commerce forbidden, and every flag driven from it, or subjected to capture and condemnation, which did not subserve the policy of the British government by paying it a tribute, and sailing under its sanction. From this period the United States have incurred the heaviest losses, and most mortifying humiliations. They have borne the calamities of war, without retorting them on its authors.

" So far your committee has presented to the view of the house, the aggressions which have been committed under the authority of the British government on the commerce of the United States. We will now proceed to other wrongs which have been still more severely felt. Among these is the impressment of our seamen, a practice which has been unceasingly maintained by Great Britain in the wars to which she has been a party since our revolution. Your committee cannot convey in adequate terms the deep sense which they entertain of the injustice and oppression of this proceeding. Under the pretext of impressing British seamen, our fellow citizens are seized in British ports, on the high seas, and in every other quarter to which the British power extends; are taken on board British men of war, and compelled to serve there as British subjects. In this mode our citizens are wantonly snatched from their country and their families ; deprived of their liberty, and doomed to an ignominious and slavish bondage ; compelled to fight the battles of a foreign country, and often to perish in them. Our flag has given them no protection ; it has been unceasingly violated, and our vessels exposed to danger by the loss of the men taken from them. "Your committee need not remark, that while this practice is continued, it is impossible for the United States to consider themselves an independent nation. Every new case is a new proof of their degradation. Its continuance is the more unjustifiable, because the United States have repeatedly proposed to the British government an arrangement which would secure to it the controul of its own people. An exemption of the citizens of the United States from this degrading oppression, and their flag from violation, is all that they have sought.————

" Your committee would be much gratified if they could close here the detail of British wrongs ; but it is their duty to recite another act of still greater malignity than any of those which have already been brought to your view. The attempt to dismember our Union, and overthrow our excellent constitution by a secret mission, the object of which was to foment discontents and excite insurrection against the constituted authorities and laws of the nation, as lately disclosed by the agent employed in it, affords full proof that *there is no bound to the hostility of the British government towards the United States : no act, however unjustifiable, which it would not commit to accomplish their ruin.* This attempt excites the greater horrour, from the consideration that it was made while the United States and Great Britain were at peace, and an amicable negotiation was depending between them for the accommodation of their differences, through public ministers regularly authorized for the purpose.

" The United States have beheld with unexampled forbearance this continued series of hostile encroachments on
their rights and interests, in the hope, that yielding to the
force of friendly remonstrances, often repeated, the British
government might adopt a more just policy towards them;
but that hope no longer exists. They have also weighed
impartially the reasons which have been urged by the
British government in vindication of those encroachments,
and found in them neither justification nor apology.

" The British government has alleged, in vindication of
the orders in council, that they were resorted to as a retaliation on France, for similar aggressions committed by
her on our neutral trade with the British dominions. But
how has this plea been supported? The dates of British
and French aggressions are well known to the world.
Their origin and progress have been marked with too
wide and destructive a waste of the property of our fellow
citizens, to have been forgotten. The decree of Berlin, of
November 21st, 1806, was the first aggression of France
in the present war. Eighteen months had then elapsed
after the attack made by Great Britain on our neutral
trade with the colonies of France and her allies, and six
months from the date of the proclamation of May, 1806.
Even on the 7th of January, 1807, the date of the first
British order in council, so short a term had elapsed after
the Berlin decree, that it was hardly possible that the
intelligence of it should have reached the United States.
A retaliation which is to produce its effect by operating on
a neutral power, ought not to be resorted to till the neutral
had justified it, by a culpable acquiescence in the unlawful
act of the other belligerent. It ought to be delayed until
after sufficient time had been allowed to the neutral to remonstrate against the measures complained of, to receive
an answer, and to act on it, which had not been done in
the present instance. And when the order of November
11th was issued, it is well known that a minister of France

had declared to the minister plenipotentiary of the United States at Paris, that it was not intended that the decree of Berlin should apply to the United States. It is equally well known that no American vessel had then been condemned under it, or seizure been made, with which the British government was acquainted. The facts prove incontestably that the measures of France, however unjustifiable in themselves, were nothing more than a pretext for those of England. And of the insufficiency of that pretext, ample proof has already been afforded by the British government itself, and in the most impressive form. Although it was declared that the orders in council were retaliatory on France for her decrees, it was also declared, and in the orders themselves, that owing to the superiority of the British navy, by which the fleets of France and her allies were confined within their own ports, the French decrees were considered only as empty threats.

"It is no justification of the wrongs of one power, that the like were committed by another; nor ought the fact, if true, to have been urged by either, as it could afford no proof of its love of justice, of its magnanimity, or even of its courage. It is more worthy the government of a great nation, to relieve than to assail the injured. Nor can a repetition of the wrongs by another power repair the violated right or wounded honour of the injured party. An utter inability alone to resist, could justify a quiet surrender of our rights, and degrading submission to the will of others. To that condition the United States are not reduced, nor do they fear it. That they ever consented to discuss with either power the misconduct of the other is a proof of their love of peace, of their moderation, and of the hope which they still indulged, that friendly appeals to just and generous sentiments would not be made to them in vain. But the motive was mistaken, if their forbearance was imputed either to the want of a just sensibility to their wrongs, or a determination, if suitable redress was not obtained, to resent them. The time has now arrived when this system of reasoning must cease. It would be insulting to repeat it. It would be degrading to hear it. The United States must act as an independent nation, and assert their rights, and avenge their wrongs, according to their own estimate of them, with the party who commits them, holding it responsible for its own misdeeds, unmitigated by those of another.

" For the difference made between Great Britain and France, by the application of the non-importation act against England only, the motive has been already too often explained, and is too well known to require further illustration. In the commercial restrictions to which the United States resorted as an evidence of their sensibility, and a mild retaliation of their wrongs, they invariably placed both powers on the same footing, holding out to each in respect to itself, the same accommodation, in case it accepted the condition offered, and in respect to the other the same restraint if it refused. Had the British government confirmed the arrangement which was entered into with the British minister in 1809, and France maintained her decrees, with France would the United States have had to resist, with the firmness belonging to their character, the continued violation of their rights. The committee do not hesitate to declare, that *France has greatly injured the United States, and that satisfactory reparation has not yet been made for many of those injuries. But that is a concern which the United States will look to and settle for themselves.* The high character of the American people is a sufficient pledge to the world that they will not fail to settle it, on conditions which they have a right to claim.

" More recently the true policy of the British government towards the United States, has been completely unfolded. It has been publicly declared by those in power, that the orders in council should not be repealed until the French government had revoked all its internal restraints on the British commerce ; and that the trade of the United States with France and her allies, should be prohibited until Great Britain was also allowed to trade with them. By this declaration it appears, that to satisfy the pretensions of the British government, the United States must join Great Britain in the war with France, and prosecute the war until France should be subdued ; for without her subjugation, it were in vain to presume on such a concession. The hostility of the British government to these states has been still further disclosed. It has been made manifest that the United States are considered by it as the commercial rival of Great Britain, and that their prosperity and growth are incompatible with her welfare. When all these circumstances are taken into consideration, it is impossible for your committee to doubt the motives which have governed the British ministry in all its measures towards the United States since the year 1805. Equally is it impossible to doubt, longer, the course which the United States ought to pursue towards Great Britain.

" From this review of the multiplied wrongs of the British government since the commencement of the present war, it must be evident to the impartial world, that the contest which is now forced on the United States, is radically a contest for their sovereignty and independence. Your committee will not enlarge on any of the injuries, however great, which have had a transitory effect. They wish to call the attention of the House to those of a permanent nature only, which intrench so deeply on our most important rights, and wound so extensively and vitally our best interests, as could not fail to deprive the United States of the principal advantages of their revolution, if submitted to. The controul of our commerce by Great Britain in regulating, at pleasure, and expelling it almost from the ocean ; the oppressive manner in which these regulations have been carried into effect, by seizing and confiscating such of our vessels, with their cargoes, as were said to

have violated her edicts, often without previous warning
of their danger ; the impressment of our citizens from on
board our own vessels on the high seas, and elsewhere, and
holding them in bondage till it suited the convenience of
their oppressors to deliver them up, are encroachments of
that high and dangerous tendency, which could not fail to
produce that pernicious effect : nor would these be the only
consequences that would result from it. The British govern
ment might, for a while, be satisfied with the ascendency
thus gained over us, but its pretensions would soon increase.
The proof which so complete and disgraceful a submission
to its authority would afford of our degeneracy, could not
fail to inspire confidence, that there was no limit to which
its usurpations, and our degradation, might not be carried.

" Your committee, believing that the freeborn sons of
America are worthy to enjoy the liberty which their fathers purchased at the price of so much blood and treasure, and seeing in the measures adopted by Great Britain,
a course commenced and persisted in, which must lead to
a loss of national character and independence, feel no hesitation in advising resistance by force ; in which the Americans of the present day will prove to the enemy and to the
world, that we have not only inherited that liberty which
our fathers gave us, but also the will and the power to·main-
tain it. Relying on the patriotism of the nation, and confi-
dently trusting that the Lord of Hosts will go with us to battle in a righteous cause, and crown our efforts with success,
your committee recommend an immediate appeal to arms."

This manifesto was followed by an act of Congress, containing a formal declaration of war, in the following words:

" *An act declaring War between the United Kingdom of
Great Britain and Ireland, and the dependencies thereof,
and the United States of America and their territories.*

" *Be it enacted,* &c. that war be and the same is hereby
declared to exist between the United Kingdom of Great

Britain and Ireland, and the dependencies thereof, and the United States of America and their territories; and that the President of the United States is hereby authorized to use the whole land and naval force of the United States to carry the same into effect, and to issue to private armed vessels of the United States commissions or letters of marque and general reprisal, in such form as he shall think proper, and under the seal of the United States, against the vessels, goods, and effects of the government of the said United Kingdom of Great Britain and Ireland, and the subjects thereof."—[Approved, June 18th, 1812.]

On the next day, viz. June 19th, 1812, the following proclamation was issued:—

" By the President of the United States of America— A Proclamation.

" Whereas the Congress of the United States, by virtue of the constituted authority vested in them, have declared by their act bearing date the 18th day of the present month, that war exists between the United Kingdom of Great Britain and Ireland, and the dependencies thereof, and the United States of America and their territories; now, therefore I, James Madison, President of the United States of America, do hereby proclaim the same to all whom it may concern: and I do specially enjoin on all persons holding offices, civil or military, under the authority of the United States, that they be vigilant and zealous in discharging the duties respectively incident thereto: and I do moreover exhort all the good people of the United States, as they love their country; as they value the precious heritage derived from the virtue and valour of their fathers; as they feel the wrongs which have forced on them the last resort of injured nations; and as they consult the best means, under the blessing of Divine Providence, of abridging its calamities, that they exert themselves in preserving order, in promoting concord, in maintaining the authority and efficacy of the laws, and in supporting and invigorat-

ing all the measures which may be adopted by the constituted authorities, for obtaining a speedy, a just, and an
honourable peace.

    " Done at Washington, the 19th day of June, 1812, &c.
                        "JAMES MADISON.
" By the President.   James Monroe, Sec. of State."

On the 18th of June, 1812, the day on which Congress
declared war against Great Britain, Mr. Russell, United
States charge d'affaires at London, wrote as follows to the
Secretary of State—

                                London, June 18, 1812.

    " I hand you herein the *Times* of yesterday, containing
the debate in the House of Commons on the preceding
evening, relative to the orders in council.   From this debate it appears that these measures are to be abandoned,
but as yet no official extinction of them has been announced.   The time already elapsed since the declaration of
Lord Castlereagh, excites a suspicion that either the promised revocation will not take place, or what is more probable, some other measure, equally unjust, is now under
consideration, to replace those which are to be revoked.

    " I hope, until the doings here are ascertained with cer-
tainty and precision, there will be no relaxation on our
part."

    On the 30th of June Mr. Russell wrote as follows—

    " I have at length had the satisfaction to announce to
you, in my letters of the 26th instant, the revocation of
the orders in council.

    " You will, without doubt, be somewhat surprised that
this is founded on the French decree of the 28th of April,
1811.

    " The real cause of the revocation is the measures of
our government.   These measures have produced a degree of distress among the manufacturers of this country
that was becoming intolerable; and an apprehension of

still greater misery, from the calamities of war, drove them to speak a language which could not be misunderstood or disregarded."

The following correspondence and documents will explain Mr. Russell's allusion to the French decree of the 28th of April, 1811.

Extract of a letter from Mr. Barlow, to the duke of Bassano, dated May 1, 1812.

"It is much to be desired that the French government would now make and publish an authentic act, declaring the Berlin and Milan decrees, as relative to the United States, to have ceased in November, 1810, declaring that they have not been applied in any instance, since that time, and that they shall not be so applied in future."

It has already been shown, that whatever our government thought of blockades in 1799, in 1806, and for some time afterwards, they were very little disturbed by that which the British government had established from the Elbe to Brest; nor, as far as their public documents show, was it ever considered worthy of serious remonstrance or complaint, until it became necessary to exercise their diplomatic skill between Great Britain and France. The importance of it, as bearing an earlier date than the Berlin decree, to the French government, has already been mentioned. It will be recollected, that in January, 1810, the French minister, in answer to a note from General Armstrong on the subject, had expressed the willingness of his majesty the emperor to repeal his decrees, on condition that the British government would revoke their blockades of France *of a date prior to the Berlin decree.* In the mean time, however, his imperial majesty had issued a third decree more extravagant in its object, and more injurious to the neutral rights of the United States than either the Berlin or Milan decree. It bears date at Rambouillet, March 23d, 1810, and is of the following tenour—

"Napoleon, &c. &c. &c. Considering that the government of the United States, by an act dated the 1st of March, 1809, which forbids the entrance of the ports, harbours, and rivers of the said states, to all French vessels, orders—

"1st. That after the 20th of May following, vessels under the French flag, which shall arrive in the United States, shall be seized and confiscated as well as their cargoes: 2d. That after the same epoch, no merchandise or produce, the growth or manufacture of France or her colonies, can be imported into the said United States from any foreign port or place whatsoever, under penalty of seizure, confiscation, and a fine of three times the value of the merchandise: 3d. That American vessels cannot go to any port of France, of her colonies, or dependencies: We have decreed, and do decree as follows:

"Art. 1. All vessels navigating under the flag of the United States, or possessed in whole or in part by any citizen or subject of that power, which, counting from the 20th of May, 1809, have entered, or shall enter into the ports of our empire, of our colonies, or of the countries occupied by our arms, shall be seized, and the product of the sales shall be deposited in the surplus fund (caisse d'amortissement.)

"There shall be excepted from this regulation, the vessels which shall be charged with despatches, or with commissions of the government of the said States, and who shall not have either cargoes or merchandise on board."

American property to a large amount was seized under this extraordinary decree, and declared forfeited. On the 5th of July following Mr. Secretary Smith addressed a letter to General Armstrong, from which the following extract is taken—

"The arrival of the John Adams brought your letters of the 1st, &c. and 16th of April.

"From that of the 16th of April it appears that the

seizures of the American property, lately made, had been followed up by its actual sale, and that the proceeds had been deposited in the emperor's *caisse privé*. You have presented in such colours the enormity of this outrage, that I have only to signify to you, that the President entirely approves the step that has been taken by you, and that he does not doubt that it will be followed by you, or the person who may succeed you, with such farther interpositions as may be deemed advisable. He instructs you particularly to make the French government sensible of *the deep impression made here by so signal an aggression on the principles of justice and of good faith,* and to demand every reparation of which the case is susceptible. If it be not the purpose of the French government to remove every idea of friendly adjustment with the United States, it would seem impossible but that a reconsideration of this violent proceeding must lead to a redress of it as a preliminary to a general accommodation of the differences between the two countries.

" At the date of the last communication from Mr. Pinkney, he had not obtained from the British government an acceptance of the condition on which the French government was willing to concur, in putting an end to all the edicts of both against our neutral commerce. If he should afterwards have succeeded, you will of course, on receiving information of the fact, immediately claim from the French government the fulfillment of its promise, and by transmitting the result to Mr. Pinkney, you will co-operate with him in completing the removal of all the illegal obstructions to our commerce.

" Among the documents now sent is another copy of the act of Congress, repealing the non-intercourse law, but authorizing a renewal of it against Great Britain, in case France should repeal her edicts and Great Britain should refuse to follow her example, and *vice versa.* You have been already informed that the President is ready to ex-

ercise the power vested in him for such a purpose, as soon
as the occasion shall arise. Should the other experiment,
in the hands of Mr. Pinkney, have failed, you will make
the act of Congress, and the disposition of the President,
the subject of a formal communication to the French
government, and it is not easy to conceive any ground,
even specious, on which the overture specified in the act
can be declined.

" If the non-intercourse law, in any of its modifications,
was objectionable to the emperor of the French, that law
no longer exists.

" If he be ready, as has been declared in the letter of
the duke of Cadore of February 14, to do justice to the
United States, in the case of a pledge on their part not to
submit to the British edicts, the opportunity for making
good the declaration is now afforded. Instead of submission, the President is now ready, by renewing the non-
intercourse act against Great Britain, to oppose to her
orders in council a measure, which is of a character that
ought to satisfy any reasonable expectation. If it should
be necessary for you to meet the question whether the
non-intercourse will be renewed against Great Britain, in
case she should not comprehend, in the repeal of her edicts,
her blockades, which are not consistent with the law of
nations, you may, should it be found necessary, let it be
understood, that *a repeal of the illegal blockades of a date
prior to the Berlin decree, namely, that of May,* 1806, *will
be included in the condition required of Great Britain,* that
particular blockade having been avowed to be comprehended in, and of course identified with the orders in
council. With respect to blockades of a subsequent date
or not, against France, you will press the reasonableness
of leaving them, together with future blockades not warranted by public law, to be proceeded against by the
United States in the manner they may choose to adopt.
As has been heretofore stated to you, a satisfactory pro-

vision for restoring the property lately surprised and seized by the order or at the instance of the French government, *must be combined with a repeal of the French edicts,* with a view to a non-intercourse with Great Britain : such a provision being an indispensable evidence of the just purpose of France towards the United States. And you will, moreover, be careful, in arranging such a provision for that particular case of spoliations, not to weaken the ground on which a redress of others may be justly pursued."

From the numerous quotations which have been made, and from a great number of passages which might be added, it is perfectly obvious, that our negotiations respecting the revocation of the British orders in council were greatly embarrassed by the form of the inquiry made of the French minister by General Armstrong, by order of the Secretary of State, in January, 1810. That inquiry was not limited to what were the conditions on which his majesty the emperor would annul the Berlin decree, but it was asked *whether he would do so if Great Britain revoked her blockades of a date anterior to that of the Berlin decree?* The subject was alluded to very often in the course of the correspondence; and on the 26th of March, 1810, Lord Wellesley, in answer to an inquiry whether the blockade of May, 1806, had been withdrawn, said—" The blockade, notified by Great Britain in May, 1806, has never been formally withdrawn. It cannot therefore be accurately stated, that the restrictions which it established, rest altogether on the order of council of the 7th of January, 1807: they are comprehended under the more extensive restrictions of that order. No other blockade of the ports of France was instituted by Great Britain, between the 16th of May, 1806, and the 7th of January, 1807, excepting the blockade of Venice, instituted on the 27th of July, 1806, which is still in force." It seems from this declaration of the British minister, that every thing except a formal revocation had taken place, the decree, as **Mr.**

Pinkney justly considered it, had been absorbed in the orders of council of January, 1807. But as this last order of council was of a subsequent date to the Berlin decree, it would not have answered the object which the French government had in view, which, as has been already remarked, was to obtain an admission, at least by implication, that the British government first adopted the policy of interfering with the rights of neutrals. For no other purpose than that of enabling the French government to gain this advantage over the British, was this subject of controversy first started, and afterwards continued between the parties; thus adding one more proof, that our government deemed it expedient at all times to keep on hand some distinct subject of controversy with Great Britain. In confirmation of the idea that the blockading order of May, 1806, was not in force, Mr. Pinkney wrote to General Armstrong on the 6th of April, 1810, in the following manner—"I do not know whether the statement contained in my letter of the 27th of last month will enable you to obtain the recall of the Berlin decree. Certainly the inference from that statement is that the blockade of 1806 is virtually at an end, being merged and comprehended in an order in council, issued after the date of the edict of Berlin. I am, however, about to try to obtain a formal revocation of that blockade (and that of Venice,) or at least a precise declaration that they are not in force.

It is not a little remarkable, that our government should have shown such a degree of meekness and humility towards France, whilst they were manifesting such a lofty air, and such a peremptory tone, in their correspondence with Great Britain. The treatment they received from the French government was not only supercilious and haughty, but the language of their official communications, in relation to the very subject in discussion, contemptuous and insulting. On the 17th of February, 1810, General Armstrong addressed a letter to the Secretary of State,

enclosing a note which he had received from **M. Cham-**
pagny, from which the following passages are extracted :

" His majesty could place no reliance on the proceedings of the United States, who having no ground of complaint against France, comprised her in their acts of exclusion, and since the month of May have forbidden the
entrance of their ports to French vessels, under the penalty
of confiscation. As soon as his majesty was informed of
this measure, he considered himself bound to order reprisals on American vessels not only in his territory, but
likewise in the countries which are under his influence.
In the ports of Holland, of Spain, of Italy, and of Naples,
American vessels have been seized, because the Americans
have seized French vessels. *The Americans cannot hesitate as to the part which they are to take. They ought
either to tear to pieces the act of their independence, and to
become again as before the revolution, the subjects of England,
or to take such measures as that their commerce and industry
should not be tariffed* (tarifés) *by the English, which renders
them more dependent than Jamaica, which at least has its assembly of representatives and its privileges. Men without just
political views,* (sans politique,) *without honour, without energy, may alledge that payment of the tribute imposed by
England may be submitted to because it is light ;* but why
will they not perceive that the English will no sooner have
obtained the admission of the principle, than they will
raise the tariff in such a way that the burden, at first light,
becoming insupportable, it will then be necessary to *fight
for interest, after having refused to fight for honour.*

" The undersigned avows with frankness, that France
has every thing to gain from receiving well the Americans
in her ports. Her commercial relations with neutrals are
advantageous to her. She is in no way jealous of their
prosperity ; great, powerful and rich, she is satisfied when,
by her own commerce, or by that of neutrals, her expor-

tations give to her agriculture and her fabricks the proper developement.

"It is now thirty years since the United States of America founded, in the bosom of the new world, an independent country, at the price of the blood of so many immortal men, who perished on the field of battle to throw off the leaden yoke of the English monarch. These generous men were far from supposing, when they thus sacrificed their blood for the independence of America, that there would so soon be a question whether there should be imposed upon it a yoke more heavy than that which they had thrown off, by subjecting its industry to a tariff of British legislation, and to the orders in council of 1807.

"If then the minister of America can enter into an engagement, that the American vessels will not submit to the orders in council of England of November, 1807, nor to any decree of blockade, unless this blockade should be real, the undersigned is authorized to conclude every species of convention tending to renew the treaty of commerce with America, and in which all the measures proper to consolidate the commerce and the prosperity of the Americans shall be provided for."

It is also remarkable, that the same Administration, whose dignity was so suddenly affronted, and whose resentment was so greatly roused, by a single expression in Mr. Jackson's letter, relating to the rejection of the arrangement with Mr. Erskine, as to refuse to hold any intercourse with that minister, should have borne, with such philosophical meekness and coolness, the foregoing language of M. Champagny. It is not easy to imagine phraseology more insolent, or sentiments more degrading to our government and country. And yet General Armstrong was not recalled; nor, in examining the correspondence relating to this subject, has any order even to remonstrate against the indignity offered to both been discovered.

In a little more than a month after the date of this letter, the Rambouillet decree, which has already been cited, was issued. No one who reads it can hesitate about its true character; which was little better than a license to commit piracy, in a manner the most base and infamous.

On the 5th of August following, General Armstrong received a note from the duke of Cadore, (Champagny) containing a formal declaration that the Berlin and Milan decrees were both revoked, and that after the 1st of November ensuing they would cease to have effect. This note is couched in language equally extraordinary with that from which we have copied the foregoing extracts. The following passages are quoted—

"Sir—I have laid before his majesty, the emperor and king, the act of Congress of the 1st of May, taken from the gazette of the United States, which you have sent to me.

"His majesty could have wished that this act, and all the other acts of the government of the United States, which interest France, *had always been officially made known to him.* In general, *he has only had a knowledge of them indirectly*, and *after a long interval of time.* There have resulted from this delay serious inconveniences, which would not have existed if these acts had been *promptly and officially communicated.*

"The emperor had *applauded the general embargo*, laid by the United States on all their vessels, because that measure, if it has been prejudicial to France, had in it at least nothing offensive to her honour."——

"The act of the 1st of March has raised the embargo, and substituted for it a measure the most injurious to the interests of France.

"This act, of which the emperor knew nothing until very lately, interdicted to American vessels the commerce of France, at the time it authorized that to Spain, Naples, and Holland, that is to say, to the countries under French influence, and denounced confiscation against all

French vessels which should enter the ports of America. *Reprisal was a right, and commanded by the dignity of France,* a circumstance on which it was impossible to make a compromise (de transigir.)   The sequester of all the American vessels in France has been the necessary consequence of the measure taken by Congress.

"Now Congress retrace their steps, (revient sur ses pas;) they revoke the act of the 1st of March; the ports of America are open to French commerce, and France is no longer interdicted to the Americans.   In short, Congress engages to oppose itself to that one of the belligerent powers which should refuse to acknowledge the rights of neutrals.

"In this new state of things, I am authorized to declare to you, sir, that the decrees of Berlin and Milan are revoked, and that after the first of November they will cease to have effect; it being understood that, in consequence of this declaration, the English shall revoke their orders in council, and renounce the new principles of blockade which they have wished to establish, or, that the United States, conformably to the act you have just communicated, shall cause their rights to be respected by the English.

"It is with the most particular satisfaction, sir, that I make known to you this determination of the emperor. His majesty loves the Americans.   Their prosperity and their commerce are within the scope of his policy.

"The independence of America is one of the principal titles of glory to France.   Since that epoch the emperor is pleased *in aggrandizing the United States,* and, *under all circumstances, that which can contribute to the independence, to the prosperity, and the liberty of the Americans, the emperor will consider as conformable with the interests of his empire.*"

On the 2d day of November, 1810, the President issued his proclamation, giving notice that the French decrees were revoked.   After the usual recital, referring to the act of Congress, authorizing him to adopt that measure, the proclamation says—

" And whereas it has been officially made known to this government, that the edicts of France violating the neutral commerce of the United States have been so revoked as to cease to have effect on the first of the present month: Now, therefore, I, James Madison, President of the United States, do hereby proclaim that the said edicts of France have been so revoked as that they ceased on the said first day of the present month to violate the neutral commerce of the United States; and that, from the date of these presents, all the restrictions imposed by the aforesaid act shall cease and be discontinued in relation to France and her dependencies."

Thus it appears, that after this long train of negotiation and effort, the French government had succeeded, in co-operation with ours, in bringing the United States to a species of issue with Great Britain. This was taking one more important step towards the open conflict which eventually occurred between the countries. A little further attention will be necessary to the correspondence of General Armstrong, relating to this adjustment.

It has been seen, that upon the issuing of the Rambouillet decree, a large amount of American property within the reach of French authority was seized and confiscated, and the avails were placed in the imperial privy purse. On the 10th of September, 1810, General Armstrong addressed a letter to the Secretary of State, in which he says, that by a letter from the duke of Cadore, a copy of which was enclosed, " it will be seen that the decree of Rambouillet is not in operation, and that American ships entering the ports of France before the 1st of November next, will be judged under the decrees of Berlin and of Milan. In a paragraph in the same letter, under the date of September 12th, he says—" I have the honour to enclose copies of two other letters from the duke of Cadore, one of which is an answer to my note of the 8th instant. To the question whether we had any thing to expect in reparation for past wrongs ? they reply, that their act being of reprisal, the law of reprisal must govern ; in other words, that *if you confiscate French property under the law of non-intercourse, they will confiscate your property under their decree of Rambouillet."* The words underscored is the verbal explanation which accompanied the letter.

" THE DUKE OF CADORE to GENERAL ARMSTRONG.

" Paris, September 7th, 1810.

" SIR,—You have done me the honour to ask of me, by your letter of the 20th of August, what will be the lot of the American vessels which may arrive in France before the 1st of November.

" His majesty has always wished to favour the commerce of the United States. It was not without reluctance that he used reprisal towards the Americans while he saw that Congress had ordered the confiscation of all French vessels which might arrive in the United States.

" It appears that Congress might have spared to his majesty and his subjects this mortification (ce désagrément) if in place of that harsh and decisive measure, which left to France no choice, they had used some palliative, such as that of not receiving French vessels, or of sending them away, after a delay of so many days.

" As soon as his majesty was informed of this hostile act, he felt that the honour of France, involved in this point, could not be cleansed (ne pouvait étre lavé) but by a declaration of war (which) could not take place but by tedious explanations.

" The emperor contented himself with making reprisals ; and in consequence, he applied to American vessels which came to France, or to countries occupied by the

French armies, word for word, the regulations of the act of Congress.

"Since the last measures by which that hostile act is repealed, his majesty hastens to cause it to be made known to you that he anticipates that which may re-establish harmony with the United States, and that he repeals his decrees of Berlin and Milan, *under the conditions* pointed out in my letter to you, of the 5th of August.

"During this interval, the American vessels which shall arrive in France will not be subjected to confiscation; because the act of Congress, which had served as a motive to our reprisals, is repealed; but these vessels will be subjected to all the effects of the Berlin and Milan decrees; that is to say, they will be treated *amicably*, if they can be considered as Americans, and *hostilely*, if they have lost their national character (s'ils se sont laissé dénationalisé) by submitting to the orders in council of the British government."

On the 7th of September, 1810, General Armstrong wrote a letter to the duke of Cadore, from which the following passages are copied—

"Your excellency will not think me importunate if I should employ the last moments of my stay in Paris, in seeking an explicit declaration on the following points:

1. Has the decree of his majesty of the 23d of March last, enjoining acts of reprisal against the commerce of the United States on account of their late law of non-intercourse, been recalled?

2. What will be the operation (on the vessels of the United States) of his majesty's decree of July last, forbidding the departure of neutral ships from the ports of France, unless provided with *imperial licenses*? Are these licenses merely substitutes for clearances? or do they prescribe regulations to be observed by the holders of them within the jurisdiction of the United States?

"Do they confine the permitted intercourse to two ports

only of the said States, and do they enjoin that all shipments be made on French account exclusively?

"Is it his majesty's will, that the seizures made in the ports of Spain and other places, on the principle of reprisal, shall become a subject of present or future negotiation between the two governments? or, are the acts already taken by his majesty to be regarded as conclusive against remuneration?

"I need not suggest to your excellency the interest that both governments have in the answers that may be given to these questions, and how nearly connected they are with the good understanding which ought to exist between them. After the great step lately taken by his majesty towards an accommodation of differences, we are not at liberty to suppose that any new consideration will arise, which shall either retard or prevent the adoption of measures necessary to a full restoration of the commercial intercourse and friendly relation of the two powers."

The following is the reply to the foregoing note—

"THE DUKE OF CADORE to GENERAL ARMSTRONG.

"*Paris, Sept.* 12*th*, 1810.

"I have received your letter of the 7th of September. That which I wrote to you the same day answered the first of the questions you put to me. I will add to what I have had the honour to write to you, that the decree of the 23d of March, 1810, which ordered reprisals in consequence of the act of Congress of the 1st of March, 1809, was repealed as soon as we were informed of the repeal of the act of *non-intercourse* passed against France.

"On your second question I hasten to declare to you, that American vessels loaded with merchandise the growth of the American provinces, will be received without difficulty in the ports of France, provided they have not suffered their flag to lose its national character, by submitting to the acts of the British council; they may in like manner depart from the ports of France. *The emperor has given licenses to American vessels.* It is the only flag which has obtained them. In this his majesty has intended to give a proof of the respect he loves to show to the Americans. If he is somewhat dissatisfied (peu satisfaite) that they have not as yet been able to succeed in causing their flag to be respected, at least he sees with pleasure that they are far from acknowledging the tyrannical principles of English legislation.

"The American vessels which may be loaded on account of Frenchmen, or on account of Americans, will be admitted into the ports of France. *As to the merchandise confiscated, it having been confiscated as a measure of reprisal, the principles of reprisal must be the law in that affair.*"

The government of Great Britain considered the revocation of the Berlin and Milan decrees as not absolute, but conditional, and therefore declined repealing their orders in council. On the 23d of July, 1811, Mr. Monroe, Secretary of State, addressed a long letter to Mr. Foster, the British minister, on the general controversy. After alluding to what occurred respecting the French decrees, he remarks, " Great Britain still declines to revoke her edicts, on the pretension that France has not revoked hers. Under that impression she infers that the United States have done her injustice by carrying into effect the non-importation against her.

" The United States maintain that France has revoked her edicts so far as they violated their neutral rights, and were contemplated by the law of May 1st, 1810, and have on that ground particularly claimed, and do expect of Great Britain a similar revocation.

" The revocation announced officially by the French minister of foreign affairs, to the minister plenipotentiary of the United States at Paris, on the 5th of August, 1810, was in itself sufficient to justify the claim of the United

States to a correspondent measure from Great Britain.
She had declared that she would proceed *pari passu* in
the repeal with France, and the day being fixed when the
repeal of the French decrees should take effect, it was reasonable to conclude that Great Britain would fix the same
day for the repeal of her orders. Had this been done, the
proclamation of the President would have announced the
revocation of the edicts of both powers at the same time ;
and in consequence thereof, the non-importation would
have gone into operation against neither. Such too is
the natural course of proceeding in transactions between
independent states ; and such the conduct which they generally observe towards each other. In all compacts between nations, it is the duty of each to perform what it
stipulates, and to presume on the good faith of the other
for a like performance. The United States having made
a proposal to both belligerents, were bound to accept a
compliance from either, and it was no objection to the
French compliance, that it was in a form to take effect at
a future day, that being a form not unusual in laws and
other public acts. Even when nations are at war and
make peace, this obligation of mutual confidence exists,
and must be respected. In treaties of commerce, by
which their future intercourse is to be governed, the obligation is the same. If distrust and jealousy are allowed to
prevail, the moral tie which binds nations together, in all
their relations, in war as well as in peace, is broken.——

  " Great Britain has declined proceeding *pari passu* with
France in the revocation of their respective edicts. She
has held aloof, and claims of the United States proof not
only that France has revoked her decrees, but that she continues to act in conformity with the revocation.——

  " You urge only as an evidence that the decrees are not
repealed, the speech of the emperor of France to the deputies from the free cities of Hamburg, Bremen, and Lubeck ; the imperial edict dated at Fontainbleau, on the

19th of October, 1810; the report of the French minister
of foreign affairs dated in December last, and a letter of
the minister of justice to the president of the council of
prizes of the 25th of that month.

" There is nothing in the first of these papers incompatible with the revocation of the decrees, in respect to the
United States. It is distinctly declared by the emperor in
his speech to the deputies of the Hanse Towns, that the
blockade of the British islands shall cease when the British
blockades cease; and that the French blockades shall cease
in favour of those nations in whose favour Great Britain revokes hers, or who support their rights against her pretension, as France admits the United States will do by enforcing the non-importation act. The same sentiment is
expressed in the report of the minister of foreign affairs.
The decree of Fontainbleau having no effect on the high
seas, cannot be brought into this discussion. It evidently
has no connection with neutral rights.

" The letter from the minister of justice to the president
of the council of prizes, is of a different character. It relates in direct terms to this subject, but not in the sense in
which you understand it. After reciting the note from
the duke of Cadore of the 5th of August last, to the American minister at Paris, which announced the repeal of the
French decrees, and the proclamation of the President in
consequence of it, it states that all causes arising under
those decrees after the 1st of November, which were then
before the court, or might afterwards be brought before it,
should not be judged by the principles of the decrees, but
be suspended until the 2d of February, when the United
States having fulfilled their engagement, the captures should
be declared void, and the vessels and their cargoes be
delivered up to their owners. This paper appears to afford
an unequivocal evidence of the revocation of the decrees,
so far as relates to the United States. By instructing the
French tribunal to make no decision until the 2d of Febru-

ary, and then to restore the property to the owners on a particular event which has happened; all cause of doubt on that point seems to be removed. The United States may justly complain of delay in the restitution of that property, but that is an injury which affects them only. Great Britain has no right to complain of it. She was interested only in the revocation of the decrees by which neutral rights would be secured from future violation ; or if she had been interested in the delay, it would have afforded no pretext for more than a delay in repealing her orders till the 2d February. From that day, at farthest, the French decrees would cease. At the same day ought her orders to have ceased."

On the 26th of July, Mr. Foster replied to Mr. Monroe. The following are extracts from his letter :—

"You urge, sir, that the British government promised to proceed *pari passu* with France in the repeal of her edicts. It is to be wished you could point out to us any step France has taken in the repeal of hers. Great Britain has repeatedly declared that she would repeal when the French did so, and she means to keep to that declaration.

"I have stated to you that we could not consider the letter of August 5th, declaring the repeal of the French edicts, provided we revoked our orders in council, or America resented our not doing so, as a step of that nature; and the French government knew that we could not ; their object was, evidently, while their system was adhered to in all its rigour, to endeavour to persuade the American government that they had relaxed from it, and to induce her to proceed in enforcing the submission of Great Britain to the inordinate demands of France. It is to be lamented that they have but too well succeeded ; for the United States government appear to have considered the French declaration in the sense in which France wished it to be taken, as an absolute repeal of her decrees, without adverting to the conditional terms which accompanied it."

" To the ambiguous declaration in M. Champagny's note, is opposed the unambiguous and personal declaration of Bonaparte himself. You urge that there is nothing incompatible with the revocation of the decrees, in respect to the United States, in his expressions to the deputies of the free cities of Hamburg, Bremen, and Lubeck; that it is distinctly stated in that speech *that the blockade of the British islands shall cease when the British blockades cease,* and that the French blockade shall cease in favour of those nations in whose favour Great Britain revokes hers, or who support their rights against her pretension.

" It is to be inferred from this and the corresponding parts of the declaration alluded to, that unless Great Britain sacrifices her principles of blockade, which are those authorized by the established law of nations, France will still maintain her decrees of Berlin and Milan, which indeed the speech in question declares to be the fundamental laws of the French empire.

" I do not, I confess, conceive how these avowals of the ruler of France can be said to be compatible with the repeal of his decrees in respect to the United States. If the United States are prepared to insist on the sacrifice by Great Britain of the ancient and established rules of maritime war practised by her, then, indeed, they may avoid the operation of the French decrees; but otherwise, according to this document, it is very clear that they are still subjected to them.

" The decree of Fontainbleau is confessedly founded on the decrees of Berlin and Milan, dated the 19th of October, 1810, and proves their continued existence. The report of the French minister of December 8, announcing the perseverance of France in her decrees, is still further in confirmation of them, and a reperusal of the letter of the minister of justice of the 25th last December, confirms me

in the inference I drew from it ; for, otherwise, why should
that minister make the prospective restoration of American vessels taken after the 1st November to be a consequence of the non-importation, and not of the French
revocation? If the French government had been sincere,
they would have ceased infringing on the neutral rights
of America after the 1st November: that they violated
them, however, after that period, is notorious.

" Your government seem to let it be understood that an
ambiguous declaration from Great Britain, similar to that
of the French minister, would have been acceptable to
them. But, sir, is it consistent with the dignity of a nation that respects itself to speak in ambiguous language?
The subjects and citizens of either country would, in the
end, be the victims, as many are already, in all probability,
who, from a misconstruction of the meaning of the French
government, have been led into the most imprudent speculations. Such conduct would not be to proceed *pari
passu* with France in revoking our edicts, but to descend
to the use of the perfidious and juggling contrivances of
her cabinet, by which she fills her coffers at the expense
of independent nations. A similar construction of proceeding *pari passu* might lead to such decrees as those of
Rambouillet or of Bayonne, to the system of exclusion or
of licenses ; all measures of France against the American
commerce, in nothing short of absolute hostility."——

"I have now followed you, I believe, sir, through the
whole range of your argument, and on reviewing the
course of it, I think I may securely say, that no satisfactory proof has as yet been brought forward of the repeal
of the obnoxious decrees of France, but on the contrary,
that it appears they continue in full force ; consequently
that no grounds exist on which you can with justice demand of Great Britain a revocation of her orders in council ; that we have a right to complain of the conduct of the
American government in enforcing the provisions of the

act of May, 1810, to the exclusion of the British trade, and afterwards in obtaining a special law for the same purpose, though it was notorious at the time that France still continued her aggressions upon American commerce, and had recently promulgated anew her decrees, suffering no trade from this country but through licenses publickly sold by her agents, and that all the suppositions you have formed of innovations on the part of Great Britain, or of her pretensions to trade with her enemies, are wholly groundless. I have also stated to you the view his majesty's government has taken of the question of the blockade of May, 1806, and it now only remains that I urge afresh the injustice of the United States' government persevering in their union with the French system, for the purpose of crushing the commerce of Great Britain."

A still more extended correspondence ensued relating to this subject, in which it was contended on the part of the American government, that the French decrees were actually repealed, and on that of the British government, that the professed act of repeal by the French emperor was a mere deception, and that the decrees were still in force; and this was urged as the reason why the British orders in council were not formally revoked. The cause which lay at the bottom of the difficulty in adjusting the controversy respecting the edicts of Great Britain, which it was contended violated our neutral rights, was the demand on our part of the revocation of the blockading order of May, 1806; the circumstances attending which have already been adverted to. In a letter from the Marquis of Wellesley to Mr. Pinkney, dated December 29th, 1810, his lordship says—" By your explanation it appears, that the American government understands the letter of the French minister as announcing an absolute repeal, on the 1st of November, 1810, of the French decrees of Berlin and Milan; which repeal, however, is not to continue in force unless the British government, within a reasonable

time after the 1st of November, 1810, shall fulfil the two
conditions stated distinctly in the letter of the French
minister. Under this explanation, if nothing more had
been required from Great Britain for the purpose of securing the continuance of the repeal of the French decrees,
than the repeal of our orders in council, I should not have
hesitated to declare the perfect readiness of this government to fulfil that condition. On these terms the British
government has always been sincerely disposed to repeal
the orders in council. It appears, however, not only by
the letter of the French minister, but by your explanation,
that the repeal of the orders in council will not satisfy
either the French or the American government. The
British government is further required, by the letter of the
French minister, to renounce those principles of blockade
which the French government alleges to be new. A reference to the terms of the Berlin decree will serve to
explain the extent of this requisition. The Berlin decree
states, that Great Britain " extends the right of blockade
to commercial unfortified towns, and to ports, harbours,
and mouths of rivers, which according to the principles and
practice of all civilized nations, is only applicable to fortified places." On the part of the American government, I
understand you to require that Great Britain should revoke
her order of blockade of May, 1806. Combining your requisition with that of the French minister, I must conclude
that America demands the revocation of that order of
blockade as a practical instance of our renunciation of those
principles of blockade which are condemned by the French
government. Those principles of blockade Great Britain
has asserted to be ancient and established by the laws of
maritime war, acknowledged by all civilized nations, and
on which depend the most valuable rights and interests of
this nation. If the Berlin and Milan decrees are to be
considered as still in force, unless Great Britain shall renounce these established foundations of her maritime

rights and interests, the period of time is not yet arrived, when the repeal of her orders in council can be claimed from her, either with reference to the promise of this government, or to the safety and honour of the nation."

Mr. Pinkney replied to Lord Wellesley on the 14th of July, 1811. In alluding to that part of his lordship's letter which has been above cited, he says—"If I comprehend the other parts of your lordship's letter, they declare in effect, that the British government will repeal nothing but the *orders in council*, and that it cannot at present repeal even them, because, in the first place, the French government has required, in the letter of the duke of Cadore to General Armstrong, of the 5th of August, not only that Great Britain shall revoke those orders, but that she shall renounce certain principles of blockade (supposed to be explained in the preamble to the Berlin decree) which France alleges to be new; and in the second place, because the American government has (as you conclude) demanded the revocation of the British order of blockade of May, 1806, *as a practical instance of that same renunciation*, or, in other words, has made itself a party, not openly indeed, but indirectly and covertly, to the entire requisition of France, as you understand that requisition.

" It is certainly true that the American government has required, as indispensable in the view of its acts of intercourse and non-intercourse, the annulment of the British blockade of May, 1806; and further, that it has through me declared its confident expectation that other blockades of a similar character (including that of the island of Zealand) will be discontinued. But by what process of reasoning your lordship has arrived at the conclusion, that the government of the United States intended by this requisition to become the champion of the edict of Berlin, to fashion its principles by those of France while it affected to adhere to its own, and to act upon some partnership in doctrines, which it would fain induce you to acknowledge, but could not prevail upon itself to avow, I am not able to conjecture. The frank and honourable character of the American government justifies me in saying that, if it had meant to demand of Great Britain an abjuration of all such principles as the French government may think fit to disapprove, it would not have put your lordship to the trouble of discovering that meaning by the aid of combinations and inferences discountenanced by the language of its minister, but would have told you so in explicit terms. What I have to request of your lordship, therefore, is that you will take our views and principles from our own mouths, and that neither the Berlin decree, nor any other act of any foreign state, may be made to speak for us what we have not spoken for ourselves."

In a letter from Mr. Pinkney to Mr. Smith, Secretary of State, of the 17th of January, 1811, in alluding to the letter from which the above passages are cited, he says— "My answer to lord Wellesley's letter was written under the pressure of indisposition, and the influence of more indignation than could well be suppressed." As the agent of his government, it was doubtless the duty of Mr. Pinkney to make the best of the case he had on hand. But it will be made apparent, before this examination is finished, that the British minister was not entirely destitute of reason for his suggestion respecting that which was called "a partnership in doctrines." It is sufficient for the present to remark, that the circumstance of the American government having introduced, as a preliminary to their negotiations respecting the appeal of the British orders in council, the British blockading order of May, 1806, prevented the adjustment of that question, and was the means of keeping alive the spirit of hostility, until it terminated in the war of 1812.

In a letter from the Marquis of Wellesley to Mr. Pinkney, dated February 11th, 1811, he again adverts to this subject, and says—"Great Britain has always insisted upon her right of self-defence against the system of commercial warfare pursued by France, and the British orders of council were founded upon a just principle of retaliation against the French decrees. The incidental operation of the orders of council upon the commerce of the United States, (although deeply to be lamented) must be ascribed exclusively to the violence and injustice of the enemy, which compelled this country to resort to adequate means of defence. It cannot now be admitted that the foundation of the original question should be changed, and that the measure of retaliation adopted against France should now be relinquished, at the desire of the United States, without any reference to the actual conduct of the enemy.

" The intention has been repeatedly declared of repealing the orders of council, whenever France shall actually have revoked the decrees of Berlin and Milan, and shall have restored the trade of neutral nations to the condition in which it stood previously to the promulgation of those decrees. Even admitting that France has suspended the operation of those decrees, or has repealed them, with reference to the United States, it is evident that she has not relinquished the conditions expressly declared in the letter of the French minister under date of the 5th of August, 1810. France therefore requires that Great Britain shall not only repeal the orders of council, but renounce those principles of blockade which are alleged in the same letter to be new ; an allegation which must be understood to refer to the introductory part of the Berlin decree. If Great Britain shall not submit to these terms, it is plainly intimated in the same letter that France requires America to enforce them.

" To these conditions, his royal highness, on behalf of his majesty, cannot accede. No principles of blockade have been promulgated or acted upon by Great Britain previously to the Berlin decree, which are not strictly conformable to the rights of civilized war, and to the approved usages and law of nations. The blockades established by the orders of council rest on separate grounds, and are justified by the principles of necessary retaliation, in which they originated."

That the French decrees were not in truth repealed on the 1st of November, 1810, was further inferred by the British government, from the fact that Bonaparte had established the practice of requiring the American vessels to take out licenses, before they could be admitted into French ports, and that they should take in for their return cargoes two-thirds of the quantity in French silks and wines. On the 16th of January, 1811, Mr. Russell, charge d'affaires of the United States at Paris, wrote to Mr. Smith, Secretary of State, as follows—

"Your letter of the 8th of November, relative to the powers given by this government to its consuls in the United States, under its decree concerning licenses, was received by me on the 11th instant, and the next day I communicated its contents to the duke of Cadore in a note, a copy of which you will find enclosed."

The following is a copy of the note above alluded to—

MR. RUSSELL to THE DUKE OF CADORE.

Paris, January 12, 1811.

"SIR,—The public journals and letters from General Armstrong have announced to the American government an imperial decree, by which permission is to be granted to a stated number of American vessels, to import into France from certain ports in the United States, the articles therein specified, and to export in return such productions of the French empire as are also enumerated in said decree. This trade, it would appear, is to be carried on under the authority of imperial licenses, and can only be perfected by the act of the French consul residing within the jurisdiction of the United States at the specified ports.

"The United States have no pretension of right to object to the operation of commercial regulations, strictly municipal, authorised by the French government to take effect within the limits of its own dominions ; but I am instructed to state to you the inadmissibility, on the part of the United States, of such a consular superintendence as that which is contemplated by this decree respecting a trade to be carried on under licenses.

" France cannot claim for her consuls, either by treaty or custom, such a superintendence. They can be permitted to enjoy such legitimate functions only as are sanctioned by public law, or by the usage of nations growing out of the courtesy of independent states.

" Besides, the decree in question professes to invest certain consuls with a power which cannot be regularly exercised in the United States without the tacit permission of the American government ; a permission that cannot be presumed, not only because it is contrary to usage, but because consuls thus acting would be exercising functions in the United States in virtue of French authority only, which the American government itself is not competent to authorise in any agents whatever.

" If the construction given by the government of the United States to this decree be correct, the government of France should not for a moment mislead itself by a belief, that its commercial agents will be permitted to exercise the extraordinary power thus intended to be given to them."

That the American government were much annoyed by this attempt of his imperial majesty of France to regulate and controul our trade with that country, in such a manner as to make it answer his own purposes, cannot be doubted. That they complain with great moderation and fear, is not a matter of surprise to any person who is acquainted with the occurrences of that period.

The duke of Cadore, in reply to the foregoing letter from Mr. Russell, on the 18th of January, 1811, said—

" I have read with much attention your note of the 12th of January, relative to the licenses *intended to favour* the commerce of the Americans in France. This system had been conceived before the revocation of the decrees of Berlin and Milan had been resolved upon. Now circumstances are changed by the resolution taken by the United States, to cause their flag and *their independence* to be respected, that which has been done before this last epoch, can no longer serve as a rule under actual circumstances."

Ten months after this, however, viz. on the 21st of November, 1811, in a letter from the Secretary of State to Mr. Barlow, then minister in France, the following language is used—

" The trade by licenses must be abrogated. I cannot too strongly express the surprise of the President, after the repeated remonstrances of this government, and more especially after the letter of the duke of Cadore of the ——————————— last, informing him that that system would fall with the Berlin and Milan decrees, that it still should be adhered to. The exequaturs of the consuls who have granted such licenses, would long since have been revoked, if orders to them to discontinue the practice had not daily been expected, or in case they were not received, the more effectual interposition of Congress to suppress it. It will certainly be prohibited by law, under severe penalties, in compliance with the recommendation of the President, if your despatches by the Constitution do not prove that your demand on this subject has been duly attended to."

The recommendation of the President here alluded to by the Secretary of State, it is presumed is in the following passage of the executive message at the opening of Congress, on the 5th of November ;—that is about a fortnight before the date of the foregoing letter—

" The justice and fairness which have been evinced on the part of the United States towards France, both before and since the revocation of her decrees, authorised an expectation that her government would have followed up that measure, by all such others as were due to our reasonable claims, as well as dictated by its amicable professions. *No proof, however, is yet given, of an intention to repair the other wrongs done to the United States;* and particularly to restore the great amount of American property seized and condemned under edicts, which though not affecting our neutral relations, and therefore not entering into questions between the United States and other belligerents, were nevertheless founded in such unjust principles, that the reparation ought to have been prompt and ample.

" In addition to this, and other demands of strict right on that nation, the United States have much reason to be dissatisfied with the rigorous and *unexpected restrictions* to which their trade with the French dominions has been subjected; *and which, if not discontinued, will require at least corresponding restrictions on importations from France into the United States.*"

There is nothing in this message like a call upon Congress to interpose and suppress the license trade under severe penalties. That trade is doubtless alluded to, though not by name, in the paragraph last quoted; but it speaks of "*rigorous and unexpected* restrictions, which, if not discontinued, will require at least *corresponding restrictions*" on our part. In other words, instead of revoking consular exequaturs, which was so boldly threatened nearly a year before, an attempt was made to frighten Bonaparte by the hint of establishing a license trade with France!

It has been the object of this work to show, by quotations from the public documents of the government, that whilst the administration were endeavoring by their language, as well as by their acts, to irritate the British government, they were manifesting towards France either a strong and unreasonable biass, or a servile and unmanly fear. Some additional evidence in support of these positions may be derived from another, but an undoubtedly correct and credible source.

In the year 1811, Mr. Robert Smith, who had held the office of Secretary of State for a number of years under Mr. Madison, in consequence of some disagreement or misunderstanding between these two personages, left that office, and retired to private life. Soon after the occurrence of that event, Mr. Smith published an address to the people of the United States, containing the reasons for his resignation. Among other statements in his publication are the following—

"The non-intercourse law of the last session was also the device of Mr. Madison. It too was introduced by presidential machinery.

"Should this statute be viewed, *as it ought to be*, in connexion with and as emanating from the law of May, 1810, then will we have to look for the "*fact*" required by that law, namely, the actual revocation of the Berlin and Milan decrees.

"If this revocation did in fact take place, as declared by the proclamation, then the act of May, communicated as it had been by the executive to the two belligerent powers, did become *ipso facto* a compact between the United States and France, and in that case neither party had a right to disregard, or by law to change, its stipulated terms and conditions, as this government confessedly did by the non-intercourse act of the last session."———

"If, however, the emperor of the French did not in fact revoke, as declared by the proclamation, the Berlin and Milan decrees, the act of May did not become a compact between the United States and France, and in that case his imperial majesty had no claim against this government, founded upon that statute, to enforce the non-intercourse against the other belligerent.

" What, then, was the evidence which had induced Congress to consider these decrees repealed, and which had accordingly induced them to pass the non-intercourse law? To the President, in this as in every other case touching our *foreign* relations, the legislature must necessarily have looked for *information* and *recommendation.* From him they had in due form received what, they imagined, they were officially bound to consider as satisfactory evidence of the repeal of these decrees, namely, *his proclamation,* and his message containing a *recommendation* to enforce the act of May, 1810. In respect then to this evidence, and in pursuance of this recommendation, did Congress pass the act called the non-intercourse law of the last session.

" This non-intercourse law, let it be distinctly kept in mind, was passed after the arrival at Washington of the new French minister, viz. on the second day of March, 1811."——

" Notwithstanding the precise protestation, solemnly communicated to the French government, and openly promulgated to the whole world, in virtue of the letters from the State Department of June and July, 1810, that "a satisfactory provision for restoring the property, lately surprised and seized by the order or at the instance of the French government, must be combined with a repeal of the French edicts, *with a view to a non-intercourse with Great Britain,* yet it is a fact, that before the passing of the non-intercourse law of the last session, viz. on the 20th of February, 1811, the French government did officially and formally, through their minister, Mr. Serrurier, communicate to this government their fixed determination *not to restore the property that had* BEEN SO SEIZED. And moreover, from the information which had been received by Mr. Madison, prior to the date of the non-intercourse law, *it was at the time of passing it, evident to my mind, that the Berlin and Milan decrees had not been revoked, as had been declared by the proclamation.*"——

" The following draught of a letter to General Arm-

strong was accordingly prepared by me immediately after
the letter of the duke of Cadore, to which it refers, had
been received. It was in the usual form laid before the
President for his approbation. He, however, objected to the
sending of it. And as there is reason to believe that this
very letter constituted part of the ground of the hostility of
Mr. Madison to me, it is but proper to give it publicity.

" *Copy of the draught of the letter proposed to be sent to*
General Armstrong.

" *Department of State, June* —, 1810.

" GEN. ARMSTRONG,—Your letters of the — with their
respective enclosures were received on the 21st day of May.

" In the note of the duke of Cadore nothing can be perceived to justify the seizure of the American property in
the ports of France and in those of her allies. The facts as
well as the arguments, which it has assumed, are confuted
by events known to the world, and particularly by that moderation of temper which has invariably distinguished the
conduct of this government towards the belligerent nations.

" After a forbearance equalled only by our steady observance of the laws of neutrality and of the immutable
principles of justice, it is with no little surprise that the
President discerns in the French government a disposition
to represent the United States as the original aggressor.
An act of violence which under existing circumstances is
scarcely less than an act of war, necessarily required an
explanation, which would satisfy not only the United States,
but the world. But the note of the duke of Cadore, instead of a justification, has not furnished even a plausible
palliation or a reasonable apology for the seizure of the
American property.

" There has never been a period of time when the
United States have ceased to protest against the British
orders in council. With regard to the resistance which
the United States may have deemed it proper to oppose

to such unlawful restrictions, it obviously belonged to the American government alone to prescribe the mode. If a system of exclusion of the vessels and merchandise of the belligerent powers from our ports has been preferred to war, if municipal prohibition has been resorted to instead of invasive retaliation, with what propriety can the emperor of the French pretend to see in that method of proceeding any thing else than a lawful exercise of sovereign power? To construe the exercise of this power into a cause of warlike reprisal is a species of dictation, which, could it be admitted, would have a tendency to subvert the sovereignty of the United States.

" France has converted our law of exclusion into a pretext for the seizure of the property of the citizens of the United States. This statute was also in force against the vessels of Great Britain. If its operation had been considered by the French government as of sufficient efficacy to justify this pretended reprisal, that very operation, as it would have been more severely felt by Great Britain, ought also to have been considered as constituting a resistance to her orders, the non-existence of which resistance has been stated by the duke of Cadore as the pretext for the act of violence exercised on the American property. The United States having resisted the British orders, the real ground of complaint would seem to be, not so much that the American government has not resisted a tax on their navigation, as that it has likewise resisted the French decrees, which had assumed a prescriptive power over the policy of the United States, as reprehensible as the attempt of the British government to levy contributions on our trade was obnoxious. Placed in a situation where a tax was proclaimed on the one hand, and a rule of action prescribed on the other, the United States owed it to their own honour to resist with corresponding measures the cupidity of the one and the presumption of the other. When the American government sees in the provisions of the British orders an assumption of maritime power in contravention of the law of nations, how can it fail also to perceive in the French decrees the adoption of a principle equally derogatory and injurious to the neutral character of the United States?

"The pretension of subjecting American navigation to a tax, as advanced by the British order of November, 1807, was in reality withdrawn by the order of the 26th of April, 1809. Yet ten months subsequent to the recall of that pretension, its alleged existence is made the basis of reproach against the American government by the emperor of the French. It would be fruitless to comment upon the disposition to insist upon the prevailing influence of a fact which no longer exists; which, when it did exist, was uniformly combated; and the final extinction of which was the manifest consequence of the measures of this government.

"If the American government had seized French vessels, as erroneously asserted in the note of the duke of Cadore, the occurrence could only have been attributed to the temerity of their owners or commanders, who, after a previous notification, from the 1st of March to the 20th of May, of the act of exclusion, would have strangely presumed upon impunity in the violation of a prohibitory municipal law of the United States. Had France interdicted to our vessels all the ports within the sphere of her influence, and had she given a warning of equal duration with that given by our law, there would have been no cause of complaint on the part of the United States. The French government would not then have had the opportunity of exercising its power in a manner as contrary to the forms as to the spirit of justice, over the property of the citizens of the United States.

"It was at all times in the power of France to suspend, with regard to herself, our acts of exclusion, of which she complains, by simply annulling or modifying her decrees.

Propositions to this effect have been made to her government through you. They were not accepted. On the contrary, a policy was preferred which was calculated to produce any other result than that of a good understanding between the two countries. By the act of Congress of the last session an opportunity is again afforded to his imperial majesty to establish the most amicable relations between the United States and France. Let him withdraw or modify his decrees ; let him restore the property of our citizens so unjustly seized, and a law of the United States exists which authorizes the President to promote the best possible understanding with France, and to impose a system of exclusion against the ships and merchandise of Great Britain in the event of her failing to conform to the same just terms of conciliation. In fine, as the emperor will now be acquainted with the fact that no French vessels have been unlawfully seized in the ports of the United States, as the law of exclusion against the commerce of France is no more in operation, there can be no longer a solitary reasonable pretext for procrastinating the delivery of the American property, detained by the French government, into the possession of the respective owners.

"These observations you will not fail to present to the view of the French government, in order that the emperor may learn that the United States insist upon nothing but their acknowledged rights, and that they still entertain a desire to adjust all differences with the government of France upon a basis equally beneficial and honourable to both nations.

"I have the honour to be, &c.
"R. SMITH."

It seems, from a passage above quoted, that Mr. Smith, who as Secretary of State had full opportunity to become acquainted with all the correspondence, and every fact in possession of the government, relative to our relations and intercourse, political and commercial, with France, had come to the conclusion that the allegation in the President's proclamation, that the Berlin and Milan decrees had been revoked, was not true. He says, "From the information that had been received *by Mr. Madison*, prior to the date of the non-intercourse law, it was, at the time of passing it, evident to my mind, that the Berlin and Milan decrees had not been revoked, as had been declared by the proclamation." It is not a little remarkable, that the President should have been convinced that those decrees had been revoked, by evidence of so slight a character as to produce a directly opposite effect upon the Secretary's mind, viz. that such a revocation had not taken place.

Mr. Smith goes on to say—

" Previously to the meeting of Congress last autumn, I expressed to Mr. Madison my apprehension that the emperor of France would not *bona fide* fulfil the just expectations of the United States; that our commerce would be exposed in his ports to vexatious embarrassments, and that tobacco and cotton would probably not be freely admitted into France. He entertained a different opinion, and, indeed, was confident that the Berlin and Milan decrees would *bona fide* cease on the first day of November, 1810, and that from that day our commercial relations with France would be incumbered with no restrictions or embarrassments whatever. I nevertheless told him that my impressions were such that I would have a conversation with General Turreau upon the subject in my interview with him in relation to certificates of origin. In the course of the correspondence which thence ensued, I was greatly checked by the evident indications of utter indifference on the part of Mr. Madison. Instead of encouraging, he absolutely discouraged the making of any animadversions upon General Turreau's letter of December 12th, 1810."

This letter was written by the Secretary of State, immediately after the receipt by our government of the letter from the duke of Cadore, which has been quoted in this work, and in which such language as the following was made use of—" The Americans cannot hesitate as to the part which *they are to take. They ought either to tear to pieces the act of their independence, and so become again as before the revolution the subjects of England.*"—" *Men without just political views, without honour, without energy,* may allege that payment of the tribute imposed by England may be submitted to because it is light "—" it will then be necessary *to fight for interest* after having refused *to fight for honour.*"

Mr. Smith's letter has been copied at length, that there may be no mistake, nor any charge of unfairness concerning its language, or its import. No dispassionate person who reads the correspondence to which it relates, and calls to mind the haughty, insolent, and rapacious conduct of the French government towards the United States, the violation of our neutral rights, and the plunder of our commerce, will be able to find any thing in it, which, in regard either to language or sentiment, under the circumstances of the case, would be considered intemperate, or even improper. And certainly, when compared with many parts of the correspondence with Great Britain, it must be viewed as tame and spiritless. Much less ought it to have been treated as if it contained a spirit of hostility in the executive department, and calling for resentment towards as high and responsible an officer as the Secretary of State. But what was the result?

" Instead of the animadversions," says Mr. Smith, " contained in the aforegoing letter, the President directed the insertion of simply the following section in my letter of the 5th of June, 1810.

" As the John Adams is daily expected, and as your further communications by her will *better enable me to adapt to the actual state of our affairs with the French government, the observations proper to be made in relation to their seizure of our property,* and to the letter of the duke of Cadore of the 14th of February, it is by the President deemed expedient *not to make at this time any such animadversions.* I cannot, however, forbear informing *you,* that a high indignation is felt by the President, as well as by the public, at this act of violence on our property, and at the outrage, both in the language and in the matter, of the letter of the duke of Cadore, so justly portrayed in your note to him of the 10th of March.

" It is worthy of notice," adds Mr. Smith, " that the last sentence of the above section was merely *a communication to General Armstrong, personally,* as to the impression made here by that outrage of the French government, and that it was not an *instruction* to him *to make the emperor of France acquainted with the high indignation felt on the occasion by the President and the nation.* It simply shows, that our executive had, at that time, but just resolution enough to impart to his own minister the sentiments of indignation that had been here excited by the enormous outrage of the Rambouillet decree, and by the insulting audacity of the duke of Cadore's letter."

Mr. Smith, in his exposition, goes on to remark——

"It is within the recollection of the American people, that the members of Congress, during the last session, were much embarrassed as to the course most proper to be taken with respect to our foreign relations, and that their embarrassments proceeded principally from the *defect in the communications to them as to the views of the emperor of the French.* To supply this defect was the great desideratum. At a critical period of their perplexities the arrival at Norfolk of an Envoy Extraordinary from France was announced. Immediately thereon all their proceedings touching our foreign relations were suspended. Their measures, as avowed by themselves and as expected by the nation, were then to be shaped according to the information that might be received from Mr. Serrurier, especially as he necessarily must have left France long after the all-important first day of November. Upon his arrival at Washington, and immediately after he had been accredited, knowing, as I did, the impatience of Congress and of my countrymen, I lost no time in having with him a conference."

At this conference, Mr. Smith informed Mr. Serruier that he would address a note to him, propounding the several questions he had put to him in conversation, and lay his answer before the President. He accordingly prepared such a letter, and submitted it to the President for his approbation, when, he says, he was "to his astonishment told by him that *it would not be expedient to send to Mr. Serrurier any such note.* His deportment throughout this interview evinced *a high degree of disquietude,* which occasionally betrayed him into fretful expressions;"—and he says he "entreated him, but in a manner the most delicate, not to withhold from Congress any information that might be useful to them at so momentous a juncture." He then gives the following as a copy of the letter which he had prepared—

" *Department of State, February* 20, 1811.

"SIR,—Desirous of laying before the President with the utmost precision the substance of our conference of this day, and knowing that verbal communications are not unfrequently misunderstood, I consider it proper to propose to you in a written form the questions which I have had the honour of submitting to you in conversation, namely :

"1st. Were the Berlin and Milan decrees revoked in *whole* or in *part* on the fifth day of last November? Or have they at any time posterior to that day been so revoked? Or have you *instructions* from your government to give to this government any assurance or explanation in relation to the revocation or modification of those decrees?

" 2d. Do the existing decrees of France admit into French ports, with or without licenses, American vessels laden with articles not the produce of the United States, and under what regulations and conditions?

"3d. Do they admit into French ports, with or without licenses, American vessels laden with articles not the produce of the United States, and under what regulations and conditions?

"4th. Do they permit American vessels with or without licenses, to return from France to the United States, and upon what terms and conditions?

"5th. Is the importation into France of any articles, the produce of the United States, absolutely prohibited? And if so, what are the articles so prohibited, and especially are *tobacco* and *cotton?*

"6th. Have you *instructions* from your government to give to this government any assurance or explanation in relation to the American vessels and cargoes seized under the Rambouillet decree?"

It will be remarked that the inquiries in this letter were intended to draw from the French minister information respecting the great points of complaint and controversy between the United States and France, viz. whether the Berlin and Milan decrees were actually repealed; whether the practice of granting licenses to the American trade was continued, and to what extent; whether American produce was admitted into French ports, and on what terms; and whether he was instructed to give any explanation respecting the American property seized under the Rambouillet decree? These were subjects of the highest interest to our citizens, and the government spent a great deal of time, in one form and another, in complaining of the treatment our country had received, that our countrymen had been plundered of their property, and interrupted in their commerce; and particularly on the subject of the repeal of the Berlin and Milan decrees, they had not only insisted upon it that such a repeal had taken place, but the President had formally and officially proclaimed it to the nation; and yet, when his confidential minister, the organ of communication and intercourse with foreign governments, proposed to make specific inquiries of the French minister on these several subjects, in order to ascertain the precise facts concerning them, he was told by the President, "that it would not be expedient to send to Mr. Serrurier any such note." Who can doubt respecting the kind and degree of influence which was exercised over Mr. Madison, when he refused to adopt the only course that existed, by which the information that was necessary could be obtained? Who can avoid the conclusion that it proceeded either from a servile fear of, or a most unwarrantable and reprehensible attachment to France?

Among the extraordinary occurrences of the period, one of the most remarkable was that which has been called the Henry plot. The history of that memorable affair may be collected from the following documents.

On the 9th of March, 1812, President Madison transmitted the following message to both houses of Congress.

" I lay before Congress copies of certain documents which remain in the department of state. They prove that, at a recent period, whilst the United States, notwithstanding the wrongs sustained by them, ceased not to observe the laws of peace and neutrality towards Great Britain, and in the midst of amicable professions and negotiations on the part of the British government, through its public minister here, *a secret agent of that government was employed in certain states*, more especially at the seat of government in Massachusetts, *in fomenting disaffection to the constituted authorities of the nation, and in intrigues with the disaffected, for the purpose of bringing about resistance to the laws, and, eventually, in concert with a British force, of destroying the Union and forming the eastern part thereof into a political connection with Great Britain.*

" In addition to the effect which the discovery of such a procedure ought to have on the public councils, it will not fail to render more dear to the hearts of all good citizens, that happy union of these states, which, under divine Providence, is the guaranty of their liberties, their safety, their tranquillity, and their prosperity."

This message was accompanied by a large number of documents, from which a few extracts only will be copied. The following is the first in the series——

" *Philadelphia, Feb.* 20, 1812.

" Sir—Much observation and experience have convinced me, that the injuries and insults with which the United States have been so long and so frequently visited, and which cause their present embarrassment, have been owing to an opinion entertained by foreign states—' *That in any measure tending to wound their pride, or provoke their hostility, the government of this country could never induce a great majority of its citizens to concur.*' And, as many of the evils which flow from the influence of this opinion on the policy of foreign nations, may be removed by any act that can produce *unanimity among all parties in America*, I voluntarily tender to you, sir, such means as I possess towards promoting so desirable and important an object; which, if accomplished, cannot fail to extinguish, perhaps forever, those expectations abroad, which may protract indefinitely, an accommodation of existing differences, and check the progress of industry and prosperity in this rising empire.

" I have the honour to transmit herewith the documents and correspondence relating to an important mission, in which I was employed by Sir James Craig, the late governor-general of the British provinces in North America, in the winter of the year 1809.

" The publication of these papers will demonstrate a

fact not less valuable than the good already proposed ; it will prove that no reliance ought to be placed on the professions of good faith of an administration, which, by a series of disastrous events, has *fallen* into such hands as a Castlereagh, a Wellesley, or a Liverpool—I should rather say, into the hands of the stupid subalterns, to whom the pleasures and the indolence of those ministers have consigned it. In contributing to the good of the United States by an exposition, which cannot (I think) fail to solve and melt all division and disunion among its citizens; I flatter myself with the fond expectation, that when it is made public in England, it will add one great motive to the many that already exist, to induce that nation to withdraw its confidence from *men, whose political career is a fruitful source of injury and embarrassment in America ; of injustice and misery in Ireland ; of distress and apprehension in England ; and contempt every where.*

" In making this communication to you, sir, I deem it incumbent on me, distinctly and unequivocally to state, that I adopt no party views ; that I have not changed any of my political opinions ; that I neither seek nor desire the patronage nor countenance of any government, nor of any party ; and that in addition to the motives already expressed, *I am influenced by a just resentment of the perfidy and dishonour of those who first violated the conditions upon which I received their confidence;* who have injured me, and disappointed the expectations of my friends ; and left me no choice, but between a degrading acquiescence in injustice, and a retaliation which is necessary to secure to me my own respect.

" This wound will be felt where it is merited ; and if Sir *James Craig* still live, his share of the pain will excite no sympathy among those who are at all in the secret of our connection.

" I have the honour to be, &c. &c.

" J. HENRY.

" To JAMES MONROE, Esq. Secretary of State."

"MR. RYLAND, SECRETARY TO SIR JAMES CRAIG, GOVER-
NOUR GENERAL OF CANADA, TO MR. HENRY.

" **Most secret and confidential.**

" *Quebec, January* 26, 1809.

" MY DEAR SIR—The extraordinary situation of things
at this time in the neighbouring states, has suggested to the
governor in chief, the idea of employing you on a secret
and confidential mission to Boston, provided an arrangement can be made to meet the important end in view,
without throwing an absolute obstacle in the way of your
professional pursuits. *The information* and political observations heretofore received from you, were transmitted
by his excellency to the secretary of state, who has expressed his particular approbation of them ; and there is
no doubt that your able execution of such a mission as I
have above suggested, would give you a claim not only on
the governour-general, but on his majesty's ministers, which
might eventually contribute to your advantage. You will
have the goodness therefore to acquaint me, for his excellency's information, whether you could make it convenient
to engage in a mission of this nature, and what pecuniary
assistance would be requisite to enable you to undertake it
without injury to yourself.

" At present it is only necessary for me to add, that the
governour would furnish you with a cypher for carrying on
your correspondence ; and that in case the leading party in
any of the states wished to open a communication with this
government, their views might be communicated through
you.

" I am, with great truth and regard, &c.

" HERMAN W. RYLAND."

" **Most secret and confidential.**

" *Quebec, February* 6, 1809.

" SIR—As you have so readily undertaken the service, which I have suggested to you, as being likely to be attended with much benefit to the public interests, I am to request that with your earliest conveniency you will proceed to Boston.

" The principal object that I recommend to your attention, is the endeavour to obtain the most accurate information of the true state of affairs in that part of the Union, which from its wealth, the number of its inhabitants, and the known intelligence and ability of several of its leading men, must naturally possess a very considerable influence over, and will indeed probably lead the other eastern states of America, in the part that they may take at this important crisis.

" I shall not pretend to point out to you the mode by which you will be most likely to obtain this important information ; your own judgment, and the connection which you may have in the town, must be your guide. I think it however necessary to put you on your guard against the sanguineness of an aspiring party ; the federalists, as I understand, have at all times discovered a leaning to this disposition, and their being under its particular influence at this moment, is the more to be expected from their having no ill founded ground for their hopes of being *nearer the attainment of their object* than they have been for some years past.

" In the general terms which I have made use of in describing the object which I recommend to your attention, it is scarcely necessary that I should observe, I include the state of the public opinions, both with regard to their internal politicks, and to the probability of a war with England ;

the comparative strength of the two great parties into
which the country is divided, and the views and designs of
that which may ultimately prevail.

" It has been supposed that if the federalists of the eastern states should be successful in obtaining that decided
influence which may enable them to direct the publick
opinion, it is not improbable that rather than submit to a
continuance of the difficulties and distress to which they are
now subject, they will exert that influence to bring about a
separation of the general union. The earliest information
on this subject may be of great consequence to our government, as it may also be, that it should be informed, *how far
in such an event they would look up to England for assistance, or be disposed to enter into a connection with us.*

" Although it would be highly inexpedient that you should
in any manner appear as an avowed agent, yet if you could
contrive to obtain an intimacy with any of the leading
party, it may not be improper that you should insinuate,
though with great caution, that *if they should wish to enter
into any communication with our government through me, you
are authorized to receive any such, and will safely transmit
it to me;* and as it may not be impossible that they should
require some document by which they may be assured that
you are really in the situation in which you represent yourself ; I enclose a credential to be produced in that view ;
but I most particularly enjoin and direct that you do not
make any use of this paper, unless a desire to that purpose should be expressed, and *unless you see good ground
for expecting that the doing so may lead to a more confidential communication* than you can otherwise look for.

"In passing through the state of Vermont, you will of
course exert your endeavours to procure all the information that the short stay you will probably make there will
admit of. You will use your own discretion as to delaying
your journey, with this view, more or less, in proportion to
your prospects of obtaining any information of consequence.

"I request to hear from you as frequently as possible; and as letters directed to me might excite suspicion, it may be as well, that you put them under cover to Mr. ———— ————, and as even the addressing letters always to the same person might attract notice, I recommend your sometimes addressing your packet to the chief justice here, or occasionally, though seldom, to Mr. Ryland, but never with the addition of his official description. I am, &c.

"JAMES H. CRAIG."

"*Copy of the 'Credentials' given by Sir James Craig to Mr. Henry.*
[Seal.]

"The bearer, Mr. John Henry, is employed by me, and full confidence may be placed in him for any communication which any person may wish to make to me *in the business committed to him.* In faith of which, I have given him this under my hand and seal at Quebec, this 6th day of February, 1809.

"J. H. CRAIG."

Mr. Henry, according to the account contained in his correspondence, after having received his instructions, proceeded to Burlington, in Vermont, where he passed a few days, apparently listening to such conversations, and chit-chat, as occurred in his hearing. In a letter from that place, he says he found the embargo laws were considered as unnecessary, oppressive, and unconstitutional; and that, in his opinion, if Massachusetts should take any bold step towards resisting their execution, Vermont would join her; and he adds—

"I learn that the governor of this state is now visiting the towns in the northern section of it; and makes no secret of his determination, as commander in chief of the militia, to refuse obedience to any command from the general government, which can tend to interrupt the good understanding that prevails between the citizens of Vermont and his majesty's subjects in Canada."

On the 19th of February he dated a letter from Windsor, Vermont, where he says the federal party declared, that in the event of a war, the state of Vermont would treat separately with Great Britain ; and that the democrats would risk every thing in preference to a coalition with that nation.

On the 5th of March, he writes from Boston, and says, " It does not yet appear necessary that I should discover to any person the purpose of my visit to Boston ; nor is it probable that I should be compelled, for the sake of gaining more knowledge of the arrangements of the federal party in these states, to avow myself as a regular authorized agent of the British government, even to those individuals who would feel equally bound with myself to preserve with the utmost inscrutability so important a secret from the public eye. I have sufficient means of information to enable me to judge of the proper period for offering the co-operation of Great Britain, and opening a correspondence between the governor-general of British America and those individuals who, from the part they take in the opposition to the national government, or the influence they may possess in any new order of things that may grow out of the present differences, should be qualified to act on behalf of the northern states. An apprehension of any such state of things as is presupposed by these remarks begins to subside, since it has appeared by the conduct of the general government that it is seriously alarmed at the menacing attitude of the northern states."

On the 7th of March, he wrote again from Boston. The following is an extract from his letter. " I have already given a decided opinion that a declaration of war is not to be expected : but, contrary to all reasonable calculation, should the Congress possess spirit and independence enough to place their popularity in jeopardy by so strong a measure, the legislature of Massachusetts will give the tone to the neighboring states; will declare itself permanent, until a new election of members; invite a Congress to be composed of delegates from the federal states, and erect a separate government for their common defence and common interest. This congress would probably begin by abrogating the offensive laws and adopting a plan for the maintenance of the power and authority thus assumed. They would by such an act be in a condition to make or receive proposals from Great Britain; and I should seize the first moment to open a correspondence with your excellency. Scarce any other aid would be necessary, and perhaps none required, than a few vessels of war, from the Halifax station, to protect the maritime towns from the little navy which is at the disposal of the national government. What permanent connection between Great Britain and this section of the Republic would grow out of a civil commotion, such as might be expected, no person is prepared to describe ; but it seems that a strict alliance must result of necessity. At present, the opposition party confine their calculations merely to resistance ; and I can assure you that at this moment, they do not freely entertain the project of withdrawing the eastern states from the Union, finding it a very unpopular topick ; although a course of events, such as I have already mentioned, would inevitably produce an incurable alienation of the New-England from the southern states.

" The truth is, the common people have so long regarded the constitution of the United States with complacency, that they are now only disposed in this quarter to treat it like a truant mistress, whom they would for a time put away on a separate maintenance, but without further and greater provocation would not absolutely repudiate."

The series of letters is continued until the 25th of May, when the 14th in number was written at Boston. By that time Mr. Henry appears to have been fully convinced that his mission was not likely to terminate successfully. He says—"I beg leave to suggest, that in the present state of things in this country, my presence can contribute very little to the interests of Great Britain." And it seems that his employers were under a similar impression; for on the 4th of May, Mr. Secretary Ryland wrote to him in a formal manner that his speedy return was hoped for, as the object of his journey seemed to be at an end. And on the 12th of June, he addressed his letter, No. 15, to the governor-general from Montreal, informing him of his arrival at that city.

These papers were referred, in the House of Representatives, to the committee on foreign relations; who made the following report—

"The committee of foreign relations, to whom was referred the President's message of the 9th instant, covering copies of certain documents communicated to him by a Mr. John Henry; beg leave to report, in part—

"That although they did not deem it necessary or proper to go into an investigation of the authenticity of documents communicated to Congress on the responsibility of a co-ordinate branch of the government, it may, nevertheless, be satisfactory to the house to be informed, that the original papers, with the evidences relating to them, in possession of the Executive, were submitted to their examination, and were such as fully to satisfy the committee of their genuineness.

"The circumstances under which the disclosures of Henry were made to the government, involving considerations of political expediency, have prevented the committee from making those disclosures the basis of any proceeding against him. And from *the careful concealment, on his part, of every circumstance which could lead to the discovery and punishment of any individuals in the United States (should there be any such) who were criminally connected with him,* no distinct object was presented to the committee by his communication, for the exercise of the power with which they were invested of sending for persons and papers.

"On being informed, however, that there was a foreigner in the city of Washington, who lately came to this country from Europe, with Henry, and was supposed to be in his confidence, the committee thought proper to send for him. His examination, taken under oath, and reduced to writing, they herewith submit to the house.

"The transaction disclosed by the President's message, presents to the minds of the committee conclusive evidence that *the British government, at a period of peace, and during the most friendly professions, have been deliberately and perfidiously pursuing measures to divide these States, and to involve our citizens in all the guilt of treason, and the horrors of a civil war.* It is not, however, the intention of the committee to dwell upon a proceeding, which, at all times, and among all nations, has been considered as one of the most aggravated character; and which, from the nature of our government, depending on a virtuous union of sentiment, ought to be regarded by us with the deepest abhorrence."

This report was accompanied by the testimony of the foreigner alluded to in it, and who signs the deposition as *Count Edward de Crillon,* taken and reduced to writing by the committee.

Upon the publication of the message and the papers connected with it, the following document was communicated to the President in the following message—

"I lay before Congress a letter from the envoy extraordinary and minister plenipotentiary of Great Britain, to the Secretary of State.

"JAMES MADISON."

"*Mr. Foster to Mr. Monroe. Washington, March 11th,* 1812.

"The undersigned, his Britannick majesty's envoy extraordinary, and minister plenipotentiary to the United States, has read in the public papers of this city, with the deepest concern, the message sent by the President of the United States to Congress on the 9th instant, and the documents which accompanied it.

"In the utter ignorance of the undersigned as to all the circumstances alluded to in those documents, he can only disclaim most solemnly, on his own part, the having had any knowledge whatever of the existence of such a mission, or of such transactions as the communication of Mr. Henry refers to, and express his conviction, that from what he knows of those branches of his majesty's government with which he is in the habit of having intercourse, no countenance whatever was given by them to any schemes hostile to the internal tranquility of the United States.

"The undersigned, however, cannot but trust that the American government and the Congress of the United States will take into consideration the character of the individual who has made the communication in question, and will suspend any further judgment on its merits until the circumstances shall have been made known to his majesty's government.

(Signed)   AUG. J. FOSTER."

John Henry was born a subject of Great Britain. For a while, he had resided in this country, and held a commission in the army of the United States. Having left the service, by his own account he resided for some time in Vermont, and afterwards returned to his natural allegiance, and became a resident of Canada. There, in the beginning of the year 1809, if his own account is to be credited, he was employed by Sir James H. Craig, governor of Canada, to repair to Boston, for the purpose of ascertaining whether the federal politicians of the New England states, particularly those of Massachusetts, were desirous of withdrawing from the Union, and forming a close connection with

Great Britain. Accordingly in the month of February of that year, he commenced his journey, and after spending some time in Vermont, and passing through New Hampshire, he reached. Boston early in the month of March. Having taken his station in the New England capital, he opened his correspondence with his employers in Canada. His first letter is dated March 5th, 1809. In that he remarked, that it had not thus far appeared necessary for him to discover to any person the object of his visit; nor was it probable that he should find it necessary, for the purpose of gaining a knowledge of the arrangements of the federal party, to avow himself as a regular authorised agent of the British government, even to those who would keep the secret—that he had sufficient means of information to enable him to judge of the proper time for offering the co-operation of Great Britain, and opening a correspondence between the governor-general of British America, and disaffected individuals in Massachusetts. Accordingly, he remained unknown at Boston till the 25th of May following, when he wrote to his principals at Quebec, that it *would be unnecessary for him in the existing state of things, and unavailing also, to attempt to carry into effect the original purposes of his mission.* He was soon recalled from that mission, and returned to Canada; and in 1811 was in England, petitioning the British government for compensation for his services abovementioned. For some cause or other, the ministry declined paying him; but referred him to the governor of Canada, on the ground that they had not discovered any wish on the part of Sir James Craig that *Henry's claims for compensation should be referred to the mother country,* and because *no allusion was made to any kind of arrangement or agreement that had been made by that officer with him.*

It is certainly a very extraordinary circumstance, that in the absence of all proof that the British government ever had the least knowledge of Henry's mission until long after it was finished, that the President should have made use of the following language, when speaking of the documents which accompanied his message to Congress—

" *They prove* that, at a recent period, whilst the United States, notwithstanding the wrongs sustained by them, ceased not to observe the laws of peace and neutrality towards Great Britain, and in the midst of amicable professions and negotiations on the part of the British government, through its public minister here, a *secret agent of that government was employed* in certain states, more especially at the seat of government in Massachusetts, *in fomenting disaffection to the constituted authorities of the nation, and in intrigues with the disaffected, for the purpose of bringing about resistance to the laws, and, eventually, in concert with a British force, of destroying the Union and forming the eastern part thereof into a political connection with Great Britain.*"

The committee on foreign relations, to whom the message and documents were referred, in their report, make the following remarks—" The transaction disclosed by the President's message, presents to the minds of the committee, *conclusive evidence, that the British government,* at a period of peace, and during the most friendly professions, *have been deliberately and perfidiously pursuing measures to divide these States, and to involve our citizens in all the guilt of treason, and the horrors of a civil war.*"

At the time of this occurrence, it is very apparent from a review of the general state of things, and from the character and course of their measures, that the government of this country had resolved on a war with Great Britain. Having formed that determination, it was natural for them to pursue such a course as would be likely to excite the public resentment towards that nation. This affair of Henry, in any other light in which it might be considered, was calculated to disgrace the American government.

Hence it was doubtless viewed as indispensable to the accomplishment of the main object, that Henry's plot should be charged over to the British government, as an attempt on their part to produce discord and division among the States. And both President Madison, and the committee on foreign relations, make the bold, unqualified, and certainly unfounded assertion, that the documents connected with the transaction prove such a flagitious attempt on the part of the British government to destroy the Union, involve the citizens in the guilt of treason, and the horrors of a civil war, and to form a political connection in the eastern states with Great Britain. But so far from this being true, there is no satisfactory evidence that the British government ever knew of the employment of Henry by the governor-general of Canada, that he ever visited Boston for such a purpose, or that they even knew there was such a man in existence. And when called upon by Henry for compensation for his services, the minister at London referred him back to the colonial government, by which he had been employed, with the remark, that it did not appear that Sir James Craig had ever expressed a wish that Henry should apply for his pay to the government of the mother country, or that any arrangement for that purpose had been even alluded to. From whence then does the inference arise, that this was a measure for which the British government was chargeable? Merely from the remark in Ryland's letter, which has been alluded to.

Is there not, however, strong ground for the belief, that one important object of this absurd, ridiculous, and disgraceful transaction, was to fix a degree of odium upon the New England states, and especially upon a certain class of New England politicians? It was well known that a large majority of the people of those states were opposed to the approaching declaration of war. It was not believed by those who were the best informed on the subject, that the real object of hostilities was avowed by those who were the most earnestly bent on bringing the war upon the nation. They were perfectly aware of the kind of influence which was exercising to bring it to pass, and as they could not justify such a measure, under such circumstances, to their consciences, they were steadily and firmly opposed to it. To excite the feelings of the country against them, no more efficacious mode could be devised, than to accuse them of being false to their country—to represent them as intrigueing with the power which was in so short a time intended to be the open and declared enemy of the United States, to destroy the Union, and to re-unite a part of its territory and inhabitants to the British nation. The miserable farce got up by Henry furnished the most plausible opportunity to accomplish the object ; and it was laid hold of for that purpose with the utmost avidity. To show how utterly unfounded this whole plot against New England was, it will be remarked, that during the whole period of Henry's residence in Boston, it does not appear that he ever conversed with a single individual respecting the object of his mission, that any overtures of the kind alluded to were ever made to him ; nor does he mention the name of even a solitary person, who ever uttered, even by accident, a sentence of disaffection to the Union of the States, or of a wish to form a connection with Great Britain. And the committee on foreign relations, in their report on this subject, say—" The circumstances under which the disclosures of Henry were made to the government, involving considerations of political expediency, have prevented the committee from making those disclosures the basis of any proceeding against him. And from the careful concealment, on his part, of every circumstance which could lead to the discovery and punishment of any individuals in the United States (should there be any such) who were criminally connected with him, no distinct object was presented to the committee by his communication for the exercise of the power with which they were invested, of sending for persons and papers."

In this state of things, without the slightest evidence, or any possible clue, which would warrant even the suspicion of guilt in a single inhabitant of Massachusetts, or of New England at large, nothing remained but to leave them exposed to the conjectures of those who seemed to consider it a species of patriotism to upbraid and reproach the inhabitants of those states as the enemies of their country.

Henry, in this transaction, was accompanied by a foreign adventurer, who called his name Crillon ; and who, to give dignity to the enterprise, added the title of count to his escutcheon. He went through a long examination, *under oath*, before the committee of foreign relations ; but for what particular purpose his testimony was published, unless it was to swell the amount of the documents, it is not easy to say. The President of the United States rewarded the profligate Henry with the sum of FIFTY THOUSAND DOLLARS, for this contemptible disclosure of his own baseness, and for the purpose of enabling himself to produce an effect upon popular feeling and opinion in favour of his favourite measure of war.

It is much to be regretted, that for the honour of the country, and the character of the government, this whole proceeding was ever suffered to see the light. It ought to have occurred in secret session, and been buried in deep oblivion. Unfortunately it was found expedient to publish the documents to the world ; and they must of course forever remain as evidence of the unworthy spirit by which the government was actuated on that memorable occasion. It must be acknowledged, however, that it was well designed to increase the animosity of the country against the British government, and to have some influence in reconciling the country to the idea of a war with that nation.

But after such an insidious attempt to vilify and traduce the inhabitants of New England, it can scarcely be a mat-

ter of surprise, that when these same New England men
were called upon to advance money, for the purpose of enabling the government to prosecute the war which they had
thus unnecessarily and rashly undertaken, they should
withhold their aid.   If any thing further was necessary to
induce them to pursue such a course, beyond a conscientious conviction that the war was unjustifiable, the treatment they had received from the government in this foul
attempt, founded on the testimony of an unprincipled and
daring foreign swindler, to blast their reputations, and render them odious to their country and the world, this transaction was sufficient to confirm them in that course.

Such was the origin of the war of 1812.   In order that
its character may be fully understood, and duly appreciated, a review of the policy and measures of the government, which finally terminated in that measure, has been
exhibited.

The first conclusion to be drawn from that review is,
that the real object in view in engaging in hostilities with
Great Britain, at the precise time when those hostilities
commenced, was not specified in the manifesto published
by the American government.   The grounds for declaring
war, as stated in that document, were twofold—*the edicts
of Great Britain which violated our neutral rights—and impressment.*   The orders in council, which were the subjects
of such loud complaints on the part of the United States,
were dated in January and November, 1807.   The war
was declared in June, 1812—four years and a half after
the date of the latest of those edicts.   The order of January was avowedly adopted by the British government, as a
measure of retaliation for the French decree of the preceding November, called the Berlin decree; and the order
of November was issued professedly in retaliation for the
French decree of Milan.   In May, 1806, the British order
for blockading the coast from the river Elbe to Brest was
adopted.   The French government declared that the

Berlin decree was issued as a measure of retaliation for the abovementioned blockading order. The order of May, 1806, was issued during the administration of Mr. Fox, the whig minister, and the great friend of this country. He declared to Mr. Monroe, at that time our minister at the court of London, that the order was intended to operate beneficially, and not injuriously to neutrals. And this view of the measure was communicated to our government by Mr. Monroe; and no complaint of its injustice was made at Washington for some years afterwards. The non-intercourse law contained a provision which authorised the President, in case either France or Great Britain *should so revoke or modify her edicts, as that they should cease to violate the neutral commerce of the United States*, to declare the same by proclamation; after which the trade suspended by said act, and by an act laying an embargo on all ships and vessels in the ports and harbours of the United States, and the several acts supplementary thereto, might be renewed with the nation so doing. Here is the ground, and the only ground on which the President was empowered by that act to adjust the existing difficulties with those nations, and renew friendly and commercial intercourse with them.

When the arrangement was made with Mr. Erskine, in April, 1809, it was stipulated by him, on the part of the British government, that in consequence of the acceptance by the President of the proposals made by him on the part of the King, for the renewal of the intercourse between the respective countries, he was authorised to declare that the orders in council of January and November, 1807, would be withdrawn, as respected the United States, on the 10th day of June then next—that is 1809. In consequence of this assurance by the British minister, the President, on the 19th of April, 1807—the day after the arrangement was completed—issued his proclamation, declaring that those orders in council would, on the 10th of

June following, have been withdrawn, and that the trade of the United States, which had been suspended by the non-intercourse act, might after that day be renewed.

In the correspondence relative to this arrangement, not a word was said on the part of the United States about the blockading order of May, 1806, nor was the slightest allusion made to the subject of impressment. The negotiation throughout was confined entirely to the abovementioned orders in council, they were considered as the only grounds on which the intercourse had been suspended; and upon their removal, the way was clear for its re-establishment. Such was the construction put upon the law by the President, when he approved the principles of the arrangement, and issued his proclamation in pursuance of the provisions of the non-intercourse act.

On the 23d of May, 1809, immediately after this arrangement had been concluded, Congress were, in consequence of it, convened, and the result of the negotiation was communicated to both houses by the President, in a message bearing that date. The following is an extract from that document.

" On this first occasion of meeting you, it affords me much satisfaction to be able to communicate the commencement of a favourable change in our foreign relations ; the critical state of which induced a session of Congress at this early period.

" In consequence of the provisions of the act interdicting commercial intercourse with Great Britain and France, our ministers at London and Paris were, without delay, instructed to let it be understood by the French and British governments, that the authority vested in the Executive, to renew commercial intercourse with their respective nations, would be exercised in the case specified by that act.

" Soon after these instructions were despatched, it was found that the British government, anticipating, from early proceedings of Congress, at their last session, the state of our laws, which has had the effect of placing the two belligerent powers on a footing of equal restrictions, and relying on the conciliatory disposition of the United States, had transmitted to their legation here, provisional instructions, not only to offer satisfaction for the attack on the frigate Chesapeake, and to make known the determination of his Britannick majesty to send an envoy extraordinary with powers to conclude a treaty on all the points between the two countries, but, moreover, to signify his willingness, in the meantime, to withdraw his orders in council, in the persuasion that the intercourse with Great Britain would be renewed on the part of the United States.

"These steps of the British government led to the correspondence and the proclamation now laid before you; by virtue of which, the commerce between the two countries will be renewable after the tenth day of June next."

"*The revision of our commercial laws, proper to adapt them to the arrangement which has taken place* with Great Britain, will doubtless engage the early attention of Congress."

In pursuance of the above suggestion, Congress immediately passed the following act—

"*Be it enacted*, &c. That from and after the passing this act, all ships or vessels owned by citizens or subjects of any foreign nation with which commercial intercourse is permitted by the act entitled 'An act to interdict the commercial intercourse between the United States and Great Britain and France, and their dependencies, and for other purposes,' be permitted to take on board cargoes of domestic or foreign produce, and to depart with the same for any port or place with which such intercourse is, or shall, at the time of their departure, respectively, be thus permitted, in the same manner, and on the same conditions, as is provided by the act aforesaid, for vessels owned by citizens of the United States; any thing in said act, or in the act laying an embargo on all ships and vessels in the ports and harbours of the United States, or in any of the several acts supplementary thereto, to the contrary notwithstanding." This act was approved May 30th, 1809.

An act was also passed at the same session, continuing in force certain sections of the non-intercourse law until the end of the then next session of Congress, with a proviso, that nothing therein contained should be construed to prohibit any trade or commercial intercourse which had been, or might be permitted in conformity with the provisions of the eleventh section of the non-intercourse act. The eleventh section was that which authorised the President to suspend the operation of the edicts of the belligerent nations, upon their revoking or modifying their edicts so that they should cease to violate our neutral rights.

Here then is a solemn declaration, in the first place, by the President, and in the second, by Congress, that *the British blockading order of May, 1806, was not an edict that violated our neutral rights in April and May, 1809,* and the inference is equally strong, that at the same time *impressment was not then considered a justifiable cause of war,* because it was not alluded to either in the arrangement with Mr. Erskine, in the President's proclamation suspending the non-intercourse law, or in that law, or in the proceedings of Congress, when engaged in adapting the commercial laws of the United States to that arrangement.

Having seen that the British blockading order of May, 1806, was not considered by our government, in the arrangement with Mr. Erskine, as one of the edicts of that nation which violated our neutral rights, but was afterwards introduced into the manifesto of the government, which laid the foundation of the President's proclamation of war, it becomes an object of importance to inquire when that decree began to be considered as a justifiable ground of hostilities. It will be recollected, that in December, 1809, General Armstrong was instructed by the

President, to inquire of the duke of Cadore, on what conditions his majesty the emperor of France would consent to annul the Berlin decree; and whether, if Great Britain revoked her blockades, of a date anterior to that decree, his majesty would consent to revoke the said decree. In a letter from Mr. Smith, Secretary of State, to Mr. Pinkney, then our minister to the British court, dated July 5th, 1810, it is said—"In explaining the extent of the repeal, which, on the British side, is required, you will be guided by the same principle. You will accordingly let it be distinctly understood, that it must necessarily include an annulment of the blockade of May, 1806, which has been avowed to be comprehended in, and identified with the orders in council; and which is palpably at variance with the law of nations. This is the explanation which will be given to the French government on this point by our minister at Paris, in case it should there be required."

The letter then proceeds to state reasons why "the British government ought to revoke every other blockade resting on proclamations or diplomatic notifications, and not on the application of a naval force adequate to a real blockade." The second of these reasons was the following—"Without this enlightened precaution, it is probable, and may indeed be inferred from the letter of the duke of Cadore to General Armstrong, that *the French government will draw Great Britain and the United States to issue on the legality of such blockades, by acceding to the act of Congress,* WITH A CONDITION, *that a repeal of the blockades shall accompany a repeal of the orders in council,* alleging that the orders and blockades differing little, if at all, otherwise than in name, a repeal of the former, leaving in operation the latter, would be a mere illusion." To ascertain the point of time, then, when the blockading order of May, 1806, began to assume the importance which it afterwards acquired, resort must be had to the negotiation between General Armstrong, in January, 1810, on the subject of revoking the Berlin and

Milan decrees, in which the French government were, in terms little short of explicit, invited to include the order of May, 1806, in their demand for the repeal of the British orders in council. And to satisfy every unprejudiced mind, that there was a full and thorough understanding between our government and that of France on this subject, the passage from the letter of Secretary Smith to Mr. Pinkney, of the 5th of July, 1810, distinctly proves. " The French government," says the letter, " will *draw Great Britain and the United States to issue on the legality of such blockades,* by acceding to the act of Congress, with a condition, that a repeal of the blockading orders shall accompany a repeal of the orders in council." Here, it is foretold, not only that the French government will draw Great Britain and the United States to issue on the legality of the blockades, but the very terms on which that issue would be made are predicted—they will accede to the act of Congress, with *a condition, that the repeal of the blockading orders shall accompany the repeal of the orders in council.* This was precisely the course pursued by the French government—they did attach a condition to their nominal revocation of the Berlin and Milan decrees, that the blockading orders, meaning emphatically that of May, 1806, should be withdrawn also.

From that time forward, this order made a prominent figure in the various correspondence and negotiations between the United States and the British governments. The British government refused to consider the French conditional revocation of their orders, as bringing themselves within the terms of a declaration that the British government had made, that they would proceed *pari passu* with the French government in removing their edicts which interfered with the rights of neutrals ; and insisted that the blockading order of May, 1806, did not violate those rights. The demand for the repeal of that order was, however, persisted in by the United States, until it was terminated by the war.

When the committee of foreign relations were engaged in drawing the manifesto, proceeding as the government did upon false principles, they felt themselves under the necessity of making as large a display of British aggressions as they could, introducing into the catalogue of grievances, a variety of subjects which had nothing to do with the causes of war. Those causes were then reduced to two—the orders in council, and impressment. In discussing the former, it was impossible for the committee to pass by the blockading order of May, 1806, as that had been one of the prime causes of the crisis which the affairs of the country had reached. To assert in the face of the facts which were publicly known to exist, and to which allusion has already been made, viz. that the order was declared by Mr. Fox, the British minister, to be intended to benefit neutrals, an opinion assented to by Mr. Monroe, —that it was not considered as violating our neutral rights in the negotiation with Mr. Erskine—and had not been complained of as such by our government, until the rejection of that arrangement by the British government. It certainly required some dexterity to work this ground of complaint into the form of such a charge against the British as to make it appear to the country, and the civilized world, as a justifiable cause of war. The passage from the manifesto of the committee has been already cited. But it is expedient to advert to it and to the subject again.

The committee say, " In May, 1806, the whole coast of the continent, from the Elbe to Brest, inclusive, was declared to be in a state of blockade." This they considered as a violation of the law of nations, as no blockade is recognized by that law, unless it is supported by an adequate force. Such a force, they contend, was not applied. But to make such a blockade a good cause of war on the part of the United States, it must, in its operations, have violated specifically the neutral rights of our country. The government of the United States could never be justified in going to war for the purpose of vindicating mere abstract principles ; nor would the country ever have supported such a war. The non-intercourse law was founded entirely upon the principle that the edicts of Great Britain and France violated our neutral rights. Pressed with this view of the subject, and conscious that the evidence of the facts to which allusion has been made were in the possession of the public, the committee were constrained to say they thought it just " to remark that *this act of the British government does not appear to have been adopted in the sense in which it has since been construed.* On consideration of all the circumstances attending the measure, and particularly the character of the distinguished statesman who announced it, we are persuaded that *it was conceived in a spirit of conciliation, and intended to lead to an accommodation of all differences between the United States and Great Britain.* His death disappointed that hope, and the act has since become subservient to other purposes. It has been made by his successors a pretext for that vast system of usurpation, which has so long oppressed and harassed our commerce."

It is very much doubted, whether the history of modern wars can produce, in all the variety of manifestoes which they have given rise to, such an extraordinary cause of war as that abovementioned. Here it is acknowledged by the committee of foreign relations, that the blockading order of May, 1806, was conceived in a spirit of conciliation, and intended to lead to an accommodation of all differences between the United States and Great Britain ; but by the construction put upon it by those who succeeded Mr. Fox in the British ministry, it has been made the pretext for the system of usurpation which has so long oppressed and harassed American commerce. For nearly four years after the adoption of this measure, it was not, as far as appears, made the subject of any complaint by the government of the United States. The manner and the occasion of its being made a ground of remonstrance, has been stated. It was after the rejection of the Erskine arrangement, and upon the commencement of negotiations with the French government, respecting the revocation of the Berlin and Milan decrees. In no instance that is recollected, was it complained of as having been the cause of positive mischief to American commerce ; but the reasoning was directed altogether to the nature of the blockade, and intended to show that it was not legitimate, because not supported by an adequate force. On this point the governments were at issue, and both appear to have depended very much upon assertion—one affirming, and the other denying the application of such a force. No evidence has been discovered, in the examination of all the correspondence upon the subject, that the successors of Mr. Fox ever put a different construction upon the measure from that which he confessedly intended it should bear. The declaration, therefore, of the committee of foreign relations, appears to have been gratuitous, and without any foundation in fact. That so important and responsible an act as that of a declaration of war by one civilized and Christian power against another, should be placed upon such a false and unfounded basis as this, can only excite surprise in the mind of every lover of truth and justice.

It will be recollected, that the orders in council, which formed one of the avowed causes of the war, were actually repealed by the British government within five days after the declaration of war. A very little delay on the part of the American government would have removed this ground of controversy, and left nothing for this country to contend for but freedom from impressment. The French emperor had authorized his minister to declare to the American government, that the Berlin and Milan decrees were revoked on the 1st of November, 1810. Upon this annunciation, application was made by our government to that of Great Britain, to follow the example set by France, and repeal their orders in council. This was refused on the part of Great Britain, on the ground that the revocation of the French decrees was not absolute, but was conditional. This question gave rise to repeated and laboured discussions between the two governments, the American negotiators maintaining with great zeal that the repeal was absolute, and those of Great Britain contending with equal pertinacity that it was conditional. It has been shown by extracts from the official correspondence, that after Mr. Barlow had arrived at Paris, as envoy from the United States, viz. in May, 1812, he pressed the French minister with great earnestness for an absolute revocation of the Berlin and Milan decrees. Such a revocation, it was known, would remove the only obstacle to a repeal of the British orders in council. On the 1st of May, 1812, Mr. Barlow addressed a letter to the duke of Bassano, in which, after adverting to the fact that the British government refused to repeal the orders in council, on the ground that the French decrees were not revoked; he says—" It is much to be desired that the French government would now make and publish an authentic act, declaring the Berlin and Milan decrees, as relative to the United States, to have ceased in November, 1810." In a letter to Mr. Monroe, Secretary of State, dated May 12th, 1812, he says—" I found from a *pretty sharp conversation* with the duke of Bassano, that *there was a singular reluctance to answering my note of the 1st of May.* Some traces of that reluctance you will perceive in the answer which finally came, of which a copy is here enclosed."

It is stated, that in the course of the conversation alluded to, the duke produced a decree of the emperor, dated April 28th, 1811, more than a year previously, declaring the Berlin and Milan decrees *definitively revoked*, and to date from the 1st of November, 1810. This, as might have been expected, surprised the American minister, though he made no comment on the fact of its concealment. Upon being inquired of by Mr. Barlow, whether the decree had ever been published, he was informed by the duke that it had not; but was assured it had been *communicated to Mr. Barlow's predecessor at that court*, and had been transmitted to *the French minister in this country*, with orders to have it communicated to our government. Mr. Barlow informed the duke, that it was not among the archives of the legation; and requested that he might be furnished with a copy; which request was complied with.

Upon receiving the information of this singular transaction, the French minister in this country was applied to, but he had no knowledge of such a decree, until he received the information from home, of what had occurred between Mr. Barlow and the duke of Bassano. Under these circumstances, a call for information was made in the House of Representatives upon the President for information, who referred the subject to the Secretary of State, and whose report has already been alluded to, as far as it related to this subject. It fully confirmed the statement made by Mr. Barlow, that nothing was known to the American government respecting the existence of such a decree, before they received the information of what had passed between the duke of Bassano and Mr. Barlow When the course which our government had pursued towards both the French and the British, is taken into consideration, it is easy to imagine that the receipt of these communications must have proved the source of severe mortification to them. The declaration of the French minister, that the decree of April 28th, 1811, had actually been passed at the time of its date, no uninterested person will for a moment believe. That it had been communicated to Mr. Barlow's predecessor at the court of France, cannot be true; and the assertion that it had been trans-

mitted to the French minister, is not to be credited. There
is no room to doubt, that it was a mere pretence, got up
for the occasion, and intended to answer a particular purpose, which will be alluded to hereafter.

The Secretary of State, in his report on the subject,
shows strong marks of chagrin, arising either from the
fact that the matter had become public, or at the unfounded declaration of the French minister, that the decree had
been passed and communicated at a period so long antecedent to its actual promulgation, in the manner as is above
related. But instead of manifesting the proper degree of
dignity and spirit, which such an attempt at imposition obviously demanded, the Secretary of State enters upon a
long and laboured series of reasoning, to prove that the
repeal of their orders in council by the British government, was not the result of the final revocation of the
French decrees, but of other causes, although "it was
made the ground of their repeal" by that government.
It is difficult to reason conclusively against facts. The
British government had uniformly declared that the French
decree of revocation of August, 1810, to take effect on the
1st of November, 1810, was conditional only, and therefore they refused to repeal their orders in council. That
it would be conditional, was declared a good while before
it took place by our government, when they predicted that
France would draw the United States and Great Britain
to issue on this subject, by revoking her decrees "with a
condition, that a repeal of the blockades should accompany
a repeal of the orders in council." That it was conditional,
was proved by the terms of the decree. But the American government insisted that it was a condition subsequent,
and therefore formed no apology for their refusal to proceed *pari passu* with the French in removing their edicts.
But the language of the French decree of the date of
April 28th, 1811, whenever it was passed, by necessary
implication admits that the decree of August, 1810, was

not such a revocation as the British demanded.   It is there called a *definitive revocation.*   A definite act of this kind, leaves room for a strong inference, that what had previously occurred was conditional, or at least not absolute.

The British government had resisted the demand of the American government, for the repeal of the orders in council, from August, 1810, to May, 1812, on the specific ground that the French decree of revocation of the former date was conditional.   But upon receiving official intelligence that France had definitively revoked her decrees, the British orders in council were repealed.   To suppose that this act was produced by the apprehension that the American government were approaching a more serious and threatening crisis towards them, appears like a mere attempt to escape from an awkward and uncomfortable dilemma, into which our administration had plunged themselves.   A more just and liberal spirit than that which adopted this construction, would have ascribed the measure to some more manly motive than that of fear.   Great Britain had braved too many dangers inconceivably greater than that of a war with the United States, to have been alarmed by the threat of a war with them.

Impressment was the second, and the only additional cause of war, set forth in the report of the committee on foreign relations.   The practice of impressing American seamen, by the British, had been a ground of just complaint, almost from the commencement of the French revolutionary wars.   The strong resemblance in the character and language of British and American seamen, rendered it somewhat difficult to discriminate between natives of the two countries.   And it is not probable that naval officers, in a time of war, and when hostilities were sharpened by the most active and powerful passions that ever influence the human mind or conduct, would be very scrupulous in deciding the question of origin, where the evidence must have been in its nature doubtful, and in its application very difficult.   Nor in such wars as those which raged so long, and with such virulence, between Great Britain and France, during that memorable period, is it strange that less regard should be had to the personal or political rights of neutrals, than the latter would have an unquestionable right to demand.   Both these nations considered themselves as struggling for existence; and of course, both acted, in a variety of exigencies, on the principle of self-preservation.   Under such circumstances, they considered the law of nations as an object of secondary importance.   A multitude of instances might be adduced in the conduct of both nations, in which a total disregard of the law of nations, and the rights of neutrals, was manifested.   As soon as the evils of impressment were seriously felt by American seamen, complaints and remonstrances from time to time were forwarded to both governments, and efforts to open negotiations were made, for the purpose of adjusting the difficulty by treaty; but all without effect.

It will be recollected, that the treaty agreed upon with Great Britain, in 1806, by Messrs. Monroe and Pinkney, was rejected by Mr. Jefferson, without ever consulting the Senate, professedly on the ground that it contained no stipulation against impressment.   In the letter which accompanied the treaty, those commissioners, when giving the reasons why they concluded to form a treaty without such a provision, remark—"On the 9th instant, we received from the British commissioners the note which they had promised us in the last interview, which we have found to correspond in all respects with what we had been taught to expect."—" When we take into view all that has passed on this subject, we are far from considering the note of the British commissioners as a mere circumstance of form.   We persuade ourselves that by accepting the invitation which it gives, and proceeding in the negotiation, we shall place the business almost, if not altogether, on as good a footing as we should have done by treaty, had the project which we offered them been adopted."

Mr. Monroe, in his letter of February, 1808, written after his return to this country, says—" I have always believed, and still do believe, that the ground on which that interest was placed by the paper of the British commissioners of November 8, 1806, and the explanations which accompanied it, was both honourable and advantageous to the United States; that it contained a concession in their favour, on the part of Great Britain, on the great principle in contestation, never before made by a formal and obligatory act of the government, which was highly favourable to their interest; and that it also imposed on her the obligation to conform her practice under it, till a more complete arrangement should be concluded, to the just claims of the United States."——

"By this paper it is evident that the rights of the United States were expressly to be reserved ; and not abandoned, as has been most erroneously supposed ; that the negotiation on the subject of impressment was to be postponed for a limited time, and for a special object only, and to be revived as soon as that object was accomplished ; and in the interim, that the practice of impressment was to correspond essentially with the views and interests of the United States."

By the rejection of this treaty, this difficult and irritating subject was left open to all the abuses to which it was unfortunately liable. The consequence was, that complaints of impressment continued, until the subject became the ground of open war with Great Britain. Indeed, within a few days after the declaration of war, it became, by the repeal of the orders in council, the only existing cause of war. That war, in the course of two years and a half, cost the United States from thirty to fifty thousand lives, and more than a hundred millions of dollars ; and when peace was determined upon, a treaty was made, and ratified, not only without any provision against impressment, but without its containing the slightest allusion to that subject. The treaty of Messrs. Monroe and Pinkney was accompanied by the note, or paper, above referred to, in which the British commissioners made the declarations already cited, and agreed to postpone the subject of impressment for a limited time, after which it was to be revived. It is remarkable, that in the last letter of instructions but one to the American commissioners who negotiated the treaty of peace in 1814, they were expressly instructed, if the British commissioners would not agree to a provision against it in the treaty, to stipulate that it should be postponed to a future opportunity; thus bringing our government back, after all its correspondence, and its multiplied attempts at negotiation, its complaints, remonstrances, and threats, and its immense expense of blood and treasure, to the precise position in which they stood when Mr. Jefferson rejected Messrs. Monroe and Pinkney's treaty in 1808. But that position was far more humiliating to the United States, than the ground they held at the period just mentioned. War had been waged to obtain security against impressment, and they had been reduced to the necessity, after a controversy of two years and a half duration for that sole object, to make a peace without obtaining the smallest degree of that security.

This review of the policy and measures of the United States government, during the administrations of Mr. Jefferson and Mr. Madison, has been undertaken for the purpose of establishing the principal proposition advanced in the early part of this work, viz. *That an ardent and overweening attachment to revolutionary France, and an implacable enmity to Great Britain, were the governing principles of those two distinguished individuals.* That their conduct at the head of the government was influenced and controlled by feelings of this description, will be admitted by all who consider the evidence adduced as sufficient to prove the truth of the proposition.

In the case of Mr. Jefferson, his own declarations contained in his posthumous works, have been cited in support of the proposition. The evidence itself cannot be contradicted or impeached. Whether it proves the point or not, the reader will determine for himself, upon carefully examining its weight and import. But much addiional proof is to be found in the public state papers of his administration. His report to Congress, just before he resigned the office of Secretary of State, in 1793, laid the foundation of the commercial resolutions, introduced to the House of Representatives of the United States, by Mr. Madison, then a member of that body, and afterwards his successor to the chief magistracy of the Union. Those resolutions were avowedly designed to detach the United States from their commercial relations with Great Britain, and transfer their foreign trade to France.

An attempt has been made to show, by an appeal to historical evidence, that it was a part of Mr. Jefferson's policy, for the purpose of influencing public feeling, and directing public opinion, to retain at all times some matter of dispute or controversy with Great Britain on hand, which might keep the feelings of the government and people of both countries in a state of fretfulness and irritation. When the treaty of 1794 was negotiated by Mr. Jay, Mr. Jefferson, though out of office, was decidedly opposed to its ratification. And when he found it had received the approbation of the Senate, and the final sanction of the Executive, he wished its execution might be defeated in the House of Representatives, though such a result would most obviously have involved the exercise of an unconstitutional power.

That treaty expired soon after he came into the admi- nistration of the government; but though the British government repeatedly offered to renew it, he instructed his minister at that court to decline the offer; thus choosing to leave the important subject of the trade to the British colonies open, and exposed to all the bickering and controversy which must naturally grow out of such an unsettled state of things.

The Convention for establishing the boundary line between the United States and the British territories adjoining them, which was negotiated and concluded by Mr. King, in the year 1803, was not ratified, leaving unsettled a dispute which has never been adjusted to this day.

In 1807, Mr. Rose was sent by the British government to this country, to make reparation for the injury we had received by the attack on the frigate Chesapeake; his instructions confined his negotiations to that subject alone, and this was well known to our government; but when, after a fruitless attempt to induce him to transcend his powers, by discussing other subjects of dispute, the negotiation was broken off, and the controversy left unadjusted.

When Mr. Jackson came as envoy from Great Britain, our cabinet very soon satisfied themselves that he was too experienced and adroit a diplomatist to be overreached or circumvented, and they accused him of insulting our government, and he was dismissed, though authorized to adjust the affair of the frigate Chesapeake.

In 1811, four years after that affair had happened, the offer to renew the negotiations on that subject was made; and finally, though with a very ill grace, and in a very undignified manner, our government accepted the same terms of reparation which they might have received from Mr. Rose if they had not broken off the negotiation with him. It is believed that this is the only controversy of any moment that was ever settled with Great Britain during the administrations of Mr. Jefferson and Mr. Madison.

In December, 1807, Messrs. Monroe and Pinkney concluded a treaty with Great Britain, on all the points in dispute between the countries, except that of impressment, and an informal understanding was agreed to on that subject. This treaty was rejected, without even submitting it to the consideration of the Senate; thereby throwing open for controversy all the questions between the governments, professedly because one was left unadjusted;—and that one remains unadjusted to this day.

The arrangement with Mr. Erskine was made under circumstances which furnish room for very strong suspicions, at least, that its ratification by Great Britain was not expected by our government. If our government were not acquainted with the nature and extent of Mr. Erskine's instructions, they were chargeable with gross negligence of duty in not previously obtaining the necessary information. If they were acquainted with them, they are justly liable to a charge of a much more heinous character.

The "restrictive system," as it was called—that is, the system of embargo and non-intercourse—was obviously adopted in pursuance of the general policy of Bonaparte, and for the purpose of furthering his views of hostility against Great Britain. It was necessarily calculated to injure the trade of Great Britain, without materially affecting that of France, as the latter was scarcely able to keep even a merchant vessel afloat on the ocean. The evidence in support of this general allegation against our government, is derived from many sources, but most specifically from Mr. Jefferson's letter to Mr. Livingston, which has been quoted.

It will be necessary to extend this recapitulation somewhat further—

Upon the failure of Erskine's arrangement, our government, as has been seen, immediately turned their attention towards the adjustment of their difficulties with France. By a series of servile and humiliating conduct towards the haughty and imperious ruler of that nation, they became involved in his unprincipled policy, and were subjected to his influence and controul. This is abundantly proved by the public documents which have been cited. In the year 1811, when it was well known that Bonaparte was making preparations upon the most extensive scale to invade the Russian dominions, for the purpose of forcing the emperor Alexander to submit to such terms as the former should prescribe, or to hurl him from his thròne, the measures of our government began to assume a warlike appearance; and advancing step by step, with the lapse of time and the progress of events, nearly at the same moment when the French army commenced its march for the north, the United States declared war against Great Britain. That the course pursued by our government was intended to operate as a diversion in favour of France, by dividing the British forces, and in some measure distracting the attention of their government from the great theatre of war in Europe, is too apparent to be questioned by any person possessed of a frank and independent mind. It might have been considered as a good political manœuvre, had it been certain that Bonaparte would succeed in his enterprise.   But he failed; and the consequences were soon seen in the change of tone assumed by our govern ment.   It is true, they endeavoured to hold out to the country the appearance of courage and confidence concerning the result of the war; but the secret history of the times shows that they were greatly alarmed at their situation, surrounded as it was with difficulties and dangers, and their conduct was obviously influenced less by courage than it was by despair; and hence alone can it be accounted for, that they so suddenly and so essentially changed their tone in the instructions given to their commissioners, who were endeavouring to negotiate for peace, and instructed them to give up all that the war was professedly made for, and to take up with a simple peace, if that could be obtained.

Coupled with these remarks, by way of recapitulation, the attempt to excite the angry passions and resentments of the country, by the disclosure of the affair of John Henry, should not be lost sight of. It was, indeed, a mere episode in the principal work, having no connection with the grievances of which our government complained, and was not even named in the government manifesto as one of the causes of war. It was, however, eagerly seized hold of by the administration as a part of the machinery which was used for the purpose of producing an effect upon the public mind—for that purpose it was set in motion, and after suffering themselves to be grossly duped and swindled by a couple of sharpers out of fifty thousand dollars, the whole plot, and its actors, were suffered to die away, and be forgotten; or remembered only to excite feelings of contempt and disgust for the policy and objects of those by whom the farce was prepared for public exhibition.

Such is a brief history of the origin and causes of the war of 1812. The evidence on which it rests is derived from the public documents of the government—from state papers published by their authority, and from other sources equally creditable. Its authenticity, therefore, cannot be doubted; and the only question that can be raised is, whether it is sufficient to establish the point for which it is adduced. On this subject, if the author is not greatly deceived, there will be little room for dispute. The chain of evidence is, in his opinion, entire, its credit unimpeachable, and its force irresistible.

The next object to which the attention of the reader will be turned is the manner in which the operations of the war were conducted.

On the 10th of April, 1812, a little more than two months before the formal declaration of war, but after it was perfectly obvious that such a measure was determined upon, Congress passed an act, of which the following are extracts—

" I. *Be it enacted*, *&c.* That the President of the

United States be, and he is hereby authorised to require of the executives of the several states and territories, to take effectual measures to organize, arm, and equip, according to law, and hold in readiness to march at a moment's warning, their respective proportions of one hundred thousand militia, officers included, to be apportioned by the President of the United States, from the latest militia returns in the department of war ; and, in cases where such returns have not been made, by such other data as he shall judge equitable.

"II. That the department of militia aforesaid shall be officered out of the present militia officers, or others, at the option and discretion of the constitutional authority in the respective states and territories; the President of the United States apportioning the general officers among the respective states and territories, as he may deem proper.

"IV. That the President of the United States be, and he hereby is, authorized to call into actual service any part, or the whole, of said detachment, in all the exigencies provided by the constitution."——

On the 15th of April, 1812, the Secretary of War wrote to the Governor of Connecticut, and it is to be presumed to the governors of the other states, as follows—

" *War Department*, 15*th April*, 1812.

" HIS EXCELLENCY THE GOVERNOR OF THE STATE OF
CONNECTICUT.

" Sir—I am instructed by the President of the United States, to call upon the executives of the several states to take effectual measures to organize, arm and equip according to law, and hold in readiness to march at a moment's warning, their respective proportions of one hundred thousand militia, officers included, by virtue of an act of Congress, passed the 10th inst. entitled, ' an act to authorize a detachment from the militia of the United States.' "

" This therefore is to require your excellency to take effectual measures for having three thousand of the militia of Connecticut (being her quota) detached and duly organized in companies, battalions, regiments, brigades and divisions, within the shortest period that circumstances will permit, and as nearly as possible in the following proportions of artillery, cavalry and infantry, viz. one twentieth part of artillery; one twentieth part of cavalry; and the residue infantry. There will, however, be no objection on the part of the President of the United States, to the admission of a proportion of riflemen, duly organized in a distinct corps, and not exceeding one tenth part of the whole quota of the states respectively. Each corps shall be properly armed and equipped for actual service.

" When the detachment and organization shall have been effected, the respective corps will be exercised under the officers set over them ; but will not remain embodied, or be considered as in actual service, until by subsequent orders they shall be directed to take the field.

" Your excellency will please to direct that correct muster rolls and inspection returns be made of the several corps, and that copies thereof be transmitted to this department as early as possible.

" I have the honor to be,
" Sir, very respectfully,
" Your obedient servant,
" WILLIAM EUSTIS."

Immediately after the declaration of war was passed, the members of the House of Representatives of the United States, who were in the minority on that question, published an address on that subject to their constituents. In that document, which is drawn up with much force of reasoning and talent, the following is given as the principal

reason for adopting that mode of communicating their sentiments to those to whom they were addressed—

"The momentous question of war with Great Britain is
decided. On this topic, so vital to your interests, the right
of public debate, in the face of the world, and especially of
their constituents, has been denied to your representatives.
They have been called into secret session on this most interesting of all your public relations, although the circumstances of the time and of the nation afforded no one
reason for secrecy, unless it be found in the apprehension
of the effect of public debate on public opinion ; or of
public opinion on the result of the vote.

"Except the message of the President of the United
States, which is now before the public, nothing confidential was communicated. That message contained no fact
not previously known. No one reason for war was intimated, but such as was of a nature public and notorious.
The intention to wage war and invade Canada, had been
long since openly avowed. The object of hostile menace
had been ostentatiously announced. The inadequacy of
both our army and navy for successful invasion, and the
insufficiency of the fortifications for the security of our sea-
board, were every where known. Yet the doors of Congress were shut upon the people. They have been carefully kept in ignorance of the progress of measures, until
the purposes of the administration were consummated, and
the fate of the country sealed. In a situation so extraordinary, the undersigned have deemed it their duty by no
act of theirs to sanction a proceeding so novel and arbitrary. On the contrary, they made every attempt, in
their power, to attain publicity for their proceedings. All
such attempts were vain. When this momentous subject
was stated, as for debate, they demanded that the doors
should be opened.

"This being refused, they declined discussion ; being
perfectly convinced, from indications too plain to be mis-

understood, that in the house, all argument with closed doors was hopeless ; and that any act giving implied validity to so flagrant an abuse of power, would be little less than treachery to the essential rights of a free people."

The allusion to the unprepared condition of the country and government for a war, and especially with Great Britain, in the abovementioned address, was perfectly well founded. Great Britain, at that time, had absolute dominion over the ocean. No other power in Europe was in a situation to annoy our commerce or invade our country. We had a sea-coast of about two thousand miles extent, exposed to hostile visits, and of course to depredations, from a maritime enemy; our principal sea-ports and harbours were in a great measure unprotected ; we had a small standing army, scattered in many directions, and over a vast extent of country, and of course incapable of being brought to act with efficiency upon any specific point, and a small navy; we were to a great degree unprovided with the ordinary materials of offensive war, and particularly with the indispensable ingredient of money. No part of the country was more open and exposed to the visits and depredations of an enemy, than the territory bordering upon the New England coast. The fortifications were hardly entitled to the name; and the garrisons employed in them were merely nominal, and so few in numbers, as to be incapable of resisting any serious attack from a well disciplined and well provided enemy. In such a state of things, letters of the following import were addressed by the Secretary of War to the governors of Massachusetts and Connecticut——

" War Department, June 12, 1812.

" SIR—I am directed by the President to request your excellency to order into the service of the United States, on the requisition of Major General Dearborn, such part of the quota of militia from the state of Massachusetts, detached conformably to the act of April 10, 1812, as he may deem necessary for the defence of the sea-coast.

" With great respect, I have the honor to be
" Your excellency's obedient servant,

" W. EUSTIS."

To the foregoing letter, Governor Griswold of Connecticut returned the following answer—

" *Lyme*, 17*th June*, 1812.

"THE HONOURABLE THE SECRETARY OF WAR.

" SIR—I had the honour, this afternoon, to receive your letter of the 12th instant, communicating to me the request of the President, that I would order into the service of the United States, on the requisition of Major General Dearborn, such part of the quota of militia from the state of Connecticut, detached conformably to the act of Congress of April 10th, 1812, as he may deem necessary for the defence of the sea-coast.

"In obedience to which request, I shall, on the requisition of General Dearborn, execute without delay the request of the President.

" With great respect, I have the honour to be
" Your obedient servant,

" ROGER GRISWOLD."

On the 22d of June, General Dearborn addressed the following letter to Governor Strong of Massachusetts—

" *Head Quarters, Boston, June* 22*d*, 1812.

"TO HIS EXCELLENCY CALEB STRONG.

" SIR—I have received instructions from the President of the United States, to call on your Excellency for such part of the quota of the militia of Massachusetts, which was detached conformably to the act of Congress of April 10, 1812, as I may deem necessary for the defence of the sea-coast : and I have now the honour of requesting your Excellency to order *fourteen companies of artillery, and twenty-seven companies of infantry* into the service of the United States, for the defence of the ports and harbours of this state, and the harbour of Newport in the state of Rhode-Island. The companies are intended for the following ports and harbours in the following proportions. For Passamaquoddy one company of artillery and two companies of infantry, to be commanded by a major. For Machias one company of artillery. For Castine one company of artillery and two companies of infantry, to be commanded by a major. For Damariscotta and Wiscasset two companies of artillery. For Kennebunk one company of artillery. For Portland two companies of artillery and two companies of infantry, to be commanded by a major. For Marblehead, Salem, Cape Ann, and Newburyport, two companies of artillery and two companies of infantry. For Boston, four companies of artillery and eight companies of infantry, with a lieutenant-colonel and one major. For the defence of Rhode-Island eight companies of infantry, with a lieutenant-colonel and one major.

" Having received official information that war has been declared by Congress against Great Britain, your Excellency will perceive the expediency of giving facility to such measures of defence as the crisis demands ; and as the defence of the sea-coast of New-England is by the general government confided to my direction, I shall with confidence rely on all the aid and support that the respective governors of the New-England states can afford ; and in a special manner on that of the Commander-in-Chief of the important state of Massachusetts. And I shall at all times receive with the greatest pleasure and readiness any advice or information that your Excellency may be pleased to communicate.

"With respectful consideration, I am, &c.

"H. DEARBORN."

The following letter of the same date, was addressed to Governor Griswold of Connecticut—

"*Head Quarters, Boston, June* 22, 1812.

"TO HIS EXCELLENCY ROGER GRISWOLD.

"SIR—Having received instructions from the President of the United States, to call on your excellency for such part of the quota of the militia, which was detached from the state of Connecticut, conformably to the act of Congress, of April the 10th, 1812, as I may deem necessary for the defence of the sea-coast; I have now the honor of requesting your Excellency to order into the service of the United States, two companies of artillery, and two companies of infantry, *to be placed under the command of the commanding officer at Fort Trumbull, near New-London;* and one company of artillery, to be stationed at the battery, at the entrance of the harbour of New-Haven. Having received official information that war has been declared by Congress against Great Britain, I shall rely with confidence on the aid and support of your Excellency, in giving effect to measures of defence on the sea-coast, which has been confided to my direction by the general government; and I shall, at any time, receive with the greatest pleasure and readiness, any advice or information you may please to communicate.

"With great respect I have the honour to be,

"Your Excellency's most obedient servant,

"H. DEARBORN, *Major-General.*"

By the letter to the governor of Massachusetts, a requisition was made for forty-one companies—fourteen of artillery, and twenty-seven of infantry. They were ordered to different places, in that state, and in Rhode-Island. Two lieutenant-colonels were called for from the militia; but no officer of a higher grade. The order to the governor of Connecticut was for five companies—two of artillery and three of infantry, but no officers of any description were included in the call. On the contrary, four of the companies were expressly directed " to be placed under the command of the commanding officer at Fort Trumbull, near New-London," who was an officer of the United States army, of the rank of captain, and the other at the battery at the entrance of New-Haven harbour, where there was a United States officer stationed.

The governor of Massachusetts did not consider the call made by the President of the United States, through General Dearborn, as warranted by the constitution, and therefore did not detach the men agreeably to his requisition. The general reasons by which he was influenced, are contained in the following extract from the speech delivered by him to the legislature of the state, who were convened in October, 1812, for the purpose of deliberating on the events which had recently occurred—

" The Constitution of the United States declares, that ' Congress may provide for calling forth the militia to execute the laws of the Union, suppress insurrections, and repel invasions,' and the act of Congress of April 10th, 1812, authorising a detachment of 100,000 of the militia, empowers the President to ' call into actual service any part, or the whole of said detachment, in all the exigencies provided by the constitution.' From these clauses in the constitution and the law of April 10th, the President derives his authority to call the militia of the states into actual service; and except in the exigencies abovementioned, he can have no authority by the constitution to do it. But there was no suggestion, either in the letter from the War Department, above referred to, or in those from General Dearborn, that this state or Rhode-Island was invaded, or in imminent danger of invasion ; or that either of the exigencies recognised by the constitutional laws of the United States existed. If such declaration could have been made with truth, it would undoubtedly have been made.

" General Dearborn plainly supposed, that in consequence of the act declaring war, he was authorized by virtue of the power given him by the President, to require any part or the whole of our detached militia to be called out and marched to such places in this and the other states as he might think proper. If this construction of the constitution is correct, the President and Congress will be able at any time, by declaring war, to call the whole militia of the United States into actual service, to march them to such places as they may think fit, and retain them in service as long as the war shall continue. It is declared indeed by the aforesaid act of April 10th, that the said detachment shall not be compelled to serve a ' longer time than six months after they arrive at the place of rendezvous.' But if the mere act of declaring war gives a right to the national government to call the militia into service, and detain them six months, it must give a right to detain them six years, if the war continues so long ; and the national government has the same authority to call out the whole, as a part of the militia."———

" Although many of the most important attributes of sovereignty are given by the constitution to the government of the United States, yet there are some which still belong to the state governments; of these, one of the most essential is the entire control of the militia, except in the exigencies above mentioned ; this has not been delegated to the United States—it is therefore reserved to the states respectively ; and whenever it shall be taken from them,

and a consolidation of the military force of the states shall
be effected, the security of the state governments will be
lost, and they will wholly depend for their existence upon
the moderation and forbearance of the national government.

"I have been fully disposed to comply with the requirements of the constitution of the United States and the
laws made in pursuance of it, and sincerely regretted that
any request should be made by an officer of the national
government to which I could not constitutionally conform.
But it appeared to me that the requisition aforesaid was
of that character; and I was under the same obligation to
maintain the rights of the state, as to support the constitution of the United States. If the demand was not warranted by the constitution, I should have violated my duty
in a most important point, if I had attempted to enforce
it, and had thereby assisted in withdrawing the militia
from the rightful authority of the state. Besides, if the
measure was not required by the constitution, it would
have been oppressive, as the militia must have been called
from their occupations to places remote from their homes,
and detained in the service during the busy season of the
year."

The governor of Connecticut, upon receiving General
Dearborn's letter of June 22d, in pursuance of the practice upon extraordinary occasions in that state, immediately convened the Council, and submitted the correspondence, and the whole subject, to their consideration, for
their opinion and advice, in the following message—

"GENTLEMEN OF THE COUNCIL,—The agitation which
has been produced by the late measures of Congress, undoubtedly requires great caution in every step which may
be taken by the government of this state. And it would
afford me particular satisfaction, if the Council would at
this meeting, direct their attention to this novel situation

of our affairs, and communicate to me their advice respecting the general course which it is proper for the Executive to pursue, under those emergencies which may probably arise. But the particular object for which I have thought it my duty to convene you at this time, is to request your advice respecting the course which it is proper to take with a requisition of the national government, communicated through the medium of General Dearborn, for detaching five companies of the drafted militia, for the defence of New-London and New-Haven.

"The order for detaching three thousand men, being the quota of this state under the act of Congress of the 10th of April, was received and immediately executed. Since which I received a letter from the Secretary of War, communicating a request from the President, that as many of the detached troops as General Dearborn should require for the defence of the sea-coast might be ordered into the service of the United States. General Dearborn has now made his requisition, and requested four companies to march for New-London, and one for New-Haven, and to be placed under the command of the officers commanding at those posts.

"My answer to the second letter from the Secretary of War was necessarily expressed in general terms that the request of the President should be executed, as I had no right to presume that any thing would be required which was not warranted by the Constitution and the law. The demand however, now made, presents several important considerations. It becomes a question whether the militia can be constitutionally and legally demanded until one of the contingencies enumerated in the Constitution shall have arisen. And whether a requisition, to place any portion of the militia under the command of a continental officer, can be executed. Other questions, especially important, may arise from the same subject.

"Relying, gentlemen, on your advice in this emergency

I have to request your serious and deliberate attention to every point connected with it.

"ROGER GRISWOLD.

"*Hartford, June* 29, 1812."

The body of men who composed the Council of Connecticut, formed one of the houses of the legislature of that state, and consisted of the lieutenant-governor, and twelve assistants. They took the matter into their consideration, and after due deliberation, came to the following result—

"*At a meeting of the governor and council of the state of Connecticut, at Hartford, on the* 29*th of June, A. D.* 1812.

"His excellency the governor has requested of this board advice respecting the course which it is proper to take on a requisition of the national government, communicated through the medium of General Dearborn, for detaching five companies of the militia, drafted under the act of Congress of the 10th of April last, for the defence of New-London and New-Haven. The order for this draft of three thousand men was received, and immediately executed. On the 12th of instant June, the Secretary of War requested of the Governor that as many of the militia thus drafted as General Dearborn should require for the defence of the sea-coast, should be ordered into the service of the United States. Presuming that nothing would be required which was not warranted by the constitution and the law, assurance was given of a compliance with this request. The council entirely approve of the promptitude with which the Governor has thus manifested his readiness to comply with all legal and constitutional requisitions, a promptitude always shown by the Government of Connecticut.

"General Dearborn now requests that four companies of the militia drafted as stated, be detached for the fort at New-London, and one company for the fort at New-Haven, *to be put under the command of the officers of the army of the United States, stationed at those posts.* His excellency the Governor has requested the 'serious and deliberate attention' of this board to the following questions, arising out of the requisition of General Dearborn,—'Can the militia be legally and constitutionally demanded until one of the contingencies enumerated in the constitution shall have arisen? And can a requisition, to place any portion of the militia under the command of a continental officer, be executed? The council, impressed with the great importance of these questions, have seriously and deliberately examined them, and in compliance with the request of the Governor, now present to him the result of their deliberations.

" The constitution of the United States has wisely ordained that Congress may provide for calling forth the militia to *execute the laws of the Union, suppress insurrections, and repel invasions.* The acts of Congress of February, 1795, and of April, 1812, in strict pursuance of the constitution, provide for calling forth the militia into the actual service, in the exigencies above named.

" This board is not informed that the requisition of General Dearborn, said to be in pursuance of that of the Secretary of War of the 12th of instant June, is grounded on a declaration made by the President of the United States, or notice by him given, that the militia are required *to execute the laws of the Union, suppress insurrections, or repel invasions, or that the United States are in imminent danger of invasion.* As none of the exigencies recognized by the constitution and laws of the United States are shown to exist, this board deem his excellency the Governor to be, of right, the commander in chief of the militia of this state, and that they cannot *thus* be withdrawn from his authority.

" The council to the second inquiry observe, that the constitution of the United States provides that the appointment of the officers of the militia shall be reserved to the states respectively. In the event of their being called forth into the actual service of the United States, in any of the exigencies specified, the laws of the United States provide, that they are to be called forth as a militia, furnished with officers by the state. The militia organized under the act of the 10th of April, from which the detachment in question is required, have been regularly, and in conformity to law, formed into a *division*, consisting of brigades, regiments, battalions, and companies. The requisition of General Dearborn is, that five companies, which constitute a battalion, be detached, four of which are required for the fort at New-London, and one for the fort at New-Haven, *to be put under the command of the officers there stationed.* The council do not perceive in the constitution or laws of the United States, any warrant for thus taking from the officers duly appointed by the state, the men under their controul, and thus impairing, and as the case may be, eventually destroying the military force of the state. Nor do they perceive any law authorizing the officers of the army of the United States to detach from a body of drafted militia, now organized with constitutional officers, a portion of its men, and thus weaken and, as the case may be, annihilate the detachment. They do perceive, however, that a compliance with such a requisition might transfer the militia of the respective states into the army of the United States, and that thus the officers of the militia might be left without any command, except in *name*, and that the respective states might thus be deprived of the militia which the constitution has granted to them. In this view of this interesting subject, the council advise his excellency the governor not to comply with the requisition of General Dearborn.

"In view of this result, made from a conviction that it is just and conformable to the constitution, the Council feel entirely disposed to give ample assurance that this state will ever support the national government in all constitutional measures, and presume that in case of invasion, or imminent danger of invasion, the governor will deem it expedient to make such provision for the protection of the sea-coast by the militia of the state, in co-operation with the military force of the United States, as the public exigency may require, and as is warranted by law.

"In regard to other matters in the governor's communication, the Council forbear to remark particularly, relying with perfect confidence on the wisdom of his Excellency, to pursue such a course, in any emergencies which may arise, as becomes the chief magistrate of a free and enlightened people, and imploring the blessings of the God of our fathers for protection in the midst of the calamities of war.

" *Passed in the Council,*
    June 29th, 1812.

"THOMAS DAY, *Secretary.*"

The call upon the governor of Massachusetts, it has been seen, was for forty-one companies. These companies, upon the most moderate estimate of their numbers, must have contained between three and four thousand men, including officers, non-commissioned officers, musicians, &c.; and of course they would have formed a division, and would have had a legal right to be commanded by a major-general. Instead of which, the highest officer named in the order was a lieutenant-colonel. The order to the governor of Connecticut was more explicit. It required five companies, which would form a battalion, and be entitled to a major's command. Instead of which, no officer of any rank or description is named or called for, but four of the companies were directed to be placed immediately under the command of the United States officer commanding at Fort Trumbull, near New-London, and the fifth under the United States officer of the garrison at New-Haven.

In both cases, the orders were not warranted by the constitution of the United States. The reasoning on the nature and objects of the requisition, in the foregoing result of the deliberations of the Council of Connecticut, is conclusive. And the principle for which they contended, is one of the most interesting description to the safety of the militia, and the rights and security of the individual states. By the constitution of the United States, Congress have power to call forth the militia of the states only in three emergencies, viz. "To execute the laws of the union, suppress insurrections, and repel invasions." But to guard against any possible mischief that might arise, either to the several states, when thus temporarily deprived of their natural protectors, or to that portion of the inhabitants who compose the militia, it was provided in the constitution, that Congress should have power "To provide for organizing, arming, and disciplining the militia, and for governing such parts of them as may be employed in the service of the United States, *reserving to the states respectively the appointment of the officers*, and the authority of training the militia according to the discipline prescribed by Congress." This provision is not only plain and explicit, but in the highest degree important to the militia, and to the states to which they belong. If when called into the service of the United States, they were to be taken from the superintendence of their own officers, and placed under the command of United States officers, they would, to all intents and purposes, become incorporated into the standing army of the nation, be shut up in garrisons, be commanded by officers of the standing army, and be subject to the same government with the standing army—or in other words, to that severe and sanguinary code, the "Rules and Articles of War." By those rules and articles it is provided,—that "All officers serving by commission from the authority of any particular state, shall on all detachments, courts-martial, or other duty, wherein they may be employed in conjunction with the regular forces of the United States, take rank next after all officers of the like grade in said regular forces, notwithstanding the commissions of such militia or state officers may be older than the commissions of the officers of the regular forces of the United States." From this provision, it is apparent, that it was intended, by the order of General Dearborn, to put the militia of Connecticut into the United States forts at New-London and New-Haven, under the immediate command of United States officers, to perform garrison duty, in the same manner as if they had been regularly enlisted into the standing army of the United States. No proposition can be more plain than this,—that if this project had succeeded, an unquestionable and most important provision of the constitution would have been violated, and the rights of the militia, in an equal degree, not have been merely infringed, but sacrificed.

The consequences of such an attempt on the part of the national government, had it been carried into effect, may perhaps be considered at the present time with a greater degree of coolness and deliberation, than could have been expected when the country was under the agitation and excitement which a state of war naturally produces, and which party feelings and passions are well calculated greatly to increase and extend. If the New-England states had given up their militia, at the requisition of the President of the United States, and in a total disregard of the federal constitution, a precedent would have been established that might, and, one day or other, in all probability would, have proved fatal to the liberties of the country. By the act of Congress of April 10th above alluded to, the President was authorized, at his own discretion, to call into the public service one hundred thousand militia. He was constituted the sole judge of the time when they should

be ordered into the field, and of the numbers that should
be called for on any given occasion. By depriving them
of their constitutional right to be commanded by their own
officers, and placing them under that of officers of the regular army, they might be pent up in garrisons, or sent to
any distant point of military operations which the President himself, or Major-General Dearborn should think
proper to designate. In this way, the several states would
have been stripped of their natural and constitutional defenders, and left exposed to all the variety of evils which
such a condition necessarily presupposes, while the militia
themselves would have been subjected to all the hardships
and degradation which are always experienced in standing
armies.

Nor was this all. By the rules and articles of war it is
provided, that—" The officers and soldiers of any troops,
whether militia or others, being mustered and in pay of
the United States, shall, at all times, and in all places,
when joined, or acting in conjunction with the regular
forces of the United States, be governed by these rules and
articles of war, and shall be subject to be tried by courts
martial, in like manner with the officers and soldiers in
the regular forces, *save only that such courts martial shall
be composed entirely of militia officers.*" By omitting in the
order issued by General Dearborn to the Governor of Connecticut, to include officers, and placing the men under the
exclusive command of United States officers, the important provision above recited from the rules and articles of
war, securing to the militia the privilege of being tried in
courts martial by militia officers, would have been entirely
evaded, because no such officers would have been in the
service, of whom such courts could have been formed. And
in the case of Massachusetts, by ordering out only officers
of a lower grade than the laws required, and a much
smaller number than the number of troops demanded, the
benefit intended to be secured to the militia by the forego-

ing provision, would have been in a great measure lost to them, because there might not have been, in various supposable cases, militia officers in the service, of whom the courts martial could have been formed.

On the 15th of July, 1812, General Dearborn wrote letters of the following tenor to the governors of Massachusetts and Connecticut—

"*Head Quarters, Boston, July* 15, 1812.

"*Having received orders to leave the sea-coast,* where I was ordered for the purpose of taking the necessary measures for placing the towns and garrisons in a state of defence against the invasion or attack of the enemy, and to repair to Albany—it becomes my duty again to request your excellency to order out such part of your states' quota of detached militia as the present state of war requires. The numbers I had the honour to state to your excellency, in my letter of the 22d ult. *As other objects will require the service of a great part of the regular troops, it will become my duty to order them from the sea-board,* and, of course, *I must leave some part of the coast with less protection against those depredating parties of the enemy, that may attempt invasion for the mere purpose of plunder, than prudence would have justified,* if a suitable number of the militia should not be ordered out in conformity with the views and intentions of the President of the United States, as heretofore expressed. If your excellency shall consider it expedient to have the militia turned out for the proposed purposes, I will with pleasure afford all the aid in my power, for effecting the intended objects, consistently with the orders I have received. As early an answer as your excellency can make convenient, will be desirable.

"I have the honor to be,

"Very respectfully, your Excellency's

"Most obedient servant,

"H. DEARBORN, *Major General.*"

It will be recollected, that when the war was declared, it was professedly for the purpose of forcing Great Britain to revoke her orders in council, and to abandon the practice of impressment. In order to accomplish these objects, the nation at large was subjected to the various calamities which an offensive war necessarily brings upon any country. But the Atlantic coast was exposed to all the evils which a powerful maritime enemy, having the absolute command of the ocean, might be disposed to inflict upon a defenceless foe. It would have been natural, under such circumstances, to expect that the government which had declared the war, would at least have taken all possible care to guard against invasions and depredations along the sea-shore;—especially as the large towns and cities, and the oldest and wealthiest settlements, lay very near to the ocean, and of course were peculiarly exposed to hostile attacks. Instead of which, within less than a month after the declaration of war, the letter above recited was forwarded by the commander in chief of the American army to the chief magistrates of two of the New-England states, informing them that he had received orders to leave the sea-coast, and to repair to Albany; and adding, that as other objects besides the defence of the coast would require the service of a great part of the regular troops, it would become his duty to order those troops from the sea-board, and that this must leave some part of the coast with less protection against those depredating parties of the enemy, who might attempt invasion for the mere purpose of plunder, *than prudence would justify.* Hence he urges the detachment of the militia, which had been previously called for. If any new or additional motive could have been necessary to induce those states to proceed with the strictest caution, and to guard against any unconstitutional demand for the militia, it might have been found in this letter. The coast of New-England, stretching from New-Brunswick to the border of the state of New-York, may be considered as between six and seven hundred miles in length; and the property upon it which would be exposed to the depredations of an enemy, was undoubtedly many times greater than lay in the same predicament upon the coast south of New-York, to the Gulf of Mexico. And yet, the small force which the national government had stationed upon that coast, was ordered away in pursuit of other objects—that is the conquest of Canada—and the inhabitants left exposed to the miseries of invasion and depredation. And this measure of depriving the eastern coast of the United States troops, in a time of war, which had been stationed there for their protection and security in a time of peace, was adopted at the very moment when, if the assertion of the chief magistrate of the Union was to be credited, there was the greatest need of their exertions for the public safety ; for in a letter from the Secretary of War to Lieutenant Governor Smith of Connecticut, dated July 14th, 1812—one day after the date of the foregoing letters to the governors of Massachusetts and Connecticut —that officer says he was instructed by the President to state to Governor Smith, that *there was at that time, imminent danger of the invasion of the country;* and this was advanced as a reason why the militia of those states should be ordered out agreeably to the call made by General Dearborn.

Could any thing be more preposterous than such conduct as this ? Had it been in the power of the government of the United States to conquer the Canadas, they would have been worthless compared with the value of the country and the settlements upon the New-England coast. And events very speedily proved the weakness and absurdity of the attempts to invade and subdue the British provinces. Disaster and disgrace overtook our forces ; and the conquest of the Canadas, weak and unprotected as they were, was soon found to be altogether chimerical. Instead of victors, our forces were led from the field as prisoners of war; and the people on the frontiers were placed in great hazard of invasion, from the very enemy against whom offensive war had been declared.

Little as the New-England states had been satisfied with the origin of the war, they had still less reason to be pleased with the manner of carrying it on. In a very short time it became apparent that they must defend themselves, or be left at the mercy of the foreign enemy. It was equally apparent, that if the President of the United States had the constitutional right to call forth the hundred thousand militia, under the act of Congress of April 10th, 1812, put them under command of United States officers, and march them to any point or station which he might think proper, the states would have been entirely deprived of their natural and legitimate means of defence, and left exposed to the inroads of the enemy wherever they should think proper to visit their coasts, and invade their territory. It therefore became a matter of not only constitutional right, but of self-security in the New-England states, exposed as they were, to meet the evils with which they were threatened at the threshold. Accordingly, in Connecticut, the opinion and advice of the council of the state were taken; and in Massachusetts, in pursuance of the practice of that state in times of emergency, the case was submitted to the supreme court of the state, for their decision upon the following questions—

" 1. Whether the commanders in chief of the militia of the several states have a right to determine whether any of the exigencies contemplated by the constitution of the United States exist, so as to require them to place the militia, or any part of it, in the service of the United States, at the request of the President, to be commanded by him, pursuant to acts of Congress?

" 2. Whether, when either of the exigencies exist authorizing the employing the militia in the service of the United States, the militia thus employed can be lawfully commanded by any officers but of the militia, except by the President of the United States ?"

The court, consisting of three very eminent judges, viz. Theophilus Parsons, Samuel Sewall, and Isaac Parker, gave it as their opinion, that the commanders in chief of the several states had the right to decide whether any of the constitutional exigencies existed, which authorized the calling forth of the militia. In our judgment, there were many strong reasons in favour of this opinion; one of which may be found in the following letter from the Secretary of War to Lieutenant-Governor Smith, of Connecticut—

" *War Department, July 14th*, 1812.

Sir,—I have the honour to acknowledge your letter of the 2d inst. The absence of his excellency Governor Griswold, ' on account of ill health,' is seriously to be regretted, particularly at this important crisis, when his prompt assurances of obeying the requisition of the President, to call into the service of the United States such detachments of militia as might be required, conformably to the act of April 10th, 1812, through General Dearborn, are interrupted and suspended by your honour.

" The reason assigned for refusing to execute the engagements of his excellency Governor Griswold, appear not less extraordinary than the act itself. After a declaration of war against a nation possessed of powerful and numerous fleets, a part of which were actually on our coast, had been promulgated, and officially communicated to the executive of the state, the assertion made by your honour, ' that the governor is not informed that *the United States are in imminent danger of invasion*,' was not to have been expected. To remove all doubt from your mind on this subject, *I am instructed by the President, to state to you that such danger actually exists ;* and to request that the requisition of General Dearborn, made by his special autho-

rity for calling into the service of the United States certain
detachments of militia from the state of Connecticut, be
forthwith carried into effect.

" The right of the state to officer the militia, is clearly
recognized in the requisition of General Dearborn. The
detachments, when marched to the several posts assigned
them, with their proper officers appointed conformably to
the laws of the state, will command, or be commanded,
according to the rules and articles of war, and the usages
of service.

" I have the honour to be,
" Respectfully, sir, your obedient servant,
" W. EUSTIS.

" His Honor John Cotton Smith,
    Sharon, Connecticut."

At the date of this letter, war had been declared but
four weeks. The fact that such an event had occurred
was not known to the government of Great Britain, and
of course, no measures could have been adopted by that
government for the invasion of our country, or even for the
prosecution of hostile measures of any description towards
the United States. With what propriety then could it be
said, that this country was in *imminent danger of invasion*
on the 14th of July, 1812? It was not true. "Imminent
danger" means danger near at hand, threatening, immediate. Under no circumstances could an order for the
invasion of the territory of the United States be expected
from Great Britain in less than five or six weeks after the
14th of July. Whatever danger, therefore, there might
have been of eventual invasion, it was then remote, and
not imminent; and therefore the declaration in the letter
above alluded to was not warranted by facts. But it is to
be presumed from the circumstances of the case, that if it
had been considered necessary at the time, the same declaration would have been made when General Dearborn

wrote his letters to the governors of Massachusetts and Connecticut, calling for the respective quotas of militia from those states, viz. on the 22d of June, four days after the declaration of war.

On the 17th of July General Dearborn addressed the following letter to Lieutenant Governor Smith—

" Head Quarters, Boston, July 17, 1812.

" HON. JOHN COTTON SMITH.

" SIR,—Being disposed to obviate as far as my authority extends, the objection to turning out the companies, required from the state of Connecticut, in my letter to Governor Griswold of the 22d June ult. I renew my requisition to your honor as acting governor in the absence of his excellency Governor Griswold, and request that you would turn out the number of companies proposed in my letter above alluded to; and that those companies destined for Fort Trumbull may be commanded by one of the majors that shall have been detached with your state's quota.

" I have the honour, Sir, to be respectfully
        " Your most obedient servant,
                " H. DEARBORN, *Major General.*"

To this letter, the following answer was returned—

" Lyme, 22d August, 1812.

" SIR,—Your two letters of the 15th and 17th of July were put into my hands immediately after my return from the state of New York; but accidentally were left at Hartford, without having been acknowledged. No inconvenience however could have resulted, as the answer to the letter of the Secretary of War, of the 14th of July, expressed the determination of the government of this state, on the points you had suggested.

" I have therefore only to express my satisfaction of the readiness with which you proposed to give the command of the companies required for New-London, to a major of our own ; together with your disposition to make every necessary provision for the defence of the sea-coast. And on all occasions, I shall be happy to co-operate with you in such measures as our defence may require.

" I have the honour to be, with high respect,
" Your obedient and humble servant,
  (Signed)   " ROGER GRISWOLD."
" GENERAL DEARBORN."

On the 4th of August, 1812, Governor Griswold again convened the council, and submitted to their consideration the letter of the Secretary of War of the 14th, and those of the 15th and 17th of July from General Dearborn, which have already been quoted, and received from them the following report—

" *At a meeting of the Governor and Council of the state of Connecticut, held at Hartford on the fourth day of August, A. D.* 1812.

" A letter from the Secretary of War addressed to his honor the Lieutenant-Governor, dated July 14th, 1812, and two letters from Major-General Dearborn, one dated July 15th, addressed to his excellency the Governor, and one dated July 17th, addressed to his honor, the Lieutenant-Governor, have been submitted by his excellency the Governor to this board, for their consideration and advice. They all relate to the subject of ordering five companies of the militia of this state into the service of the United States. It is obvious that the claim for the services of the militia is made on the ground that war has been declared by the Congress of the United States against Great Britain. No place in this state, or in the United States, has been particularly designated as in danger of being invaded. The danger which exists is that alone which arises from a state of war thus declared ; and exists throughout the

United States, and will continue, so long as the war shall last. To provide against this supposed danger of invasion five companies of militia are required.

" They are required to do ordinary garrison duty at the forts at New-London and New-Haven. Upon the same principle, that the militia may be called for, to march to these places and do this duty, they may be called for, to march to any place within the United States, to perform the same duty, and this, from time to time, and at all times, during the continuance of the war. It will not escape attention that this requisition is not made for a portion of the militia, *most convenient to the place of danger or scene of action*, pursuant to the act of Congress, approved February 28th, 1795, but is made upon the Governor of this state, for a portion of the militia detached, pursuant to an act of Congress passed the 10th day of April, 1812, and liable by the terms of that act, to be called into the service of the United States, when, and only when one of the *exigencies provided by the Constitution shall occur*. By the Constitution of the United States, those exigencies are, *to execute the Laws of the Union, suppress Insurrections, and repel Invasions*. It is believed that the militia of this state would be among the first to perform their constitutional duties, and not among the last to understand and justly appreciate their constitutional rights. Should any portion of this state be invaded or menaced with invasion by a foreign power, the militia would not wait for a requisition, but hasten with alacrity to the place invaded or threatened, to meet and repel it. Of this spirit his excellency the Governor would doubtless receive prompt evidence, in the execution of the laws of this state, should the necessity unhappily arise. But if the Congress of the United States have seen fit to exercise the power *to declare war*, before they have carried into execution another provision of the Constitution *to raise and support armies*, it does not follow that the militia are bound to enter their forts and garrisons to perform ordinary garrison duty, and wait for an invasion, which may never happen.

"Whatever may be the disposition of this state, or the militia thereof, to render voluntary services under state authority to carry on the war in which this country is unhappily engaged, it is surely important that when *demands* are made by the administration of the government of the United States, they should be found to be strictly within the constitution of the United States, and while obedience shall be promptly yielded to all its requirements, that the constitution and sovereignty of this state should not be impaired or encroached upon—That the powers '*delegated to the United States*' may be exercised, and the powers '*reserved to the states respectively*' may be retained. And as no information has been given, and none is in possession of this board, that any part of this state is invaded, or that any other danger exists than that which arises from a declaration of war made by the Congress of the United States against Great Britain, and the suggestion that a part of her fleet has been on the coast of the United States, and as the militia are called for, not to repel invasion, but to perform ordinary garrison duty, the Council are of opinion that it does not consist with 'the powers retained' by this state to order its militia into the service of the United States, on the requisition of any of the officers of the United States, in a case not demanded by the constitution. And until such case occurs, the Council advise his excellency the Governor to retain the militia of this state under his own command, and decline a compliance with the requisition of the Secretary of War and Major-General Dearborn. Passed in the Council.

"Attest.   THOMAS DAY, *Secretary.*"

In this state of things, Governor Griswold called an extra session of the General Assembly of Connecticut, on the fourth Tuesday of August, 1812, on which occasion he transmitted to them the following message—

" Message of his Excellency Governor Griswold, to the General Assembly, with the Documents accompanying the same.

" GENTLEMEN OF THE COUNCIL, MR. SPEAKER, AND GENTLEMEN OF THE HOUSE OF REPRESENTATIVES.

" Several important matters, growing out of the war in which we are unhappily engaged, appear to demand the immediate attention of the legislature ; and although aware of the expense and inconvenience attending a meeting of the General Assembly at this season of the year, and at a time so near the fall session, yet, I trust, that on a full examination of all the circumstances, it will appear that the measure has become highly expedient. To render our public concerns, however, intelligible, it will be necessary to unfold the events which have attended us.

" It is known to the Assembly, that on the 10th of April last, Congress passed an act to detach one hundred thousand militia for the service of the United States, and that three thousand men, the quota of this state, agreeably to the orders of the President, were promptly detached, and held in readiness, for the exigencies pointed out by the constitution and the law.

" The act of Congress, and the measures regarding it, were communicated at the last session, and will be again laid before you. After your adjournment, a letter was received from the War Department, dated June 12th, transferring the duty of calling for the men to General Dearborn, and requesting that his requisition might therefore be complied with.

" As nothing appeared in this communication, but a wish of the President to confide this duty to an officer of rank, who it was understood, would be charged with the general command of the troops in the northern states, and as it could not be expected that the President would authorize an order which should be repugnant to the constitution ; I did not hesitate to inform the Secretary of War, that any requisition which the President might make through General Dearborn should be complied with.

" Soon after these transactions, at a time when I was pursuing a journey for my health, a letter was received from General Dearborn, requiring four companies of the drafted militia to march, and to be placed under the command of the officer commanding at Fort Trumbull at New-London, and one company to march for the battery near New-Haven. An attention to the terms of General Dearborn's letter fully satisfied me, that the requisition was unconstitutional and could not be complied with. I had long noticed that important provision in the constitution of the United States, which authorizes the President to call into service the militia, ' to repel invasions, suppress insurrections, and to aid in the execution of the laws ;' and it was with satisfaction I had noticed that the act of Congress had strictly followed the principle of the constitution.

"But although I entertained no doubts regarding my duty, yet as I viewed the step which it became necessary to take, highly important, it became proper for me to obtain the reasonings and opinions of the Council on the occasion.

" That body was accordingly convened at Hartford, and it gave me great satisfaction to find that their opinions concurred with my own. Thinking it necessary, however, to pursue my journey, his honor, Governor Smith, was so good as to take the charge of the correspondence which had become necessary on the occasion ; and by his letter to the Secretary of War of the 2d of July, communicated the opinion entertained in this state, and our determination respecting the requisition.

" The Secretary in reply, dated July 14th, in language unusual, and altogether unexpected, appeared to claim a promise, contained in my letter of the 12th of June, to execute any requisition which should be made by General

Dearborn. This strange insinuation, which originated in expressions of civility to the President, and could not with decency have been omitted, was repelled. .

"In a letter from the War Department, the subject was also placed in a point of view which appeared to require a new consideration; and a second meeting of the Council was accordingly deemed necessary. The gentlemen comprising that body were again fully consulted, and every view of the subject has been taken of which it appeared susceptible, and we have been confirmed in the opinion which we first formed, and the Council has again advised that nothing has taken place to justify me in executing the requisition of General Dearborn.

"All the papers, to which I have referred, together with a general proclamation, concisely explaining the facts which have taken place, and the views which have been entertained at this important period, will be now communicated for your inspection.

"The importance of this measure, both as it regards the security of the state, and as it may also form a precedent on future occasions, rendered it highly important to consult the General Assembly.

"But the inconvenience of convening so large a body, and the early period of the fall session, induced me to submit to the temporary disadvantage of a delay, rather than subject the immediate representatives of the people to so much inconvenience. Several new circumstances, however, having arisen, which it appeared to me could not with propriety admit of delay; I have thought it my duty at this time to convene the legislative body, and I avail myself of the occasion to solicit your immediate attention to the proceedings of the council, and your deliberate opinion on the measure which has been taken. This becomes more immediately important, from the consideration, that if any errors have been committed, they may, at this time, be corrected without much inconvenience.

" The necessity of obtaining supplies of military stores on this emergency, in addition to those already on hand, will be universally felt ; and finding the price and scarcity rapidly increasing, I thought no consideration could justify a delay in calling the attention of the legislature immediately to that subject. It can scarcely be necessary to inform you that military stores are not to be expected from the general government ; and that we have reason to expect that the regular troops will be principally called from the sea-coast, and of course the state will be left to defend itself, if exposed to foreign invasion.

" It may also be observed that it is unwise to depend altogether upon the general government for the defence of our sea-coast.

" The extensive territory which it has been the national policy to grasp within our jurisdiction, and the great number of points requiring defence, together with an unhappy disposition to enlarge our extended frontier by new conquests, will probably demand all the military force in the power of government for similar objects. This appears to be the determination at this time, and the important business of garrisoning the coast must be left to the militia, or neglected.

" But if these essential interests are disregarded, we must not neglect ourselves ; and I trust that the present occasion will furnish the best reasons for improving the militia both in organization and discipline, and for obtaining ample supplies of arms and military stores, and placing ourselves on the best footing for defence. It is also proper to avail ourselves of every principle in the constitution for rendering our means effectual and the least inconvenient.

" Among other provisions in the constitution, it will be found, that in time of war the states may organize and support a military force of their own, and which cannot, under any circumstances, be controlled by the general government, and which may undoubtedly be applied in all cases to the defence of the State. Whether such a force will become immediately necessary, the general assembly will judge ; but as the subject can be examined and a plan partially digested without expense, and measures commenced for the speedy execution of the principle at an early but future session, I feel it my duty to recommend that subject to your consideration.

" In recommending this measure, it is far from my intention to propose that the state troops should at any time during the war be withheld from aiding the national and neighbouring state forces in the common defence ; but to increase the strength of those corps, and particularly to apply that body of men to our own defence, should our frontier at any future time be unhappily abandoned.

" Nor will it be understood that whilst I feel it my duty to recommend the necessary preparation for arraying every description of constitutional and military force which may be proper for our defence, that I wish to urge a step which may interfere with any liberal measure which the general government may take for the same object.

" To the general government we must and ought to look for our security ; and I trust that the time will come when a full knowledge of our resources will place the safety of our sea-coast on that naval defence which alone is capable of giving it complete security.

" Although it has been thought correct in this state, on ordinary occasions, for the state government to leave the national councils to pursue their own measures without interference, yet I submit to your consideration whether this is not an occasion on which that principle should be dispensed with, and whether it is not proper that the general assembly should, by a plain and decisive address to the President, express their own opinion and that of their constituents on the important questions which have recently occurred.

" It is certainly necessary that the public opinion should

be known by the President on the question of war; and it is presumed, when expressed by the legislature of a state, it will be respected.

"Whatever events, however, may take place, you may be satisfied that the faithful preservation of the public peace, a rigid and prompt execution of the laws under which we happily live, and which form our security, together with a strict adherence to our form of government and of the constitution of the United States, will compose the basis of the administration of government in this state.

"Trusting, gentlemen, that the God of our fathers will not desert us on this occasion, and that our safety is in Him, I have only to implore his guidance in all our proceedings, and his smiles on all our deliberations.

"ROGER GRISWOLD.

"*Extra Session, 4th Tuesday of August,* 1812."

This message was accompanied by the correspondence between the United States officers, civil and military, to which reference has been made, and extracts from which have been copied; and thus the whole was placed before the legislature of that state for their consideration. These documents were referred to a joint committee of the two houses, who made a long and able report on the general subject, and concluded by recommending the following resolution—

"Resolved, that the conduct of his excellency the governor, in refusing to order the militia of this state into the service of the United States, on the requisition of the Secretary of War and Major-General Dearborn, meets with the entire approbation of this assembly."

This resolution was adopted and passed by both houses. The general assembly also, in pursuance of the suggestion in the executive message, united at the same session in a declaration, in which they say, that "they believe it to be the deliberate and solemn sense of the people of the state," that "the war was unnecessary." The following passage is extracted from the abovementioned document—

"To the United States is delegated the power to call forth the militia to execute the laws, to suppress insurrection, and repel invasion. To the states respectively is reserved the entire controul of the militia, except in the cases specified. In this view of that important provision of the constitution, the legislature fully accord with the decision of his excellency the governor in refusing to comply with the requisition of the general government for a portion of the militia. While it is to be regretted that any difference of opinion on that subject should have arisen, the conduct of the chief magistrate of this state, in maintaining its immunities and privileges, meets our cordial approbation. The legislature also entertain no doubt that the militia of the state will, under the direction of the captain-general, be ever ready to perform their duty to the state and nation in peace or war. They are aware that in a protracted war, the burden upon the militia may become almost insupportable, as a spirit of acquisition and extension of territory appears to influence the councils of the nation, which may require the employment of the whole regular forces of the United States in foreign conquest, and leave our maritime frontier defenceless, or to be protected solely by the militia of the states.

" At this period of anxiety among all classes of citizens, we learn with pleasure that a prominent cause of the war is removed by a late measure of the British cabinet. The revocation of the orders in council, it is hoped, will be met by a sincere spirit of conciliation on the part of our administration, and speedily restore to our nation the blessings of a solid and honourable peace."

Almost immediately after the close of this session of the general assembly of Connecticut, an election of members of the house of representatives of that state occurred, when the returns showed, as far as evidence of public opinion can be derived from such a source, that the people of the state, by a very large majority, approved the course pursued by the governor and council with regard to the militia, and the measures adopted by the legislature at the extra session in the preceding month of August. The parties in the house stood—Federalists 163, Democrats 36 —leaving a majority of Federalists of 127.

At the regular session, which was held in October following, an act was passed to establish a military corps for the defence of the state. By it, the commander in chief of the state was authorised to raise, by voluntary enlistments, a military corps for the defence and protection of the state, to suppress insurrections and repel invasion, and compel obedience to the laws of the state, and of the United States, to consist of two regiments of infantry, four companies of artillery, and four troops of horse, to serve during the war, unless sooner discharged by law.

This act of the legislature was carried into effect, and a corps of about two thousand men was raised under it, who were completely officered and equipped, and in the course of the war performed very essential services to the United States, as well as to the state to which they belonged.

In July, 1812, the governor of Massachusetts issued a general order to the militia of that state, in which, after some preliminary remarks on the state of the country, and directing that the detachment of ten thousand men should be completed without delay—it is added,—that as that body of men, being to be raised throughout the state, could not be assembled to repel a sudden invasion, and it would be extremely burdensome to keep them constantly in service, and if they were assembled, they would not be adequate to the defence of the exposed points on a coast of several hundred miles in extent,—it was ordered that the officers of the whole militia of the state hold themselves, and the militia under their command, in constant readiness to assemble, and march to any part or parts of the state.

Congress assembled at Washington on the 4th of November, 1812. In the message to the houses on that occasion, the disputes with the New-England states relative to the militia were referred to in the following manner :—

" Among the incidents to the measures of the war, I am constrained to advert to the refusal of the governors of Massachusetts and Connecticut, to furnish the required detachments of militia towards the defence of the maritime frontier. The refusal was founded on a *novel* and *unfortunate exposition* of the provisions of the constitution relating to the militia. The correspondences which will be before you, contain the requisite information on the subject. It is obvious that if the authority of the United States to call into service and *command the militia* for the public defence, can be thus frustrated, even in a state of declared war, and of course *under apprehensions of invasion preceding war*, they are not one nation for the purpose most of all requiring it ; and that the public safety may have no other resource, than in those large and permanent military establishments which are forbidden by the principles of our free government, and against the necessity of which the militia were meant to be a constitutional bulwark."

This part of the message, which wears somewhat the appearance of a denunciation, was referred to a committee of the Senate, of which William B. Giles, of Virginia, was chairman, whose feelings were strongly in favour of the administration, and in support of their measures, and particularly of the war. That this gentleman, from the peculiarity of his temper, as well as the feelings and sentiments entertained by him, would gladly have seized this opportunity to manifest his animosity against the New-England politicians, no one acquainted with him can doubt. But after keeping the subject before the committee during the whole session, it was suffered to pass away without any report, or even the recommendation of a resolution of censure upon the course pursued by the governments of the New-England states.

And it is apparent, from the language of the message itself, that the President found some difficulty in placing the subject in a satisfactory manner before the national legislature. It says, " the refusal of the governors of Massachusetts and Connecticut to furnish the required detachments of militia towards the defence of the maritime frontier, was founded on *a novel and unfounded exposition of the provisions of the constitution relating to the militia.*" If the exposition given by those governors was novel, it was probably owing to the fact, that no such call for the militia had previously been made. Being made under such circumstances, it must necessarily have been novel. That it was unfortunate, depends upon the question whether it was sound, and conformable to the letter and spirit of the constitution ? If such was its character, however unfortunate it may have been for the policy of the administration, or the objects they had in view, it must be considered as quite otherwise for the country, and emphatically so for the militia—which will be allowed to be objects of much higher moment than the views or the popularity of any individuals for the time entrusted with the administration of the government.

The militia are composed of the whole male inhabitants of the states, between the ages of eighteen and forty-five— that is, of the active physical force of the union. They are the inhabitants of the states in which they reside, and they belong to the several states. By the second section of the second article of the constitution of the United States, it is provided that—" The President shall be commander in chief of the navy and army of the United States, and of *the militia of the several states,* when called into the actual service of the United States." Here the militia are described, in the constitution itself, as *belonging to the several states,* and the national government have no authority over them, beyond that which the several states have relinquished to them in the constitution. Any attempt on the part of the national government, or of the President, to exercise such authority beyond that granted to them in the constitution, would be usurpation, and would render the individuals exercising it liable to the consequences of an usurpation of power.

The only cases mentioned in the constitution, in which the congress have the power to call the militia of the states into their service, are " to execute the laws of the Union, suppress insurrections, and repel invasions." These are cases in which the existence of the government and the safety of the country are in danger, and to preserve them this extraordinary power was vested in the national government. But aware of the danger that might arise in placing the whole military force of the country under the command of the national executive, it was wisely and prudently, and it may be added, fortunately provided, that the appointment of the officers of the militia should be reserved to the states respectively. By this reservation, the individual states were secured against the danger of having their own military forces taken from under their own immediate authority and controul, and placed under the command of men who, if so disposed, might turn them against the governments to which they belonged, and the communities of which they formed a part, and thus subvert and destroy their freedom and independence. It was manifestly the object of President Madison, when he called upon the governors of Massachusetts and Connecticut for their quotas of militia, under the act of Congress of April 10th, 1812, to take them away from their own officers, appointed under state authority, and put them under the command of United States officers, because, as has been shown, he took care in the call upon the first of those magistrates, to designate no officer of the rank which the number of troops required ; and in the call upon the second of them, to designate no officer of any rank, but to order the men to be placed immediately under the command of the United States officers in the garrisons at New-London and New-Haven. That such was his object appears to be clear and unquestionable, not only from the circumstances already alluded to, but from the language of the message above recited. It is there said—" It is obvious that if the authority of the United States to call into service *and command* the militia for the public defence, can be thus frustrated, even in a state of declared war, and of course under apprehensions of invasion preceding war, they are not one nation for the purpose most of all requiring it." The object was not only to call the militia into service, but into *the command* of the United States. A defeat in the attempt to accomplish these objects, President Madison says, would show that the United States were not one nation for the purpose most of all requiring it. " In such a state of things," he adds, "the public safety may have no other resource than in those large and permanent military establishments which are forbidden by the principles of our free government, and against the necessity of which the militia were meant to be a constitutional bulwark." What is meant by the expression of " *apprehensions of invasion preceding war*," is not very apparent. The constitution contains no provision for calling forth the militia, in the case of " apprehension of invasion preceding war." The language of that instrument is " to repel invasion." It does not require a military force to repel an invasion which exists only in the fears or imagination of an individual, even if that individual should be placed at the head of the government ; and above all things, when such an invasion is apprehended *before war takes place.*

As it regards the militia, no doubt can be entertained by those who are uninfluenced by party feelings or selfish interests, the conduct of the governors of Massachusetts and Connecticut will be considered as of the highest im-

portance. The duties of the militia of the several states
to the United States, are described in the clause of the
constitution which has been quoted. They are few, and
easily understood. When there occurs, in any portion of
the Union, such a degree of resistance to the execution of
the laws of the United States, as cannot be overcome by
the ordinary means which the laws provide, it is the duty
of the national government to call forth the militia to enforce that execution. In the event of a domestic insurrection against the government, which is too formidable to
be quelled in any other mode, resort must be had to the
militia for the accomplishment of the object. And when
the country is invaded by a foreign enemy, upon a constitutional call from the national government, it is the duty
of the militia to repair to the place where the hostile in-
road has occurred, and repel the invader. Beyond these
specific services, the United States have not, and cannot
have, any claim upon the militia for military services.
But there is nothing in the constitution that implies a
power in the President of the United States to call the
militia into the field, when there are in his mind *apprehensions of an invasion* by a foreign nation, *preceding war.*
Much less is there any authority in the constitution to take
the militia from their homes, and away from their officers,
shut them up in garrisons, under the command of United
States officers, subject to the services and the duties of a
standing army, and liable to the provisions and penalties
of the "Rules and Articles of War." If there is any
thing valuable in being secured against any future attempt
to exercise this unconstitutional power over the militia, if
there is any gratification to the minds of free citizens of a
free republic, in being exempt from all liability to the de
gradation of being forced into a standing army, and held
in bondage under the despotic government which always
controuls and regulates standing armies, they will be indebted for these privileges and this security to the firm,

independent, dignified stand taken by those virtuous and upright New-England magistrates.

On the 2d of August, 1812, the United States frigate Constitution, commanded by Captain Isaac Hull, sailed on a cruise from the harbour of Boston. On the 19th of that month he fell in with the British frigate Guerriere, Captain Dacres, and after a short but severe engagement captured her. This brilliant achievement, as was perfectly natural, caused great exultation throughout the country, and particularly among the friends of the administration; and much merit was claimed on their behalf for such a splendid victory over the "Empress of the ocean." No person probably doubted that the Constitution, as well as others of our ships of war, had been ordered to cruise in quest of the enemy, in order to give them specimens of our skill and bravery upon their favourite element. As far as can be ascertained, no such orders were given, certainly in the case of the abovementioned vessel.

At the time when war was declared, the Constitution lay at Annapolis in Maryland. On that day, the following letter was addressed from the Navy Department to Captain Hull—

" Navy Department, 18th of June, 1812.

" This day war has been declared between the United empire of Great Britain, Ireland, and their dependencies, and the United States of America, and their territories. And you are, with the force under your command, entitled to every belligerent right—to attack, and capture, and to defend. You will use the most despatch to reach New-York, after you have made up your complement of men, &c. at Annapolis. In your way from thence, you will not fail to notice the British flag, should it present itself. I am informed that the Belvidera is on our coast, but you are not to understand me as *impelling you to battle*, previously to your having confidence in your crew, unless attacked; or with a reasonable prospect of success, of which you are to be, at your discretion, the judge.

" You are to reply to this, and inform me of your progress.

"P. HAMILTON.

"Captain Hull, of the United States Frigate Constitution."

On the 3d of July, 1812, the following letter was written to Captain Hull—

"*Navy Department, 3d July,* 1812.

" As soon as the Constitution is ready for sea, you will weigh anchor, and proceed to New-York.

" If on your way thither, you should fall in with an enemy's vessel, you will be guided in your proceedings by your own judgment, bearing in mind however, that you are not voluntarily to encounter a force superior to your own. On your arrival at New-York, you will report yourself to Commodore Rodgers. If he should not be in that port, you will remain there till further orders.

"P. HAMILTON.

"Captain Isaac Hull, Annapolis."

These orders extended no further than to sailing the Constitution from Annapolis to New-York ; and great care is taken by the Secretary of the Navy to let Captain Hull understand, that upon the passage to the latter port, he must *act upon his own discretion,* if he should fall in with any British vessels—that he was not to be understood as *impelling Captain Hull to battle, previously to having confidence in his crew, unless attacked ;* that he must *act upon his own judgment,* at the same time *not voluntarily to encounter a force superior to his own.* Here is certainly a praise-worthy degree of precaution, manifested by the Secretary of the Navy, against risk and responsibility, but no encouragement to fighting. That any further orders were given to Captain Hull, between the 3d of July and the 2d of August, is hardly to be supposed. If there were such, they can be produced. If there were not, all the credit of this gallant exploit is due to Captain Hull, and not the slightest portion of it to the administration.

No special credit, however, was ever given to that brave and meritorious officer, on the score of his having gone upon this enterprise upon his own responsibility, and without the orders of the government. A satisfactory reason may be given for this reserve on the part of the latter on this subject. The Constitution having sailed without orders, had she been unsuccessful, the misfortune would have been justly ascribed to the rashness of her commander; if successful, the country would of course suppose that she had been ordered by the government on the cruise, and the glory of the victory would redound to their credit, as well as to that of the officers and crew.

This sketch of the manner in which the government of the United States commenced their warlike operations in the eastern states, will satisfy any person that it was not calculated to render the war, or the administration, popular in that portion of the Union. The plan of removing the United States troops from the Atlantic coast, in order to march them to the frontiers of Canada, and thus leave the inhabitants for several hundred miles upon the coast exposed to the horrors of invasion, could not, in the nature of things, reconcile them to a war which they originally considered unnecessary and extremely impolitic. The result of the choice of representatives for the state legislature in Connecticut, in September, 1812, showed what was the tone of public feeling in that state. Governor Griswold died during the October session of the general assembly, and of course was placed beyond the reach of human applause or censure, for the share he had borne in the transactions which have been alluded to. But the votes of the freemen of that state, during the remainder of the war, showed, in the most conclusive manner, their decided approbation of the measures he had recommended, and the course he had pursued, for the security of the militia, and for the protection and preservation of the constitutional rights of the state.

And such also was the state of things in Massachusetts. In 1812, at an election which was held more than two months before the declaration of war, Governor Strong was chosen by a majority of 1,370 votes only. In 1813, he received a majority of 13,974. In 1814, though opposed by a federalist of distinguished talents and character, his majority was 10,421. In October, 1814, the house of representatives of the state legislature passed a resolution approving of Governor Strong's conduct, in relation to the defence of the state, by a vote of 222 to 59. At the same session, a resolution authorising the governor to raise ten thousand men for the defence of the state, passed the same body by a vote of 252 to 71.

In the month of June, 1813, a detachment of ships from the United States navy, consisting of the frigates United States and Macedonian, and the sloop of war Hornet, under the command of Commodore Decatur, in attempting to pass through Long Island Sound to the ocean, found a British squadron at the entrance into the Sound, of such force that it became necessary for the former to take refuge in New-London harbour. As the garrisons in and near that port were not sufficient to resist the British squadron on that station, strong apprehensions were entertained that the latter would force their way into the harbour, for the purpose of destroying the United States ships. Those ships, by way of precaution, were moved up the river Thames, several miles above New-London; and application was immediately made to Governor Smith, the successor to Governor Griswold, for a military force to defend the city of New-London, and to protect the United States squadron. Orders were issued without delay for the detachment of a large body of militia, to be stationed at and near New-London. This detachment, drawn partly from the troops raised for the defence of the state, and the residue from the militia, were speedily in the field, and were placed under the command of Major-General Williams of the militia; and from that time until the departure of the squadron from the harbour of New-London, which was not until after the peace, a large military force was kept in service by the state, for the security of the United States ships of war blockaded at New-London.

During the year 1813, Brigadier General Burbeck, of the United States army, commanded in the "military district," in which Connecticut was included. This means that he resided as titular commander of a certain portion of country which for the occasion was called a "military district," but in which the United States had very few troops,—the appointment having been, beyond a doubt, for the purpose of having a United States officer on the spot, to take the command of the militia whenever they might be ordered into the service of the nation. No difficulty, however, occurred during that year, between General Williams and General Burbeck on the score of precedence; and at the close of the year, the expenses of the campaign were allowed and paid by the United States.

In 1814, General Burbeck having been removed to another station, the command at New-London was placed in the hands of Brigadier-General Cushing. The harbour of New-London was still blockaded, and the United States' squadron still required protection. In the month of April, a body of sailors and marines from the British fleet in the Sound, entered Connecticut river, and landed at a village in the town of Saybrook, a few miles above the mouth of the river, where they destroyed a considerable number of merchant vessels, which were there laid up, and retreated before any force was brought to attack or resist them. At this time Long-Island Sound was under the absolute controul of the British cruizers. In August following, an attack was made upon Stonington, the easternmost town in Connecticut, bordering on the sea-shore, by a number of British armed ships under the command of Commodore Hardy, which was repulsed with great gallantry by a small body of militia, hastily assembled there for the purpose. This movement of the enemy excited strong apprehensions for the safety of the squadron in the Thames; and a call was forthwith made by General Cushing upon Governor Smith for a detachment of militia for its security.

On the 4th of July, 1814, the following circular was addressed to the governors of several of the states—

"*War Department, July* 14th, 1814.

"Sir,—The late pacification in Europe, offers to the enemy a large disposable force, both naval and military, and with it the means of giving to the war here, a character of new and increased activity and extent.

"Without knowing with certainty that such will be its application, and still less that any particular points will become the objects of attack, the President has deemed it advisable, as a measure of precaution, to strengthen ourselves on the line of the Atlantic, and (as the principal means of doing this will be found in the militia) to invite the executive of certain states to organize and hold in readiness, for immediate service, a corps of 93,500 men, under the laws of February, 1795, and the 18th of April, 1814.

"The enclosed detail will show your excellency what, under this requisition, will be the quota of ——

"As far as uniform volunteer companies can be found, they will be preferred.

"The expediency of regarding (as well as in the designations of the militia as of their places of rendezvous) the points, the importance or the exposure of which will be most likely to attract the views of the enemy, need but be suggested.

" A report of the organization of your quota, when completed, and of its place or places of rendezvous, will be acceptable.

" I have the honour to be, &c.

" JOHN ARMSTRONG."

" His Excellency the Governor of ——."

" Detail of militia service, under the requisition of July 4th, 1814. Connecticut, 3 regiments, viz. 300 artillery, 2,700 infantry, total 3,000. General staff, 1 Major General, 1 Brigadier General, 1 Deputy Quartermaster General, 1 Assistant Adjutant General."

By this order from the War Department, it appears that 3,000 men were considered as forming a division, or in other words, a Major General's command. This would of course make 1,500 a brigade, or Brigadier General's command. The requisition from General Cushing, upon Governor Smith, was for seventeen hundred of the three thousand men specified in the official call from the Secretary of War—outnumbering a brigade, and therefore having a legal claim to be commanded by a Major General;—and this more especially as there was but one Brigadier General detailed in that order. Doubtless Brigadier General Cushing believed that no officer of higher rank than himself was necessary, and therefore took care in his requisition, not to call for any officer who should take rank above himself. In the course of the summer, in consequence of the alarm produced by the hostile operations of the British, other detachments of the militia were ordered to various other points, until the whole number in the service amounted to twenty-three or twenty-four hundred men. This was considerably larger than that of the preceding year. Being therefore warranted in the measure by the example of 1813, when the whole number of men was smaller, and by the conduct of the national government in paying the troops of that year, as well as by the large body of men in the field, a Major General was ordered to take the command. And when, in addition to these considerations, it is recollected that all, or nearly all the expense of both years was incurred in defence of the national property vested in Decatur's squadron, no person could have suspected that so material a distinction could have been drawn between the cases, as that the expenses of one year would have been paid without hesitation, and those of the other peremptorily refused. Such, however, was the fact; and the state was left, after all the burdens which had been thrown upon them by a war, the justice of which they questioned, and the policy of which they entirely condemned, to provide for the support of the whole body of militia ordered into the service of the United States, and essentially for the security of their ships of war, during the year 1814. The change of conduct in the government of the United States on the foregoing subject, may perhaps be accounted for, at least in part, by the occurrence of peace just after the close of the year 1814. The intelligence that peace had been concluded, relieved them from all apprehensions of further embarrassments from the continuance of hostilities; and this afforded an opportunity for the administration to manifest their resentment for the measures pursued in the New-England states, on the subject of the war, and particularly in regard to the militia.

In the year 1817 agents were appointed by the state of Massachusetts, to present the claim of that state for a remuneration for the expenditure which had been incurred for the various detachments of militia for the defence of the state, during the war. After alluding to the call by General Dearborn, in 1812, which has already been adverted to, those agents, in the representation accompanying their claim, remark—

" The next request received by the governor, was in

July, 1814, when the probability of attack having increased, the general requested eleven hundred men might be
ordered out for the defence of the more exposed parts of
the sea-coast—this order was complied with, the troops
placed under the authority of the United States, and the
service performed ; part of the said troops, to the number
requested by General Dearborn, having been stationed at
Castine and Machias, prior to the capture of those places
by the enemy.

"On the 5th of September, 1814, General Dearborn
again made a requisition on the governor of Massachusetts,
for a body of militia, when the general order No. 2, herewith presented, was issued on the 6th of the same month,
and every measure taken to guard against the attacks of
the enemy,—a considerable body of the elite of the militia from the interior, was ordered into immediate service,
and marched and encamped on the sea-board, and the
whole of the militia were enjoined to hold themselves in
constant readiness, and were called upon ' by every motive
of the love of country, of honour, and sympathy for their
fellow-citizens, who might be suffering the perils of war,
to maintain the most perfect state of preparation, and to
move when called to the scene of action with the utmost
celerity ;' but the difficulties which had arisen, and the
complaints that had been made, from placing the militia
in the immediate service of the United States, under United States officers, on former occasions, had been such as
to induce the belief, it would be inexpedient, if not hazardous, to repeat the order, without having the power to
enforce it ; an arrangement was, however, subsequently
made with General Dearborn, to place part of the militia
in the forts of the United States in the harbour of Boston,
under the direction of his son, General H. A. S. Dearborn,
and the very efficient body of troops beforementioned, were
stationed in the vicinity of the forts.

"A fourth requisition was made by General Dearborn

to guard the prisoners at Pittsfield, but the same causes as in the other case, in addition to the belief, that in the midst of a thickly settled population, the danger of escape from the existing guard, or of insurrection, did not require a compliance with the call—the event verified the soundness of the opinion.

"These are all the calls for the militia which are known to have been made, and it is believed it can be shown, that the omission to place the militia in the service of the United States was a matter of form rather than of fact—that the protection of the country was never for a moment abandoned, and that the militia were assembled and in readiness to act, whenever emergencies appeared to require them, that the arrangements adopted were judicious, and in several instances predicated upon the wishes of the officers of the United States, or of those who had the confidence of the general government."—

The authorities of Massachusetts and Connecticut have been so often charged with having refused to order out the militia of those states, upon the call of the President of the United States, and they have been so frequently and so loudly reproached for this conduct, that there are good reasons for believing that a great proportion of the inhabitants of the United States, and especially that large number of them who have come upon the stage of active life since the close of the war of 1812, have been fully impressed with the idea that the militia of those states were never in the field during the war, but were entirely withheld from the public service. The facts which have been stated will serve to remove such an impression, wherever it may exist. The militia were never withheld from the public service, but in both states, when the exigencies of the times required, were in large numbers in the field. And in Connecticut, they were not merely encamped for the purpose of preventing or repelling invasion, but they were out in large numbers, for two successive seasons, for the purpose of defending the property of the United States, and preventing the destruction of the squadron of armed ships in the harbour of New-London. The refusal of the governors of those states to order out the militia, at the requisition of General Dearborn, in 1812, was on widely different ground. That ground has been already alluded to. It was solely because an attempt was made to take the militia away from their own officers, and to place them under the command of officers of the United States, thus depriving the states of their natural defenders, and the militia of their constitutional right, and in fact incorporating them into the standing army. Probably they were induced to take this course, by a wish to change the character of the war from defensive to offensive; and to accomplish this object, the absurd and ridiculous project of attempting to conquer the Canadas was devised. The result proved, that the character of the war was not easily altered. The first campaigns on that frontier, showed it to be as truly defensive on the inland frontier, as it was upon the Atlantic coast.

There was nothing in the mode of conducting the war that was in the slightest degree calculated to secure the confidence of the country, and especially of that part of it where it was the most unpopular. Neither the plan of general operations, nor the character of the men appointed to carry them into effect, had any tendency to convince the opponents of the war, that it would prove to be either honourable or advantageous to the United States. The military operations against Upper Canada, which was the first object of hostile movements, were not only disastrous, but in the highest degree disgraceful. One army, with its commander-in-chief, was captured almost without firing a shot; and very little reputation was gained the first season along the whole line of the inland frontier.

Instances of great bravery and good conduct occasionally occurred; but nothing appeared which manifested dis-

tinguished military talents, skill, or experience. In the
President's message at the opening of Congress in November, 1812, it is said—

"With these blessings [that is health, plenty, &c.] are
mingled the pressures and vicissitudes incident to the state
of war into which the United States *have been forced*, by
the perseverance of a foreign power in its system of injustice and aggression.

"Previous to its declaration it was deemed proper, as a
measure of precaution and forecast, that a considerable
force should be placed in the Michigan territory, with a
general view to its security, and, in the event of war, such
operations in the uppermost Canada as would intercept
the hostile influence of Great Britain over the savages,
obtain the command of the lake on which that part of
Canada borders, and maintain co-operating relations with
such forces as might be most conveniently employed against
other parts. Brigadier General Hull was charged with
this provisional service; having under his command a body
of troops, composed of regulars, and of volunteers from
the state of Ohio. Having reached his destination after
his knowledge of the war, and possessing discretionary
authority to act offensively, he passed into the neighbouring
territory of the enemy, with a prospect of easy and victorious progress. The expedition nevertheless terminated
unfortunately, not only in a retreat to the town and fort of
Detroit, but in the surrender of both, and of the gallant
corps commanded by that officer. The causes of this painful reverse will be investigated by a military tribunal.

" Our expectation of gaining the command of the lakes,
by the invasion of Canada from Detroit, having been disappointed, measures were instantly taken to provide on
them a naval force superior to that of the enemy. From
the talents and activity of the officer charged with this
object, every thing that can be done may be expected.
Should the present season not admit of complete success,

the progress made will ensure for the next a naval ascen-
dancy, where it is essential to our permanent peace with,
and control over the savages."

The mortification arising from the disasters on the
Canada frontier, were in some measure alleviated by the
success of some of our armed ships upon the ocean. The
victory obtained by the frigate Constitution, under the
command of Captain Hull, over the British frigate Guerriere, in the month of August, had a tendency to soothe
the irritable feelings of the administration, as well as those
of their friends who were ardently devoted to the prosecution of the war. Other brilliant achievements at sea
occurred, in a high degree honourable to our naval character ; but the capture o.' a few armed ships was calculated rather to prolong, than to shorten the contest ; and
to heighten, rather than allay the fears of the states upon
the sea-coast, of hostile visits and depredations from the
enemy.

No doubt can rest on any mind, that the government of
the United States expected to make a serious impression
on Great Britain, by carrying the war into the British
provinces. It appears by the above quotation from the
President's message, that General Hull was entrusted
"with discretionary powers to act offensively," and that
the object was to get "the command of the lakes by the
invasion of Canada from Detroit." And this may serve
to explain the reasons why orders were given to General
Dearborn, at so early a stage of the war, to march the
regular troops away from the Atlantic coast to the Canada
frontier, leaving the former entirely exposed to the invasions of the enemy, unless repelled by the forces of the
individual states adjoining that coast. Eventually those
invasions were made. It has been seen that Saybrook
and Stonington in Connecticut were the subjects of them,
and attempts were made to effect landings at other places
bordering upon Long Island Sound. In Massachusetts,

Castine, Machias, and Eastport, in the District of Maine, were all taken possession of by British forces, and the adjoining country, to a considerable extent, was threatened with subjugation, and of course was kept in a state of great alarm and apprehension.

In 1814, when invasions had actually occurred, and depredations were threatened along the New-England coast, and those states were left to depend exclusively upon their own means of defence, while the burdens arising from the military arrangements for their own security were becoming more and more severe, at such a moment, when the legal pecuniary demands of the government were fully exacted, the supplies and pay of the militia were withdrawn by the orders of the national government, and the whole weight of supporting them was, in a petulant fit of resentment, thrown upon the states. By this time defensive measures had become absolutely necessary, not only to secure the property, but the persons of the inhabitants along the coast. The character of the war, whether that war was originally necessary or unnecessary, just or unjust, had ceased to be an object of discussion or consideration. The inhabitants of the states where the declaration of war had been most pointedly condemned, were now placed in situations where considerations of a different nature came home with full force to their circumstances and feelings. Self-defence, the protection of their families and fire-sides, became objects of immediate and pressing necessity to the people near the Atlantic shore; and no sacrifices of a pecuniary nature, or of personal feeling, could stand in the way of individual or domestic security.

It would not be practicable, without far transcending the limits of this work, to give a minute and circumstantial history of the manner in which the military operations in the New-England states were conducted. In July, 1813, the British squadron off New-London was reinforced by the addition of several armed vessels, and consisted of two ships of the line, two frigates, a brig, and a number of transports. This, of course, excited great alarm among the inhabitants, as that city was far more exposed to an attack from the water, than the ships belonging to Decatur's squadron. On the first week in July Governor Smith had been employed in detaching a body of militia to New-London, and had left Hartford, the seat of government, for his residence in the western part of the state, when he received information from General Burbeck, the United States officer commanding at New-London, informing him that orders had been received from the Secretary of War for the discharge of the militia at that place. In less than a week after the receipt of the order, and the consequent dismission of the troops, the additional force which has been mentioned, arrived, and joined the British squadron. The alarm produced by this event, and the exposure of the city of New-London to an attack, induced General Burbeck to dispatch an express to Governor Smith, and request a detachment of militia for the protection of that city. A similar application was made on behalf of the inhabitants of New-London; and orders were immediately issued for a strong body of the militia to repair to that station. On the 20th of the same month Governor Smith convened the council, to confer with them on the state of affairs, and to submit to them the measures he had adopted in the emergency which had so recently occurred. They unanimously approved of his conduct; and advised him to detach an additional body of men for the defence of New-London.

How this dismission of the militia, and the subsequent sudden call for a new detachment, all occurring within the compass of a single week, is to be accounted for, has not been explained. Whether it was owing to a fit of caprice, or to some other cause which it was thought on the score of prudence required concealment, remains among the mysteries of the period. Until an explanation is made, the public must be left to form their own conclusions. To whatever other cause it may be ascribed, no person will charge it to the account of an eager solicitude, on the part of the national government, to protect the inhabitants on the sea-coast of the state, against the inroads of the enemy.

In his speech at the opening of the session of the general assembly of that state in October, 1813, Governor Smith alluded to the occurrences which have been mentioned, in the following manner—

" The cause which first occasioned the array of a military force at New-London has not ceased to operate. Accordingly, at the request of the general government, a considerable body of troops has been kept at that station. I have endeavoured, conformably to the advice of the council, to divide the duty between the militia and the military corps, and to spread detachments of the former over the several brigades. To men, however, who are accustomed to different pursuits, the service could not be otherwise than burdensome. The remark is particularly applicable to the regiments in the neighbourhood of New-London. From their proximity to the scene of action, they were of course first brought into the field, and although they were dismissed as speedily as circumstances would permit, yet the frequent alarms, produced by sudden augmentation of the enemy's force, as frequently compelled them to return. They have therefore suffered losses and privations which could be equalled only by the patience and magnanimity with which they were endured. Their hardships were unhappily increased by an occurrence, which, as it is intimately connected with these events, ought not to pass unnoticed. An order from the war department for the dismission of all the militia then on duty, arrived at the moment a detachment from the distant brigades was on the march to relieve those who had been so repeatedly called into service. Believing the general government had the right of determining what degree of force would suffice to protect the national property, and unwilling to obtrude the services of our citizens upon the public when they were not desired, especially in a season so very important to our husbandmen, I issued instructions giving full effect to the order. Scarcely however had the disbanded troops reached their several homes, before a request for the militia was renewed, enforced by an urgent petition from the principal inhabitants of New-London and Groton. This combined application I felt no disposition to refuse. The requisite aid was immediately ordered; but from the necessity of the case, men who had been just discharged, were obliged to repair again to the post of danger, and to remain until a new detachment could be levied and brought to their relief. The ground of this procedure is hitherto unexplained."

In the course of the session, a joint committee of the two houses was appointed to take into consideration the subject of the war, who made a report, from which the following passage is copied—

" The committee cannot forbear to express their opinion on a subject intimately connected with the object of their appointment. They consider the general plan of warfare adopted by the Administration of the National Government, as not conformable to the spirit of the constitution of the United States. That instrument was formed, and adopted, among other things, for the EXPRESS PURPOSE OF PROVIDING FOR THE COMMON DEFENCE OF THE NATION. The war in which we are now engaged, was *declared by the government of the United States.* The contest is with a nation possessed of an immense naval force, and capable of annoying us in no other manner than by means of that force. To its attacks a long extent of sea-coast, stretching from one extremity of the nation to the other, and containing a vast proportion of its population and wealth, was peculiarly exposed. Against the dangers and calamities of a war *thus declared*, and with such an enemy, the inhabitants of the cities, towns, villages, and plantations along that coast, had an undoubted and imperative right to such protection as the nation could provide Instead of which, the regular forces have been, almost without exception, ordered away from the Atlantic frontier, to the interior of the country, for the purpose of carrying hostilities into the territory of unoffending provinces, and in pursuit of conquests, which, if achieved, would probably produce no solid benefit to the nation; while the seacoast is left exposed to the multiplied horrors usually produced by an invading and exasperated enemy."

The events and transactions of 1814, immediately connected with the military operations in Connecticut, have been already adverted to. The burthens thrown upon the New-England states at the commencement of the war in 1812, had been increasing in weight and severity through the two following years, until, by the refusal of the national government to furnish supplies and pay for the troops employed in the defence of the coast, and particularly in Connecticut to protect the naval squadron near New-London, had become nearly intolerable. In the meantime the national government, embarrassed by the fruits of their own rashness, in declaring war when they were totally unprepared with the means of carrying it on with the least prospect of success, were driven to the necessity of raising money by loans, and this at an extravagant rate of premiums to the lenders. As a large portion of the wealth of the country was in the hands of men who considered the war not only unnecessary but unjust, application was of course made to this description of persons to advance the means of defraying the expenses to which it necessarily subjected the government. Voluntary loans by individuals who viewed the controversy in the light which has been alluded to, were to a great extent declined, and much clamour was raised, throughout a large part of the country, against them, for their want of patriotism in this course of conduct. It is a little remarkable that a charge of this description should be preferred, under the circumstances of the case, against individuals who were situated as the capitalists in the New-England states were. The government had, in their opinion, plunged the nation into a war unnecessarily, and without having previously made the requisite preparations for carrying it on with any reasonable hope of success. The war had exposed them to the most serious calamities from a naval enemy; and to increase the evils under which they laboured, the government had withdrawn their troops from the sea-coast, more immediately liable to hostile visitation, and left them to defend themselves, or to suffer all the horrors of invasion, while the national forces which ought to have defended and protected them, were despatched to a distant region, on a quixotic expedition, after adventures in no way likely to raise the reputation of the government, or to promote the substantial interests of the country. And to add to all these, during the year 1814, when the dangers were the most threatening, and the fears of the inhabitants on the coast were excited to the highest pitch, the government, in a fit of splenetic resentment, withheld all supplies of provisions and pay from the large bodies of militia thus forced into the field in self-defence. It certainly was presuming much when that government called upon the wealthy men of the eastern states to lend them money to expend in attempts to subdue the British provinces, at the same moment that the families and firesides of the latter were exposed to the inroads and devastations of an exasperated foe. Nor would an appeal to the feelings of patriotism be likely to add much force to a call of this description.

But on what ground is it, that men are bound by feelings of patriotism, to lend their money to the government to carry on a war, the effects of which are in the most ex-

treme degree disastrous to them, and the principle of which
they conscientiously and utterly condemn? As good citi
zens, they will of course yield obedience to the laws; and
if the laws exact money from them to support the war,
they will pay it.   But voluntary loans stand upon a very
different basis.   As honest men, they cannot, consistently
with their integrity, voluntarily contribute their aid in prosecuting an unjust and unnecessary war, because such a
course of conduct would involve them in the guilt, as well
as the calamities of the controversy.   Besides, is a man
to be *forced*, under any circumstances, to lend money to
his government?   The idea is incompatible with the plain-
est principles of freedom.   In the dark ages, the despotic
sovereigns of Europe did not hesitate, by the most cruel
tortures, to force one class of their subjects to advance
them money, whenever they thought proper to make such
a requisition.   But in modern times, the practice of forcing contributions, from members of civilized communities, is left exclusively to highway robbers and associations of banditti.   Civilized governments dare not raise
money in this mode.   On the broad principle of freedom,
freemen have a perfect and unquestionable right to withhold their contributions of money from any object, let the
requisition proceed from what source it may.   It has been
urged in reference to this subject, that the character of the
country was at stake, and every man was bound, let his
political principles or feelings have been what they might,
to bury those principles and feelings, and support the war,
and save the reputation of the country.   The opposers of
the war viewed the matter in a somewhat different light.
The administration of the national government, and their
immediate partizans and supporters, made the war.   It
was their war, and not that of the country.   A large portion of the country was opposed to it, and used every effort
to prevent its occurrence.   Their remonstrances were not
listened to, and the war was declared.   The responsibility

of it, therefore, rested upon those who brought it upon the nation. It was not, then, the character of the country that was at stake, except so far as the country was responsible for the acts of its government—but it was *the character of the administration.* It is probable that the opposers of the war did not, under the peculiar circumstances of the case, consider themselves bound to make any extraordinary efforts or sacrifices to save the reputation of an administration in whom they never placed confidence, and whose misuse of the powers with which they had been entrusted, had reduced them to a state of great peril, and subjected them to the most lively apprehensions. The principle contended for by those who claimed it to be the duty of capitalists, whether they approved or disapproved of the war, upon the broad ground of public spirit and patriotism to advance their money to carry on the war, may be brought to a test respecting which there is very little room for mistake. Laws were passed early in the controversy, authorising the government to accept the services of volunteer troops. Probably such services were offered in a variety of instances ; but did any man ever pretend that the great body of the militia throughout the Union, were bound, by a regard to the character of the country, voluntarily to shoulder their muskets and march into the field ? It is certain that men are of more importance in a war than even money, because the latter is wanted almost exclusively for the purpose of obtaining the former. But what proportion even of the able-bodied men of the United States, who were the supporters of the administration, and of course of the war, ever tendered their personal services in the field to the government ? And who ever thought of reproaching and reviling them, because they preferred staying at home, to risking their lives in the camp, as enemies to their country, or even as wanting in the proper feelings of patriotism ? When the war in Europe was brought to a close by the downfall of Bonaparte, and the overthrow of his imperial power and tyranny, then the authors of the war between the United States and Great Britain became seriously alarmed for their popularity, as well as for the safety of the country.   Under the excitement which their well grounded fears for their own safety produced, they made every exertion in their power to enlist the nation at large in the contest.   The means adopted for this purpose, were not of the most reputable kind.   Instances of gross imposition upon the people at large are exhibited in the course of this work, which will justify this assertion ; while the original policy which led to the war, and the objects for which it was professedly declared, must satisfy every reasonable and dispassionate mind, that its character was not national.   In addition to this, the fact that it was political, and intended to answer the purposes of politicians of a daring and ambitious character, was well known at the time to those most intimately acquainted with the public affairs of the nation.

In the course of the year 1814, the progress of the war upon the sea-coast became in the highest degree alarming and destructive.   It appeared to be the object of the British to render hostilities as distressing to the inhabitants, especially upon the southern division of the Union, as the ravages of invading armies could make them.   It is not the object of this work to give a history of the war.   The subject is alluded to for the purpose of showing how miserably it was conducted on the part of the United States, and how the inhabitants along the Atlantic shore were left exposed to its depredations and miseries, while the national government were either totally unable, or not disposed to yield them any protection.   In the month of August, having entire command of the Chesapeake Bay, the British landed a force in the state of Maryland, and moved forward towards the city of Washington, the seat of the United States government.   An attempt was made by the militia of that state to resist them, particularly at

Bladensburgh, but without success; and their progress towards the capital was so rapid, that the President, and other high officers of the government, were under the necessity of fleeing into the country with great precipitation, to avoid falling into the hands of the enemy. During the time in which they held possession of the city of Washington, they destroyed the public buildings, and committed other depredations, in a manner and to an extent, that would have better characterized an armed body of Vandals, than the well disciplined forces of a modern civilized government. At the same time, a squadron of armed ships sailed up the Potomac, and took possession of the city of Alexandria, where they contented themselves with carrying away all public and private naval stores, the shipping then in port, and merchandise of every description. These enterprises were followed by an attack upon the city of Baltimore, where the British were repulsed with considerable loss; and among the officers who were killed on that occasion, was General Ross, the commanding officer of the expedition. It was also well understood, that the plan of their operations included attacks upon the other principal cities and towns upon the sea-coast, such as Charleston, Savannah, &c. and the character of the war was rapidly degenerating into a system of barbarous invasion of towns and villages, the plundering of private inhabitants, and the burning of vessels, stores, &c. and spreading ruin and desolation along the sea-shore.

The disasters of 1814 showed, in the most conclusive manner, the incapacity, or indisposition of the national government to protect the country against the calamities brought upon it by the war into which they had plunged it; and the uncivilized manner in which it was carried on during that year, greatly alarmed the fears of the people, who could not but see that the inhabitants more immediately exposed to the inroads of naval squadrons, were in danger of experiencing the most severe misfortunes and sufferings

And what added much to the general anxiety, was the publication of a message from the President to congress, in the month of October of that year, containing an account from the American commissioners for negotiating peace at Ghent, of the extravagant demands of the British commissioners, of certain principles as the basis of negotiation. By a despatch from the former, dated August 19th, 1814, it was stated, that it was demanded as a *sine qua non* on the part of Great Britain, that the Indians who had been engaged in hostilities on the side of that nation, and against the United States, " should be included in the pacification ; and as incident thereto, the boundaries of their territories should be permanently established." The object of this requisition was stated to be, "that the Indians should remain as a permanent barrier between our western settlements and the adjacent British provinces, to prevent them from being conterminous to each other : and that neither the United States nor Great Britain should ever thereafter have the right to purchase or acquire any part of the territory, thus recognized as belonging to the Indians."

It was stated further, that there should be a revision of the boundary line between the dominions of Great Britain and the United States ; and in explanation of this requisition, it was said that—" Experience had proved that *the joint possession of the lakes, and a right, common to both nations, to keep up a naval force on them, necessarily produced collisions, and rendered peace insecure.* As Great Britain could not be supposed to expect to make conquests in that quarter, and as that province was essentially weaker than the United States, and exposed to invasion, it was necessary for its security that Great Britain should require that *the United States should hereafter keep no armed naval force on the western lakes, from Lake Ontario to Lake Superior, both inclusive ; that they should not erect any fortified or military post or establishment on the shores of those lakes ; and*

that they should not maintain those which are already exist-
ing. This must be considered, they said, as a moderate
demand, since Great Britain, if she had not disclaimed
the intention of any increase of territory, might, with propriety, have asked a cession of the adjacent American
shores. The commercial navigation and intercourse would
be left on the same footing as heretofore. It was expressly stated, in answer to a question (by the American
commissioners) that Great Britain was to retain the right
of having an armed naval force on those lakes, and of
holding military posts and establishments on their shores."

This last demand, respecting the exclusive occupation
of the lakes, was not stated as a *sine qua non ;* the British
commissioners, when inquired of respecting that point,
declined giving a positive answer.

The message and documents relating to this subject, so
far as the executive thought proper to make them public,
were published without delay ; and as was doubtless expected and intended, they excited much feeling throughout the Union. Not an individual in the United States,
however decidedly he might originally have been opposed
to the declaration of war, and however strongly he might
have disapproved the general policy and measures of the
administration, could fail of rejecting such extravagant
demands as the basis of a treaty of peace. Overlooking
what had passed, there was a general determination to
resist such a requisition at every hazard. Some other
facts relating to this subject, of which the community at
large have, even to this day, been kept in ignorance, may
now with much propriety be adverted to. A letter from
Washington, dated October 15th, 1814, from a gentleman
of the highest respectability, and directed to his friend,
contains the following passage—

" The instructions to our commissioners were communicated and read on the 14th. They are voluminous, and
contain a great deal of reasoning. *The greatest part are*

ordered to be printed.   The subjects of blockade and impress-
ment, after the fall of Bonaparte, were entirely abandoned.
With respect to security on the lakes, our commissioners were
instructed to make the same demands of the British, as they
have made on us—that is, that the British shall keep no force
there, while we might keep as large a force as we thought
proper.   Some of the party say, that the British must have
had a knowledge of these instructions, and that ———,
instead of finding out other people's secrets at London,
has probably lost his own."

It is doubted whether a more singular occurrence than
this ever took place in the history of any government. The
war was declared against Great Britain, at a time, and
under circumstances as irritating to that government, as
can well be imagined. It was also against the decided
opinions and feelings of a large portion of our own countrymen.   But events had occurred which had changed the
face of things, and gave that nation the vantage ground
against us; and it therefore became necessary to excite
the resentment of the people of the United States, and
unite them in opposition to the extravagant demands of
the enemy as the price of peace.   For those purposes the
instructions containing these demands, were communicated to Congress, and the country, as the *sine qua non*, the
only basis on which Great Britain would consent to negotiate for a treaty of peace ; and as has been remarked, it
produced the intended effect—the country was greatly excited, and manifested a determination, under no circumstances, to yield to such requisitions.   Now it seems that
though we declared the war, and were in a state of alarm
for the result, yet *our commissioners were instructed to make*
the same extravagant demands of the British, that they
made of us ; but the instructions to our commissioners
were never presented to the British negotiators, and were
kept back from the public, while those of the British were
distributed through the country, to rouse the public indig-

nation. Nor have the instructions relating to this particular subject ever been published to this time.

The facts now disclosed warrant the belief, that the
British government had, by some means or other, become
acquainted with the nature of the instructions to our commissioners, and therefore shaped theirs to meet them.
But the British commissioners having disclosed their instructions, ours had address enough to keep their own out
of sight, doubtless for the purpose of enabling the President to produce a strong effect upon the public mind, and
to induce all descriptions of people to unite in opposition
to such extravagant demands. The effect was produced;
but it was the result of a gross imposition, not to say
fraud, upon the people of the United States.

The situation in which the state of Connecticut was
placed early in the year 1814, may be in some measure
ascertained from the following extract from the speech
delivered by Governor Smith to the legislature of that
state, at the opening of their session in the month of May.

"I am not informed that any effectual arrangements
are made by the national government to put our sea-coast
into a more respectable state of defence. Should the plan
of the last campaign be revived, and especially should the
war retain the desolating character it has been made to
assume, the states on the Atlantic border cannot be insensible to the dangers which await them. ' To provide for
the common defence' was an avowed, and it may with
truth be said the chief purpose for which the present constitution was formed. How far this object is promoted by
aiming at foreign conquest, and resigning our most wealthy
and populous frontier to pillage and devastation, becomes
a momentous inquiry. Whatever measures, gentlemen,
you may think proper to adopt on the occasion, I feel assured they will flow from an equal regard to your own
rights and to the interests of the Union. In any event, I
am persuaded that we shall place no reliance on the for-

bearance of a declared enemy, and that if the aid to which we are entitled is withheld, the means which God has given us will be faithfully employed for our safety.

"It is with concern I lay before you an official account of the destruction of a very considerable number of private vessels at Saybrook, by a detachment from the British squadron. The misfortune is embittered by the reflection that it would probably have been prevented by a small force stationed at Fort Fenwick, at the entrance of Connecticut river. It will be recollected that a guard, authorised by the United States, was kept at that post nearly the whole of the last season. It was dismissed early in December. Information of the exposed condition of these vessels, and of the consequent apprehensions of the town for its own safety, was duly transmitted to the war department, and the attention of the government to the important objects was earnestly solicited. It was presumed, as there were regular troops in the vicinity, either that the request would be promptly complied with, or if such an arrangement was inconvenient, that this government would be frankly and seasonably apprized of it. In the latter event the force of the state would have been applied not less readily to the protection of the persons and property of our citizens, than it had been to the defence of the national squadron. Under these circumstances then existing, the Council, whom I particularly consulted, could not think it adviseable for the state government to interfere."

The war having been declared for the reasons assigned, and hostilities having commenced, and prosecuted, it has not been an object of importance to trace the course of the administration with regard to the mode of conducting it, but to ascertain the principles on which they would be willing to bring it to a close. It will be borne in mind, that immediately after the declaration of war was published, and long before the news of that event could have reached England, the orders in council were repealed by the British government, leaving no other acknowledged cause of war except the subject of impressment. The strong language used by the President, and the Secretary of State, on various occasions, has been noticed. After the offer of mediation by the emperor of Russia, the President, professing to entertain no doubts that Great Britain would accede to the proposition, nominated commissioners to negotiate under that mediation, and furnished them with a long set of instructions, relative to the formation of a treaty of peace. Those instructions related principally to the subject of impressment. In the course of them it is said—" I have to repeat, that the great object which you have to secure, in regard to impressment, is, that *our flag shall protect the crew.*"—Again—" Upon the whole subject I have to observe, that your first duty will be *to conclude a peace with Great Britain,* and *that you are authorized to do it, in case you obtain a satisfactory stipulation against impressment, one which shall secure, under our flag, protection to the crew.* The manner in which it may be done has been already stated, with the reciprocal stipulations which you may enter into, to secure Great Britain against the injury of which she complains. *If this encroachment of Great Britain is not provided against, the United States have appealed to arms in vain.* If your efforts to accomplish it should fail, *all further negotiations will cease,* and *you will return home without delay.*"

These instructions bear date April 15th, 1813.

The British government having declined the offer of Russian mediation, a proposition was made to open a negotiation at Gottenburg. This having been agreed to, instructions were made out to the United States commissioners accordingly. In those instructions, after a reference to those previously given, when it was supposed the negotiations would have been held at St. Petersburgh, and a declaration that they were to be considered as applicable, except where modified by the present, to the negotiations about to take place; the following passage occurs—" On impressment, as to the right of the United States to be exempted from it, I have nothing new to add. *The sentiments of the President have undergone no change on that important subject. This degrading practice must cease; our flag must protect the crew, or the United States cannot consider themselves an independent nation.*"

On the 14th of February, 1814, additional instructions were forwarded to the commissioners, in which the following passage appears—" By an article in the former instructions, you were authorised in making a treaty to prevent impressment from our vessels, to stipulate, provided a certain specified term could not be agreed on, that it might continue in force for the present war in Europe only. At that time it seemed probable that the war might last many years. Recent appearances, however, indicate the contrary. Should peace be made in Europe, as the practical evil of which we complain in regard to impressment would cease, it is presumed the British government would have less objection to a stipulation to forbear that practice for a specified term, than it would have, should the war continue. In concluding a peace with Great Britain, even in case of a previous general peace in Europe, it is important to the United States to obtain such a stipulation."

It will be recollected, that the letter from which the preceding passage is copied, was written after the failure of Bonaparte's Russian expedition, and the disastrous retreat of his forces from Moscow. On the 24th of March, 1814, the Secretary of State wrote a short letter to the commissioners, in which he says—" If a satisfactory arrangement can be concluded with Great Britain, the sooner it can be accomplished the happier for both countries. If such an arrangement cannot be obtained, it is important for the United States to be acquainted with it without delay."

When the war was declared by the United States, in

1812, Bonaparte was just preparing to invade Russia with an immense army, and with every expectation of humbling, at least, if not of dethroning the sovereign of that vast and powerful empire. It requires the exercise of much charity towards this government to believe that they did not seize that opportunity to throw their weight into the scale against Great Britain, who was supporting Russia against France, and whose influence and power had up to that time prevented the absolute subjugation of the whole continent of Europe by the French. Hence it may be accounted for, that after the defeat which the ambitious emperor of that nation experienced in Russia, the tone of the United States government so suddenly changed on the subject of the negotiations for peace, and the still greater change after he was dethroned in 1814. This will be manifest from the style of the letter just quoted, and still more so from one from the Secretary of State to the commissioners, dated June 25th, 1814—

"It is impossible, with the lights which have reached us, to ascertain the present disposition of the British government towards an accommodation with the United States. We think it probable that the late events in France may have had a tendency to increase its pretensions.

"At war with Great Britain, and injured by France, the United States have sustained the attitude founded on those relations. No reliance was placed on the good offices of France, in bringing the war with Great Britain to a satisfactory conclusion. Looking steadily to an honourable peace, and the ultimate attainment of justice from both powers, the President has endeavoured, by a consistent and honourable policy, *to take advantage of every circumstance that might promote that result. He, nevertheless, knew that France held a place in the political system of Europe and of the world, which, as a check on England, could not fail to be useful to us.* What effect the late events

may have had, in these respects, is the important circumstance *of which* you are doubtless better informed than we
can be.

" It was inferred from the general policy of Russia, and
the friendly sentiments and interposition of the emperor,
that a respect for both would have much influence, with
the British cabinet, in promoting a pacific policy towards
us. The manner, however, in which it is understood that
a general pacification is taking place; the influence Great
Britain may have in modifying the arrangements involved
in it; the resources she may be able to employ exclusively
against the United States; and the uncertainty of the
precise course which Russia may pursue in relation to the
war between the United States and Great Britain, naturally claim attention, and raise the important question, in
reference to the subject of impressment, on which it is presumed your negotiations will essentially turn, whether
your powers ought not to be enlarged, so as to enable you
to give to those circumstances all the weight to which they
may be entitled. On full consideration, it has been decided, that in case no stipulation can be obtained from the
British government at this moment, when its pretensions
may have been much heightened by recent events, and
the state of Europe be most favourable to them, either
relinquishing the claim to impress from American vessels,
or discontinuing the practice, even in consideration of the
proposed exclusion from them of British seamen, *you may
concur in an article, stipulating, that the subject of impressment*, together with that of commerce between the two
countries, be referred to separate negotiation, to be undertaken without delay, at such place as you may be able
to agree on, *preferring* this city, if to be obtained."

Two days after the date of the preceding letter, viz.
June 27th, 1814, the Secretary of State addressed a letter
to the American commissioners, in which is the following
passage—

" On mature consideration it has been decided, that under all the circumstances above alluded to, incident to a prosecution of the war, *you may omit any stipulation on the subject of impressment, if found indispensably necessary to terminate it.* You will, of course, not recur to this expedient until all your efforts to adjust the controversy in a more satisfactory manner have failed. As it is not the intention of the United States, in suffering the treaty to be silent on the subject of impressment, to admit the British claim thereon, or to relinquish that of the United States, it is highly important that any such inference be entirely precluded, by a declaration or protest in some form or other, that the omission is not to have any such effect or tendency. Any modification of the practice to prevent abuses, being an acknowledgment of the right in Great Britain, is utterly inadmissible."

On the 11th of August, 1814, the Secretary of State, in a letter to the commissioners, says—" By my letters of the 25th and 27th of June, of which another copy is now forwarded, the sentiments of the President, as to the conditions on which it will be proper for you to conclude a treaty of peace, are made known to you. It is presumed that either in the mode suggested in my letter of the 25th of June, which is much preferred, or by permitting the treaty to be silent on the subject, as is authorized in the letter of the 27th of June, the question of impressment may be so disposed of, as to form no obstacle to a pacification. This government can go no further, because it will make no sacrifice of the rights or honour of the nation."

It is worthy of notice, that the negotiations between the British and American commissioners, related almost exclusively to subjects which had no connection with the causes of the war. The declaration of war was founded on the orders in council, and impressment. The first were repealed within a week from the date of the declaration of war, leaving nothing to contend about but impressment.

In one of the earliest communications from the commissioners of the United States to those of Great Britain,
when the negotiations opened at Ghent, and which was
dated the 24th of August, 1814, is contained the following
passage—" *The causes of the war between the United States
and Great Britain having disappeared by the maritime pacification of Europe, the government of the United States does
not desire to continue it in defence of abstract principles,
which have, for the present, ceased to have any practical effect.*
The undersigned have been accordingly instructed to agree
to its termination, both parties restoring whatever they
may have taken, and both reserving all their rights, in
relation to their respective seamen."

It is to be presumed that the commissioners made use
of this language, in pursuance of the powers contained in
their instructions. But who will undertake to reconcile it
with that adopted by the committee of foreign relations in
January, 1813? Referring to the repeal of the orders of
council in June, 1812, as having removed one of the causes
of the war, leaving only that of impressment, the committee say—" Had the executive consented to an armistice on
the repeal of the orders in council, without a satisfactory
provision against impressment, or a clear and distinct understanding with the British government to that effect,
your committee would not have hesitated to disapprove it.
The impressment of our seamen being deservedly considered a principal cause of the war, the war ought to be prosecuted until that cause was removed."—" War having
been declared, and the case of impressment being necessarily included as one of the most important causes, it is
evident that it must be provided for in the pacification :
the omission of it in a treaty of peace would not leave it
on its former ground: it would in effect be an absolute
relinquishment."—" It is an evil which ought not, which
cannot be longer tolerated."—" It is incompatible with
their (the United States) sovereignty. It is subversive of

the main pillars of their independence. The forbearance of the United States under it has been mistaken for pusillanimity."

Notwithstanding these, and many other specimens of strong language, and a professed predetermination, on the part of our government, to prosecute the war until a specific agreement, in a formal treaty, should be obtained from Great Britain, renouncing both the right and the practice of impressment, the moment Bonaparte was overthrown, and his power subverted, the subject dwindled into an abstract principle, not worth the trouble of further controversy.

In September, 1814, Congress were convened by the executive at an earlier day than had been fixed at the previous adjournment; and on the 20th of that month the President's message was received by the houses. After alluding to the reasons for the early meeting, one of which was the manner in which the war was carried on, manifesting a spirit of hostility more violent than ever, the President remarks—

" This increased violence is best explained by the two important circumstances, that the great contest in Europe, for an equilibrium guarantying all its states against the ambition of any, has been closed without any check on the overbearing power of Great Britain on the ocean ; and that it has left in her hands disposable armaments, with which, forgetting the difficulties of a remote war against a free people, and yielding to the intoxication of success, with the example of a great victim to it before her eyes, she cherishes hopes of still further aggrandizing a power already formidable in its abuses to the tranquillity of the civilized and commercial world.

" But, whatever may have inspired the enemy with these more violent purposes, the public councils of a nation, more able to maintain than it was to acquire its independence, and with a devotion to it, rendered more ardent by the experience of its blessings, can never deliberate but on the means most effectual for defeating the extravagant views or unwarrantable passions with which alone the war can now be pursued against us."

It is very apparent from the language above cited, that President Madison had become seriously alarmed by the course of events in Europe, the downfall of Bonaparte, and the destruction of his imperial despotism, and that he therefore considered it necessary to excite the country to make more vigorous exertions in carrying on the war, the folly and fruitlessness of which now stared him full in the face. That he expected the war would render powerful assistance in the accomplishment of the great object which the French emperor had in view—viz. the humiliation, if not the absolute subjugation of Great Britain, cannot be doubted. And that the disappointment in his expectations from this quarter not only mortified, but alarmed him, is very apparent. " The closing of the great contest in Europe," he says, " without producing any check on the overbearing power of Great Britain on the ocean, has left in her hands disposable armaments, with which, forgetting the difficulties of a remote war against a free people, she cherishes hopes of still further aggrandizing a power already formidable to the tranquillity of the civilized and commercial world." That our government expected to have an important agency in producing that check to the power of Great Britain, when they undertook the war, nobody who is acquainted with the history and circumstances of the case can doubt. But it is a little extraordinary that the President should allude to the war as if it were one for which they were responsible, apparently desirous of keeping out of sight the fact, that it was forced upon them by us, and that under circumstances calculated greatly to excite their feelings, and enkindle their resentment against this country.

But the language of the next paragraph is still more

extraordinary. The message, with apparent gratification, states, that as a nation, we were, in 1814, more able to *maintain our independence* than *we were originally to acquire it;* and that having experienced the blessings of independence, we could deliberate on nothing " but the most effectual means of defeating the extravagant views and unwarrantable passions with which alone the war could be pursued against us." It was understood that the war, when declared, was to vindicate our rights, not to defend our independence. Whatever encroachments might have been committed against our neutral character, and those were the injuries complained of, there was no attempt on the part of Great Britain to destroy our national independence, and reduce us to the condition of colonies. If our political character as a foreign independent people was in danger, it was the effect of the indiscreet declaration of a war by our government, at a time when they were entirely unprepared to prosecute it with vigour, or with any reasonable prospect of success. And if at the end of the second year after the commencement of hostilities, instead of an offensive, it had become a defensive war, it was in the most emphatical manner disgraceful to those by whom it was forced upon the country.

After reviewing the events of the war, the message, in terms not the most explicit, but sufficiently clear, when taken in connection with other circumstances, to be understood, speaks in the following language :—

" To meet the extended and diversified warfare adopted by the enemy, great bodies of militia have been taken into service, for the public defence, and great expenses incurred. That the defence every where may be both more convenient and more economical, Congress will see the necessity of immediate measures for *filling the ranks of the regular army*, and of enlarging the provision for special corps, mounted and unmounted, to be engaged for longer periods of service than are due from the militia. I ear-

---

nestly renew, at the same time, a recommendation of *such changes in the system of the militia,* as by *classing and disciplining for the most prompt and active service the portions the most capable of it,* will give to that great resource for the public safety, all the requisite energy and efficiency."

This subject was referred by the house of representatives to the military committee, who of course applied to the Secretary of War for the purpose of ascertaining the views and wishes of the administration with regard to these suggestions. That office was then filled by James Monroe, afterwards President of the United States. Having but recently entered upon the duties of his office, he was not able to reply to the committee until the 17th of October, at which time he submitted his report, of which the following is an extract:—

"1. That the present military establishment, amounting to 62,448 men, be preserved and made complete, and that the most efficient means authorised by the constitution and consistent with the general rights of our fellow citizens be adopted, to fill the ranks, with the least possible delay.

"2. That a permanent force, consisting of at least 40,000 men, in addition to the present military establishment, be raised for the defence of our cities and frontiers, under an engagement by the executive with such corps that it shall be employed in that service within certain specified limits, and that a proportional augmentation of general officers of each grade, and other staff, be provided for."

This report was accompanied by a long letter from the Secretary, addressed to the chairman of the military committee, explaining the views and sentiments of the executive department on the subject at large, under the general head of "Explanatory Observations."

"In providing a force necessary to bring this war to a happy termination, the nature of the crisis in which we are involved, and the extent of its dangers, claim particular attention. If the means are not fully adequate to the end, discomfiture must inevitably ensue.

"It may be fairly presumed, that it is the object of the British government, by striking at the principal sources of our prosperity, to diminish the importance, if not to destroy the political existence of the United States. If any doubt remained on this subject, it has been completely removed by the despatches from our ministers at Ghent, which were lately laid before Congress.

"A nation contending for its existence against an enemy powerful by land and sea, favoured in a peculiar manner by extraordinary events, must make great sacrifices. Forced to contend again for our *liberties and independence*, we are called on for a display of all the patriotism which distinguished our fellow citizens in the first great struggle. It may be fairly concluded, that if the United States *sacrifice any right, or make any dishonourable concession to the demands of the British government, the spirit of the nation will be broken, and the foundations of their union and independence shaken. The United States must relinquish no right, or perish in the struggle. There is no intermediate ground to rest on. A concession on one point, leads directly to the surrender of every other.* The result of the contest cannot be doubtful. The highest confidence is entertained that the stronger the pressure, and the greater the danger, the more firm and vigorous will be the resistance, and the more successful and glorious the result.

"It is the avowed purpose of the enemy to lay waste and destroy our cities and villages, and to desolate our coast, of which examples have already been afforded. It is evidently his intention *to press the war along the whole extent of our sea-board, in the hope of exhausting equally the spirit of the people and the national resources.* There is also reason to presume, that it is the intention to press the war from Canada on the adjoining states, while attempts are made on the city of New-York, and other important points, with a view to the main project of dismemberment or subjugation. It may be inferred likewise to be a part of the scheme, to continue to invade this part of the Union, while a separate force attacks the state of Louisiana, in the hope of taking possession of the city of New-Orleans, and of the mouth of the Mississippi, that great inlet and key to all that portion of the United States lying westward of the Alleghany mountains. The peace in Europe having given to the enemy a large disposable force, has essentially favoured these objects.

"The advantage which a great naval superiority gives to the enemy, by enabling him to move troops from one quarter to another, from Maine to Mississippi, a coast of two thousand miles extent, is very considerable. Even a small force moved in this manner for the purposes avowed by the British commanders, cannot fail to be sensibly felt, more especially by those who are most exposed to it. It is obvious, if the militia are to be relied on principally for the defence of our cities and coasts against their predatory and desolating incursions, wherever they may be made, that by interfering with their ordinary pursuits of industry, it must be attended with serious interruption and loss to them, and injury to the public, while it greatly increases the expense. It is an object, therefore, of the highest importance, to provide a regular force, with the means of transporting it from one quarter to another along our coast, thereby following the movements of the enemy with the greatest possible rapidity, and repelling the attack wherever it may be made. These remarks are equally true as to the militia service generally under the present organization of the militia, and the short terms of service prescribed by law. It may be stated with confidence, that at least three times the force in the militia has been employed at our principal cities along the coast, and on the frontier, in marching to and returning thence, that would have been necessary in regular troops; and that the expense attending it has been more than proportionably augmented, from the difficulty, if not the impossibility, of preserving the same degree of system in the militia, as in the regular service.

"But it will not be sufficient to repel these predatory and desolating incursions. To bring the war to an honourable termination, we must not be contented with defending ourselves. Different feelings must be touched, and apprehensions excited in the British government. By pushing the war into Canada, we secure the friendship of the Indian tribes, and command their services, otherwise to be turned by the enemy against us; we relieve the coast from the desolation which is intended for it, and we keep in our hands a safe pledge for an honourable peace.

"It follows from this view of the subject, that it will be necessary to bring into the field the next campaign, not less than 100,000 regular troops. Such a force, aided, in extraordinary emergencies, by volunteers and militia, will place us above all inquietude as to the final result of this contest. It will fix on a solid and imperishable foundation our union and independence, on which the liberties and happiness of our fellow citizens so essentially depend. It will secure to the United States an early and advantageous peace.

"The return of the regular force now in service, laid before you, will show how many men will be necessary to fill the present corps; and the return of the numerical force of the present military establishment, will show how many are required to complete it to the number proposed. The next and most important inquiry is, how shall these men be raised? Under existing circumstances, it is evident that the most prompt and efficient mode that can be devised, consistent with the equal rights of every citizen, ought to be adopted. The following plans are respectfully submitted to the consideration of the committee. Being distinct in their nature, I will present each separately, with the considerations applicable to it."

By the extreme consternation which it is manifest from the language of this document the administration felt, at facing the dangers and calamities they had brought upon the country, it would seem that they must have engaged in the war without the remotest idea that they could fail of success in its progress and termination. This confidence of theirs undoubtedly rested upon the full assurance they entertained, that Bonaparte would succeed in his expedition against Russia, and after having subdued his great northern foe, that he would have nothing to do but to turn his whole force against Great Britain, in which event, the downfall of the latter might be considered as absolutely certain. The circumstances of the case were, by an untoward series of occurrences, reversed, and instead of the emperor of Russia having been humbled and subdued, that calamity fell upon the emperor of France; and thus Great Britain became extricated from the European controversy, and was at liberty to bring all her force to bear upon the United States. It was not unnatural that men, whose views were at the outset so shortsighted, and who took so much for granted should, at such a material change of circumstances, when their eyes were opened upon the dangers and difficulties with which they were surrounded, become seriously alarmed and perplexed with such unexpected embarrassments. From the lofty ground of a nation which had declared an offensive war, at the end of a little more than two years, we were reduced to one " contending for existence, against an enemy powerful by land and sea," and " favoured in a peculiar manner by extraordinary events." Let it be remembered, that the British nation were, in October, 1814, no more powerful by land or sea, than they were in June, 1812. And if those who precipitated the United States into the war, had possessed a little more moderation of feeling, had entertained a smaller degree of devotion to France, and not quite so much animosity against Great Britain, they would not have rushed headlong, influenced by a mad calculation of future events, into a contest which might so easily and so speedily bring them to the extreme of danger, and this when so absolutely unprovided with the means of carrying on the war, and bringing themselves honourably out of the conflict.

But a most extraordinary sentiment is contained in this document—extraordinary, when the facts connected with it are taken into consideration. The President of the United States, speaking through the medium of the Secretary of War, says in this letter—"It may be fairly concluded, that if the United States *sacrifice any right*, or make any dishonourable concession to the demands of the British government, *the spirit of the nation will be broken, and the foundation of their union and independence shaken.* The United States must *relinquish no right, or perish in the struggle.* There is *no intermediate ground to rest on.* It will be borne in mind, that the war was declared in order to force the British government to revoke their orders of council, and to give up the practice of impressment. The orders of council were revoked within five days after the declaration of war, leaving no avowed subject of controversy but that of impressment. A determination not to submit to this any longer, was manifested throughout the conflict; and our public agents of all descriptions, who had any thing to do with the subject of the controversy, were instructed never to agree to any treaty of peace which did not contain a specific provision, that the British government should relinquish that practice. And in a great number of instances, many of which have been quoted, instructions to this effect were given to their commissioners, appointed to negotiate for peace, and language equally strong with that just cited from the letter of the Secretary of War, was used in their instructions on the subject. Now let it be remembered, *that on the 27th of*

June, 1814, *nearly four months before the date of this report of the Secretary of War, instructions had been sent by the President of the United States, to the commissioners at Ghent, through the medium of James Monroe, then Secretary of State, and in October following Secretary of War,* in which those commissioners are told that—" *On mature consideration it has been decided, that under all the circumstances above alluded to, incident to a prosecution of the war, you may omit any stipulation on the subject of impressment, if found indispensably necessary to terminate it.*" That is, the only subject of controversy, about which the country had been engaged in a war for nearly two years and a half, at an expense of more than a hundred millions of dollars, and from thirty to fifty thousand lives, was formally abandoned in June ;—and in October following, it was declared that *rather than relinquish any right, we ought to make up our minds to perish in the struggle.* This can be viewed in no other light than that of an attempt, on the part of the administration, to impose upon Congress the belief, that we were fighting for existence, and that we ought to perish, rather than surrender a single right, when at the same moment, *the only ground of controversy had been long previously abandoned* by that same administration, for the sole purpose of extricating themselves from the war.

The following is Mr. Secretary Monro's " First Plan."

" Let the free male population of the United States, between eighteen and forty-five years, be formed into classes of one hundred men each, and let each class furnish   men for the war, within thirty days after the classification, and replace them in the event of casualty.

" The classification to be formed with a view to the equal distribution of property among the several classes.

" If any class fails to provide the men required of it, within the time specified, they shall be raised by draft on the whole class ; any person being thus drafted being allowed to furnish a substitute.

" The present bounty in land being allowed to each recruit, and the present bounty in money, which is paid to each recruit by the United States, to be paid to each draft by all the inhabitants within the precinct of the class within which the draft may be made, equally according to the value of the property which they may respectively possess; and if such bounty be not paid within   days, the same to be levied on all the taxable property of the whole precinct.

" The recruits to be delivered over to the recruiting officer in each district, to be marched to such places of general rendezvous as may be designated by the department of war.

" *That this plan will be efficient cannot be doubted.* It is evident, that the men contemplated may soon be raised by it. Three modes occur, by which it may be carried into effect. 1st. By placing the execution of it in the hands of the county courts throughout the United States. 2d. By relying on the militia officers in each county. 3d. By appointing particular persons in each county for that purpose. It is believed that either of these modes would be found adequate.

" Nor does there appear to be any well-founded objection to the right in Congress to adopt this plan, or to its equality in its application to our fellow-citizens individually. Congress have a right, by the constitution, to raise regular armies, and no restraint is imposed in the exercise of it, except in the provisions which are intended to guard generally against the abuse of power, with none of which does this plan interfere. It is proposed, that it shall operate on all alike, that none shall be exempt from it except the chief magistrate of the United States, and the governors of the several states.

" It would be absurd to suppose that Congress could not carry this power into effect, otherwise than by accepting the voluntary service of individuals. It might happen that an army could not be raised in that mode, whence the power would have been granted in vain. The safety of the state might depend on such an army. Long continued invasions conducted by regular well disciplined troops, can best be repelled by troops kept constantly in the field, and equally well disciplined. Courage in an army is in a great measure mechanical. A small body well trained, accustomed to action, gallantly led on, often breaks three or four times the number of more respectable and more brave, but raw and undisciplined troops. The sense of danger is diminished by frequent exposure to it without harm, and confidence, even in the timid, is inspired by a knowledge that reliance may be placed on others, which can grow up only by service together. The grant to Congress to raise armies was made with a knowledge of all these circumstances, and with the intention that it should take effect. The framers of the constitution, and the states who ratified it, knew the advantage which an enemy might have over us, by regular forces, and intended to place their country on an equal footing.

" The idea that the United States cannot raise a regular army in any other mode than by accepting the voluntary service of individuals, is believed to be repugnant to the uniform construction of all grants of power, and equally so to the first principles and leading objects of the federal compact. An unqualified grant of power gives the means necessary to carry it into effect. This is an universal maxim which admits of no exception. Equally true is it that the conservation of the state is a duty paramount to all others. The commonwealth has a right to the service of all its citizens, or rather, the citizens composing the commonwealth have a right collectively and individually to the service of each other, to repel any danger which may be menaced. The manner in which the service is to be apportioned among the citizens, and rendered by them, are objects of legislation. All that is to be dreaded in such case, is the abuse of power, and happily our constitution has provided ample security against that evil.

"In support of this right in Congress, the militia service affords a conclusive proof and striking example. The organization of the militia is an act of public authority, not a voluntary association. The service required must be performed by all, under penalties which delinquents pay. The generous and patriotic perform them cheerfully. In the alacrity with which the call of the government has been obeyed, and the cheerfulness with which the service has been performed throughout the United States by the great body of the militia, there is abundant cause to rejoice in the strength of our republican institutions, and in the virtue of the people.

"The plan proposed is not more compulsive than the militia service, while it is free from most of the objections to it. The militia service calls from home, for long terms, whole districts of country. None can elude the call. Few can avoid the service, and those who do are compelled to pay great sums for substitutes. This plan fixes on no one personally, and opens to all who choose it a chance of declining the service. It is a principal object of this plan to engage in the defence of the state the unmarried and youthful, who can best defend it, and best be spared, and to secure to those who render this important service, an adequate compensation from the voluntary contribution of the more wealthy in every class. Great confidence is entertained that such contribution will be made in time to avoid a draft. Indeed it is believed to be the necessary and inevitable tendency of this plan to produce that effect.

"The limited power which the United States have in organizing the militia may be urged as an argument against their right to raise regular troops in the mode proposed. If any argument could be drawn from that circumstance, I should suppose that it would be in favour of an opposite conclusion. The power of the United States over the militia has been limited, and that for raising regular armies granted without limitation. There was doubtless some object in this arrangement. The fair inference seems to be, that it was made on great consideration; that the limitation in the first instance was intentional, the consequence of the unqualified grant of the second.

"But it is said that by drawing the men from the militia service into the regular army, and putting them under regular officers, you violate a principle of the constitution, which provides that the militia shall be commanded by their own officers. If this was the fact, the conclusion would follow. But it is not the fact. The men are not drawn from the militia, but from the population of the country: when they enlist voluntarily, it is not as militia men that they act, but as citizens. If they are drafted, it must be in the same sense. In both instances they are enrolled in the militia corps, but that, as is presumed, cannot prevent the voluntary act in one instance, or the compulsive in the other. The whole population of the United States within certain ages belong to these corps. If the United States could not form regular armies from them, they could raise none.

"In proposing a draft as one of the modes of raising men in case of actual necessity, in the present great emergency of the country, I have thought it my duty to examine such objections to it as occurred, particularly those of a constitutional nature. It is from my sacred regard for the principles of our constitution that I have ventured to trouble the committee with any remarks on this part of the subject.

"Should it appear that this mode of raising recruits was justly objectionable on account of the tax on property, from difficulties which may be apprehended in the execution, or from other causes, it may be advisable to decline the tax, and for the government to pay the whole bounty."

Large extracts have been made from this extraordinary document, for the purpose of placing before the community a state paper, which is probably but little known, and which contains sentiments and doctrines of the most extravagant and dangerous description.

The proposition here made is, to divide the free male population of the United States into classes of 100 men each, each class to furnish   men. This classification to be made with a view to an equal distribution of property among the classes. If any class should fail to provide the men within 30 days after the classification, they were to be raised by draft on the class. The bounty given to recruits by the United States *in money*, was to be paid by the inhabitants belonging to the class within which the draft was made, according to the value of the property they might possess; and if not paid within the time specified by law, it was to be levied on all the taxable property of the said inhabitants. The recruits thus obtained, were to be delivered over to the recruiting officer in each district, and marched to such places of general rendezvous as the Secretary of War might direct.

This whole system is founded upon the simple basis of arbitrary power in the national government over the militia of the states. Voluntary enlistments are entirely discarded, and a hundred men, arbitrarily classed together, and their property as arbitrarily assessed, are to be forced to raise a specified number of soldiers from the list of names in their class, and pay them their bounty-money, and, in case of failure, to pay a round sum of money, in fact as a penalty, to be levied and collected from their property, and applied, of course, to the use and benefit of the United States. This was a conscription of the most detestable kind, intended to be introduced into a nation living under a written constitution of government, and nominally enjoying the benefit of laws to protect their persons and property against the arbitrary exactions of despotic power.

Although rather more insidious in the manner, it was intended to be equally efficacious in its effects with the conscription established in France by Bonaparte,—the object of it being two-fold—first, to recruit the regular army by force from the militia, and secondly, to replenish the treasury of the United States, not by a forced loan, but by an exaction from a certain portion of the community, equally unwarranted by the constitution of the country as is the demand of a man's purse upon the highway by a footpad.

In the first place, the attempt to force the militia into the regular service of the United States, to perform duty as soldiers of the standing army, was in direct violation of the national constitution.   It has already been contended, and it is believed has been shown in this work, that the militia belong to the several states, and not to the United States—that the latter have only a limited power over the militia, in certain cases specified in the constitution, and that beyond those cases, the United States have no authority whatever over them.   A statesman of distinguished talents, a few weeks after the date of this letter of the Secretary of War, made the following remarks in the House of Representatives of the United States—"One general principle is, that the militia of the several states belong to the people and government of the states—and not to the government of the United States.   I consider this as a proposition too clear to require illustration, or to admit of doubt.   The militia consist of the whole people of a state, or rather of the whole male population capable of bearing arms; including all of every description, avocation, or age.   Exemption from militia duty is a mere matter of grace.   This militia, being the very people, belong to the people or to the state governments, for their use and protection.   They were theirs at the time of the revolution, under the old confederation—and when the present form of government was adopted.   Neither the people nor their state governments have ever surrendered this their property in the militia to the general government, but have carefully kept and preserved their general dominion or control, for their own use, protection, and defence. They have, it is true, granted *or lent* (if I may use such an expression) to Congress a special concurrent authority or power over the militia in certain cases; which cases are particularly set down—guarded—limited and restricted, as fully as the most scrupulous caution, and the use of the most apt and significant words our language affords could limit and restrict them. The people have granted to Congress a right to call forth the militia in certain cases of necessity and emergency—a right to arm and organize them—and to prescribe a plan, upon which they shall be disciplined and trained. When they are called into the service of the United States (and they cannot be called unless upon the happening of one of the contingencies enumerated) they are to be under the command of the President. Hence it follows, that the general power, authority, or jurisdiction, remains in the state governments. A special, qualified, limited, and concurrent power is vested in Congress, to be exercised when the event happens, and in the manner pointed out, prescribed, and limited in the constitution. And hence it also follows, that this delegated power cannot be executed upon any other occasions, nor in any other ways, than those prescribed by the constitution."*

This reasoning may challenge refutation. If its force is admitted, or if it cannot be overthrown, it must necessarily follow that there is no authority in the constitution, under this or any other mask, to draft the militia away from the states, and force them into the standing army of the United States, to do duty as regular soldiers of that army.

But, says the Secretary of War—" Congress have a right, by the constitution, to raise regular armies, and *no*

* Speech of the Hon. Richard Stockton, in the House of Representatives, United States, December 10, 1814.

restraint is imposed in the exercise of it, except in the provisions which are intended generally to guard against the
abuse of power, with none of which does this plan interfere." This is a broad and sweeping declaration. What
is the usual mode of raising or recruiting armies? By
voluntary enlistments ; and there can be no other mode
adopted in this free country, compatible with the rights
and liberties of the citizens. Would the Secretary of War
have contended for the authority in the general government, under the power to raise armies, to issue an order
to the several states to send into the service of the United
States four able-bodied soldiers from every hundred men
between the ages of 18 and 45, to be placed in the ranks
of the standing army, and under the command of the officers of that army, to pay each man a hundred dollars
bounty, or in failure to do so, to pay to the national government a hundred dollars for each man? But both are
equally constitutional; and if the power for which he con-
tends is warranted by the constitution, the case above
stated is warranted also.

Another constitutional difficulty lay in the way of the
Secretary of War, and it was so important, as well as so
obvious, that he could not avoid bestowing a moment's
attention to it. " But it is said, that by drawing the men
from the militia service into the regular army, and putting
them under regular officers, you violate a principle of the
constitution, which provides that the militia shall be commanded by their own officers. *If this was the fact, the
conclusion would follow.* But it is not the fact. The men
are not drawn from the militia, but from *the population of
the country:* when they enlist voluntarily, it is not as militiamen that they act, but as citizens. If they are drafted,
it must be in the same sense. In both instances they are
enrolled in the militia corps, but that, as is presumed, cannot prevent the voluntary act in one instance, or the compulsive in the other. The whole population of the United

States, within certain ages, belong to these corps. If the United States could not form regular armies from them, they could raise none."

To establish the constitutionality of his plan, then, it was incumbent on the Secretary of War to establish the position, that there is a real and substantial difference between the citizens as a body, and the militia. He says the men who by his plan were to be drafted for the regular army, "were not to be drawn from *the militia,* but from *the population of the country."* And his argument rests entirely upon the soundness of this proposition. Who then are the militia? The militia, in the most extensive sense of the word, consist of the whole male population of a state capable of bearing arms. According to the laws of congress, they are made up of all the able-bodied men of the country, between the ages of 18 and 45. This restriction of the meaning of the term is founded upon the idea that those who are under the age of 18 are too young to endure the fatigues and perform the services of a military life, and those above 45 are too old. If the first are too young, and the last are too old, as militiamen, certainly they are equally so as citizens. And the Secretary of War adopts the same language with that of the law, in describing that part of the population from which his conscripts, or drafts, are to be taken. He says, let the free male population of the United States, *between* 18 *and* 45 *years, be formed into classes.* Now, when the whole male population between those ages are formed into classes *as citizens,* for the purpose of making the drafts, it may be asked *where are the militia?* Suppose the plan had provided, that instead of four or six recruits from each class, the whole number of the class had been included. Where would the militia of the states have been in that case? But if the constitution gave authority to congress to draft four from every hundred of the citizens, in a greater emergency, by the same mode of reasoning, it could have authorised a draft of fifty, or even the whole hundred.

The most abstruse logic, the nicest metaphysical reasoning that the human mind is capable of devising, can never raise this argument above the level of gross and obvious absurdity. It therefore, as a necessary consequence, leaves the administration liable to the charge of a second attempt to force the militia into the service of the United States, in violation of the constitution, by taking them away from the states to which they belong, depriving them of their constitutional right to be commanded by their own officers, ordering them to be marched where the Secretary of War might direct, and reducing them to the degraded condition of regular soldiers in a standing army. The Secretary of War acknowledges that such will be the conclusion, if the men thus drafted are taken from the militia. That they must be taken from the militia, if taken at all, has, it is believed, been demonstrated. It then must follow that the plan violated the constitution.

"But," says the Secretary of War, "it would be absurd to suppose that Congress could not carry this power into effect, otherwise than by accepting the voluntary service of individuals. It might happen that an army could not be raised in that mode, whence the power would have been granted in vain. The safety of the state might depend on such an army." The language of the constitution is—"Congress have power to raise and support armies." The argument of the Secretary is, that having the power to raise armies, if it cannot be done by voluntary enlistment, it may, as a matter of necessity, be done by force; and hence the attempt to establish this system. There is no allegation in this letter, that the militia had refused to enlist. Indeed, such an allegation could not have been truly made on the occasion, for this was a mere project before a committee, not having been reported, and of course no call could have been made under it upon the militia to enlist. As far, therefore, as the soundness of the argument depends on necessity, it must fail, because no experiment to obtain voluntary enlistments had been made. It is, however, perfectly obvious, that there was a further object in view, in driving this measure with so much force. Money was wanted as well as men; and in one mode or the other the government intended to obtain it. They meant to force the inhabitants to advance them money in the shape of a bounty to the conscripts, or in the character of a penalty if they failed in procuring the men. If the bill for raising the eighty thousand men, which was brought before the Senate by Mr. Giles, had in the first place provided for opening recruiting quarters, the men might have voluntarily enlisted, and then there would have been no opportunity to extort the money from the inhabitants.

The very next clause of the constitution after that for raising and supporting armies, is in the following words— " Congress shall have power to provide and maintain a navy." *Providing a navy*, is exactly equivalent to *raising an army;* and *maintaining a navy* to *supporting an army.* " Congress have a right," says the Secretary of War, " by the constitution, to raise regular armies, and no restraint is imposed by the exercise of it." Hence he infers the right, if men do not voluntarily enlist, to force them by a draft, in other words, by a conscription, into the ranks of the regular army. Congress have the power also to provide a navy, and there is no restraint imposed upon its exercise. By the same course of reasoning, they might order each state to provide, that is to build and equip, a seventy-four gun ship, and hand it over to the United States, as a constituent part of their naval force. And as in the case of the conscript, the bounty was to be paid by the classes, so in the case of the ships, it might be ordered that the states should lay in the stores, or furnish the means to pay the men. This would fall distinctly within the idea of maintaining a navy ; and therefore, agreeably to the mode of reasoning adopted by the Secretary of War, would be constitutional.

The Secretary of War carries his doctrine to a still greater length. He says—" An unqualified grant of power gives the means necessary to carry it into effect. This is an universal maxim which admits of no exception. Equally true is it that the conservation of the state is a duty paramount to all others." These are latitudinarian sentiments, especially when it is considered that.they come from a source which has always contended obstinately for the doctrine of " strict construction," and for the principle that all power not expressly granted to the United States, is reserved to the several states. However, they serve to show, that men who in some situations are the most pertinacious in their adherence to certain general principles, will, when placed in different situations, bend easily to circumstances, and adopt those of a more liberal description. In this case, however, the construction is very liberal, under the maxim that " the conservation of the state is a duty paramount to all others ;" and, therefore, men may be forced not only without constitutional authority, but in the very face of it, from the militia of the states, into the regular army, under the pretence that the commonwealth is in danger. An inquiry naturally arises here, what composes the state ? The answer of course is, *the people of the state.* The state is made up of the people ; and the government belongs to the people. This is so universally acknowledged, that it has become a mere truism. And it is founded upon the fundamental principle of our system, that the people are the source of power. No man dare dispute the soundness of this maxim. On the contrary, the very rulers of our country, those in whose hands the powers of government, from time to time are placed, call themselves the servants of the people. However solemn or momentous, then, the duty of *conserving* the state may be, it is very questionable whether the servants of the people have the right to insist upon it that their masters shall, under all circumstances, be forced to perform the duty of conserving *themselves* and *their government*—that the question whether they will or will not, should not even be put to them, but they are ordered by the power of conscription to march to the field, for the purpose of taking care of their own interests, at the command of their servants.

The mode proposed by the Secretary of War, for carrying this project into effect, is indicative not only of a great want of judgment and discretion in its abettors, but of a total disregard of the constitutional rights of the citizens. " Three modes occur," says that officer, " by which it may be carried into effect. 1. By placing the execution of it in the hands of the county courts throughout the United States. 2. By relying on the militia officers in each county. 3. By appointing particular persons in each county for that purpose." Suppose each of these bodies should decline to execute their commission, what would in that case become of the conscription? If the county courts, or the militia officers, had undertaken the task in some states, or at least in one, viz. in Connecticut, the legislature of the state would, without ceremony, have revoked their commissions, and thus deprived them of all authority.

But suppose either conscript body had accepted the commission, and had gone on to class the militia, and made the drafts, in what mode would they have levied and collected the bounty in the one case, or the penalty in the other? The plan says, the bounty shall be " paid to each draft by all the inhabitants within the precinct of the class, equally, according to the value of the property they may respectively possess;" and if " not paid within days, the same to be levied on all the taxable property of the said inhabitants." The property of one hundred men is to be assessed.   One might be worth half a million of dollars, and one not more than ten dollars, and the other ninety-eight would be set at various sums between the two extremes.   In what manner is this to be levied and collected?   Who is to decide the legal questions that may arise, render the judgment, and issue the execution?   Is the property to be taken according to the different degrees of indebtedness in the class, and sold at auction, or by private sale?   The constitution says—"In suits at common law, where the value in controversy shall exceed twenty dollars, the right of trial by jury shall be preserved."   This, however, may not be considered as a civil claim, but as partaking more of a criminal nature. The right of trial by jury is also secured to all persons in criminal cases.

The truth is, the whole scheme was not only unconstitutional, and oppressive in the most extravagant degree, and totally at variance with the rights and liberties of the citizens, but it was in an equal degree preposterous and absurd.   And when it was modified, and reduced somewhat to form, in a bill introduced by Mr. Giles into the senate, for the purpose of raising eighty thousand men for the army, after long debate, and great efforts by the friends of the administration, and the zealous supporters of the war, the measure could not be carried through the houses, and of course failed.

But it served to show to the nation at large, that those who plunged the country into the war, when they found their popularity in danger, were prepared to adopt the boldest and the most unconstitutional measures to save their own reputations, and to preserve their power.   And it was equally well calculated to excite the greatest alarm in the citizens at large, not merely for the preservation of the constitutional authority of the government, but for their own personal security, rights, and liberties ; and to teach them the absolute necessity of watching over their own freedom and safety.

In pursuance of what appears to have been the general plan of operations, viz. forcing men into the service, the Secretary of the Navy also made a report, in answer to a resolution of the senate, " for the better organization of the navy of the United States." Among many other things contained in that document, is the following passage—

" There is another branch of the service which appears to me to merit the serious deliberation of the legislature, with regard to the establishment of some regular system, by which the voluntary enlistments for the navy may derive occasional enforcement from the services of those seamen who, pursuing their own private occupations, are exempt, by their itinerant habits, from public service of any kind. In my view, there would be nothing incompatible with the free spirit of our free institutions, or the rights of individuals, if registers, with a particular descriptive record, were kept in the several districts, of all the seamen belonging to the United States, and provision made by law for classing and calling into the public service, in succession, for reasonable stated periods, such portions or classes as the public service might require ; and if any individual so called should be absent at the time, the next in succession should perform the tour of duty of the absentee, who should, on his return, be liable to serve his original tour, and his substitute be exempt from his succeeding regular tour of duty.

" In the military service, should the ranks not be filled by recruits, the deficiency of regular force may be filled up by drafts of militia to assemble at a *given* time and place ; not so in the naval service, it depends exclusively upon voluntary enlistments, upon which there is no reliance for any given object, at any time or place. Hence the most important expeditions may utterly fail, though every possible exertion shall have been made to carry them into effect."

This was advancing another step in the policy of conscription. Having, as was probably supposed, devised a plan for forcibly turning the militia into regular soldiers, and recruiting the standing army by a large body of conscripts, the next attempt was to supply the deficiencies of the navy by a similar process. That was, in effect, to establish by law, what even in Great Britain has never had any higher sanction than that of practice, viz.—*a system of impressment*—that very abuse, for which, when proceeding from another nation towards us, we had carried on a most expensive and disastrous war of nearly two years and a half continuance. And it is worthy of notice, that the Secretary of the Navy speaks of the right of drafting the militia, proposed by the Secretary of War, as an established legal right, and makes use of it as an argument to justify his plan of impressment.

At the same time that these attempts were making by the administration to establish conscription and impressment by law, a measure was brought before the Senate of a kindred character, and of a common origin. It was called a bill, "making further provision for filling the ranks of the army of the United States." The first section of the bill provided, that recruiting officers should be authorised to enlist into the army of the United States any free, effective, able-bodied men, between the age of eighteen and fifty years.

The second section repealed so much of former acts, as required the consent in writing of the parent, master, or guardian, to authorise the enlistment of persons under twenty-one years of age, provided masters of apprentices who enlist should receive a certain portion of the bounty-money.

This measure excited great alarm in many parts of the country. It was considered as aiming a direct blow at the legislative prerogatives of the several states, by the assumption of a power never granted to the United States, but most clearly belonging to the several states. By the laws of the individual states, parents have an absolute right to the services of their children, until they arrive at the age of twenty-one years. This right is founded on the duty of protection and support on the one side, and of obedience and service on the other. In the case of apprentices, the relationship is formed by positive contract between the parties; and the constitution contains no authority for Congress to interfere in the private concerns of individuals under the jurisdiction of the several states, to destroy the nearest and most interesting and important relationships of domestic life, or to vacate contracts entered into between individuals, concerning the ordinary business of life. But the fears of parents were excited to the highest degree, by this bold and arbitrary attempt to destroy the moral character and welfare of their children—to take them from under parental care and controul, and place them in the purlieus of a camp, and in the midst of the contaminating atmosphere of a regular army.

It was clearly perceived, that if Congress could thus interfere with the internal affairs of the states, annul the authority of their laws in cases of such importance as the domestic relations of the inhabitants, and set aside obligations, legal, moral, and social, of the most interesting and momentous character, there could be no further question about the nature of the government. It must be considered as a fearful and unrelenting despotism, restrained by no constitutional authority, and regulated and controuled solely by its absolute and sovereign will and pleasure.

The legislature of Connecticut were in session when information was received of the propositions before Congress for establishing a conscription and for enlisting minors. That information produced a great degree of excitement, and the constitutional means of guarding the rights of the militia, and of parents, guardians, and masters, became an object of serious consideration and examination. In the course of the session the following measure was adopted unanimously in the council, and in the House of Representatives by a vote nearly unanimous, there being but six in the minority.

"RESOLUTION.

" *Whereas* a plan of the Secretary of the Department of War, for filling up the regular army of the United States, has been submitted to the Congress of the United States, now in session, and a bill for an act to carry a part of the same into execution is pending before the House of Representatives of the United States, the principles of which plan and bill, if adopted, will place at the disposal of the administration of the United States government, not only all the militia of this state, but the troops raised for the defence of this state at a period when the state was left unprotected—and by the principles of which our sons, brothers, and friends, are made liable to be *delivered against their will, and by force,* to the marshals and recruiting officers of the United States, to be employed, not for our own defence, but for the conquest of Canada, or upon any foreign service upon which the administration may choose to send them; or impose upon the people of this state '*a capitation or other direct tax,*' limited by no rules but the will of officers appointed by the President of the United States.

" *And whereas* the principles of the plan and bill aforesaid, are, in the opinion of this assembly, not only intolerably burdensome and oppressive, but utterly subversive of the rights and liberties of the people of this state, and the freedom, sovereignty, and independence of the same, and inconsistent with the principles of the constitution of the United States.

" *And whereas* it will become the imperious duty of the

legislature of this state to exert themselves to ward off a
blow so fatal to the liberties of a free people—

"*Resolved by this Assembly*—that in case the plan and
bill aforesaid, or any other bill on that subject, containing
the principles aforesaid, shall be adopted, and assume the
form of an act of Congress, the Governor of this state is
hereby requested forthwith to convoke the General Assembly; and to avoid delay, he is hereby authorised to issue
his proclamation, requiring the attendance of the members
thereof, at such time and place as he may appoint, to the
end that opportunity may be given to consider what measures may be adopted to secure and preserve the rights
and liberties of the people of this state, and the freedom,
sovereignty and independence of the same."

The events of 1814 have been already referred to.
They had excited strong consternation throughout a large
portion of the country, and particularly in the New-England states, where the exposure to invasion was pre-emi-
nently great, and where the consequences which must
ensue such a hostile visitation, must necessarily prove in
the highest degree disastrous.   The national government
had withdrawn almost all their troops from the Atlantic
frontier, and had provided nothing for the safety of the
inhabitants beyond a single military officer of some rank,
(and perhaps a small number of soldiers,) to take the
oversight of a certain specified portion of territory which
was called a "military district."   In a pamphlet published
in Boston in 1823, it is said—" In the summer of 1814,
the war, which before had not approached nearer than the
great northern lakes, at length fell unexpectedly and in
an alarming manner upon the borders of Massachusetts.
The English, in considerable force, captured Castine, a
small town at the mouth of the Penobscot, and in a short
time had the absolute control of all that part of Maine
which lies to the eastward of that great river.   Intelligence was shortly received by express at head quarters in

Boston, that the enemy was preparing to execute without delay a more extensive invasion, and it therefore became necessary to take measures of immediate and vigorous defence. Under these distressing and disastrous circumstances, Governor Strong resolved to assemble the members of the legislature. The general court accordingly met on the 5th day of October of the same year; and his excellency commenced his message in the following words:—"Since your last adjournment such important changes have taken place in the state of our public affairs, and the war in which we have been unhappily involved has assumed an aspect so threatening and destructive, that the council unanimously concurred with me in opinion that an extraordinary meeting of the legislature was indispensable."———"Two days after the session began, viz. on the 7th of October, a resolution approving the governor's conduct as it related to the defence of the state, passed the house by a *vote of 222 to 59*. On the 13th of October another resolution, authorising the governor to raise ten thousand men for the defence of the state, passed the house by a *vote of 252 to 71*."

In addition to all the other calamities with which the country was visited, in the year 1814, a large proportion of the banks in the states south of New-England had refused to pay their notes in specie, in consequence of which the paper currency issued by such banks greatly depreciated, strong fears prevailed that they were insolvent, and the alarm became almost universal. As a natural result of the excitement which was caused by this state of things, business of all kinds was greatly impeded and embarrassed, if not entirely suspended; to such a degree had the fears of the community been raised, that the individual who was under the necessity of travelling from New-York to Boston, found himself subjected to serious loss, as well as great inconvenience, in consequence of the doubts entertained of the security of the notes circulated by the banks of the former city. The state of Connecticut, bordering upon the state of New-York, and having a constant intercourse with its inhabitants, and especially relying upon the city of New-York as the great market for their marketable commodities, received New-York bank paper almost exclusively in payment for those commodities; and it soon became a question of much importance, whether it was safe for the state of Connecticut to receive a depreciated and depreciating currency of another state, in payment of taxes, which, by the extraordinary expenditures in support of the war, and especially in paying the militia, had become extremely burthensome. From the high tone which, in their public communications, the American government had assumed, when treating of the subject of peace, it was impossible to foresee, or even to calculate the probable duration of the war. If they adhered to their demands, it appeared likely to be interminable, for the British, having been extricated from the war with France, were left at full liberty to devote their undivided attention to that with the United States. And had our government held out—had they not in their instructions to their agents, who were employed in negotiating for peace, empowered them to abandon every ground and principle for which the war was professedly undertaken, there is no room to doubt that the year 1815 would have been the most fearful period that had ever marked our national history. The events of 1814 manifested a spirit of resentment on the part of the British, from which it was easy to perceive that the worst passions would attend, and the most vindictive spirit be exhibited, in the further prosecution of the war. There was nothing, therefore, in the prospect, that was calculated to afford the slightest relief to the apprehensions of the country, respecting the hostile movements of the enemy, during the approaching season. On the contrary, as the means for carrying on the war were in a great measure exhausted, the government had become alarmed for their own popularity, and were obviously preparing to resort to the most desperate, as well as the most unconstitutional measures, to save themselves from the odium which they could scarcely hope to avoid, if hostilities should continue through another year, and the utmost alarm prevailed concerning the result. The situation of the New-England states was in the highest degree critical and dangerous. The services of the militia, for two years, had been extremely severe, they were constantly taken from their farms and their ordinary occupations, and in addition to all the losses which such a state of things must necessarily produce, they were subjected to the hardships and hazards of a camp, and the life of a soldier. In the mean time, the United States had withheld all supplies for the maintenance of the militia for the year 1814, both in Massachusetts and Connecticut, and thus forced upon the states the burden of supporting the troops employed in defending their coasts from invasion, and their towns from being sacked and pillaged. And all this time, the taxes laid to carry on the war were exacted from those states with the most rigorous strictness ; and when, under all these circumstances, the monied institutions in a large part of the country were stopping payment, when their credit was shaken, their notes depreciated, and their solvency doubted, the capitalists of the New-England states, because they did not deem it expedient to risk their private fortunes by loaning money to the government, which had wilfully and against all remonstrances, brought these multiplied calamities upon themselves, as well as upon the nation, were reviled as enemies to their country and as traitors to its government. It had become perfectly apparent, that if the New-England states were rescued from the effects of these calamities at all, it must depend, as far as human means were concerned, upon their own exertions, and that they could not place the least dependance on the national government. Indeed, they had been repeatedly told that such was the state of things by the national government.

In Massachusetts, the danger to which the inhabitants near the sea-coast were exposed, had spread an alarm throughout the commonwealth. Early in the year 1814, memorials from a great number of towns, from the interior as well as near the coast, were forwarded to the legislature, praying that body to exert their authority to protect the citizens in their constitutional rights and privileges, and suggesting the expediency of appointing delegates, "to meet delegates from such other states as might think proper to appoint them, for the purpose of devising proper measures to procure the united efforts of the commercial states, to obtain such amendments and explanations of the constitution as will secure them from further evils."

These memorials were referred to a joint committee of the Senate and House of Representatives, who made a report, of which the following, in relation to the proposed convention, is an extract—" The committee are convinced of the right, and think the legislature ought to vindicate it, of acting in concert with other states, in order to produce a powerful, and, if possible, an irresistible claim for such alterations as will tend to preserve the Union, and restore violated privileges, yet they have considered that there are reasons which render it inexpedient at the present moment to exercise this power.

" The committee entertain no doubt, that the sentiments and feelings expressed in the numerous memorials and remonstrances which have been committed to them, are the genuine voice of a vast majority of the citizens of this commonwealth."

This report bears date February 4th, 1814, and was adopted in the Senate by a vote of 23 to 8, and in the House of Representatives, of 178 to 43.

On the 16th of October the House of Representatives passed the following resolution, by a vote of 260 to 90—

" Resolved, That twelve persons be appointed as delegates from this Commonwealth, to meet and confer with delegates from the other New-England states, or any other, upon the subject of their public grievances and concerns ; and upon the best means of preserving our resources ; and of defence against the enemy ; and to *devise and suggest for adoption by those respective states* such measures as they may deem expedient ; and also to take measures, if they shall think it proper, for procuring a convention of delegates from all the United States, in order to revise the Constitution thereof, and more effectually to secure the support and attachment of all the people, by placing all upon the basis of fair representation."

The Senate having concurred in passing this resolution, on the 18th of October the Houses in convention elected the delegates by a vote of 226 to 67. The legislature directed the President of the Senate, and the Speaker of the House of Representatives, to make known as speedily as possible, to the different governments of the Union the proceedings of the government of that state. Accordingly the following letter was written by those two officers of the government to the executive magistrates of the other states.—

" *Boston, October* 17*th,* 1814.

" Sir,—Your Excellency will herewith receive certain resolutions of the legislature of Massachusetts, which you are respectfully requested to take the earliest occasion to lay before the legislature of your state, together with this letter, which is intended as an invitation to them, to appoint delegates, if they shall deem it expedient, to meet such others as may be appointed by this and other states, at the time and place expressed in these resolutions.

" The general objects of the proposed conference are,

first, to deliberate upon the dangers to which the eastern section of the Union is exposed by the course of the war, and which there is too much reason to believe will thicken round them in its progress, and to devise, *if practicable,* means of security and defence which may be consistent with the preservation of their resources from total ruin, and adapted to their local situation, mutual relations and habits, and NOT REPUGNANT TO THEIR OBLIGATIONS AS MEMBERS OF THE UNION. When convened for this object, which admits not of delay, it seems also expedient to submit to their consideration, the inquiry, whether the interests of these states demand that persevering endeavours be used by each of them to procure such *amendments,* to be effected in the national constitution, as may secure to them equal advantage, and whether, if in their judgment this should be deemed impracticable, under the existing provisions for amending that instrument, an experiment may be made without disadvantage to the nation, for obtaining a convention from all the states in the Union, or such of them as approve of the measure, with *a view to obtain such amendment.*

" It cannot be necessary to anticipate objections to the measure which may arise from jealousy or fear. This legislature is content, for its justification, to repose on the purity of its own motives, and upon *the known attachment of its constituents to the national union, and to the rights and independence of their country.*

" We have the honor to be, &c.
" JOHN PHILLIPS,
" *President of the Senate of the Commonwealth of Massachusetts.*
" TIMOTHY BIGELOW,
" *Speaker of the House of Representatives of said Commonwealth.*"

The documents from the legislature of Massachusetts, which have just been quoted, were transmitted to the legislatures of Connecticut and Rhode Island. The General

Assembly of Connecticut were then in session, and the documents were communicated to the two houses, and by them were referred to a joint committee, who thereupon made the following report—

" At a General Assembly of the State of Connecticut, holden at New-Haven, in said state, on the second Thursday of October, in the year of our Lord one thousand eight hundred and fourteen.

" To the Honourable the General Assembly now in session. The committee to whom was referred the speech of his excellency the governor, with the documents accompanying the same, and also his excellency's message, presenting a communication from the governour of Massachusetts; further report,—

" That the condition of this state demands the most serious attention of the Legislature. We lately enjoyed, in common with the other members of the national confederacy, the blessings of peace. The industry of our citizens, in every department of active life, was abundantly rewarded; our cities and villages exhibited indications of increasing wealth; and the foreign relations of the Union secured our safety and nourished our prosperity.

" The scene is now reversed. We are summoned to the field of war, and to surrender our treasures for our defence. The fleets of a powerful enemy hover on our coasts; blockade our harbours; and threaten our towns and cities with fire and desolation.

" When a commonwealth suddenly falls from a state of high prosperity, it behoves the guardians of its interests to inquire into the cause of its decline, and, with deep solicitude, to seek a remedy.

" In the latter part of the last century, a spirit of daring enterprise—impatient of restraint—regardless of the sanctions of religion—hostile to human happiness, and aspiring to supreme power—overturned many ancient governments; made Europe a scene of carnage, and threatened with ruin all which was valuable in the civilized world. The history of its progress and decline is familiar to every mind. Nations without the reach of the immense physical power which it embodied, were tainted by its corruptions; and every state and province in christendom has felt its baneful influences. By the pure principles inherited from our fathers, conducive, at once, to the preservation of liberty and order, this state has been eminently exempt, in its interior policy, from this modern scourge of nations. In thus withstanding this potent adversary of all ancient establishments, while many monarchies have been subverted, we have exhibited to the world the highest evidence that a free constitution is not inconsistent with the strength of civil government, and that the virtue of a people is the best preservation of both.

" Occupying a comparatively small territory, and naturally associating, during the revolutionary war, with states whose views were identified with ours, our interests and inclinations led us to unite in the great national compact, since defined and consolidated by the constitution of the United States. We had justly anticipated, from that union, the preservation and advancement of our dearest rights and interests; and while the father of his country, and those other great and wise men,—who, mindful of their high duties, and regardless of local and party considerations, consulted the happiness of the commonwealth, guided our councils, we were not disappointed in our expectations. The federal government, in which our own venerable statesmen were conspicuous, was revered in every nation. An American in foreign lands, was honoured for his country's sake : a rich and virtuous population was rapidly reducing the limits of our extensive wilderness ; and the commerce of America was in every sea.

" But a coalition, not less evident than if defined by the articles of a formal treaty, arose between the national administration and that fearful tyrant in Europe, who was

aspiring to the dominion of the world. No means, however destructive to the commerce and hazardous to the
peace of this country, were left unattempted, to aid his
efforts and unite our interests and destinies with his.
From this fatal cause, we are bereft of the respectable
standing we once held in the councils of the nation ; im-
poverished by a long course of commercial restrictions;
involved in an odious and disastrous war ; and subjected
to all the complicated calamities which we now deplore.

" Thus driven from every object of our best hopes, and
bound to an inglorious struggle in defence of our dwellings.
from a public enemy; we had no apprehension, much as
we had suffered from the national government, that it
would refuse to yield us such protection as its treasures
might afford. Much less could we doubt, that those disbursements, which might be demanded of this state, would
be passed to our credit on the books of the treasury. Such
however has not been the course adopted by the national
agents. All supplies have been withdrawn from the militia of this state, in the service of the United States. The
groundless pretext for this unwarrantable measure, was,
their submission to an officer assigned them by the commander in chief, in perfect conformity with military usage,
and the principles of a request from the President himself,
under which a party of them were detached. The injustice of that measure, by which we were compelled to sustain alone the burden of supplying and paying our own
forces, in the service of the United States—a service rendered necessary to defend our territory from invasion—is
highly aggravated by the consideration, that the dangers
which called them to the field, and the concentration of
the enemy's forces on our coasts, have resulted from the
ships of the United States having taken refuge in our waters. Were this the only instance evincive of the disregard of the administration to the just claims and best interests of this state,—the only ground to fear that we are

forgotten in their councils, except as subjects of taxation and oppression,—we should choose to consider it an instance anomalous and solitary—still yield them our confidence, and hope for protection to the extent of their power, in this season of unusual calamity.

"Protection is the first, and most important claim of these states on the government of the nation. It is a primary condition, essential to the very obligation of every compact between rulers and their subjects. To obtain that, as a principal object, Connecticut became a member of the national confederacy. In a defensive war, a government would stand justified, after making a fair application of its powers to that important end;—for it could do no more. But when a government hastily declares war, without providing the indispensable means of conducting it—want of means is no apology for refusing protection. In such a case, the very declaration of war, is, of itself, a breach of the sacred obligation; inasmuch as the loss of protection by the subject, is the natural and inevitable consequence of the measure. When that war annihilates the only revenues of the nation, the violation of the original contract is still more palpable. If waged for foreign conquest, and the wreck of the national treasures devoted to a fruitless invasion of the enemy's territory, the character of the act is more criminal, but not more clear.

"Whatever may be the disposition of the national Executive towards this state, during the sequel of the war, such is the condition of the public finances, that constant and very great advances must be made from our state treasury, to meet the expenditures necessary for our own defence.

"But the utmost efforts of this state, under the most favourable circumstances for raising revenue, would be hardly adequate to the costly operations of defending, against a great naval power, a sea-coast of more than one hundred and twenty miles in length; much less, at this inauspicious period, when the distresses of the people are enhanced by the embarrassments of our monied institutions, and the circulating medium constantly diminishing, can any thing be spared consistently with our safety. Yet the national government are dooming us to enormous taxation, without affording any just confidence that we shall share in the expenditures of the public revenue. The invasion of Canada is perseveringly pursued, our coasts left defenceless, and the treasures of the country exhausted on more favoured points of the national frontier. To meet those demands, and, at the same time, to defend ourselves, is impossible. Whatever we may contribute, we have no reasonable ground to expect protection in return.

"The people of this state have no disloyalty to the interests of the Union. For their fidelity and patriotism, they may appeal, with confidence, to the national archives from the commencement of the revolutionary war.

"In achieving the independence of the nation, they bore an honourable part. Their contingent in men and money has ever been promptly furnished, when constitutionally required. Much as they lament the present unnatural hostilities with Great Britain, they have, with characteristic obedience to lawful authority, punctually paid the late taxes imposed by the general government. On every lawful demand of the national Executive, their well-disciplined militia have resorted to the field. The public enemy, when invading their shores, has been met at the water's edge, and valiantly repulsed. They duly appreciate the great advantages which would result from the federal compact, were the government administered according to the sacred principles of the constitution. They have not forgotten the ties of confidence and affection, which bound these states to each other during their toils for independence;—nor the national honour and commercial prosperity, which they mutually shared, during the happy years of a good administration. They are, at the same time, conscious of their rights and determined to defend them. Those sacred liberties—those inestimable institutions, civil and religious, which their venerable fathers have bequeathed them, are, with the blessing of Heaven, to be maintained at every hazard, and never to be surrendered by tenants of the soil which the ashes of their ancestors have consecrated.

"In what manner the multiplied evils, which we feel and fear, are to be remedied, is a question of the highest moment, and deserves the greatest consideration. The documents transmitted by his excellency the Governor of Massachusetts, present, in the opinion of the committee, an eligible method of combining the wisdom of New-England, in devising, on full consultation, a proper course to be adopted, consistent with our obligations to the United States. The following resolutions are, therefore, respectfully submitted.

"Signed by order,
"HENRY CHAMPION, *Chairman*."

" *General Assembly, October Session,* 1814.

"In the House of Representatives, the foregoing report is accepted and approved.
"Attest.   CHARLES DENISON, *Clerk*."
" Concurred in by the Upper House.
"Attest.   THOMAS DAY, *Secretary*."

" Resolved, That seven persons be appointed Delegates from this state, to meet the delegates of the Commonwealth of Massachusetts, and of any other of the New-England states, at Hartford, on the 15th day of December next, and confer with them on the subjects proposed by a resolution of said Commonwealth, communicated to this legislature, and upon any other subjects which may come before them, for the purpose of devising and recommending such measures for the safety and welfare of these states, AS MAY CONSIST WITH OUR OBLIGATIONS AS MEMBERS OF THE NATIONAL UNION.

" Resolved, That his excellency the Governor be requested to transmit the foregoing report and resolutions
to the Executives of the New-England states.

" This Assembly do appoint his honour Chauncey Goodrich, the honourable James Hillhouse, the honourable
John Treadwell, the honourable Zephaniah Swift, the honourable Nathaniel Smith, the honourable Calvin Goddard
and the honourable Roger M. Sherman, Delegates from
this state, to meet the Delegates of the Commonwealth of
Massachusetts and of any other of the New-England states,
at Hartford, on the fifteenth day of December next, and
confer with them on the subjects proposed by a resolution
of said Commonwealth, communicated to this Legislature,
and upon any other subjects which may come before them,
for the purpose of devising and recommending such measures for the safety and welfare of these states as may consist with our obligations as members of the national Union.

" The above and foregoing are true copies of record,
examined and certified under the seal of the state, by

" THOMAS DAY, *Secretary.*"

The following is an account of the proceedings of the
legislature of Rhode-Island on this subject—

" State of Rhode-Island and
Providence Plantations.

" *In General Assembly, October Session, A. D.* 1814.

" Whereas this General Assembly, having long witnessed with regret and anxiety, the defenceless situation of
this state, did, at their last session, request his excellency
the governor to communicate with the executives of our
neighbouring sister states upon the subject of our common
defence by our mutual co-operation : and whereas those
states feeling equally with us the common misfortunes,
and the necessity of united exertions, have appointed and

invited us to appoint delegates to meet and confer upon our calamitous situation, and to devise and recommend wise and prudent measures for our common relief.

" *Resolved,* That this General Assembly will appoint four delegates from this state, to meet at Hartford in the state of Connecticut, on the fifteenth day of December next, and confer with such delegates as are or shall be appointed by other states, upon the common dangers to which these states are exposed, upon the best means of co-operating for our mutual defence against the enemy, and upon the measures which it may be in the power of said states, consistently with their obligations to adopt, to restore and secure to the people thereof, their rights and privileges under the constitution of the United States.

" True copy—witness,

" HENRY BOWEN, *Sec'ry.*"

" Both houses having joined in grand committee, chose Daniel Lyman, Samuel Ward, Benjamin Hazard, and Edward Manton, Esquires, delegates from this state, to meet at Hartford in the state of Connecticut, on the fifteenth day of December next, and confer with delegates from other states, pursuant to a resolution for this purpose passed at the present session.

" True copy—witness

" HENRY BOWEN, *Sec'ry.*"

On the 15th of December, 1814, the Convention met at Hartford, in the state of Connecticut. There were twelve members from Massachusetts, viz. George Cabot, Nathan Dane, William Prescott, Harrison Gray Otis, Timothy Bigelow, Joshua Thomas, Samuel Sumner Wilde, Joseph Lyman, George Bliss, Stephen Longfellow, Jun. Daniel Waldo, and Hodijah Baylies. From Connecticut there were seven members, viz. Chauncey Goodrich, John Treadwell, James Hillhouse, Zephaniah Swift, Nathaniel

Smith, Calvin Goddard, and Roger Minot Sherman. From Rhode Island there were four, viz. Daniel Lyman, Samuel Ward, Edward Manton, and Benjamin Hazard. Three persons, viz. Benjamin West and Mills Olcott, from New-Hampshire, and William Hall, Jun. of Vermont, who appeared as delegates chosen by local conventions in those states, were also admitted as members. Immediately upon being assembled, they proceeded to the choice of officers. George Cabot, a member from Massachusetts, was chosen president, and the author of this work secretary. Having thus become organized, they proceeded in the performance of the business for which they had been delegated; and after a session of three weeks, embodied the result of their labours in the following report—

"REPORT, &c.

" *The delegates from the legislatures of the states of Massachusetts, Connecticut, and Rhode-Island, and from the counties of Grafton and Cheshire in the state of New-Hampshire and the county of Windham in the state of Vermont, assembled in convention, beg leave to report the following result of their conference.*

" The convention is deeply impressed with a sense of the arduous nature of the commission which they were appointed to execute, of devising the means of defence against dangers, and of relief from oppressions proceeding from the acts of their own government, without violating constitutional principles, or disappointing the hopes of a suffering and injured people. To prescribe patience and firmness to those who are already exhausted by distress, is sometimes to drive them to despair, and the progress towards reform by the regular road, is irksome to those whose imaginations discern, and whose feelings prompt, to a shorter course. But when abuses, reduced to a system, and accumulated through a course of years, have pervaded every department of government, and spread corruption through every region of the state ; when these are clothed with the forms of law, and enforced by an executive whose will is their source, no summary means of relief can be applied without recourse to direct and open resistance. This experiment, even when justifiable, cannot fail to be painful to the good citizen; and the success of the effort will be no security against the danger of the example. Precedents of resistance to the worst administration, are eagerly seized by those who are naturally hostile to the best. Necessity alone can sanction a resort to this measure; and it should never be extended in duration or degree beyond the exigency, until the people, not merely in the fervour of sudden excitement, but after full deliberation, are determined to change the constitution.

" It is a truth, not to be concealed, that a sentiment prevails to no inconsiderable extent, that administration have given such constructions to that instrument, and practised so many abuses under colour of its authority, that the time for a change is at hand. Those who so believe, regard the evils which surround them as intrinsic and incurable defects in the constitution. They yield to a persuasion, that no change, at any time, or on any occasion, can aggravate the misery of their country. This opinion may ultimately prove to be correct. But as the evidence on which it rests is not yet conclusive, and as measures adopted upon the assumption of its certainty might be irrevocable, some general considerations are submitted, in the hope of reconciling all to a course of moderation and firmness, which may save them from the regret incident to sudden decisions, probably avert the evil, or at least insure consolation and success in the last resort.

" The constitution of the United States, under the auspices of a wise and virtuous administration, proved itself competent to all the objects of national prosperity comprehended in the views of its framers. No parallel can be found in history, of a transition so rapid as that of the United States from the lowest depression to the highest felicity—from the condition of weak and disjointed republics, to that of a great, united, and prosperous nation.

"Although this high state of public happiness has undergone a miserable and afflicting reverse, through the prevalence of a weak and profligate policy, yet the evils and afflictions which have thus been induced upon the country, are not peculiar to any form of government. The lust and caprice of power, the corruption of patronage, the oppression of the weaker interests of the community by the stronger, heavy taxes, wasteful expenditures, and unjust and ruinous wars, are the natural offspring of bad administrations, in all ages and countries. It was indeed to be hoped, that the rulers of these states would not make such disastrous haste to involve their infancy in the embarrassments of old and rotten institutions. Yet all this have they done; and their conduct calls loudly for their dismission and disgrace. But to attempt upon every abuse of power to change the constitution, would be to perpetuate the evils of revolution.

"Again, the experiment of the powers of the constitution to regain its vigour, and of the people to recover from their delusions, has been hitherto made under the greatest possible disadvantages arising from the state of the world. The fierce passions which have convulsed the nations of Europe, have passed the ocean, and finding their way to the bosoms of our citizens, have afforded to administration the means of perverting public opinion, in respect to our foreign relations, so as to acquire its aid in the indulgence of their animosities, and the increase of their adherents. Further, a reformation of public opinion, resulting from dear-bought experience, in the southern Atlantic states, at least, is not to be despaired of. They will have felt, that the eastern states cannot be made exclusively the victims of a capricious and impassioned policy. They will have seen that the great and essential interests of the people are common to the south and to the east. They will realize the fatal errors of a system which seeks revenge for commercial injuries in the sacrifice of commerce, and aggravates by needless wars, to an immeasurable extent, the injuries it professes to redress. They may discard the influence of visionary theorists, and recognize the benefits of a practical policy. Indications of this desirable revolution of opinion, among our brethren in those states, are already manifested. While a hope remains of its ultimate completion, its progress should not be retarded or stopped, by exciting fears which must check these favourable tendencies, and frustrate the efforts of the wisest and best men in those states, to accelerate this propitious change.

"Finally, if the Union be destined to dissolution, by reason of the multiplied abuses of bad administrations, it should, if possible, be the work of peaceable times, and deliberate consent. Some new form of confederacy should be substituted among those states which shall intend to maintain a federal relation to each other. Events may prove that the causes of our calamities are deep and permanent. They may be found to proceed, not merely from the blindness of prejudice, pride of opinion, violence of party spirit, or the confusion of the times; but they may be traced to implacable combinations of individuals, or of states, to monopolize power and office, and to trample without remorse upon the rights and interests of commercial sections of the Union. Whenever it shall appear that these causes are radical and permanent, a separation, by equitable arrangement, will be preferable to an alliance by constraint, among nominal friends, but real enemies, inflamed by mutual hatred and jealousy, and inviting, by intestine divisions, contempt and aggression from abroad. But a severance of the Union by one or more states, against the will of the rest, and especially in a time of war, can be justified only by absolute necessity. These are among the principal objections against precipitate measures tending to disunite the states, and when examined in connection with the farewell address of the Father of his country, they must, it is believed, be deemed conclusive.

" Under these impressions, the convention have proceeded to confer and deliberate upon the alarming state of public affairs, especially as affecting the interests of the people who have appointed them for this purpose, and they are naturally led to a consideration, in the first place, of the dangers and grievances which menace an immediate or speedy pressure, with a view of suggesting means of present relief; in the next place, of such as are of a more remote and general description, in the hope of attaining future security.

" Among the subjects of complaint and apprehension, which might be comprised under the former of these propositions, the attention of the convention has been occupied with the claims and pretensions advanced, and the authority exercised over the militia, by the executive and legislative departments of the national government. Also, upon the destitution of the means of defence in which the eastern states are left; while at the same time they are doomed to heavy requisitions of men and money for national objects.

" The authority of the national government over the militia is derived from those clauses in the constitution which give power to Congress ' to provide for calling forth the militia to execute the laws of the Union, suppress insurrections and repel invasions ;'—Also ' to provide for organizing, arming, and disciplining the militia, and for governing such parts of them as may be employed in the service of the United States, reserving to the states respectively the appointment of the officers, and the authority of training the militia according to the discipline prescribed by Congress.' Again, ' the President shall be commander in chief of the army and navy of the United States, and of the militia of the several states, *when called into the actual service of the United States.'* In these specified cases only, has the national government any power over the militia ; and it follows conclusively, that for all general and ordinary purposes, this power belongs to the states respectively, and to them alone. It is not only with regret, but with astonishment, the convention perceive that under colour of an authority conferred with such plain and precise limitations, a power is arrogated by the executive government, and in some instances sanctioned by the two houses of congress, of control over the militia, which if conceded will render nugatory the rightful authority of the individual states over that class of men, and by placing at the disposal of the national government the lives and services of the great body of the people, enable it at pleasure to destroy their liberties, and erect a military despotism on the ruins.

" An elaborate examination of the principles assumed for the basis of these extravagant pretensions, of the consequences to which they lead, and of the insurmountable objections to their admission, would transcend the limits of this report. A few general observations, with an exhibition of the character of these pretensions, and a recommendation of a strenuous opposition to them, must not, however, be omitted.

" It will not be contended that by the terms used in the constitutional compact, the power of the national government to call out the militia is other than a power expressly limited to three cases. One of these must exist, as a condition precedent to the exercise of that power—Unless the laws shall be opposed, or an insurrection shall exist, or an invasion shall be made, congress, and of consequence the President as their organ, has no more power over the militia than over the armies of a foreign nation.

" But if the declaration of the President should be admitted to be an unerring test of the existence of these cases, this important power would depend, not upon the truth of the fact, but upon executive infallibility. And the limitation of the power would consequently be nothing more than merely nominal, as it might always be eluded. It follows therefore that the decision of the President in this particular cannot be conclusive. It is as much the duty of the state authorities to watch over the rights *reserved*, as of the United States to exercise the powers which are *delegated*.

"The arrangement of the United States into military districts, with a small portion of the regular force, under an officer of high rank of the standing army, with power to call for the militia, as circumstances in his judgment may require; and to assume the command of them, is not warranted by the constitution or any law of the United States. It is not denied that Congress may delegate to the President of the United States the power to call forth the militia in the cases which are within their jurisdiction—But he has no authority to substitute military prefects throughout the Union, to use their own discretion in such instances. To station an officer of the army in a military district without troops corresponding to his rank, for the purpose of taking command of the militia that may be called into service, is a manifest evasion of that provision of the constitution which expressly reserves to the states the appointment of the officers of the militia; and the object of detaching such officer cannot be well concluded to be any other than that of superseding the governor or other officers of the militia in their right to command.

"The power of dividing the militia of the states into classes, and obliging such classes to furnish by contract or draft, able-bodied men, to serve for one or more years for the defence of the frontier, is not delegated to Congress. If a claim to draft the militia for one year for such general object be admissible, no limitation can be assigned to it, but the discretion of those who make the law. Thus, with a power in Congress to authorize such a draft or conscription, and in the Executive to decide conclusively upon the existence and continuance of the emergency, the whole militia may be converted into a standing army disposable at the will of the President of the United States.

"The power of compelling the militia, and other citizens of the United States, by a forcible draft or conscription, to serve in the regular armies as proposed in a late official letter of the Secretary of War, is not delegated to Congress by the constitution, and the exercise of it would be not less dangerous to their liberties, than hostile to the sovereignty of the states. The effort to deduce this power from the right of raising armies, is a flagrant attempt to pervert the sense of the clause in the constitution which confers that right, and is incompatible with other provisions in that instrument. The armies of the United States have always been raised by contract, never by conscription, and nothing more can be wanting to a government possessing the power thus claimed to enable it to usurp the entire control of the militia, in derogation of the authority of the state, and to convert it by impressment into a standing army.

"It may be here remarked, as a circumstance illustrative of the determination of the Executive to establish an absolute control over all descriptions of citizens, that the right of impressing seamen into the naval service is expressly asserted by the Secretary of the Navy in a late report. Thus a practice, which in a foreign government has been regarded with great abhorrence by the people, finds advocates among those who have been the loudest to condemn it.

"The law authorising the enlistment of minors and apprentices into the armies of the United States, without the consent of parents and guardians, is also repugnant to the spirit of the constitution. By a construction of the power to raise armies, as applied by our present rulers, not only persons capable of contracting are liable to be impressed into the army, but those who are under legal disabilities to make contracts, are to be invested with the capacity, in order to enable them to annul at pleasure contracts made in their behalf by legal guardians. Such an interference with the municipal laws and rights of the several states, could never have been contemplated by the framers of the constitution. It impairs the salutary control and influence of the parent over his child—the master over his servant —the guardian over his ward—and thus destroys the most important relations in society, so that by the conscription of the father, and the seduction of the son, the power of the Executive over all the effective male population of the United States is made complete.

" Such are some of the odious features of the novel system proposed by the rulers of a free country, under the limited powers derived from the constitution. What portion of them will be embraced in acts finally to be passed, it is yet impossible to determine. It is, however, sufficiently alarming to perceive, that these projects emanate from the highest authority, nor should it be forgotten, that by the plan of the Secretary of War, the classification of the militia embraced the principle of direct taxation upon the white population only ; and that, in the house of representatives, a motion to apportion the militia among the white population exclusively, which would have been in its operation a direct tax, was strenuously urged and supported.

" In this whole series of devices and measures for raising men, this convention discern a total disregard for the constitution, and a disposition to violate its provisions, demanding from the individual states a firm and decided opposition. An iron despotism can impose no harder servitude upon the citizen, than to force him from his home and his occupation, to wage offensive wars, undertaken to gratify the pride or passions of his master. The example of France has recently shown that a cabal of individuals assuming to act in the name of the people, may transform the great body of citizens into soldiers, and deliver them over into the hands of a single tyrant. No war, not held in just abhorrence by the people, can require the aid of such stratagems to recruit an army. Had the troops already raised, and in great numbers sacrificed upon the frontier of Canada, been employed for the defence of the country, and had the millions which have been squandered with shameless profusion, been appropriated to their payment, to the protection of the coast, and to the naval service, there would have been no occasion for unconstitutional expedients. Even at this late hour, let government leave to New-England the remnant of her resources, and she is ready and able to defend her territory, and to resign the glories and advantages of the border war to those who are determined to persist in its prosecution.

" That acts of Congress in violation of the constitution are absolutely void, is an undeniable position. It does not, however, consist with respect and forbearance due from a confederate state towards the general government, to fly to open resistance upon every infraction of the constitution. The mode and the energy of the opposition, should always conform to the nature of the violation, the intention of its authors, the extent of the injury inflicted, the determination manifested to persist in it, and the danger of delay. But in cases of deliberate, dangerous, and palpable infractions of the constitution, affecting the sovereignty of a state, and liberties of the people ; it is not only the right but the duty of such a state to interpose its authority for their protection, in the manner best calculated to secure that end. When emergencies occur which are either beyond the reach of the judicial tribunals, or too pressing to admit of the delay incident to their forms, states which have no common umpire, must be their own judges, and execute their own decisions. It will thus be proper for the several states to await the ultimate disposal of the obnoxious measures recommended by the Secretary of War, or pending before Congress, and so to use their power according to the character these measures shall finally assume, as effectually to protect their own sovereignty, and the rights and liberties of their citizens.

" The next subject which has occupied the attention of the convention, is the means of defence against the common enemy. This naturally leads to the inquiries, whether any expectation can be reasonably entertained, that adequate provision for the defence of the eastern states will be made by the national government? Whether the several states can, from their own resources, provide for self-defence and fulfil the requisitions which are to be expected for the national treasury ? and, generally, what course of conduct ought to be adopted by those states, in relation to the great object of defence.

" Without pausing at present to comment upon the causes of the war, it may be assumed as a truth, officially announced, that to achieve the conquest of Canadian territory, and to hold it as a pledge for peace, is the deliberate purpose of administration. This enterprize, commenced at a period when government possessed the advantage of selecting the time and occasion for making a sudden descent upon an unprepared enemy, now languishes in the third year of the war. It has been prosecuted with various fortune, and occasional brilliancy of exploit, but without any solid acquisition. The British armies have been recruited by veteran regiments. Their navy commands Ontario. The American ranks are thinned by the casualties of war. Recruits are discouraged by the unpopular character of the contest, and by the uncertainty of receiving their pay.

" In the prosecution of this favourite warfare, administration have left the exposed and vulnerable parts of the country destitute of all the efficient means of defence.

The main body of the regular army has been marched to
the frontier. The navy has been stripped of a great part
of its sailors for the service of the lakes. Meanwhile the
enemy scours the sea-coast, blockades our ports, ascends
our bays and rivers, makes actual descents in various and
distant places, holds some by force, and threatens all that
are assailable with fire and sword. The sea-board of
four of the New-England states, following its curvatures,
presents an extent of more than seven hundred miles,
generally occupied by a compact population, and accessi-
ble by a naval force, exposing a mass of people and property to the devastation of the enemy, which bears a great
proportion to the residue of the maritime frontier of the
United States. This extensive shore has been exposed
to frequent attacks, repeated contributions, and constant
alarms. The regular forces detached by the national
government for its defence are mere pretexts for placing
officers of high rank in command. They are besides confined to a few places, and are too insignificant in number
to be included in any computation.

" These states have thus been left to adopt measures for
their own defence. The militia have been constantly kept
on the alert, and harassed by garrison duties, and other
hardships, while the expenses, of which the national government decline the reimbursement, threaten to absorb
all the resources of the states. The President of the United States has refused to consider the expense of the militia detached by state authority, for the indispensable defence of the state, as chargeable to the Union, on the
ground of a refusal by the Executive of the state to place
them under the command of officers of the regular army.
Detachments of militia placed at the disposal of the general government, have been dismissed either without pay,
or with depreciated paper. The prospect of the ensuing
campaign is not enlivened by the promise of any alleviation of these grievances. From authentic documents,

extorted by necessity from those whose inclination might lead them to conceal the embarrassments of the government, it is apparent that the treasury is bankrupt, and its credit prostrate. So deplorable is the state of the finances, that those who feel for the honour and safety of the country, would be willing to conceal the melancholy spectacle, if those whose infatuation has produced this state of fiscal concerns had not found themselves compelled to unveil it to public view.

"If the war be continued, there appears no room for reliance upon the national government for the supply of those means of defence which must become indispensable to secure these states from desolation and ruin. Nor is it possible that the states can discharge this sacred duty from their own resources, and continue to sustain the burden of the national taxes. The administration, after a long perseverance in plans to baffle every effort of commercial enterprize, had fatally succeeded in their attempts at the epoch of the war. Commerce, the vital spring of New-England's prosperity, was annihilated. Embargoes, restrictions, and the rapacity of revenue officers, had completed its destruction. The various objects for the employment of productive labour, in the branches of business dependent on commerce, have disappeared. The fisheries have shared its fate. Manufactures, which government has professed an intention to favour and to cherish, as an indemnity for the failure of these branches of business, are doomed to struggle in their infancy with taxes and obstructions, which cannot fail most seriously to affect their growth. The specie is withdrawn from circulation. The landed interest, the last to feel these burdens, must prepare to become their principal support, as all other sources of revenue must be exhausted. Under these circumstances, taxes, of a description and amount unprecedented in this country, are in a train of imposition, the burden of which must fall with the heaviest pressure upon the states east of the Potomac. *The amount of these taxes for the ensuing year cannot be estimated at less than five millions of dollars upon the New-England states, and the expenses of the last year for defence, in Massachusetts alone, approaches to one million of dollars.*

" From these facts, it is almost superfluous to state the irresistible inference that these states have no capacity of defraying the expense requisite for their own protection, and, at the same time, of discharging the demands of the national treasury.

" The last inquiry, what course of conduct ought to be adopted by the aggrieved states, is in a high degree momentous. When a great and brave people shall feel themselves deserted by their government, and reduced to the necessity either of submission to a foreign enemy, or of appropriating to their own use those means of defence which are indispensable to self-preservation, they cannot consent to wait passive spectators of approaching ruin, which it is in their power to avert, and to resign the last remnant of their industrious earnings to be dissipated in support of measures destructive of the best interests of the nation.

"This convention will not trust themselves to express their conviction of the catastrophe to which such a state of things inevitably tends. Conscious of their high responsibility to God and their country, solicitous for the continuance of the Union, as well as the sovereignty of the states, unwilling to furnish obstacles to peace—resolute never to submit to a foreign enemy, and confiding in the Divine care and protection, they will, until the last hope shall be extinguished, endeavor to avert such consequences.

" With this view they suggest an arrangement, which may at once be consistent with the honour and interest of the national government, and the security of these states. This it will not be difficult to conclude, if that government should be so disposed. By the terms of it these states might be allowed to assume their own defence, by the militia or other troops. A reasonable portion, also, of the taxes raised in each state might be paid into its treasury, and credited to the United States, but to be appropriated to the defence of such state, to be accounted for with the United States. No doubt is entertained that by such an arrangement, this portion of the country could be defended with greater effect, and in a mode more consistent with economy, and the public convenience, than any which has been practised.

" Should an application for these purposes, made to Congress by the state legislatures, be attended with success, and should peace upon just terms appear to be unattainable, the people would stand together for the common defence, until a change of administration, or of disposition in the enemy, should facilitate the occurrence of that auspicious event. It would be inexpedient for this Convention to diminish the hope of a successful issue to such an application, by recommending, upon supposition of a contrary event, ulterior proceedings. Nor is it indeed within their province. In a state of things so solemn and trying as may then arise, the legislatures of the states, or conventions of the whole people, or delegates appointed by them for the express purpose in another Convention, must act as such urgent circumstances may then require.

" But the duty incumbent on this Convention will not have been performed, without exhibiting some general view of such measures as they deem essential to secure the nation against a relapse into difficulties and dangers, should they, by the blessing of Providence, escape from their present condition, without absolute ruin. To this end a concise retrospect of the state of this nation under the advantages of a wise administration, contrasted with the miserable abyss into which it is plunged by the profligacy and folly of political theorists, will lead to some practical conclusions. On this subject, it will be recollected,

that the immediate influence of the Federal Constitution
upon its first adoption, and for twelve succeeding years,
upon the prosperity and happiness of the nation, seemed
to countenance a belief in the transcendency of its perfec-
tion over all other human institutions. In the catalogue
of blessings which have fallen to the lot of the most favoured nations, none could be enumerated from which our
country was excluded—a free Constitution, administered
by great and incorruptible statesmen, realized the fondest
hopes of liberty and independence—The progress of agriculture was stimulated by the certainty of value in the
harvest—and commerce, after traversing every sea, returned with the riches of every clime. A revenue, secured by a sense of honour, collected without oppression, and
paid without murmurs, melted away the national debt;
and the chief concern of the public creditor arose from its
too rapid diminution. The wars and commotions of the
European nations, and their interruptions of the commercial intercourse afforded to those who had not promoted,
but who would have rejoiced to alleviate their calamities,
a fair and golden opportunity, by combining themselves to
lay a broad foundation for national wealth. Although occasional vexations to commerce arose from the furious collisions of the powers at war, yet the great and good men
of that time conformed to the force of circumstances which
they could not control, and preserved their country in security from the tempests which overwhelmed the old
world, and threw the wreck of their fortunes on these
shores. Respect abroad, prosperity at home, wise laws
made by honoured legislators, and prompt obedience yielded by a contented people, had silenced the enemies of republican institutions. The arts flourished—the sciences
were cultivated—the comforts and conveniences of life
were universally diffused—and nothing remained for succeeding administrations but to reap the advantages and

cherish the resources flowing from the policy of their predecessors.

" But no sooner was a new administration established in the hands of the party opposed to the Washington policy, than a fixed determination was perceived and avowed of changing a system which had already produced these substantial fruits. The consequences of this change, for a few years after its commencement, were not sufficient to counteract the prodigious impulse towards prosperity, which had been given to the nation. But a steady perseverance in the new plans of administration, at length developed their weakness and deformity, but not until a majority of the people had been deceived by flattery, and inflamed by passion, into blindness to their defects. Under the withering influence of this new system, the declension of the nation has been uniform and rapid. The richest advantages for securing the great objects of the constitution have been wantonly rejected. While Europe reposes from the convulsions that had shaken down her ancient institutions, she beholds with amazement this remote country, once so happy and so envied, involved in a ruinous war, and excluded from intercourse with the rest of the world.

" To investigate and explain the means whereby this fatal reverse has been effected, would require a voluminous discussion. Nothing more can be attempted in this report than a general allusion to the principal outlines of the policy which has produced this vicissitude. Among these may be enumerated—

" *First.*—A deliberate and extensive system for effecting a combination among certain states, by exciting local jealousies and ambition, so as to secure to popular leaders in one section of the Union, the controul of public affairs in perpetual succession. To which primary object most other characteristics of the system may be reconciled.

" *Secondly.*—The political intolerance displayed and

avowed in excluding from office men of unexceptionable merit, for want of adherence to the executive creed.

" *Thirdly.*—The infraction of the judiciary authority and rights, by depriving judges of their offices in violation of the constitution.

" *Fourthly.*—The abolition of existing taxes, requisite to prepare the country for those changes to which nations are always exposed, with a view to the acquisition of popular favour.

" *Fifthly.*—The influence of patronage in the distribution of offices, which in these states has been almost invariably made among men the least entitled to such distinction, and who have sold themselves as ready instruments for distracting public opinion, and encouraging administration to hold in contempt the wishes and remonstrances of a people thus apparently divided.

" *Sixthly.*—The admission of new states into the Union formed at pleasure in the western region, has destroyed the balance of power which existed among the original States, and deeply affected their interest.

" *Seventhly.*—The easy admission of naturalized foreigners, to places of trust, honour or profit, operating as an inducement to the malcontent subjects of the old world to come to these States, in quest of executive patronage, and to repay it by an abject devotion to executive measures.

" *Eighthly.*—Hostility to Great Britain, and partiality to the late government of France, adopted as coincident with popular prejudice, and subservient to the main object, party power.   Connected with these must be ranked erroneous and distorted estimates of the power and resources of those nations, of the probable results of their controversies, and of our political relations to them respectively.

" *Lastly and principally.*—A visionary and superficial theory in regard to commerce, accompanied by a real hatred but a feigned regard to its interests, and a ruinous perseverance in efforts to render it an instrument of coercion and war.

" But it is not conceivable that the obliquity of any administration could, in so short a period, have so nearly consummated the work of national ruin, unless favoured by defects in the constitution.

" To enumerate all the improvements of which that instrument is susceptible, and to propose such amendments as might render it in all respects perfect, would be a task which this convention has not thought proper to assume. They have confined their attention to such as experience has demonstrated to be essential, and even among these, some are considered entitled to a more serious attention than others. They are suggested without any intentional disrespect to other states, and are meant to be such as all shall find an interest in promoting. Their object is to strengthen, and if possible to perpetuate, the union of the states, by removing the grounds of existing jealousies, and providing for a fair and equal representation, and a limitation of powers, which have been misused.

" The first amendment proposed, relates to the apportionment of representatives among the slave holding states. This cannot be claimed as a right. Those states are entitled to the slave representation, by a constitutional compact. It is therefore merely a subject of agreement, which should be conducted upon principles of mutual interest and accommodation, and upon which no sensibility on either side should be permitted to exist. It has proved unjust and unequal in its operation. Had this effect been foreseen, the privilege would probably not have been demanded; certainly not conceded. Its tendency in future will be adverse to that harmony and mutual confidence which are more conducive to the happiness and prosperity of every confederated state, than a mere preponderance of power, the prolific source of jealousies and controversy, can be to any one of them. The time may therefore arrive, when a sense of magnanimity and justice will reconcile those states to acquiesce in a revision of this article, especially as a fair equivalent would result to them in the apportionment of taxes.

" The next amendment relates to the admission of new states into the Union.

" This amendment is deemed to be highly important, and in fact indispensable. In proposing it, it is not intended to recognize the right of Congress to admit new states without the original limits of the United States, nor is any idea entertained of disturbing the tranquillity of any state already admitted into the Union. The object is merely to restrain the constitutional power of Congress in admitting new states. At the adoption of the constitution, a certain balance of power among the original parties was considered to exist, and there was at that time, and yet is among those parties, a strong affinity between their great and general interests.—By the admission of these states that balance has been materially affected, and unless the practice be modified, must ultimately be destroyed. The southern states will first avail themselves of their new confederates to govern the east, and finally the western states, multiplied in number, and augmented in population, will control the interests of the whole. Thus for the sake of present power, the southern states will be common sufferers with the east, in the loss of permanent advantages. None of the old states can find an interest in creating prematurely an overwhelming western influence, which may hereafter discern (as it has heretofore) benefits to be derived to them by wars and commercial restrictions.

"The next amendments proposed by the convention, relate to the powers of Congress, in relation to embargo and the interdiction of commerce.

" Whatever theories upon the subject of commerce have hitherto divided the opinions of statesmen, experience has at last shown that it is a vital interest in the United

States, and that its success is essential to the encouragement of agriculture and manufactures, and to the wealth,
finances, defence, and liberty of the nation. Its welfare
can never interfere with the other great interests of the
state, but must promote and uphold them. Still those
who are immediately concerned in the prosecution of commerce, will of necessity be always a minority of the nation. They are, however, best qualified to manage and
direct its course by the advantages of experience, and the
sense of interest. But they are entirely unable to protect
themselves against the sudden and injudicious decisions of
bare majorities, and the mistaken or oppressive projects of
those who are not actively concerned in its pursuits. Of
consequence, this interest is always exposed to be harassed,
interrupted, and entirely destroyed, upon pretence of securing other interests. Had the merchants of this nation
been permitted by their own government to pursue an innocent and lawful commerce, how different would have
been the state of the treasury and of public credit! How
short-sighted and miserable is the policy which has annihilated this order of men, and doomed their ships to rot
in the docks, their capital to waste unemployed, and their
affections to be alienated from the government which was
formed to protect them! What security for an ample and
unfailing revenue can ever be had, comparable to that
which once was realized in the good faith, punctuality,
and sense of honour, which attached the mercantile class
to the interests of the government! Without commerce,
where can be found the aliment for a navy; and without
a navy, what is to constitute the defence, and ornament,
and glory of this nation! No union can be durably ce-
mented, in which every great interest does not find itself
reasonably secured against the encroachment and combinations of other interests. When, therefore, the past system of embargoes and commercial restrictions shall have
been reviewed—when the fluctuation and inconsistency of

public measures, betraying a want of information as well as feeling in the majority, shall have been considered, the reasonableness of some restrictions upon the power of a bare majority to repeat these oppressions, will appear to be obvious.

"The next amendment proposes to restrict the power of making offensive war. In the consideration of this amendment, it is not necessary to inquire into the justice of the present war. But one sentiment now exists in relation to its expediency, and regret for its declaration is nearly universal. No indemnity can ever be attained for this terrible calamity, and its only palliation must be found in obstacles to its future recurrence. Rarely can the state of this country call for or justify offensive war. The genius of our institutions is unfavourable to its successful prosecution; the felicity of our situation exempts us from its necessity. In this case, as in the former, those more immediately exposed to its fatal effects are a minority of the nation. The commercial towns, the shores of our seas and rivers, contain the population whose vital interests are most vulnerable by a foreign enemy. Agriculture, indeed, must feel at last, but this appeal to its sensibility comes too late. Again, the immense population which has swarmed into the west, remote from immediate danger, and which is constantly augmenting, will not be averse from the occasional disturbances of the Atlantic states. Thus interest may not unfrequently combine with passion and intrigue, to plunge the nation into needless wars, and compel it to become a military, rather than a happy and flourishing people. These considerations, which it would be easy to augment, call loudly for the limitation proposed in the amendment.

"Another amendment, subordinate in importance, but still in a high degree expedient, relates to the exclusion of foreigners hereafter arriving in the United States from the capacity of holding offices of trust, honour, or profit.

"That the stock of population already in these states is amply sufficient to render this nation in due time sufficiently great and powerful, is not a controvertible question. Nor will it be seriously pretended, that the national deficiency in wisdom, arts, science, arms, or virtue, needs to be replenished from foreign countries. Still, it is agreed, that a liberal policy should offer the rights of hospitality, and the choice of settlement, to those who are disposed to visit the country. But why admit to a participation in the government aliens who were no parties to the compact— who are ignorant of the nature of our institutions, and have no stake in the welfare of the country but what is recent and transitory? It is surely a privilege sufficient, to admit them after due probation to become citizens, for all but political purposes. To extend it beyond these limits, is to encourage foreigners to come to these states as candidates for preferment. The Convention forbear to express their opinion upon the inauspicious effects which have already resulted to the honour and peace of this nation, from this misplaced and indiscriminate liberality.

"The last amendment respects the limitation of the office of President to a single constitutional term, and his eligibility from the same state two terms in succession.

"Upon this topic it is superfluous to dilate. The love of power is a principle in the human heart which too often impels to the use of all practicable means to prolong its duration. The office of President has charms and attractions which operate as powerful incentives to this passion. The first and most natural exertion of a vast patronage is directed towards the security of a new election. The interest of the country, the welfare of the people, even honest fame and respect for the opinion of posterity, are secondary considerations. All the engines of intrigue, all the means of corruption are likely to be employed for this object. A President whose political career is limited to a single election, may find no other interest than will be promoted by making it glorious to himself, and beneficial to his country. But the hope of re-election is prolific of temptations, under which these magnanimous motives are deprived of their principal force. The repeated election of the President of the United States from any one state, affords inducements and means for intrigues, which tend to create an undue local influence, and to establish the domination of particular states. The justice, therefore, of securing to every state a fair and equal chance for the election of this officer from its own citizens is apparent, and this object will be essentially promoted by preventing an election from the same state twice in succession.

" Such is the general view which this Convention has thought proper to submit, of the situation of these states, of their dangers and their duties. Most of the subjects which it embraces have separately received an ample and luminous investigation, by the great and able assertors of the rights of their country, in the national legislature; and nothing more could be attempted on this occasion than a digest of general principles, and of recommendations suited to the present state of public affairs. The peculiar difficulty and delicacy of performing even this undertaking, will be appreciated by all who think seriously upon the crisis. Negotiations for peace are at this hour supposed to be pending, the issue of which must be deeply interesting to all. No measures should be adopted which might unfavourably affect that issue ; none which should embarrass the administration, if their professed desire for peace is sincere ; and none which on supposition of their insincerity, should afford them pretexts for prolonging the war, or relieving themselves from the responsibility of a dishonourable peace. It is also devoutly to be wished, that an occasion may be afforded to all friends of the country, of all parties, and in all places, to pause and consider the awful state to which pernicious counsels and blind passions have brought this people. The number of those who perceive, and who are ready to retrace errors, must, it is believed, be yet sufficient to redeem the nation. It is necessary to rally and unite them by the assurance that no hostility to the constitution is meditated, and to obtain their aid in placing it under guardians who alone can save it from destruction. Should this fortunate change be effected, the hope of happiness and honour may once more dispel the surrounding gloom. Our nation may yet be great, our union durable. But should this prospect be utterly hopeless, the time will not have been lost which shall have ripened a general sentiment of the necessity of more mighty efforts to rescue from ruin, at least some portion of our beloved country.

" THEREFORE RESOLVED,

" That it be and hereby is recommended to the legislatures of the several states represented in this Convention, to adopt all such measures as may be necessary effectually to protect the citizens of said states from the operation and effects of all acts which have been or may be passed by the Congress of the United States, which shall contain provisions, subjecting the militia or other citizens to forcible drafts, conscriptions, or impressments, not authorised by the constitution of the United States.

" *Resolved*, That it be and hereby is recommended to the said Legislatures, to authorize an immediate and earnest application to be made to the government of the United States, requesting their consent to some arrangement, whereby the said states may, separately or in concert, be empowered to assume upon themselves the defence of their territory against the enemy; and a reasonable portion of the taxes, collected within said States, may be paid into the respective treasuries thereof, and appropriated to the payment of the balance due said states, and to the future defence of the same. The amount so paid into the said treasuries to be credited, and the disbursements made as aforesaid to be charged to the United States.

"*Resolved*, That it be, and hereby is, recommended to the legislatures of the aforesaid states, to pass laws (where it has not already been done) authorizing the governors or commanders-in-chief of their militia to make detachments from the same, or to form voluntary corps, as shall be most convenient and conformable to their constitutions, and to cause the same to be well armed, equipped, and disciplined, and held in readiness for service; and upon the request of the governor of either of the other states to employ the whole of such detachment or corps, as well as the regular forces of the state, or such part thereof as may be required and can be spared consistently with the safety of the state, in assisting the state, making such request to repel any invasion thereof which shall be made or attempted by the public enemy.

"*Resolved*, That the following amendments of the constitution of the United States be recommended to the states represented as aforesaid, to be proposed by them for adoption by the state legislatures, and in such cases as may be deemed expedient by a convention chosen by the people of each state.

"And it is further recommended, that the said states shall persevere in their efforts to obtain such amendments, until the same shall be effected.

"*First.* Representatives and direct taxes shall be apportioned among the several states which may be included within this Union, according to their respective numbers of free persons, including those bound to serve for a term of years, and excluding Indians not taxed, and all other persons.

"*Second.* No new state shall be admitted into the Union by Congress, in virtue of the power granted by the constitution, without the concurrence of two thirds of both houses.

" *Third.* Congress shall not have power to lay any embargo on the ships or vessels of the citizens of the United States, in the ports or harbours thereof, for more than sixty days.

" *Fourth.* Congress shall not have power, without the concurrence of two thirds of both houses, to interdict the commercial intercourse between the United States and any foreign nation, or the dependencies thereof.

" *Fifth.* Congress shall not make or declare war, or authorize acts of hostility against any foreign nation, without the concurrence of two thirds of both houses, except such acts of hostility be in defence of the territories of the United States when actually invaded.

" *Sixth.* No person who shall hereafter be naturalized, shall be eligible as a member of the senate or house of representatives of the United States, nor capable of holding any civil office under the authority of the United States.

" *Seventh.* The same person shall not be elected president of the United States a second time ; nor shall the president be elected from the same state two terms in succession.

" *Resolved,* That if the application of these states to the government of the United States, recommended in a foregoing resolution, should be unsuccessful, and peace should not be concluded, and the defence of these states should be neglected, as it has been since the commencement of the war, it will, in the opinion of this convention, be expedient for the legislatures of the several states to appoint delegates to another convention, to meet at Boston in the state of Massachusetts, on the third Thursday of June next, with such powers and instructions as the exigency of a crisis so momentous may require.

" *Resolved,* That the Hon. George Cabot, the Hon. Chauncey Goodrich, and the Hon. Daniel Lyman, or any two of them, be authorized to call another meeting of this

convention, to be holden in Boston, at any time before
new delegates shall be chosen, as recommended in the
above resolution, if in their judgment the situation of the
country shall urgently require it.

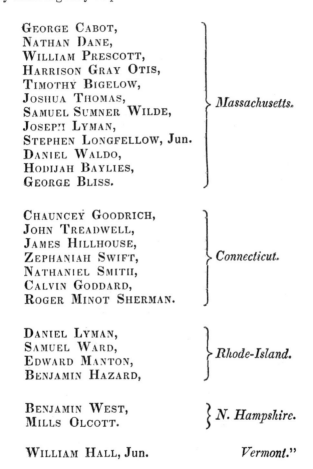

GEORGE CABOT,
NATHAN DANE,
WILLIAM PRESCOTT,
HARRISON GRAY OTIS,
TIMOTHY BIGELOW,
JOSHUA THOMAS,
SAMUEL SUMNER WILDE,   } *Massachusetts.*
JOSEPH LYMAN,
STEPHEN LONGFELLOW, Jun.
DANIEL WALDO,
HODIJAH BAYLIES,
GEORGE BLISS.

CHAUNCEY GOODRICH,
JOHN TREADWELL,
JAMES HILLHOUSE,
ZEPHANIAH SWIFT,   } *Connecticut.*
NATHANIEL SMITH,
CALVIN GODDARD,
ROGER MINOT SHERMAN.

DANIEL LYMAN,
SAMUEL WARD,
EDWARD MANTON,   } *Rhode-Island.*
BENJAMIN HAZARD,

BENJAMIN WEST,   } *N. Hampshire.*
MILLS OLCOTT.

WILLIAM HALL, Jun.   *Vermont.*"

This document was immediately published, and extensively circulated through the country. It was looked for
with much anxiety, and of course was read with great avidi-

ty. The expectations of those who apprehended it would contain sentiments of a seditious, if not of a treasonable character, were entirely disappointed. They looked in vain for either the one or the other, and were obliged to acknowledge that no such sentiments were to be found in it. Equally free was it from advancing doctrines which had a tendency to destroy the union of the states. On the contrary, it breathed an ardent attachment to the integrity of the republic. Its temper was mild, its tone moderate, and its sentiments were liberal and patriotic. Many leading members of the party who had always adhered to the administration and supported the war, did not hesitate to declare that it was an able and unexceptionable document ; and politicians of every party, and of all descriptions, agreed that it displayed great ability, and contained principles and sentiments of much importance to the welfare of the nation.

In a very short time after the publication of the report, the country was surprised with the news of peace. The manner in which the intelligence of this event was received throughout the country, afforded a striking commentary upon the character of the war, and the light in which it was viewed by the nation at large. Without waiting to learn what were the provisions of the treaty, or to ascertain whether the objects for which the war was professedly declared had been accomplished, a general spirit, not merely of rejoicing, but of exultation, broke out in every part of the country. Mutual congratulations at the restoration of peace were exchanged by all descriptions of politicians, bonfires were kindled, and illuminations were exhibited over a large portion of the Union. Nobody seemed to manifest any anxiety about the provisions of the treaty—the war was at an end, and peace was established ; and beyond those main points, scarcely any individual appeared to be disposed to inquire or examine.

Almost at the same moment of time when the news of

peace reached the seat of government, intelligence was received of the repulse of the British forces at New-Orleans. Although this event occurred some time after the treaty of peace was signed, and the war was ended, yet its brilliancy was considered as a proof of merit in the administration in the manner of conducting the war. The flush of feeling which this victory occasioned, drew the public attention away from the treaty of peace, and the vast expense of treasure and blood which the war had given rise to; and the administration and their devoted friends, with their usual skill, turned it to their own account. As a never-failing source of profit to the leaders of the party in power, the public resentment was excited against the opposers of the war, and particularly against the New-England states, and the Hartford Convention became the theme of universal calumny and reproach. The report, dignified, able, and unobjectionable as it was so generally acknowledged to be, had no efficacy in shielding the states from the most opprobrious charges, and the Convention from the foulest reproaches. Not being able to find any thing to justify this virulence in the report, it was alleged with as much apparent confidence as if it had been known to be a matter of fact, that although the report itself contained no evidence of treason, or even of sedition, yet the history of their secret proceedings, whenever they should be made public, would disclose an abundance of proof of the existence of both. When the Convention adjourned on the 5th of January, 1815, it was supposed that it might be necessary for them to hold a second meeting. With that expectation, when they adjourned, they did not think it expedient to remove the injunction of secrecy under which the members had been laid at the commencement of the session; and the journal was sealed, and placed for safe keeping in the hands of the President. When it was found that it was not likely to be published, the charge of meditated sedition and treason was repeated in every quarter, certain specific measures partaking of such a character were boldly asserted to have been brought before the Convention, and urged upon the members for their adoption. And to give plausibility to their declarations, some of the stories went so far as to state the manner in which the mischievous propositions were rejected, and to name the individual member or members by whose exertions and influence the intended object was defeated. Notwithstanding the impossibility that facts of this kind could be disclosed, except by some of the members, or by the secretary, as no others were ever present at any of the proceedings, the tale, in spite of its absurdity, appeared to gain credit abroad in the community, and added one more item to the long catalogue of falsehoods and slanders that were circulated about the proceedings and character of the Convention. At length it was thought expedient to place the journal in the office of the Secretary of State of Massachusetts, for the inspection of all persons who might feel curiosity enough to examine it. It was afterwards published in pamphlets, and in newspapers; but it did not stop the clamours of those who were unwilling to lose so powerful an engine of partizan warfare as this had long been. Like the name of "Federalist," it answered the most valuable purpose among demagogues, and unprincipled politicians; it was used with great effect; the weak, the designing, and the wicked, still made use of the Hartford Convention as a countersign of party, and as a watchword to rally the ignorant and the vicious around the standard of the ambitious; and even now, there is an apparent uneasiness among that description of people, at the idea that they may be obliged to give up this their favourite topic of reproach upon their political opponents.

The following is a copy of that document.

Secret Journal of the Hartford Convention.

" Hartford, Thursday, Dec. 15, 1814.

"This being the day appointed for the meeting of the Convention of Delegates from the New-England states, assembled for the purpose of conferring on such subjects as may come before them, the following persons, from those states, met in the council chamber of the state house, in Hartford, in the state of Connecticut, viz.—

" From the state of Massachusetts, Messrs. George Cabot, William Prescott, Harrison Gray Otis, Timothy Bigelow, Nathan Dane, George Bliss, Joshua Thomas, Hodijah Baylies, Daniel Waldo, Joseph Lyman, Samuel S. Wilde, and Stephen Longfellow, Jun.

" From the state of Rhode-Island, Messrs. Daniel Lyman, Benjamin Hazard, and Edward Manton.

" From the state of Connecticut, Messrs. Chauncey Goodrich, James Hillhouse, John Treadwell, Zephaniah Swift, Nathaniel Smith, Calvin Goddard, and Roger M. Sherman.

" From the state of New-Hampshire, Messrs. Benjamin West, and Mills Olcott.

" Upon being called to order by Mr. Cabot, the persons present proceeded to choose, by ballot, a President— Messrs. Bigelow and Goodrich were appointed to receive and count the votes given in for that purpose, who reported that Mr. George Cabot, a member from Massachusetts, was unanimously chosen.

" On motion, voted, that the Convention proceed to the choice of a person to be their Secretary, who is not a member of the Convention ; and the votes having been received and counted, Theodore Dwight, of Hartford, was declared to be chosen unanimously.

" Messrs. Otis, Hillhouse, and Lyman, were appointed a committee to examine the credentials of the members returned to serve in the convention, and report the names of such as they should find duly qualified ; who, having attended to the subject of their said appointment, made the following report :—

" The committee appointed to examine the credentials of the members returned to serve in the convention now assembled at Hartford, have attended to that service, and find the following persons to have been elected members thereof by the respective legislatures of the following states ;—From *Massachusetts*, George Cabot, William Prescott, Harrison Gray Otis, Timothy Bigelow, Stephen Longfellow, Jun. Daniel Waldo, George Bliss, Nathan Dane, Hodijah Baylies, Joshua Thomas, Joseph Lyman, and Samuel S. Wilde. From *Rhode-Island*, Daniel Lyman, Samuel Ward, Benjamin Hazard, and Edward Manton. From *Connecticut*, Chauncey Goodrich, James Hillhouse, John Treadwell, Zephaniah Swift, Calvin Goddard, Nathaniel Smith, and Roger Minot Sherman.

" The committee also report, that at a conventional meeting of twenty towns in the county of Cheshire, in the state of New-Hampshire, Hon. Benjamin West was elected to meet in this convention ; and at a conventional meeting of delegates from most of the towns in the county of Grafton, and from the town of Lancaster, in the county of Coos, Mills Olcott, Esq. was elected to meet in this convention ; and the committee are of opinion, that the above named persons are entitled to take their seats as members of this convention.

" On motion, voted, that said report be accepted and approved.

" On motion of Mr. Otis, voted, that the convention be opened with prayer, and that the delegates from the state of Connecticut be requested to invite a clergyman belong ing to the town of Hartford to perform that service.

" On motion, voted, that Messrs. Goddard, Bigelow, and

the purpose of defending the property of the United States, and preventing the destruction of the squadron of armed ships in the harbour of New-London. The refusal of the governors of those states to order out the militia, at the requisition of General Dearborn, in 1812, was on widely different ground. That ground has been already alluded to. It was solely because an attempt was made to take the militia away from their own officers, and to place them under the command of officers of the United States, thus depriving the states of their natural defenders, and the militia of their constitutional right, and in fact incorporating them into the standing army. Probably they were induced to take this course, by a wish to change the character of the war from defensive to offensive; and to accomplish this object, the absurd and ridiculous project of attempting to conquer the Canadas was devised. The result proved, that the character of the war was not easily altered. The first campaigns on that frontier, showed it to be as truly defensive on the inland frontier, as it was upon the Atlantic coast.

There was nothing in the mode of conducting the war that was in the slightest degree calculated to secure the confidence of the country, and especially of that part of it where it was the most unpopular. Neither the plan of general operations, nor the character of the men appointed to carry them into effect, had any tendency to convince the opponents of the war, that it would prove to be either honourable or advantageous to the United States. The military operations against Upper Canada, which was the first object of hostile movements, were not only disastrous, but in the highest degree disgraceful. One army, with its commander-in-chief, was captured almost without firing a shot; and very little reputation was gained the first season along the whole line of the inland frontier.

Instances of great bravery and good conduct occasionally occurred; but nothing appeared which manifested dis-

" On motion, voted, that said report be accepted and approved.

"On motion, voted, that a committee of five be appointed to inquire what subjects will be proper to be considered by this Convention, and report such propositions for that purpose, as they may think expedient, to the Convention, to-morrow morning.

" The following persons were appointed on that committee: Messrs. Goodrich, Otis, Lyman, of Rhode Island, Swift, and Dane.

" On motion, voted, that this Convention be adjourned to 10 o'clock to-morrow morning; then to meet at this place.

" *Friday, December* 16, 1814.

" The Convention met, agreeably to adjournment.

" The Convention was opened with prayer by the Rev. Dr. Strong.

" Mr. Ward, a member from the State of Rhode Island, attended, and took his seat in the Convention.

" The committee appointed to inquire what subjects will be proper to be considered by the convention, and to report such propositions for that purpose, as they may think expedient, respectfully report :

" ' That your committee deem the following to be proper subjects for the consideration of the Convention :— The powers claimed by the executive of the United States, to determine, conclusively, in respect to calling out the militia of the states into the service of the United States ; and the dividing the United States into military districts, with an officer of the army in each thereof, with discretionary authority from the executive of the United States, to call for the militia to be under the command of such officer. The refusal of the executive of the United States to supply, or pay the militia of certain states, called out for their defence, on the grounds of their not having been called out under the authority of the United States, or not having been, by the executive of the state, put under the command of the commander over the military district. The failure of the government of the United States to supply and pay the militia of the states, by them admitted to have been in the United States' service. The report of the Secretary of War to Congress, on filling the ranks of the army, together with a bill, or act, on that subject. A bill before Congress, providing for classing and drafting the militia. The expenditure of the revenue of the nation in offensive operations on the neighbouring provinces of the enemy. The failure of the government of the United States to provide for the common defence; and the consequent obligations, necessity and burdens, devolved on the separate states, to defend themselves; together with the mode, and the ways and means, in their power for accomplishing the object.'

" On motion, voted, that said report be accepted and approved. On motion, voted, that a committee of three be appointed to obtain such documents and information as may be necessary for the use and consideration of the Convention, and may be connected with their proceedings. Mr. Hillhouse, Mr. Bliss, and Mr. Hazard, were appointed on that committee. On motion, voted, that the Rev. Dr. Perkins be invited to attend in turn with the other gentlemen already invited, as chaplains. On motion, voted, that the injunction of secrecy, as to the proceedings of yesterday, be removed. On motion, voted, that the convention be adjourned to 3 o'clock, P. M. of this day, then to meet in this place.

" *Three o'clock, P. M.*—The Convention met agreeably to adjournment. After spending the afternoon in various discussions of important subjects, on motion, voted, that this Convention be adjourned till to-morrow, 10 o'clock, A. M. then to meet at this place.

"*Saturday, December* 17, 1814.

" The Convention met, agreeably to adjournment.

" The Convention was opened with prayer, by the Rev. Dr. Strong. After spending the forenoon in discussing the first section of the report of the committee made on Friday, on motion, voted, that when this Convention adjourn, it be adjourned till Monday next. On motion, voted, that this Convention be adjourned till Monday next, at 10 o'clock, A. M. then to meet at this place.

"*Monday, December* 19, 1814.

" The Convention met, agreeably to adjournment. The Convention was opened with prayer, by the Rev. Mr. Chase.

" On motion, voted, that a committee of five be appointed to prepare and report a general project of such measures as it may be proper for this Convention to adopt.

" Messrs. Smith, Otis, Goddard, West, and Hazard, were appointed to be of that committee.

" On motion, voted, that this Convention be adjourned till 3 o'clock this afternoon, then to meet at this place.

" *Three o'clock, P. M.*—The Convention met agreeably to adjournment. On motion, voted, that the Rev. Mr. Cushman be invited to attend in turn with the other gentlemen already invited, as chaplains.

" After spending the afternoon in discussing the report, the committee, on motion, voted, that this Convention be adjourned till to-morrow morning, 10 o'clock, then to be held at this place.

" *Tuesday, December* 20, 1814.

" The Convention met, agreeably to adjournment. The Convention was opened with prayer, by the Rev. Dr. Strong. The committee appointed to prepare and report a general project of such measures as it may be proper for this Convention to adopt, made a report, which was laid in and read. After discussing several articles of the said report, the further consideration of it was postponed until the afternoon. On motion, voted, that this Convention be adjourned till 3 o'clock this afternoon, then to meet at this place.

" *Three o'clock, P. M.*—The Convention met, pursuant to adjournment. The Convention resumed the consideration of the report of the committee, which was postponed in the forenoon ; and after discussion through the afternoon, the same was postponed until the morning. On motion, voted, that this Convention be adjourned until to-morrow morning, 10 o'clock, A. M. then to meet at this place.

" *Wednesday, December* 21, 1814.

" The Convention met, pursuant to adjournment. The Convention was opened with prayer, by the Rev. Mr. Chase. The Convention resumed the consideration of the report postponed yesterday. After spending the time of the forenoon in the discussion of the report of the committee, the further consideration was postponed to the afternoon. On motion, voted, that this Convention be adjourned to 3 o'clock this afternoon, then to meet at this place.

" *Three o'clock, P. M.*—The Convention met, pursuant to adjournment. The Convention resumed the consideration of the report of the committee, which was postponed in the forenoon. On motion, voted that a committee of seven be raised to prepare a report illustrative of the principles and reasons which have induced the Convention to adopt the results to which they have agreed. Mr. Otis, Mr. Smith, Mr. Sherman, Mr. Dane, Mr. Prescott, Mr. West, and Mr. Hazard, were appointed on that committee. On motion, voted, that this Convention be adjourned til to-morrow morning, 10 o'clock.

" Thursday, December 22, 1814.

" The Convention met, pursuant to adjournment. The Convention was opened with prayer, by the Rev. Dr. Perkins. The Convention resumed the consideration of the report of the committee, postponed last evening. After spending the forenoon in discussing said report, the further consideration was postponed till this afternoon. On motion, voted, that this Convention be adjourned till 3 o'clock, then to meet at this place.

" *Three o'clock, P. M.*—The Convention met agreeably to adjournment. The Convention resumed the consideration of the report of the committee, which was postponed in the forenoon. After spending the afternoon in discussing said report, the further consideration thereof was postponed. On motion, voted, that this Convention be adjourned till to-morrow morning, 10 o'clock, then to meet at this place.

" *Friday, December* 23, 1814.

" The Convention met pursuant to adjournment. The Convention was opened with prayer by the Rev. Mr. Chase. The Convention resumed the consideration of the report of the committee, which was postponed yesterday. After spending the forenoon in discussing the report of the committee, the further consideration thereof was postponed until to-morrow. On motion, voted, that this Convention be adjourned until to-morrow morning, 10 o'clock, then to meet at this place.

" *Saturday, December* 24, 1814.

" The Convention met, pursuant to adjournment. The Convention was opened with prayer, by the Rev. Dr. Perkins. The president communicated an address from a number of citizens belonging to the county of Washington, in the state of New-York, which was read. On motion, voted, that the said address be referred to the committee appointed on the 21st inst.

" The Convention resumed the consideration of the report of the committee, which was postponed yesterday. On motion, voted, that another member be added to the committee appointed on the 21st inst. Mr. Sherman being necessarily absent. Mr. Swift was appointed on said committee.

" The report of the committee which was laid in on the 20th instant, having been under discussion at the several meetings of the Convention, and having been amended, was adopted, and referred to the committee appointed on the 21st to report ; which report is as follows, viz.

" The committee appointed to prepare and report a general project of such measures as it may be proper for this Convention to adopt, respectfully report :

" 1. That it will be expedient for this convention to prepare a general statement of the unconstitutional attempts of the executive government of the United States to infringe upon the rights of the individual states, in regard to the militia, and of the still more alarming claims to infringe the rights of the states, manifested in the letter of the Secretary of War, and in the bills pending before Congress, or acts passed by them, and also to recommend to the legislatures of the states, the adoption of the most effectual and decisive measures, to protect the militia and the states from the usurpations contained in these proceedings.

" 2. That it will be expedient, also, to prepare a statement, exhibiting the necessity which the improvidence and inability of the general government have imposed upon the several states, of providing for their own defence, and the impossibility of their discharging this duty, and at the same time fulfilling the requisitions of the general government ; and also, to recommend to the legislatures of the several states, to make provision for mutual defence, and to make an earnest application to the government of the United States, with a view to some arrangement, whereby the states may be enabled to retain a portion of the taxes levied by Congress, for the purposes of self-defence, and for the reimbursement of expenses already incurred, on account of the United States.

" 3. That it is expedient to recommend to the several state legislatures, certain amendments to the constitution of the United States, hereafter enumerated, to be by them adopted and proposed. (The remainder of this article in the report was postponed.)

" 1. That the power to declare or make war, by the Congress of the United States, be restricted.

" 2. That it is expedient to attempt to make provision for restraining Congress in the exercise of an unlimited power, to make new states, and admit them into this Union.

" 3. That the powers of Congress be restrained in laying embargoes, and restrictions on commerce.

" 4. That a president shall not be elected from the same state two terms successively.

" 5. That the same person shall not be elected president a second time.

" 6. That an amendment be proposed, respecting slave representation, and slave taxation.

" On motion, voted, that this Convention be adjourned to Monday afternoon, three o'clock, then to meet at this place.

" *Monday, December* 26, 1814.

" The Convention met, pursuant to adjournment. The Convention was opened with prayer, by the Rev. Mr. Woodbridge, of Hadley, Massachusetts. The committee not being prepared to lay in their report, on motion, voted, that this Convention be adjourned till to-morrow morning, ten o'clock, then to meet at this place.

" *Tuesday, December* 27, 1814.

"The Convention met, pursuant to adjournment. The Convention was opened with prayer, by the Rev. Dr. Perkins. The committee not being prepared to lay in their report, on motion, voted, that this Convention be adjourned till this afternoon, three o'clock, then to meet at this place.

" *Three o'clock*, *P. M.*—The Convention met pursuant to adjournment. The committee not being prepared to lay in their report, on motion, voted, that this Convention be adjourned till to-morrow morning, ten o'clock, then to meet at this place.

" *Wednesday, December* 28, 1814.

" The Convention met, pursuant to adjournment. The Convention was opened with prayer, by the Rev. Mr. Chase. A certificate of the proceedings of a Convention in the county of Windham, in the state of Vermont, appointing the Hon. William Hall, Jun. to represent the people of that county in this Convention, was read. On motion, voted, that the Hon. William Hall, Jun. is entitled to a seat in this Convention; and that the Hon. Mr. Olcott, of New-Hampshire, be requested to introduce Mr. Hall, for the purpose of taking his seat.

" Mr. Hall, a member from the county of Windham, in the state of Vermont, attended, and took his seat in the Convention. The report of the committee not being prepared, on motion, voted, that this Convention be adjourned to three o'clock, this afternoon; then to meet at this place.

" *Three o'clock*, *P. M.*—The Convention met pursuant to adjournment. The report of the committee not being prepared, upon motion, voted, that this Convention be adjourned till to-morrow morning, ten o'clock.

" *Thursday, December* 29, 1814.

" The Convention met, pursuant to adjournment. The Convention was opened with prayer, by the Rev. Dr. Strong. On motion, voted, that the following proposition be referred to the committee appointed on the 21st instant.

" ' That the capacity of naturalized citizens to hold offices of trust, honour, or profit, ought to be restrained; and that it is expedient to propose an amendment to the Constitution of the United States, in relation to that subject.'

" The report of the committee not being prepared, on motion, voted, that this Convention be adjourned till three o'clock this afternoon, then to meet at this place.

" *Three o'clock, P. M.*—The Convention met, pursuant to adjournment. The report of the committee not being prepared, on motion, voted, that this Convention be adjourned till to-morrow morning, ten o'clock, then to meet at this place.

" *Friday, December* 30, 1814.

" The Convention met, pursuant to adjournment. The Convention was opened with prayer, by the Rev. Dr. Perkins. The committee appointed on the 21st instant presented their report, which was read twice. The forenoon having been spent in reading the report, on motion, voted, that this Convention be adjourned till three o'clock this afternoon, then to meet at this place.

" *Three o'clock, P. M.*—The Convention met, pursuant to adjournment. After spending the afternoon in discussing the report, the subject was postponed. On motion, voted, that this Convention be adjourned till to-morrow morning, ten o'clock, then to meet at this place.

" *Saturday, December* 31, 1814.

" The Convention met, pursuant to adjournment. The Convention was opened with prayer, by the Rev. Mr.

Chase. The Convention resumed the consideration of the report, postponed yesterday. On motion, voted, that a committee, to consist of three, be appointed to procure that part of the report which relates to the militia, printed confidentially. Messrs. Goodrich, Lyman, of Massachusetts, and Goddard, were appointed on that committee. After having spent the forenoon in considering the report, the further consideration thereof was postponed. On motion, voted, that this Convention be adjourned till half past two o'clock this afternoon, then to meet at this place.

" *Three o'clock, P. M.*—The Convention met, pursuant to adjournment. The Convention resumed the consideration of the report of the Committee, which was postponed in the forenoon. After having spent the afternoon in discussing the report of the committee, the further consideration thereof was postponed. On motion, voted, that a committee of three persons be appointed to ascertain what expenses have been incurred in this Convention, which it is necessary for them to defray, and to report the mode of discharging them. Mr. Goddard, Mr. Prescott, and Mr. Ward, were appointed on that committee. On motion, voted, that the first eight pages of the report be recommitted to the committee which reported it, to reconsider the same. On motion, voted, that the same committee report such documents and articles as they may think proper, to compose an appendix to the report.

" On motion, voted, that this Convention be adjourned till Monday morning, ten o'clock, then to meet at this place.

" *Monday, January* 2, 1815.

" The Convention met, pursuant to adjournment. The Convention was opened with prayer, by the Rev. Mr. Chase. The Convention resumed the consideration of the report of the committee which was postponed from Saturday. After spending the forenoon in discussing the report, the further consideration thereof was postponed. On motion, voted, that this Convention be adjourned till half past two o'clock this afternoon, then to meet at this place.

"*Half past two o'clock, P. M.*—The Convention met, pursuant to adjournment. The Convention resumed the consideration of the report of the committee which was postponed in the forenoon. After spending the afternoon in discussing the report of the committee, the further consideration thereof was postponed. On motion, voted, that this Convention be adjourned till to-morrow morning, nine o'clock, then to meet at this place.

"*Tuesday, January 3, 1815.*

"The Convention met, pursuant to adjournment. The Convention was opened with prayer, by the Rev. Dr. Perkins. The Convention resumed the consideration of the report of the committee which was postponed yesterday. After spending the forenoon in discussing the report of the committee, the same was postponed till the afternoon. On motion, voted, that this Convention be adjourned till three o'clock this afternoon, then to meet at this place.

"*Three o'clock, P. M.*—The Convention met, pursuant to adjournment. The Convention resumed the consideration of the report of the committee, which was postponed in the forenoon. After discussing and amending the report of the committee, voted, that the same be accepted and approved. On motion, resolved, that the injunction of secrecy, in regard to all the debates and proceedings of this Convention, except in so far as relates to the report finally adopted, be, and hereby is, continued. On motion, voted, that a committee of three persons be appointed to consider and report what measures it will be expedient to recommend to the states, for their mutual defence. Mr. Prescott, Mr. Wilde, and Mr. Manton, were appointed on the committee.

"On motion, voted, that Mr. Sherman be added to the committee for superintending the printing of the report.

On motion, voted, that this Convention be adjourned till to-morrow morning, ten o'clock, then to meet at this place.

" *Wednesday, January* 4, 1815.

" The Convention met, pursuant to adjournment. The Convention was opened with prayer, by the Rev. Mr. Chase. On motion, voted, that certain documents before the Convention, be published, with the following title, ' *Statements prepared and published, by order of the Convention of delegates, held at Hartford, Dec.* 15, 1814, *and printed by their order.*'

" On motion, voted, that Mr. Goodrich be discharged from any further services on the committee to superintend the printing of the report, &c. On motion, voted, that another member be added to that committee. Mr. Otis was appointed to that place. The committee appointed to report what measures it will be expedient to recommend to the states, for their mutual defence, presented a report, which was read. On motion, voted, that the said report be accepted and approved. On motion, voted, that this Convention be adjourned till three o'clock this afternoon, then to meet at this place.

" *Three o'clock, P. M.*—The Convention met, pursuant to adjournment On motion, voted, that two copies of the report of the Convention, subscribed by all the members who shall be disposed to sign the same, be forwarded to each of the governors of the states of Massachusetts, Connecticut, Rhode Island, New-Hampshire, and Vermont ; one of which to be for the private use of the said governors, and with a request that the other, at some proper time, may be laid before the legislatures of the states aforesaid.

" Mr. Goodrich submitted the following resolution to the Convention. Resolved, That the thanks of the Convention be presented to the Hon. George Cabot, in testimony of the respectful sense they entertain of his conduct whilst presiding over their deliberations.

" On the question being put by the secretary, it passed in the affirmative, *unanimously*. On motion, voted, that the Convention be adjourned till 7 o'clock, this evening, then to meet at this place.

" *Seven o'clock, P. M.*—The committee met, pursuant o adjournment. On motion, voted, that the report, as amended, and the resolves accompanying the same, be accepted and approved. On motion, voted, that the delegates from Massachusetts, Connecticut, and Rhode Island, take two copies of the report of the Convention, and deliver the same to the governors of those states, agreeably to the vote of the Convention passed this day, and that the president be requested to transmit two copies of the report to the governors of the states of New-Hampshire and Vermont, together with a copy of the vote of the Convention aforesaid.

" On motion, voted, that at the close of the Convention, the journal be committed to the care of the president. On motion, voted, that the Convention be adjourned till to-morrow morning, 9 o'clock, then to meet at this place.

" *Thursday, January 5, 1815—9 o'clock, A. M.*

" The Convention met, pursuant to adjournment—after solemn prayer, by the Rev. Dr. Strong, on motion, voted, that this Convention be adjourned without day.

" Attest,   THEODORE DWIGHT, *Secretary.*"

This document, when placed in the secretary's office at Boston, was accompanied by a certificate of the following tenor, viz.

" I George Cabot, late president of the Convention, assembled at Hartford, on the fifteenth day of December, 1814, do hereby certify, that the foregoing is the original and only journal of the proceedings of that Convention ; and that the twenty-seven written pages, which compose it, and the printed report, comprise a faithful and complete record of all the motions, resolutions, votes, and proceedings, of that Convention. And I do further certify, that this journal has been constantly in my exclusive custody, from the time of the adjournment of the Convention, to the delivery of it into the office of.the Secretary of this Commonwealth.

"*Boston, Nov. 16th*, 1819."   " GEORGE CABOT.

By adverting to the Report, it will be seen that the Convention, in their proceedings, and in the result, kept strictly within the limits of their commissions. They *conferred* upon the general subjects referred to them for consideration ; and after mature deliberation, and the exercise of the utmost caution, discretion, and sound judgment, they embodied their views, their sentiments, and their conclusions, in a document which has been admired, and which will be admired, even by future generations, as one of the ablest for wisdom and talent that our country has ever produced.

After a concise, but forcible review of the policy of the government previously to the declaration of war, the Convention take a survey of the state of things after that event, and of the calamities which it had brought upon the nation ; and close with recommending to the legislatures by whom they were appointed, the following resolutions :

" *Resolved*, That it be and is hereby recommended to the legislatures of the several states represented in this Convention, to adopt all such measures as may be necessary effectually to protect the citizens of said states from the operation and effects of all acts which have been or may be passed by the Congress of the United States, which shall contain provisions subjecting the militia or other citizens to forcible drafts, conscriptions, or impressments, not authorised by the Constitution of the United States.

" *Resolved*, That it be and hereby is recommended to the said legislatures to authorise an immediate and earnest application to be made to the Government of the United States, *requesting their consent* to some arrangement, whereby the said states may separately or in concert, be empowered to assume upon themselves the defence of their territory against the enemy ; and a reasonable portion of the taxes collected within said states, may be paid into the respective treasuries thereof, and appropriated to the payment of the balance due said states, and to the future defence of the same. The amount so paid into the said treasuries to be credited, and the disbursements made as aforesaid, to be charged to the United States.

" *Resolved*, That it be, and it hereby is recommended to the legislatures of the aforesaid states, to pass laws (where it has not already been done) authorising the Governors or Commanders in chief of their militia, to make detachments from the same, or to form voluntary corps, as shall be most convenient and conformable to their constitutions, and to cause the same to be well armed, equipped, and disciplined, and held in readiness for service ; and upon the request of the Governor of either of the other states, to employ the whole of such detachment or corps, as well as the regular forces of the state, or such part thereof as may be required, and can be spared consistently with the safety of the state, in assisting the state making such request, to repel any invasion thereof which shall be made or attempted by the public enemy."

The other resolutions recommended by the Convention to their several legislatures, consisted of various propositions for amending the Constitution of the United States, a practice which has been extensively engaged in by different states, almost throughout the Union, and which is harmless in itself; and as the mode of amending that instrument is pointed out by itself, it is not necessary to allude to them in the present work. Nor have the others which we have copied been considered as reprehensible in themselves. To recommend to the legislatures of the states to adopt such measures as might be necessary to protect their citizens from forcible drafts, conscriptions, and impressment, cannot fail to meet with the approbation not only of that great body of citizens who are immediately exposed to the effects of such unconstitutional measures, but of all upright, just, and virtuous people, of every age, and in whatever circumstances of life.

The next resolution falling directly within the provision which has been quoted, will be as little likely to meet with objections from any quarter. It recommends an application to Congress, for permission to assume upon themselves the defence of their own territory, and to appropriate a portion of the taxes collected within those states, to pay the balance due the states for money already advanced in defending their coasts, and to defray any further expenses attending their future efforts for the same object.

The third resolution recommends to the legislatures of the several states which they represented, to pass laws for forming volunteer corps, and to cause them to be armed and equipped, and held in readiness for service, and if necessity required, to assist each other in defending themselves against the inroads of the enemy.

This recommendation pursues the course pointed out by the administration, soon after the commencement of the war, when they called upon Massachusetts to send a body of militia to Rhode Island, to defend the town and port of Newport in the latter state.

The case of the Hartford Convention appears, then, to be summarily as follows :—It was legitimate in its origin, in no respect violating any provisions of the constitution of the United States, either in its letter or its spirit. The commissions given to the members were scrupulously guarded against any unconstitutional conduct on the part

of the Convention, giving them authority only to confer
together, and recommend such measures to their principals
as they might deem expedient, taking care to govern themselves by a regard to the duties and obligations which the
states owed to the United States. The account of their
proceedings shows that they punctiliously observed the in-
junctions contained in their instructions ; and the result of
their deliberations proves their conduct to have been, in
every respect, strictly constitutional.

Notwithstanding the vast amount of calumny and reproach that has been bestowed upon the Hartford Convention by the ignorant and the worthless, it will not be a
hazardous assumption to say, that henceforward no man
who justly estimates the value of his character for truth
and honesty, and who, of course, means to sustain such a
character, will risk his reputation by the repetition of such
falsehoods respecting that body, as have heretofore been
uttered with impunity. No man, with the facts before him,
can do this, without sacrificing all claim to veracity, and,
of course, to integrity and honour. Nor will the subter-
fuge that the journal and report of the Convention do not
contain the whole of their proceedings, save him from the
disgrace of wilfully disregarding the truth. Nearly nine-
teen years have elapsed since the Convention adjourned,
and no proof has been adduced, and nothing nearer proof,
than the unsupported assertions of the corrupt journals of
political partizans, of any measure having been adopted
or recommended by the Convention, besides those contained in the journal and the report. If there was any
treason, proposed or meditated, against the United States,
at the Convention, it must have been hidden in as deep
and impenetrable obscurity, as the fabulous secrets of free
masonry are said to be buried, otherwise some traces of
it would have been discovered and disclosed to the public
before this late period. No such discovery having been

made, the inference must necessarily be, that no such treasonable practice or intention existed.

But, in the nature of things, nothing could have been transacted by the Convention, beyond what appears in their journal and report. They were a public body—a grand committee appointed by the legislatures of three distinct states, to confer, and report. The subjects of their conference must appear in their journal, otherwise they could never obtain a legitimate existence. And the report must. in like manner, contain the entire result of their deliberations, because nothing that did not appear embodied in that document, could, in the nature of things, form a part of their proceedings, and be laid before their principals. It is then absurd to pretend that there were other proceedings, which have been kept out of sight, or suppressed, and never revealed, because nothing that was thus kept back could have formed any part of their proceedings.

The internal evidence of the case is therefore sufficient to show the groundlessness of the charge that a part of the proceedings of the Convention were suppressed. But the certificate of Mr. Cabot has been quoted, which asserts in direct and positive terms, that the journal contains "a *faithful and complete record of all the motions, resolutions, votes, and proceedings of that Convention.*" If this certificate is false, there were, at the time it was made, at least twenty individuals of the highest respectability in existence, who would have been able to prove its falsity. There are no less than twelve such individuals now living, who are able to impeach its correctness, if it asserts that which is not true. Mr. Cabot was a man of the highest respectability for understanding, integrity, and talents. He had more reputation to lose than scores together of those who would impeach his veracity can lay claim to or boast of. His declaration on any subject would have been taken for truth, wherever he was well known, with as much confidence as if it had been sanctioned by the most solemn oath. Here it is impeached by nothing but the unsupported assertions or suggestions of political partizans—men without manners, without principles, and of course without reputation.

In January, 1831, the publisher of a newspaper in the State of Connecticut, was prosecuted before the Superior Court of that State for a libel. The article which was the foundation of the prosecution, contained an allusion to the Hartford Convention. Although that allusion was not the basis of the charge, yet the opportunity was improved to draw from one of the members of that body some facts respecting its character and conduct. The member referred to was Roger Minot Sherman, a lawyer of great eminence, and a gentleman of the highest respectability of character, both professional and personal. He was regularly summoned as a witness, on a collateral point, and not material to the issue before the court, and was examined at length. There is very little doubt that the object was, to ascertain from this source, whether there was any thing treasonable, or seditious, in the proceedings of the Convention. In the course of his testimony he said—

"There was not, to the best of my recollection, *a single motion, resolution, or subject of debate, but what appears in the Journal.*" In answer to a question put to him, he replied—" I believe I know their proceedings perfectly, and that *every measure, done or proposed, has been published to the world.*"

But it may be said, that both Mr. Cabot and Mr. Sherman were members of the Convention, and however high their standing in the community, as men of the purest morals, and the most unsullied integrity, may have been, still they must be considered as involved in its guilt, if guilt actually existed, and therefore they are witnesses interested in the question, and not entitled to the full measure of credit which would otherwise be due to them. It then only remains for the only individual who was present at the Convention, and was not a member, and who alone had the opportunity to be fully acquainted with all their proceedings, to give his testimony. This testimony is not offered because the exigencies of the case in any sense require it. If a hundred disinterested individuals of the most unquestioned integrity could be found, who were as well acquainted with the facts as the two persons who have already been named, and who should concur in their declarations, their united testimony would not add a particle of strength to that of Messrs. Cabot and Sherman, where the characters of the latter were known. But if a disinterested witness should be kept back, who might be produced, an inference might be drawn by some caviller, from that circumstance, unfavourable to the character and conduct of the Convention. Such a witness is the author of this work—the Secretary of the Convention ; and he feels it a duty which he owes to truth, and the characters of as respectable, patriotic, and virtuous a body of men, as ever were collected on any occasion, to say, in the most positive and unhesitating manner, and with all the solemnity which the nature of the case requires, that the JOURNAL AND THE REPORT OF THE CONVENTION, CONTAIN A FULL, COMPLETE, AND SPECIFIC ACCOUNT OF ALL THE MOTIONS, VOTES, AND PROCEEDINGS OF THE CONVENTION. And he will add, that no proposition was made in the Convention to divide the Union, to organize the New England States into a separate government, or to form an alliance with Great Britain, or any other foreign power ; on the contrary, every motion that was made, every resolution that was offered, and every measure that was adopted, was, in principle and in terms, strictly confined within the limits of the instructions from the several legislatures by whom the delegates were appointed. And when the Report was adopted, it was by an unanimous vote, sanctioned by the signature of every member.

The effect of this declaration upon the public mind, will of course be left to the decision of the public.

The legislative acts of Massachusetts, Connecticut, and Rhode Island, containing provisions for the appointment of Delegates to meet in Convention, and stating the general objects of the measure, specifying the powers and authorities by which their conduct should be regulated, and prescribing the limits within which they were to be confined, it will be recollected were passed in the month of October, 1814. The condition of the country at large, and particularly that of the New England States upon the Atlantic coast, has been alluded to and explained. At that time, the towns upon the sea-shore were exposed to hostile invasion by the enemy's naval forces—several of the towns had been captured, some places had been attacked by their ships, property to a great amount destroyed, the whole extent of the coast, from the border of New-York to Eastport, had been essentially abandoned by the United States troops, and the defence of it thrown upon the individual states—those states had large bodies of men in the field, guarding the towns, defending the forts, and protecting the inhabitants, at a most enormous sacrifice of time and money ; and in the darkest and most threatening period of the war, the United States government had withdrawn their supplies for the militia, and forced the states to support their own men in the national service. At the same time, the taxes imposed and collected by the government of the United States, for the expenses of the war, were extremely burthensome ; and to add to the general mass of calamity, the currency of the country had become deranged, and depreciated to such a degree, that the most extensive distress was threatened from that fruitful source of evil.

Just at this moment, the despatches from the Commissioners at Ghent were published, showing that such extravagant demands were made by the British, as the basis of negotiation, that there was scarcely a ray of hope that peace would be obtained. And such was the language of the executive members of our government. The letter of the Secretary of War to the military Committee of the House of Representatives, from which extracts have been made, was dated October 17th, 1814. In that extraordinary document, every effort was made to alarm the country, not only with regard to the continuance of the war, and the hopelessness of peace, but to convey the idea that it would thenceforward be a war of the most violent, desperate, and dangerous description—that we were fighting, not only for our liberty and independence, but for existence—and that if we made any dishonourable concession to Great Britain, the spirit of the nation would be broken, and the foundation of our liberty and independence shaken.

In addition to all these considerations, the manner of conducting the war had been such from the beginning, as to manifest great inability in the administration and their agents, and to destroy all confidence, not only in their principles, but in their capacity for conducting the affairs of the nation.

Under such circumstances, and with such a prospect for the ensuing year, the New England States were under the necessity, for their self-preservation, to consult together, for the purpose, if practicable, of devising and adopting some system of operations which might conduce to their own safety. The situation of Massachusetts, Rhode Island, and Connecticut, rendered it indispensably necessary that they should take preliminary measures of this description, previously to the opening of another campaign. The President had directed a call to be made upon Massachusetts, at a very early stage of the war, to furnish men for the defence of Newport, in Rhode Island. At that time the danger of invasion was inconceivably less than it was in

October, 1814. What part of the New England coast would be the object of the next hostile visit, could not be known, or conjectured. But that there was at that time "imminent danger of invasion," could not be denied, or doubted. And that the whole extent of the coast was left destitute of the means of defence, was a fact not to be questioned.

Under circumstances like these, the general subject was presented to the consideration of those states. If defended at all, they must defend themselves. This was the import of the correspondence which the national government had carried on with those states from the beginning. The danger was common to them, and it was therefore absolutely necessary, in the performance of the duty which the national government had forced upon them, that some general plan of operations should be devised, which would be the most likely to accomplish the object in view. The New England States, therefore, in adopting the course they were pursuing, were not volunteers. The national government had withdrawn from them all the means of defence which they possessed, and then informed them they must defend themselves. And having brought those states into this predicament, they did not even furnish them with their advice in regard to the manner in which their defence was to be conducted. They left it to themselves to supply the means, and to use them in the manner which they might suppose would best accomplish the object in view. They adopted the plan of holding a convention of delegates, who should meet and consult upon the great subject of defending their coasts from invasion, their towns from being sacked and plundered, their property from being wasted and destroyed, their houses and their homes from being pillaged and broken up, and their families from being scattered or massacred. To proceed with the utmost prudence and caution, they selected the wisest and most virtuous members of their several communities

—men of great experience, sound principles, mature age, holding large stakes in the public welfare, and highly esteemed for integrity, public services, and patriotism. And to render the matter perfectly secure, the legislatures by whom the delegates were appointed, took care to furnish them with commissions, specifically prescribing the duties which they were to perform, and the limits within which they were to operate. In Massachusetts, their delegates were instructed " *to devise, if practicable, means of security and defence which may be consistent with the preservation of their resources from total ruin, and adapted to their local situation, mutual relations and habits,* not REPUGNANT TO THEIR OBLIGATIONS AS MEMBERS OF THE UNION." The resolution of the legislature of Connecticut was equally specific and guarded. Their delegates were instructed to meet those of the Commonwealth of Massachusetts and of other states who should appoint, and " confer with them on the subjects proposed by a resolution of said Commonwealth, and upon any other subjects which may come before them, for the purpose of devising and recommending such measures for the safety and welfare of these states AS MAY CONSIST WITH OUR OBLIGATIONS AS MEMBERS OF THE NATIONAL UNION." The Rhode Island legislature instructed their delegates to confer with such delegates as are or shall be appointed by other states, upon the common dangers to which these states are exposed, upon the best means of co-operating for our mutual defence against the enemy, and upon the measures which it may be in the power of said states, CONSISTENTLY WITH THEIR OBLIGATIONS, *to adopt, to restore and secure to the people their rights and privileges under the Constitution of the United States.*"

The great object of the states, then, in calling a convention, was, *to confer on the practicability of devising means of security and defence*—that is, to perform the task which the national government had thrown upon them in 1812, and which had been left upon them down to the time of appointing delegates to meet in convention, and which had now become so imperative that there was no room to avoid it. But, at the same time, in holding this conference, nothing was to be done that was not compatible with the duties and obligations of the states as members of the Union. These commissions were precisely similar in their character to powers of attorney, in which the principals give the agents authority to perform certain acts specified in the instruments. To the extent of that authority the agents may act, and no further. If the agents transcend those limits, whatever they may attempt to perform beyond the scope of their authority is not binding upon the principals, and of course is void. In these commissions, however, the delegates were not clothed with power to do any thing except to confer with their associates, for the purpose of devising means for the defence and security of the states which they represented. Whatever conclusions they might eventually come to, must of course be reported to the legislatures by whom they were appointed and commissioned, for them to adopt or reject, as they might think expedient. Here, it will be recollected, were the representatives of three states. Upon receiving their report, one state might adopt, another might reject, and a third might not do either, but adopt in part, and reject in part ; or the three might reject the whole report.

But whatever was done, or recommended to be done, was to be governed by the principles of loyalty to the Union and Government of the United States. This limitation of power confined the Convention strictly within constitutional limits. The constitution provides that " No state shall, without the consent of Congress, lay any duty on tonnage, keep troops or ships of war in time of peace, enter into any agreement or compact with another state, or with a foreign power, or engage in war, unless actually invaded, or in such imminent danger as will not admit of delay." Had the Convention disregarded their authority so far as to recommend the adoption of either of these prohibited acts, without the previous consent of Congress, their recommendation would have been void, for the want of power in themselves even to advise such a course. In addition to which, their recommendation of any course would not have bound the legislatures. To give it any validity, the latter bodies must have adopted it, and made it their own.

Having given a history of the war, and of the manner in which it was conducted on the part of the United States, with the view of placing before the public a correct account of the events which led to the assembling of the Hartford Convention, it may be well to devote a few moments to its termination by the treaty of peace.

On the 18th of February, 1815, the President of the United States transmitted a message to both houses of Congress, of which the following is an extract—

" I lay before Congress copies of the treaty of peace and amity between the United States and his Britannic majesty, which was signed by the commissioners of both parties at Ghent, on the 24th of December, 1814, and the ratifications of which have been duly exchanged.

" While performing this act, I congratulate you, and our constituents, upon an event *which is highly honourable to the nation*, and *terminates with peculiar felicity, a campaign signalized by the most brilliant successes.*

" The late war, although reluctantly declared by Congress, had become a necessary resort, to assert the rights and independence of the nation. It has been waged with *a success which is the natural result of the wisdom of the legislative councils*, of the patriotism of the people, of the public spirit of the militia, and of the valour of the military and naval forces of the country. Peace, at all times a blessing, is peculiarly welcome, therefore, at a period when the causes for the war have ceased to operate, when the government has demonstrated the efficiency of its powers of defence, and when the nation can review its conduct without regret, and without reproach."

The only cause of war, at the end of five days after its declaration, was that of the impressment of our seamen by British cruisers. The prevention of this evil was considered by our government an object of sufficient importance to justify the expenditure of the treasure and blood which was caused by the war. Many declarations of the government have been quoted in this work, from both the executive and legislative departments, intended to impress upon the minds of the public at large, as well as upon those of the commissioners for negotiating a peace, the indispensable importance of obtaining security against the further adoption of the practice. As late as January, 1814, the Secretary of State informed the plenipotentiaries at Gottenburg that " The sentiments of the President had undergone no change on that important subject. This degrading practice must cease; our flag must protect the crew, or the United States cannot consider themselves an independent nation." In January, 1813, the committee of foreign relations of the House of Representatives say, " War having been declared, and the case of impressment being necessarily included as one of the most important causes, it is evident that *it must be provided for in the pacification: the omission of it in a treaty of peace would not leave it on its former ground: it would in effect be an absolute relinquishment*"—" It is *an evil which ought not, which cannot be longer tolerated*"—" *It is incompatible with their sovereignty. It is subversive of the main pillars of their independence.*" But the case of impressment was not provided for in the pacification. So far from it, the subject is not once mentioned, or even alluded to in the whole course of the treaty. So far, then, from gaining this, which was avowedly the sole object of the war when it was declared, as well as when these various declarations were made, and this strong language was used, it must, according to those declarations, be considered as having been left on worse ground than that on which it stood upon before the war;—indeed, as having been absolutely relinquished; for no stipulation was entered into, no agreement made, not even an informal understanding was had with regard to it, and the evil which could not be longer tolerated, which was incompatible with our sovereignty, and subversive of the main pillars of our independence, was entirely unnoticed at the conclusion of the war and the negotiations for peace. And this was, in fact, the effect of an "absolute relinquishment" of the subject by the positive order of the President. It has been seen, that in a letter of instructions from the Secretary of State to the commissioners, dated June 27th, 1814, the latter were informed, that if they should find it indispensably necessary in order to terminate the war, they might omit any stipulation in the treaty on the subject of impressment. And yet notwithstanding all this—notwithstanding no single object for which the war was declared was accomplished, and the treaty of peace has no reference to such object, the President, in a public message to Congress, declares, that the peace was an event "highly honourable to the nation," and that it terminated "with peculiar felicity a campaign *signalized by the most brilliant successes.*"

Even the subject of impressment, for the purpose of getting rid of which it had been exclusively maintained, almost from the beginning, had been formally abandoned, and the controversy had in October, 1814, in fact, though secretly, assumed its true character, which was that of a war for the support of the personal popularity of the national administration, and not for the protection of the rights and honour of the nation. Having in terms relinquished the idea of obtaining security against impressment in the treaty of peace, the only object was to retire from the contest with as little loss of reputation, to those who involved the country in it, as the nature of the case would admit. To accomplish this object, the attempt to force the militia into the regular army, in defiance of the express provisions and principles of the constitution, was made. It was defeated by the patriotic and independent stand taken at the outset by the New-England governments; and to those governments is it solely owing, that a precedent so dangerous to the liberties of the country was not established.

It is not an easy matter to reconcile the foregoing declarations of the chief magistrate of the United States with the facts which have been alluded to. How is it possible that a peace could be "highly honourable to the nation," when the single object for which the war was carried on was not accomplished? The fact that we gained splendid naval victories, and that the British were repulsed at New-Orleans, do not prove it. M'Donough's victory on Lake Champlain was a brilliant achievement, as well as the repulse of the British at New-Orleans. But the latter event occurred in January, 1815, two weeks after the treaty of peace was signed, and therefore could not with propriety be considered as having terminated the campaign. But against these signal victories the capture of the city of Washington, the destruction of the public buildings, and the flight of the officers of the government, must be placed as a set-off. Besides, it must be borne in mind, that the war was on our part an offensive war; and was waged professedly for the vindication of national rights. The victory of New-Orleans, which has been considered as the most brilliant event achieved by our land forces during the war, was the fruit of a defensive battle merely, fought upon our own ground, and for the protection of one of our own cities. The event, therefore, however reputable to those by whom the battle was fought, reflects no credit on the administration and their friends, who declared the war.

To have gained honour to themselves, required something more than mere defensive operations. That we were able in that one instance to defend ourselves, furnishes very slight evidence of the wisdom of our legislative councils, by whom the war was declared. As far as it went, it proved the efficiency of the powers of the government in self-defence. But there were many events in the course of the war which demonstrated the opposite fact—which showed its inefficiency for defence. And this inefficiency was acknowledged in the calls made by the administration for the militia, in which it was stated expressly, that the regular troops were ordered from the Atlantic coast, and of course, that the coast would be left without defence, unless the militia were detailed upon the service.

The truth is, the peace, so far from being highly honourable to the country, was in an equal degree disgraceful. The mere circumstance that "the causes for the war had ceased to operate," proves nothing. Those causes would have ceased to operate in the same manner, whenever a peace should take place in Europe, as certainly without a war on our part against Great Britain, as with it. Such a peace, it was well known, must first or last occur, because a perpetual war was not in the nature of things to be expected. War between this country and Great Britain, at the time, was calculated to put off the peace in Europe, rather than to accelerate it. Peace eventually occurred, by the final overthrow of the great DISTURBER of that quarter of the globe—the man in whose favour the war was intended to operate—a short time after the treaty of Ghent between the United States and Great Britain, and was brought to pass by the great and decisive battle of Waterloo, on the 18th day of June, 1815—*the anniversary of the Declaration of War by the United States against Great Britain.* This country is in a worse condition as it regards security in any future war, against impressment by the British, than it would have been if the treaty negotiated by Messrs. Monroe and Pinkney had been ratified; and much worse than it would have been if the war had not been declared. That treaty was accompanied by an informal understanding entered into by the commissioners, that at some future time impressment should become the subject of further negotiation. Now we have no security even for that privilege; but if an occasion should ever hereafter occur, which should render it convenient for the British to engage anew in the practice, they could do it without infringing the stipulations of a treaty, or even violating an informal understanding. The United States would then have as strong an inducement to engage in a second war, for the purpose of forcing Great Britain to give up the practice, as they had in that of 1812—that is, if impressment was the real cause of the war. In that event, they may have another opportunity to go through a warfare of two years and a half more; and then make a peace " highly honourable to the country," without gaining the object for which the war was made, and ascribe the result to "the wisdom of the legislature," and "the cessation of the causes of the war."

But this result proves, in the most conclusive manner, the correctness of the views of those who were opposed to the war. They contended that the country was utterly unprepared for war, and therefore ought not to rush into it, foreseeing that its effects would be disastrous, and its termination disreputable to the government, and the country. They did not believe that the real causes of the war were alleged in the manifesto which preceded it; and the event showed that their belief was well founded. In short, judging of the character of the war, the capacity of those who were the appointed agents to conduct it, and the fact of its being brought to a close without securing one of its avowed objects, and all intelligent and upright people must justify the opposers of the war in withholding their sanction from its justice, and their approbation

from the sentiment that peace was " HIGHLY HONOURABLE
TO THE COUNTRY."

The readers of this work have now had a full opportunity to become acquainted with the causes which gave rise
to the Hartford Convention, the duties which that Convention were called upon to perform, the principles by which
they were governed in their proceedings, and the manner
in which they performed those duties. It will also have
been perceived, that it has not been the object of the author to frame an apology either for the Convention, or for
the legislative authorities by whom the Convention was
appointed. His object has been by the simple force of
truth, to stop the mouth of calumny, to turn the current
of falsehood back upon its authors, to free historical evidence from the mists in which it has for so many years
been involved and obscured, and if possible, to kindle a
blush of shame on the cheek of political fraud and profligacy. Instead of apologizing for the New-England States
for their conduct during the late unprincipled war, he entertains not a doubt that the example which was set by
those states, when they were drawn into competition with
the national government, the unshaken resolution which
they manifested in support of their own rights, and particularly in defence of the rights of the militia, will be the
means of protecting that large and most important class
of citizens from all future attempts to deprive them of
their constitutional rights, and to force them, at the will
of a despotic administration, into the ranks of a standing
army. Had not the New-England States made a firm stand
in defence of their constitutional privileges and prerogatives, the next war in which the nation shall be engaged,
would have reduced the individual states under the power
and placed them at the mercy of the national government.
All that would have been necessary to the accomplishment
of the object, would be a declaration, whether true or false,
that the country was in danger of invasion, and a demand

for any number of the militia which the Executive might
think proper to order, to be placed under the command of
United States officers, and made liable to be marched to
any rendezvous which the President, or any subordinate
officer under him should direct. This would at a stroke
deprive the states of their militia—their only safeguard
against tyranny and oppression ; and the national government would at once be in possession of a power sufficient
to overthrow their liberties and independence.

Mr. Giles's bill, introduced into the Senate, in October,
1814, was founded upon Mr. Monroe's plan for a conscription. It provided for raising eighty thousand men for the
United States service. The manner in which they were to
be obtained has been stated. The object was to make
them regular soldiers, to be placed under the command of
United States officers, and of course to remove them beyond the limits and controul of state authority, put them
in garrisons, march them to the frontiers, or to any other
point to which they might be ordered by the Secretary of
War. This would of course subject them to the military
despotism which is centered in, and exercised under the
"Rules and Articles of War." This vast body of men,
far more numerous than the United States ever had in the
field on any former occasion, either in the revolutionary
war, or since, would have been under the absolute direction and controul of the President of the United States,
and liable to be employed in any service upon which he
might think proper to detach them. What security would
the country have had against such a formidable force, in
the hands of a daring, ambitious, unprincipled warrior,
who was disposed to plant the standard of his own authority on the ruins of his country's freedom ? The question
need not be answered. The condition of the New-England states may be alluded to, in the room of a more specific reply to this inquiry. Pressed along the whole length
of the coast by the fleets and forces of a flushed and vin-

dictive foe, robbed of their militia, and exhausted of their means for carrying on military operations against either a foreign or domestic enemy, they would have been at the mercy of whatever " Military Chieftain " might have happened to be commander-in-chief. What would, under such circumstances, have been their fate, might, under different circumstances, have been the fate of other states. Nor would it be a difficult task for an ambitious soldier, at the head of such a force, to subvert every vestige of republicanism in our national government, and place himself at the head of a military despotism.

Speculations of this kind, in a time of peace, and when neither war, nor even rumours of war, exist, may be considered extravagant. But as the last war was undertaken for political and personal interests, another may be waged for reasons equally unwarrantable and reprehensible. The measures of the administration during the war of 1812, will justify the remarks that have been made, and the speculations that have been suggested. It is true that Mr. Madison was not much of a hero, and in all probability would have hesitated, even under the circumstances supposed, before he would have placed himself at the head of the army, the raising of which Mr. Giles's bill contemplated, and made a daring effort to conquer and enslave his country. But he had nerve enough to commence his military career, by a series of bold attempts to violate the constitution of his country. And as the war advanced, and difficulties and dangers multiplied around him, his courage rose to a higher pitch, until he was, in a desperate moment, induced to aim a fatal blow at some of the most important provisions and principles of the great charter of its freedom.

It is, however, believed, that it was not originally his wish to plunge the nation into a war. He received the government from the hands of his immediate predecessor, embarrassed with all the difficulties which the latter had planted around it; and in conducting its foreign affairs, it was next to impossible for him to change its course, without sacrificing his popularity with the leaders of the party which had placed him at its head. The first four years of his presidential life would expire in 1813; and unfortunately some bold and ambitious politicians had set their minds on war—with what expectation of advantage it is difficult to imagine. Apprehensive that his nerves might shrink from such a fearful responsibility, it was asserted at the time, and is not known ever to have been contradicted, or questioned, that he was informed by the individuals alluded to, that unless he recommended a war with Great Britain, the Western States would not support his re-election. The declaration of war was accordingly recommended, and proclaimed. The consequence was, the whole Union was agitated and distressed for two years and a half, by the calamities and the fears necessarily attendant on a state of war. The nation incurred a debt of more than a hundred millions of dollars, the payment of which, at the end of eighteen years, has scarcely been completed, and the country lost, according to the best estimate that could be made, more than thirty thousand lives. Considering the war, then, as intended to secure an election, and not to vindicate the rights, nor to promote the general welfare of the country, it would not be safe reasoning to conclude, that merely because Mr. Madison was not bred in a camp, and did not like to "look on scenes of blood and carnage," that he had not nerve enough to prostrate the constitution and liberties of his country. The facts which have been adduced in this history have shown, that when the aspect of things became darkened, and the war began to assume a more threatening and formidable appearance to the country at large, and of course to his personal popularity, he did not hesitate to recommend a series of measures, which, had they been carried into effect, would have been as complete and fatal a triumph over the constitution, as could have been effected by a dispersion, with force and arms, of the legislative houses, and shutting up the halls of Congress. Had Mr. Giles's bill passed into a law, the power of accomplishing these results would have been placed in the hands of the executive. It would be but a poor answer to say that he would not have abused the power. The argument will carry but little force, when it is recollected, that the power which was in his hands was abused; and in one instance, the very existence of the constitution was placed in extreme jeopardy. But the precedent would have remained; and the first "Military Chieftain" who had been bred in a camp, and was not afraid to " look on blood and carnage," and who had succeeded in taking the reins of government into his own hands, would have it in his power, under its sanction, after having plunged the nation into a war, to conquer and enslave his country.

For the escape from these evils, the United States are indebted to the firm and patriotic stand taken by the New England States, in defence of their constitutional rights and privileges. There is very little probability, at least for half a century to come, that another such attempt will be made against their liberties and independence. . That probability is much strengthened by the consideration, that the attempt which was made during the late war was so signally defeated. Deeply concerned as all the individual states in fact were in the result of the controversy between the New England States and the United States, in 1812, and during the war, no particular class of inhabitants were so directly and deeply interested, as the whole body of militia throughout the Union. Nothing saved them from being forced, during the late war, into the ranks of the regular army, but the independent conduct of the chief magistrates of the three New England States, viz. Massachusetts, Connecticut, and Rhode Island. The firmness of those public officers, approved and supported as they were by the legislatures of their several jurisdictions, checked the progress of the national government towards the establishment of Conscription and Impressment, by legislative acts wearing the forms of law. And it should be borne in mind, that when these efforts were made to violate the constitutional rights of the states, and of the militia, the war had ceased to be a contest for the vindication of any national right whatever.

APPENDIX.

It may not be uninteresting, to give the community at large some general information respecting the characters of the individuals who composed the Hartford Convention. For that purpose, the following very brief sketches have been prepared.

George Cabot was a native of Massachusetts, and a descendant of one of the discoverers of a portion of this continent. He was a man of strong powers of mind, extensive knowledge, dignified manners, the strictest integrity, and the purest morals. He was a warm friend to the independence of his country during the revolutionary contest ; and soon after the adoption of the constitution of the United States, he was appointed a senator in Congress from the state of Massachusetts. He was an able, upright, judicious, and disinterested statesman, and had a thorough knowledge of the principles of the government, and the great interests of the country. His mind was elevated far above the arts of intrigue ; he disdained political cunning and chicanery ; his principles were sound and pure, and his conduct disinterested and independent.

For many years previously to 1814, he had declined public office, and had taken no active part in politics, until the dangers of the country, and particularly those by which New-England was surrounded, induced him to consent to attend the Convention at Hartford. He was unanimously chosen to preside in that assembly; and throughout its session, he performed the duties of his office in the most acceptable and dignified manner. His life was prolonged several years after the close of the war; and he maintained the same high reputation that he had previously acquired to the end of his days, enjoying the universal esteem and respect of his friends, and of the community where he had passed a long and virtuous life. Few men understood more thoroughly the principles of the government, or the important interests of the country; and no man was ever more divested of selfishness, in his exertions to promote its welfare.

NATHAN DANE was bred to the bar, and practised law for many years with a high reputation for learning, integrity, and talents. He was a firm friend to his country during the revolutionary war, and was a member of Congress from Massachusetts, under the confederation, where he performed eminent services,—particularly in procuring the insertion of a provision in the ordinance establishing territorial governments over the territories northwest of the Ohio river, which forever excluded slavery from those regions. He was also for many years a member of the state legislature; and at all times, through a long and useful life, enjoyed extensively the confidence of his fellow-citizens in the town, county, and state where he resides. He is still living; and though at a very advanced age, is still engaged in rendering important services to the community, by the publication of valuable works on subjects of an interesting nature, and by distributing with a liberal hand the fruits of his own industry and talents, in support of the public institutions of the state.

WILLIAM PRESCOTT was a son of Colonel Prescott, so distinguished in the annals of his country for heroic bravery and conduct,—especially at the battle of Bunker's Hill, on the 17th of June, 1775,—for devoted patriotism, and an ardent zeal for the independence of his native land. Mr. Prescott was educated for the bar, and settled early in life in the town of Salem, in the county of Essex. Here he rose to great distinction as a learned counsellor, and an able advocate. He then removed to Boston, where he attained to great eminence as one of the most distinguished members of the profession. He has been a member of the House of Representatives, and of the senate of the state legislature, and was sure of an election whenever he would consent to be a candidate. No man ever had a higher reputation for strict integrity, personal worth, or public virtue; and very few men of his elevated standing for talents, or moral worth, were more entirely free from every feeling of ambition, or the desire of official distinction or influence.

HARRISON GRAY OTIS was born at Boston, and is a branch of the same family with James Otis, one of the most active and eloquent patriots of that city, at the beginning of the revolution. He was bred to the bar, and was distinguished for his talents and eloquence in his profession. He came young into public life ; has been a representative to congress, often a member of the legislature of the state, a senator to congress, and finally mayor of the city. In all these stations, he was highly respected and esteemed as an eloquent speaker, an able statesman, and an upright politician.

Few individuals have been placed more frequently in conspicuous stations before the public than this gentleman. Possessed of fine talents, of captivating oratory, and persuasive eloquence, he has always been able to command the respect, and to a great extent the esteem of his political opponents; while he has possessed in an eminent degree the attachment and the confidence of his political friends and associates.

TIMOTHY BIGELOW was a highly respectable lawyer, esteemed for his integrity in his professional pursuits; was for many years elected a member of the state legislature, and for nearly an equal period was annually chosen speaker of the house of representatives; and having declined a further election to that office, was appointed a member of the executive council of the state. Few men have more fully possessed the confidence of their constituents than Mr. Bigelow.

JOSHUA THOMAS held the office of judge of probate in the county of Plymouth, in Massachusetts, the duties of which he executed for many years with much reputation, enjoying the confidence of the community in an uncommon degree. This office rendered him inelegible to the legislature, otherwise there is no doubt he would have been elected to a seat in one house or the other, as often as he would have consented to become a candidate for popular favour.

JOSEPH LYMAN was by profession a lawyer, and pursued the practice for many years with a respectable character for integrity and talents. For a very considerable period he has held the office of sheriff of the county to which he belongs, which renders him ineligible to a seat in the legislature. He was elected a member of the convention, which was held a number of years since, for the purpose of suggesting amendments to the state constitution. He has always enjoyed the respect and confidence of the community, particularly that part of it where he has always resided, and still is esteemed for his public and private virtues.

GEORGE BLISS was an eminent lawyer, distinguished in the profession for extensive learning, unwearied industry, uncommon intelligence, the strictest integrity, and the most unshaken independence both of principle and of conduct. In private life he possessed a most estimable and exemplary character. He was repeatedly elected to the state legislature, and was often a member of the executive council of the state. No man ever passed through life with a fairer reputation for integrity, or in a more entire possession of the confidence of the community in which he resided.

DANIEL WALDO is an inhabitant of Worcester, in the state of Massachusetts, where he was early in life established as a merchant. In all the business and intercourse of life, he has maintained a most respectable and irreproachable character. He has been a member of the state senate, and could always be elected when he would suffer himself to be named as a candidate for that office. Affluent in his circumstances, he has usually found sufficient employment in superintending his private affairs. Being of an unambitious disposition, he has, to a great extent, left the political concerns of the country to others, contenting himself with the quiet pursuits and occupations of private life, and in doing good to his fellow men.

SAMUEL SUMNER WILDE was bred to the bar, where he maintained a highly respectable character for learning, talents, and integrity. No better evidence of his high standing in the profession could be given, than his appointment to a seat on the bench of the supreme court of Massachusetts—a court which has always ranked among the most distinguished in our country, and which within a few years previously had been ornamented by a Parsons, a Strong, a Sedgwick, a Sewall, and other jurists of an eminent character. This place Mr. Wilde has filled for many years, with reputation to himself, and with the full approbation of the community.

HODIJAH BAYLIES was an officer of much merit in the revolutionary army, and served with reputation until the establishment of his country's independence. For many years he has held the office of judge of probate, in the county in which he resided, which disqualified him for legislative employment, otherwise from his well established character for sound understanding, solid talents, and unimpeachable integrity, he would doubtless have been often selected by his fellow citizens for places of trust and importance.

STEPHEN LONGFELLOW, Jun. was bred to the bar, and resided in the city of Portland, now in the state of Maine. As a lawyer, he has been considered as at the head of his profession, for talents and integrity. He has also been elected to the house of representatives of the United States, where his talents were fully displayed, the respectability of his character acknowledged, and his disinterestedness and integrity duly appreciated.

CHAUNCEY GOODRICH was educated for the bar, and was for many years a practitioner of the highest respectability, for learning, talents, and integrity. He was repeatedly a member of the legislature of Connecticut, and held successively a seat in both of its branches. Early in life he was several times elected a member of the house of representatives of the United States, and subsequently was appointed a senator in congress. From the latter station he was chosen Lieutenant-Governor of the state—an office which he held till his death. Rarely has any individual passed through so many scenes in public life with a higher reputation, and a more unimpeachable character. Thoroughly acquainted with the public concerns, both of the state to which he belonged, and of the United States, no statesman ever pursued with a more single eye the interests of his country. Unshaken in his principles, cool and determined in his conduct, nothing could induce him to deviate a hair's-breadth from the path of rectitude, or swerve in the slightest degree from the most strict integrity of purpose. On all occasions, even during the highest strife of party spirit, and in the most animating and exciting moments of debate, he never lost sight of the most rigid decorum of manners ; and his political op ponents involuntarily yielded him their esteem and respect.

JOHN TREADWELL, in private life, was a model of personal worth, and in public, was universally esteemed for his sound understanding, unquestionable integrity, and sterling worth. He spent a great part of his life in the service of the public—having filled successively the places of representative and councillor in the state legislature, and the offices of lieutenant-governor and governor of the state. He was also for a long period a judge of the court of common pleas, in the county in which he resided, and for a good many years was the presiding judge of that tribunal. In all the offices which he filled, and in all the public services which he performed, his life passed without a stain. He was a whig in the revolution, a patriot of the Washington school in politics, a plain republican in his principles and manners, conscientiously upright in all his intercourse with his fellow men, and he possessed, in a very extensive degree, the respect and confidence of the great body of the community in whose service he spent his days.

JAMES HILLHOUSE. Very few men in the United States have been more extensively known in public life than this gentleman. He was for many years a practising lawyer of celebrity, a member of the state legislature, and for nearly twenty years connected with the national government, either as a representative, or a senator in Congress. In both those stations his character stood high for integrity, firmness, and independence. During the revolutionary war he fought bravely for his country; and in the pursuit of peace, he was distinguished for activity, intelligence, and public spirit. Few men ever possessed greater energy of character—no man ever excelled him in industry and perseverance, in whatever pursuit and employment he might be engaged.

ZEPHANIAH SWIFT was a lawyer, distinguished for learning and talents. For many years he was actively and extensively engaged in the duties of his profession; during which he was successively a member of the state legislature, speaker of the house of representatives, and a representative in congress. Subsequently he was a judge, and for a number of years chief judge of the supreme court of the state, where he acquired a high reputation for learning, talents, integrity, and independence.

NATHANIEL SMITH was one of the most extraordinary men of his time. With few advantages of early education, he became a student of law; and after a regular period of preparation was admitted to the bar. By the force of great native powers of mind, and a most commanding forensic eloquence, he soon rose to the head of the profession, and was for a number of years considered as one of the most distinguished lawyers and advocates in the state. He was elected a member of the house of representatives of the United States; and afterwards, for a number of years, was a judge of the supreme court of the state. In every situation in which he was called to act, the extraordinary talents with which he was endued were manifest; whilst his whole life was marked for purity of morals, strict integrity, and a devoted attachment to the interests of the state to which he belonged, and to the welfare of the United States.

CALVIN GODDARD was born in Massachusetts, but was educated for the bar in Connecticut, where he first settled in the practice of law, and almost immediately rose to eminence in the profession. Possessed of distinguished talents, his practice soon became extensive, when at an early period he was elected a member of the house of representatives of the United States, where he served with much reputation for four successive years. At the end of that time he declined a third election. Upon leaving Congress he resumed the practice of law, which he followed with great success for a number of years. He was repeatedly elected to the state legislature, and for a number of years was an active and influential member of the council, the higher branch of that body. Whilst a member of that house, he was appointed a judge of the supreme court of the state, and continued on the bench until the formation of the new state constitution, when he returned to the bar, and has been engaged till the present time in the business of his original profession, with a high character for learning, talents, and integrity.

ROGER MINOT SHERMAN was bred to the bar; and immediately upon his admission to practice became distinguished for abilities of a superior order. He has been repeatedly elected to the state legislature, and for a number of years was a member of the council. Few men in the profession in any part of the country have a higher reputation, or possess forensic talents of a more distinguished description. Such has been his reputation for purity of morals, strict professional and personal integrity, and for the unimpeachableness of his character, that he has always possessed the confidence of the community,

all parties having paid him the tribute of their esteem and
respect.

DANIEL LYMAN was a native of Connecticut. Early in
the revolutionary war he joined the army, and served till
the establishment of independence by the peace of 1783.
He rose to the rank of major, and sustained a high reputation for military talents and bravery. After the peace
he settled in the practice of law in Rhode Island, where
he became distinguished for integrity and talents in the
profession, and was eventually appointed Chief-Justice of
the Supreme Court of the state; a place that he filled for
a number of years with much reputation, and to the entire satisfaction of the community whose laws he was
called to administer.

SAMUEL WARD was the son of Governor Ward of Rhode
Island. He received his education at the university of
that state; and in the year 1774 joined the army of the
United States, having received the commission of captain
at eighteen years. In 1775 he joined General Arnold on
his expedition against Quebec, and went with him on that
most severe and dangerous enterprize; and after enduring
hardships almost inconceivable, he arrived before Quebec
in December of that year. In the subsequent attack upon that city he was made a prisoner; but afterwards was
exchanged, and returned to his country, and served in the
army, having been promoted to the rank of colonel, till
peace was restored, and our independence was acknowledged. He afterwards became engaged in trade, and
visited the East Indies and Europe.

In the year 1786, Colonel Ward was elected, with Colonel Bowen, a delegate to the convention, which met at
Annapolis, in Maryland, in September of that year, for
the purpose of taking into consideration the trade and commerce of the United States, and to endeavour to agree on

some uniform system in their commercial intercourse. Colonel Ward proceeded as far as Philadelphia, where he ascertained that the convention had adjourned.

In private life Colonel Ward sustained a most estimable character ; and as a soldier and patriot, his reputation was without a stain.

BENJAMIN HAZARD was a native of Rhode Island, and was educated to the bar. In the profession, he has long ranked among the most respectable practitioners in the state for integrity aud talents. He has for many years been elected by his fellow-citizens of Newport to a seat in the state legislature, and is justly considered as one of the most distinguished members of that body. His private worth is universally acknowledged, and he is justly considered as one of the most respectable citizens of his native state.

EDWARD MANTON was a native of Rhode Island. He was of an unambitious disposition, and rarely mingled in the political discussions and agitations. His principles were sound, stable, and independent—such as were common to the friends of the Union and Constitution of the United States. His character as a man and a patriot was marked by sterling integrity, strict probity, and great moral worth ; and he enjoyed the respect and confidence of the community in a degree proportioned to his modest and unobtrusive merit.

BENJAMIN WEST was a native of New-Hampshire, and was bred to the bar. He practised for many years with distinguished reputation, and was considered as at the head of the profession in that state. His integrity was universally admitted, and his talents as generally acknowledged. In his intercourse with the community he was greatly esteemed ; and in the private relations of life his character was in a high degree estimable and interesting.

Mills Olcott was a native of New-Hampshire, and a son of the Hon. Chief-Justice Olcott of that state. He is himself a lawyer of respectable talents and character, and much esteemed for his private worth, his unimpeachable integrity, and estimable character. It is understood that he has for a good many years withdrawn from political life, enjoying in retirement the advantages of social intercourse, and the unobtrusive round of domestic tranquility and happiness.

William Hall, Jun. was an inhabitant of Vermont, and his business that of a merchant. In the midst of extensive concerns he found leisure to devote his attention occasionally to public affairs. He was frequently a member of the state legislature; and might have been much more extensively employed in the service of his fellow citizens, if he had been disposed to pursue the life of a politician. No man ever enjoyed a reputation more entirely free from all reproach than this gentleman. He was universally esteemed and respected by all good men, who had the opportunity to become acquainted with his character, manners, and moral excellence.

It may not be amiss to compare the conduct of the New-England States during the war of 1812, with that of another state, at a much later period. It is well known, that a portion of the inhabitants of South Carolina were, for a considerable time, greatly excited on the subject of what has been familiarly called the "tariff policy" of the national government. That policy had for its object the encouragement and protection of domestic manufactures. For this purpose laws were passed laying heavy duties upon certain kinds of foreign manufactures, with the view of enabling American citizens to foster and support their own industry. For a number of years very little complaint of injustice, or even of hardship, in the operation of the system, was heard from any quarter. At length, however, it became the subject of clamour among politicians, who resided in those parts of the country where manufacturing is not pursued, and where, from the peculiar situation and circumstances of the community, there is very little reason to expect that the industry of the labouring class of the inhabitants will take that direction. By the unwearied efforts of some of their influential citizens, and particularly of those whose attention was devoted to their political concerns, a great degree of warmth was enkindled, loud and threatening complaints were uttered, the laws laying duties on merchandise for the encouragement of American industry were openly denounced as unconstitutional, and therefore not obligatory upon the people, and threats of open and direct opposition to the execution of the laws alluded to were heard from every quarter. At the same time, the constitutional authority of the national judiciary to determine questions of this description was denied, the power of the individual states to decide, each for itself, was avowed, and the right of seceding from the Union, as the necessary consequence of these doctrines, was claimed and vindicated.

Among the distinguished leaders in this crusade against the Union and constitution of the United States, was Robert Y. Hayne, then a senator from South Carolina in the congress of the United States, and now governor of that state. In the year 1830, and whilst he was a member of the senate, the celebrated debate on the nominal subject of the public lands occurred in that body. This gentleman took an active and decided part in that debate ; and in two successive speeches, put forth the whole strength of his talents, and the full powers of his eloquence. In the course of one of those speeches he alluded. among a multitude of other subjects, to that of the Hartford Convention ; and after depicting the calamities of the country, at the time the Convention assembled, in glowing colours, he represented the conduct of the eastern states, in relation to the war, in as reprehensible a light as the force of language would enable him. For the facts to support his statements, he relied principally upon a book entitled " *The Olive Branch*," published at a time not far distant from the meeting of the Convention—a work of almost all others intended to subserve party purposes, the least entitled to credit. On such an authority, he proceeded in a strain of great vehemence to make the following remarks :

" As soon as the public mind was sufficiently prepared for the measure, the celebrated Hartford Convention was got up ; not as the act of a few unauthorized individuals, but by authority of the legislature of Massachusetts ; and as has been shown by the able historian of that Convention, in accordance with the views and wishes of the party of which it was the organ. Now, sir, I do not desire to call in question the motives of the gentlemen who composed that assembly ; I knew many of them to be in private life accomplished and honourable men, and I doubt not there were some among them who did not perceive the dangerous tendency of their proceedings. I will even go further, and say, that if the authors of the Hartford Convention believed, that ' gross, deliberate, and palpable violations of the constitution ' had taken place, utterly destructive of their rights and interests, I should be the last man to deny their right to resort to any constitutional measures for redress. But, sir, in any view of the case, the time when, and the circumstances under which that Convention assembled, as well as the measures recommended, render their conduct, in my opinion, wholly indefensible.

" Let us contemplate, for a moment, the spectacle then exhibited to the view of the world. I will not go over the disasters of the war, nor describe the difficulties in which the government was involved. It will be recollected, that its credit was nearly gone, Washington had fallen, the whole coast was blockaded, and an immense force collected in the West Indies, was about to make a descent, which it was supposed we had no means of resisting. In this awful state of our public affairs, when the government seemed to be almost tottering on its base, when Great Britain, relieved from all her other enemies, had proclaimed her purpose of 'reducing us to unconditional submission'—we beheld the peace party in New-England (in the language of the work [The Olive Branch] before us) pursuing a course calculated to do more injury to their country, and to render England more effective service than all her armies. Those who could not find it in their hearts to rejoice at our victories, sang ' Te Deum' at the King's chapel in Boston at the restoration of the Bourbons. Those who would not consent to illuminate their dwellings for the capture of the Guerriere, could give visible tokens of their joy at the fall of Detroit. The ' beacon fires' of their hills were lighted up, not for the encouragement of their friends, but as signals to the enemy; and in the gloomy hours of midnight the very lights burned blue. Such were the dark and portentous signs of the times which ushered into being the renowned Hartford Convention. That Convention met, and from their proceedings it appears that their chief object was to keep back the men and money of New-England from the service of the Union, and to effect radical changes in the government—changes that can never be effected without a dissolution of the Union."

In adverting to Mr. Hayne's speech on this occasion, the object has not been to examine into the justice of his remarks, the correctness of his statements, or the soundness of his conclusions. The subject has been noticed for a very different purpose. It is to give that gentleman, and the state of South Carolina, an opportunity to view them-

selves in their own mirror. The ground on which the
Hartford Convention stood, is to be found in the preceding
pages of this work. If the facts and evidence which have
been adduced do not justify the New-England States in
convening that assembly, and in the fullest manner warrant their proceedings, and the result of their deliberations
and labours, they will doubtless be condemned. But if,
in any of these particulars, they suffer in a comparison with
the state of South Carolina, in the measures more recently
adopted by the latter in opposition to the laws of the United
States, it will certainly excite no small degree of surprise.

In South Carolina, though for a few years past, there
have been great complaints of oppression arising from the
operation of the revenue laws of the United States, yet the
actual degree of suffering could not be easily and precisely ascertained. The real ground of complaint appeared to
be against the acts of Congress laying what are called pro-
tective duties upon foreign merchandise, for the purpose
of encouraging and protecting domestic manufactures.
The constitutional authority to lay duties of this description was denied by the politicians of that state; and having failed after various attempts in Congress to obtain
a repeal of those acts, the state determined to take the
matter into their own hands, and force the national government to yield to their demands, or to secede from the
Union, and establish an independent government. Accordingly the legislature of the state passed an act, calling
upon the people to elect delegates to a Convention, to take
the subject into consideration, and provide a remedy for
the evils which they experienced. Under the authority
of this act delegates were chosen, and the Convention
assembled; and after due deliberation, they adopted the
following ordinance :—

" An ordinance to nullify certain acts of the Congress
of the United States, purporting to be the laws laying duties
and imposts on the importation of foreign commodities.

" Whereas the Congress of the United States, by various acts purporting to be acts laying duties and imposts on foreign imports, but in reality intended for the protection of domestic manufactures, and the giving of bounties to classes and individuals engaged in particular employment, at the expense and to the injury and oppression of other classes and individuals, and by wholly exempting from taxation certain foreign commodities, such as are not produced or manufactured in the United States, to afford a pretext for imposing higher and excessive duties on articles similar to those intended to be protected, hath exceeded its just powers under the constitution, which confers on it no authority to afford such protection, and hath violated the true meaning and intent of the constitution, which provides for equality in imposing the burdens of taxation upon the several states and portions of the confederacy. And whereas the said Congress, exceeding its just power to impose taxes and collect revenue for the purpose of effecting and accomplishing, hath raised and collected unnecessary revenues, for objects unauthorised by the constitution.

" We, therefore, the people of the State of South Carolina in convention assembled, do declare and ordain, and it is hereby declared and ordained, that the several acts and parts of acts of the Congress of the United States, purporting to be laws for the imposing of duties and imposts on the importations of the United States, and more especially an act entitled 'An act in alteration of the several acts imposing duties on imports,' approved on the nineteenth day of May, one thousand eight hundred and twenty-eight, and also an act entitled 'an act to alter and amend the several acts imposing duties on imports,' approved on the fourteenth day of July, one thousand eight hundred and thirty-two, are unauthorised by the constitution of the United States, and violate the true meaning thereof, and are null and void, and no law, not binding upon this state, its officers or citizens; and all promises, contracts, and obligations, made or entered into, with the purpose to secure the duties imposed by said acts, and all judicial proceedings which shall be hereafter had in affirmance thereof, are, and shall be, held utterly null and void.

"And it is further ordained, that it shall not be lawful for any of the constituted authorities, whether of this state or of the United States, to enforce the payment of duties imposed by the said acts within the limits of this state; but that it shall be the duty of the legislature to adopt such acts as may be necessary to give full effect to this ordinance, and to prevent the enforcement and arrest the operation of the said acts and parts of acts of the Congress of the United States within the limits of this state, from and after the first day of February next, and the duty of all other constituted authorities, and of all persons residing or being within the limits of this state, and they are hereby required and enjoined to obey and give effect to this ordinance, and such acts and measures of the legislature as may be passed or adopted in obedience thereto.

"And it is further ordained, that in no case of law or equity, decided in the courts of this state, wherein shall be drawn in question the authority of this ordinance, or the validity of such act or acts of the legislature as may be passed for the purpose of giving effect thereto, or the validity of the aforesaid acts of Congress, imposing duties, shall any appeal be taken, or allowed, to the Supreme Court of the United States, nor shall any copy of the record be permitted or allowed for that purpose; and if any such appeal shall be attempted to be taken, the courts of this state shall proceed to execute and enforce their judgments, according to the laws and usages of the state, without reference to such attempted appeal; and the persons attempting to take such appeal may be dealt with for a contempt of the court.

"And be it further enacted, that all persons now holding any office of honor, profit, or trust, civil or military, under this state, shall within such time as the legislature may prescribe, take, in such manner as the legislature may direct, an oath well and truly to obey, execute, and enforce this ordinance, and such act or acts of the legislature as may be passed in pursuance thereof, according to the true intent and meaning of the same; and on the neglect or omission of any such person or persons so to do, his or their office or offices shall be forthwith vacated, and shall be filled up, as if such person or persons were dead, or had resigned; and no person hereafter elected to any office of honour, profit, or trust, civil or military, shall, until the legislature shall otherwise provide and direct, enter on the execution of his office, or be in any respect competent to discharge the duties thereof, until he shall in like manner have taken a similar oath; and no juror shall be impannelled in any of the courts of this state, in any cause in which shall be in question this ordinance, or any act of the legislature passed in pursuance thereof, unless he shall first, in addition to the usual oath, have taken an oath that he will well and truly obey, execute, and enforce this ordinance, and such act or acts of the legislature as may be passed to carry the same into operation and effect, according to the true intent and meaning thereof.

"And we, the people of South Carolina, to the end that it may be fully understood by the government of the United States, and the people of the co-states, that we are determined to maintain this, our ordinance and declaration, at every hazard, do further declare that we will not submit to the application of force, on the part of the federal government, to reduce this state to obedience; but that we will consider the passage by Congress of any act authorising the employment of any military or naval force against the state of South Carolina, her constituted authorities or citizens, or any act abolishing or closing the ports of this state, or any of them, or otherwise obstructing the free ingress and egress of vessels to and from the said ports; or any other act on the part of the federal government to coerce the state, shut up her ports, destroy her commerce, or to enforce the acts hereby declared to be null and void, otherwise than through the civil tribunals of the country, as inconsistent with the longer continuance of South Carolina in the Union: and that the people of this state will thenceforth hold themselves absolved from all further obligation to maintain or preserve their political connection with the people of other states, and will forthwith proceed to organize a separate government, and do all other acts and things which sovereign and independent states may of right do."

Mr. Hayne found himself under the necessity of making a concession in his speech, in favour of the New England States, in consequence of the general principles which he maintained, and the course that the state to which he belonged were about to pursue. " If," said he, " the authors of the Hartford Convention *believed* that ' gross, deliberate, and palpable violations of the constitution' had taken place, utterly destructive of their rights and interests, I should be the last man to deny their right to resort to any constitutional measures for redress." The authors of the Hartford Convention not only believed, but they had positive and undeniable proof, that such violations of the constitution had *in fact* taken place. The evidence of this is contained in the body of this work. The President of the United States violated the constitutional rights and privileges of the New England States, in demanding detachments of their militia, to be placed under the command of United States officers—in attempting to raise troops from the militia by a conscription, and seamen by impressment—and to enlist minors without the consent of their parents, guardians, and masters. These are plain, specific cases—they were "gross, deliberate, and palpable"—and they were calculated utterly to destroy the rights against which they were directed. The argument then is finished, as far as that statement is concerned.

But this is not the principal object to be accomplished in adverting to the case of South Carolina. The design is to compare the conduct of that state, in the year 1832, with that of the New England States, in the year 1814.

The New England States "believed" that the national government had not only violated the constitution, in the several particulars above-mentioned, but they had, by their mode of carrying on the war, thrown upon those states the necessity of defending their coast, their towns, and their families, against the hostile visits and invasions of the enemy, and at the same time refused to furnish them with either men or money for their own protection. From the commencement of hostilities, those states had been informed that they must defend themselves—and this had been repeated from time to time, until, in the language of Mr. Hayne, " the credit of the government was nearly gone, Washington had fallen, the whole coast was blockaded, and an immense force, collected in the West Indies, was about to make a descent, which it was supposed we had no means of resisting." This was a state of things as fully understood and realized in New England, in the autumn of 1814, as it was by Mr. Hayne when this speech was delivered in the Senate, in 1830. They had seven hundred miles of sea-coast to defend, with no other means than those which they were able themselves to furnish; and even of those, the national government, by the most unconstitutional and despotic measures, were endeavouring to deprive them. Under such circumstances, the Hartford Convention was appointed, and instructed to devise and recommend the best means in their power of preserving their resources, to enable the states to fulfil the task which the national government had imposed upon them, but, to let every thing be done in a manner consistent with their duties and obligations to the United States. And the

most important measure recommended by the Convention
was, that the New England States, thus deserted and
abandoned by the government of the United States, should
make application to Congress, for permission to use their
own men, and their own money, in defence of their own
territory—their towns, their property, and their fire-sides,
against the invasions of the enemy. " Their chief object,"
says Mr. Hayne, " was to keep back the men and the
money of New England from the service of the Union.
The history of the case proves incontestibly, that this was
an unfounded assertion. " Their chief object was," to employ their men and their money in the service of the United States—for it was the duty of the United States to
provide both men and money, for the defence of the states
against the enemy which they had brought upon them.

" But," says Mr. Hayne, " the time when, and the circumstances under which, that Convention assembled, as
well as the measures they recommended, render their conduct wholly indefensible." This is seriously narrowing the
ground of complaint against the Convention, yielding the
right, at least by necessary implication, and objecting only to the expediency of the time when they were convened.
But so far from this being a well founded objection against
calling the Convention, it was the time, and the circumstances, which not only justified the measure, but which
rendered it indispensably necessary. The danger which
hung over the states was immediate ; and the circumstances were of so threatening and alarming a character,
that preparation to ward off that danger could not safely
be postponed for a single day. And such was the import
of the language used by the administration, in all the calls
they made upon the New England States, to provide the
means for their own defence.

But what says the " Ordinance " of the South Carolina
Convention ? That document declares the laws of Congress therein referred to, and which are commonly called

the tariff laws, null and void, and not binding upon the people of that state—it declares all promises, contracts, and obligations, for the securing of the duties imposed by those laws, and all judicial proceedings in affirmance of such promises, contracts, and obligations, also null and void—that it shall not be lawful for the constituted authorities of South Carolina, or of the United States, to enforce the payment of such duties within that state, but it shall be the duty of the legislature to adopt measures for preventing the collection of the duties, and to arrest the operation of the acts of Congress within that state, and all the authorities and all the people are enjoined to obey and give effect to the Ordinance. It then proceeds to declare, that the validity of the Ordinance shall not be drawn in question in any court in the state, that no appeal shall be allowed from the state court to the Supreme Court of the United States, that no copy of the record of the state court shall be allowed to be taken for the purposes of an appeal; and if any attempt to appeal should be made, the state court should proceed to execute their own judgments without regard to such appeal, and the person attempting to take it should be punishable for a contempt of court. The Ordinance advances still further, and declares, that all officers, civil and military, shall take an oath to obey the Ordinance, and for omitting to do so, their offices shall be vacated, and filled anew, as in the case of death or resignation; and no juror shall be impannelled, in any cause in which the Ordinance shall be drawn into question, without having first taken an oath to obey and enforce the Ordinance. And, finally, it is declared, that the state will not submit to the application of force, on the part of the United States, to reduce them to obedience; but if Congress should undertake to employ military or naval force against them, to shut up their ports, destroy their commerce, or resort to any other means of enforcing the laws which the Ordinance orders to be null and void, other than through the civil tribunals of the country, such a course will render the longer continuance of South Carolina in the Union inconsistent, and that they will thenceforth hold themselves absolved from all further connection with the other states, and will proceed to organize a separate independent government.

This is the case of South Carolina, placed in contrast with that of the New England States. The document which contains these provisions, was prepared under the eye, if not by the hand of the same Mr. Hayne, who pronounced the conduct of the authors of the Hartford Convention "utterly indefensible." This declaration referred to the time when, and the circumstances under which, the Hartford Convention assembled. That time, and those circumstances, have been repeatedly alluded to and described in the course of this work. They were alarming and portentous, fraught with danger and distress to the country, and foreboding ruin to the Union and Constitution. Far different were the times and the circumstances when the South Carolina Convention passed their ordinance. Their time was a time of peace and prosperity. The country was pressed by no enemy from without, and by no tumult or insurrection within. Agriculture, commerce, and manufactures, were flourishing beyond all former example, and the country was advancing in numbers, wealth, and power, in a degree surprising to ourselves, and astonishing to all other nations. If there is any peculiar merit on the part of South Carolina, in choosing this halcyon period, for making such arrogant claims, and for throwing the Union into a state of discord, fermentation, and animosity, when all things else were at peace, it would not be amiss if those grounds were more explicitly stated. At present, they will be disallowed by every virtuous, intelligent, and patriotic mind. The Hartford Convention recommended no measure which had the slightest tendency to prostrate the national constitution, or to destroy the

Union. Every sentiment expressed in the South Carolina ordinance was hostile to the constitution, and every measure proposed or adopted, was calculated to dissolve the Union. The propositions of the Hartford Convention, were to obtain the consent and approbation of the general government to their principal measures; the South Carolina ordinance denied the authority of that government to controul them in the case about which they complained, and defied their power to execute their laws. The Hartford Convention recommended an application to Congress for permission to raise troops for the defence of their coasts; the South Carolina ordinance provided for the raising of a body of men to oppose by force of arms the execution of the laws of Congress, and to raise the standard of rebellion against the government of the nation.

If Mr. Hayne thought the conduct of the authors of the Hartford Convention " utterly indefensible," what must he think of the authors of the South Carolina Ordinance? About the facts in the two cases there is no room for dispute. The conclusions which those facts will fairly warrant, will be drawn by the community.

ERRATA.

The reader is requested to correct the following errors in the foregoing pages.

Page 28, line 14 from the top, read *king* instead of *kings*.
32, line 8 from the bottom, read *strain* instead of *train*.
46, line 9 from the top, read 1804 instead of 1801.
126, line 19 from the top, after the word *France*, the words *was conducted* are omitted.
166, line 7 from the top, instead of " *is*," after "underscored," read *contain*.
218, line 4 from the top, omit the words " *and*," to the end of the line.
219, line 14 from the top, insert at the beginning of the sentence, *It required some assurance*.
221, line 4 from the top, read *have* been stated.
225, line 2 from the top, read *definitive* instead of *definite*.
302, line 8 from the bottom, read hostilities having *been* commenced.
361, line 17 from the bottom, read with *the* respect.